Rhetoric in Ancient China
Fifth to Third Century B.C.E.

The Warring States
475 – 221 B.C.E.

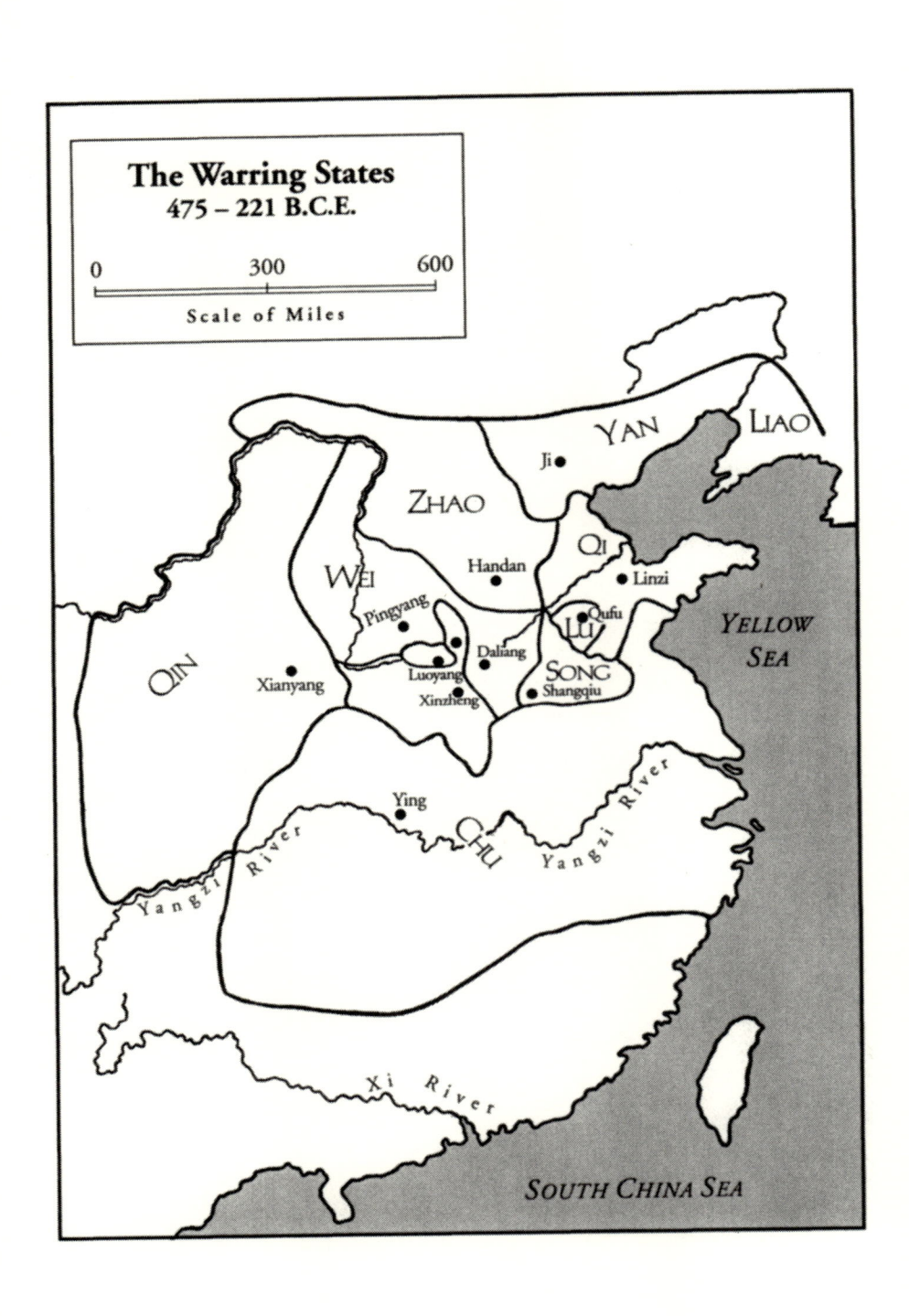

Rhetoric in Ancient China
Fifth to Third Century B.C.E.
A Comparison with Classical Greek Rhetoric

Xing Lu
呂行

UNIVERSITY OF SOUTH CAROLINA PRESS

Studies in Rhetoric/Communication
Thomas W. Benson, Series Editor

©1998 University of South Carolina

Cloth edition published by the University of South Carolina Press, 1998
Paperback edition published in Columbia, South Carolina,
by the University of South Carolina Press, 2011

www.sc.edu/uscpress

20 19 18 17 16 15 14 13 12 11   10 9 8 7 6 5 4 3 2 1

The Library of Congress has cataloged the cloth edition as follows:

Lu, Xing, 1956–
    Rhetoric in ancient China, fifth to third century, B.C.E. : a comparison with classical Greek rhetoric / Xing Lu.
    p. cm.—(Studies in rhetoric/communication)
    Includes bibliographical references (p.) and index.
    ISBN 1-57003-216-5
    1. Chinese language—Rhetoric. 2. Chinese language—To 600. 3. Greek language—Rhetoric. 4. Rhetoric, Ancient. 5. Comparative linguistics. I. Title. II. Series.
  PL1271.L84   1997
  808'.04951—dc21   97-33916

ISBN: 978-1-61117-053-5 (pbk)

To Lulu

Contents

Editor's Preface	ix
Preface	xi
Acknowledgments	xv
A Chronology of Chinese Dynasties from Xia to the Warring States Period	xvii
Chinese Schools of Thought and Major Thinkers	xviii
Abbreviations	xix
Introduction	1
CHAPTER ONE Perceptions and Methodology in the Study of Classical Chinese Rhetoric	14
CHAPTER TWO Cultural Contexts and Rhetorical Practices of the Pre-Qin Period	44
CHAPTER THREE Chinese Terminology of Rhetoric	68
CHAPTER FOUR Rhetorical Features in Literary and Historical Texts	94
CHAPTER FIVE Conceptualization of Ming Bian: The School of Ming	127
CHAPTER SIX Conceptualization of Yan and Ming Bian: The School of Confucianism	154
CHAPTER SEVEN Conceptualization of Ming Bian: The School of Mohism	195
CHAPTER EIGHT Conceptualization of Yan and Ming Bian: The School of Daoism	225
CHAPTER NINE Conceptualization of Shui and Ming Bian by Han Feizi	258
CHAPTER TEN Conclusions and Implications	288
Notes	311
Bibliography	327
Index	341

Editor's Preface

Is rhetoric a universal discipline, present in every culture and time, or is it a unique, historically situated invention that appeared in Greece and worked its way into a fitful relation with Western culture? Perhaps, if we are to be able to respect human cultural diversity and yet at the same time satisfy the needs of multicultural communication, we must answer "both" and sometimes more than "both."

Professor Xing Lu argues that the study of rhetoric is incomplete if it does not take into account the ways in which non-Western cultures have studied the human use of symbols. She brings her training in classical Chinese and her study of Western rhetoric to bear on the implicit, and sometimes explicit, views of human communication set forth in ancient Chinese texts written in the period when classical Greek rhetoric was formulated—the fifth to third century B.C.E. She finds that these Chinese texts on history, politics, ethics, and epistemology are rich with theoretical implications about language, persuasion, and argument. Although the ancient Chinese had no word for rhetoric as such, they had, according to Professor Lu, what amounted to a highly developed sense of rhetoric clustered in a set of key terms and texts and situated in the cultural traditions and historical practices of ancient China.

Professor Lu's book surveys ancient Chinese rhetorical theory, compares that theory with classical Greek rhetoric, and discusses the implications of Chinese patterns of communication for multicultural rhetoric. Professor Lu concludes her book with a call for the building of such a multicultural rhetoric, which, she writes, is crucial to "the survival of humankind." Her own contribution to the effort is a fascinating and compelling work of scholarship.

Thomas W. Benson

Preface

I was born and raised in China. Growing up during the so-called "Cultural Revolution" launched by Mao Zedong that took place between 1966 and 1976, I witnessed rhetorical practices of the "red guards" in the forms of oral debates, public speeches, and big-character posters intended to persuade, propagate, and provoke the mass audience. Without knowing much about the weight and impact of this massive and destructive movement, I was impressed by the power of language, means of persuasion, and eloquence of the Chinese people. I guess I unconsciously planted a seed for a career of rhetoric and communication at the time.

This book on classical Chinese rhetoric was conceived as a result of my experience as a graduate student at the University of Oregon. While reading and taking courses on Western rhetoric, I became fascinated by the role of the Western rhetorical tradition in shaping Western thought and culture. At the same time, however, I became increasingly frustrated by the lack of information on Chinese rhetoric, or, for that matter the other non-Western rhetorical traditions. Driven by a desire to trace my own rhetorical roots and to contribute to an intercultural understanding of rhetoric, I began to search for "a Chinese rhetoric." Evidence uncovered during the course of my research, along with a few previous studies, strongly indicated that China possesses a rich rhetorical tradition. Moreover, while retaining certain characteristics uniquely Chinese, Chinese rhetoric appears to share many striking similarities with the Greek rhetorical tradition.

Specifically, it is my hope in writing this book to contribute to the study of the history of rhetoric in several ways. First and foremost, my intention is to offer Western readers, as well as those Chinese readers who can read English, a more complete and authentic account of ancient Chinese rhetorical theories and practices. I will accomplish this task through an exhaustive survey and analysis of ancient Chinese texts on history, ethics, politics, and epistemology by Chinese thinkers from the fifth to third century B.C.E. In so doing, I wish to dispel certain misconceptions regarding Chinese rhetoric held by Western scholars. Such misconceptions tend to fall under the umbrella of Orientalism. I chose to compare classical Chinese rhetoric with classical Greek rhetoric in order to illuminate both Eastern and Western rhetorical traditions better. This study also aims to shed light on contemporary Chinese communication patterns and dynamics inherited from and affected by the Chinese rhetorical tradition. My final intention is to suggest a methodology for the pursuit of a multicultural rhetoric in order to enrich the scope of discursive possibilities and language art while enhancing the general understanding of diverse rhetorical experiences and concepts.

The first challenge I encountered in undertaking this ambitious project pertained to methodology. My training in Western rhetoric has helped me be more sensitive to rhetorical expressions and theories in Chinese texts and contexts, but at the same time, I am aware of the importance of not imposing Western rhetorical categories upon the Chinese tradition. To safeguard this tendency, I have embedded my analysis in the context of ancient China. As there are no explicitly identifiable works of ancient Chinese rhetoric, I refer to literary, historical, and philosophical works by classical Chinese writers. In order to understand as accurately as possible the rhetorical meanings embedded in these texts, I have interpreted the philosophical views and principles of the various thinkers in rhetorical terms and considered the social and cultural conditions under which each text was produced and in which each writer lived. When these texts and their authors are put into their proper social, political, and intellectual contexts, the rhetorical theories and practices identified therein become more meaningful and clear.

One particularly problematic area in the study of non-Western rhetoric is the issue of key terms. While it is more convenient simply to borrow the English word *rhetoric* in the discussion of the Chinese art of discourse, such a practice would run the risk of obscuring the authentic meaning of Chinese persuasive discourse and language art by imposing Western rhetorical assumptions upon the Chinese experience. To avoid this pitfall, I have surveyed the Chinese terms pertaining to speech, language, persuasion, and argumentation as they appear in their original texts. This methodology may pose certain challenges to Western readers but is linguistically and culturally more precise and helpful in capturing and explaining the Chinese rhetorical experience. Subsequently, I have compared the ancient Chinese rhetorical perspectives with those of the ancient Greeks. In fact, quite naturally, in the writing of this book, I have been made aware of various similarities and differences between Chinese and Greek rhetorical traditions. I consider such meaningful comparison a necessary component in the understanding and construction of a multicultural rhetoric which recognizes both culturally specific and transcultural elements of rhetoric.

According to conventional wisdom, Eastern ontology and epistemology favor integrated, holistic, and implicit modes of speech and argumentation, while Western ontology and epistemology give primacy to the discrete and explicit. This study attempts to follow intercultural hermeneutical models in that the conceptual construction and reconstruction of Chinese rhetorical studies will be guided by an integration of Chinese and Western methodological orientations rather than favoring one over the other. My ultimate purpose is to contribute to a multicultural vision of rhetoric residing in multiple forms of rhetoric, as well as in multiple modes of inquiry that are calibrated for diverse contexts and contents.

Acknowledgments

I am indebted to many people for the completion of this project, which was conceived during my time as a graduate student at the University of Oregon. I wish to thank my former professors Sonja Foss, Dominic LaRusso, Charley Leistner, and Carl Carmichael for opening my eyes to the scope and dimensions of rhetoric. My deepest appreciation goes to David Frank, who inspired, advised, and encouraged me in the completion of my dissertation, which amounted to an early version of this manuscript. Throughout the writing of this manuscript, which has undergone much expansion and revision, Professor Frank has offered his insights and invaluable suggestions for improvement. I am grateful to Judy Bowker, who kindly and generously offered to proofread my dissertation and was there when I needed help. Regarding the completion of this manuscript, I wish to thank my colleagues in the communication department at DePaul University for their kind and consistent support. Particularly, I want to thank my colleague Bruno Tebul for translating works of French language into English for me. I am especially grateful to Jacqueline Taylor, the former chair of the department, for her strong support and encouragement throughout my completion of the project. My gratitude also goes to the College of Arts and Sciences and the University Research Council at DePaul University for the travel grant to China to collect relevant materials for the project, as well as for granting me a one-year academic leave, without which I would not have completed the project in a timely manner.

I am very grateful to Professor Vernon Jensen, one of the pioneers on this subject, for his generous and consistent support since the beginning of this project. I am indebted to Mary Garrett, whose work on Chinese rhetoric inspired and encouraged me to venture further into the topic. With her impressive knowledge in Chinese philosophy and language, Professor Garrett provided invaluable suggestions for the improvement of the work from my dissertation to the current manuscript. I would also like to express my gratitude to Edward Schiappa, whose work in classical Greek rhetoric has informed my study of Chinese rhetoric. When I first contacted him about my dissertation, he kindly and generously sent me his work along with a list of helpful references. His works on Greek rhetoric have been inspiring sources for me, and his suggestions for the improvement of this manuscript were very helpful and valuable. I appreciate especially Professor Martin Bernal's offer to read the entire manuscript. His solid knowledge of Chinese ancient history, philosophy, and language made his comments most valuable and suggestions most helpful. I am also thankful to Tara McKinney for her careful proofreading and excellent editing in the preparation of this manuscript.

In the course of my two trips to Beijing, I was privileged to consult with several Chinese scholars about this project. Among them I wish to thank Liu Baochen 劉寶臣, Li Jiangzhe 李江浙, and Wang Caimei 王采梅 from Beijing Academy of Social Sciences for their enthusiastic encouragement and insightful guidance. In particular, I wish to thank Sun Miao 孫淼 from Beijing University for giving me a copy of his book on the history of the Xia and Shang dynasties. I also appreciate very much the assistance I received from Professor Wang Keng 王鏗 of Beijing University concerning verification of the meanings of key classical Chinese terms in the texts under consideration. In addition, I wish to thank Warren Slesinger from the University of South Carolina Press for his enthusiastic response to my book proposal and confidence in my ability to complete the project. Thanks are also in order for Joyce Harrison and Bill Adams from the University of South Carolina Press for their fine editorial guidance.

I wish to express my profound gratitude to my husband, Gu Licheng (Richard) 顧利程, who is also a professor of Chinese language at Northwestern University, for his many sacrifices that made it possible for me to find the time to write. Moreover, I appreciate very much his assistance in the verification of translations from Chinese to English and for technically word processing most of the Chinese characters which appear in this book. Finally, I wish to thank my five-year-old daughter, Wendi Lulu Gu, for her love, patience, and understanding. Knowing "Mommy is working all the time," she has learned to entertain herself more than any five year old could be expected to.

Chinese Dynasties from Xia to the Warring States Period

Dates (B.C.E.)	Dynasties
21st–16th Century	Xia
16th–11th Century	Shang
1027–770	Zhou
722–481	Chun Qiu (the Spring Autumn)
475–221	Zhan Guo (the Warring States)

Chinese Schools of Thought and Major Thinkers

	Mingjia	Confucianism	Daoism	Mohism	Legalism
B.C.E.					
600	Deng Xi (546–501)	Confucius (551–479)	Laozi (500–?)		
500				Mozi (480–420)	
400	Hui Shi (380–320)	Mencius (390–305)			
			Zhuangzi (369–286)		
	Gong-sun Long (328–295)				
300		Xunzi (298–238)		Later Mohists (300–?)	
					Han Feizi (280–233)

Abbreviations

The abbreviations below are only applied to the editions of texts under consideration and editions of ancient texts relevant to the study. Full information of the primary sources is given in the bibliography.

Ancient Texts under Consideration

DDJ	*Dao De Jing* 道德經
DXZ	*Deng Xizi* 鄧析子
GSL	*Gong-Sun Longzi* 公孫龍子
GY	*Guo Yu* 國語
HF	*Han Feizi* 韓非子
LY	*Lun Yu* 論語
M	*Mengzi* 孟子
MB	*Mo Bian* 墨辯
SJ	*Shi Jing* 詩經
SS	*Shang Shu* 尚書
X	*Xunzi* 荀子
Z	*Zhuangzi* 莊子
ZGC	*Zhan Guo Ce* 戰國策
ZZ	*Zuo Zhuan* 左傳

Ancient Texts Relevant to the Study

DX	*Da Xue* 大學
HN	*Huai Nanzi* 淮南子
HS	*Han Shu* 漢書
L	*Liezi* 列子
LSCQ	*Lu Shi Chun Qiu* 呂氏春秋
S	*Sunzi* 孫子
SY	*Shuo Yuan* 說苑
YJ	*Yi Jing* 易經
ZL	*Zhou Li* 周禮
ZY	*Zhong Yong* 中庸

Rhetoric in Ancient China
Fifth to Third Century B.C.E.

Introduction

Ignorance and denial of non-Western cultures' rhetorical traditions have led to the mistaken notion that rhetoric is the sole property and invention of the West, fueling cultural prejudice and bigotry with regard to the intellectual histories of other cultures. In recovering the rhetorical traditions of non-Western cultures, we gain new information about rhetorical theories and practices, challenging the Eurocentric views of rhetoric and expanding our knowledge of the history of rhetoric in the process. This book informs rhetorical scholars about Chinese rhetorical experiences, expressions, and conceptualizations, assisting not only in assembling the missing pieces of the puzzle of rhetorical history but also in promoting understanding, recognition, and appreciation of diverse rhetorical practices and communication patterns.

The Western rhetorical tradition has been explored and surveyed in countless studies offering information about Western civilization, the Western development of thoughts and ideas, and Western theories of speech and argumentation. Moreover, these studies further our understanding of how people in Western cultures make sense of their world and derive meaning from their surroundings through symbolic creations and interactions. However, the study of human rhetoric is not complete if it does not include the rhetorical traditions of non-Western cultures that can offer both diverse and unified views of human experience in the formulation and use of symbols. This survey of classical Chinese rhetoric, in the context of ancient Chinese philosophy and history, is a serious attempt toward this end.

The history of rhetoric is conventionally believed to have begun in ancient Greece, with the first codification of rhetorical themes credited to Corax and Tisias in the fifth century B.C.E. Following the codification of rhetoric, the Greek rhetorical tradition developed along three streams of thought: technical rhetoric, sophistic rhetoric, and philosophical rhetoric, placing different emphasis on the effectiveness of speech, the speaker, and audience analysis (Kennedy 1980). The term *rhetoric* is defined in various ways. It is most commonly perceived, however, as the art of persuasion, the artistic use of oral and written expressions, for the purpose of changing thought and action at social, political, and individual levels.

In recent years some prominent scholars, such as Brian Vickers (1980, 471–74) and Vernon Jensen (1987, 219), have called the rhetorical scholars to explore the rhetoric of non-Western cultures both for disciplinary interest and for contemporary significance in rhetoric and communication. Moreover, challenges have been made to established modes of knowledge, and the field of rhetorical studies has gradually expanded its vision. For example, in his book *Black Athena* Martin Bernal (1987) has called for a critical examination of the Aryan Model, which views Greece and Europe as the cradle of civilization, along with a return to the Ancient Model rooted in Egyptian and Phoenician cultures. Similarly, the conventional belief that rhetoric was first invented by ancient Greeks has been challenged by Michael Fox (1983) in his study of ancient Egyptian rhetoric. Furthermore, since Robert Oliver's (1971) first account of Chinese rhetoric and communication, Vernon Jensen (1992) and Mary Garrett (1993) have continued to research Asian rhetoric, in general, and Chinese rhetoric, in particular.

Even within the realm of Greek rhetoric, a revised version of the history of rhetoric has been proposed. According to recent studies by Thomas Cole (1991), Edward Schiappa (1993), and Richard Enos (1993), respectively, various rhetorical sensibilities and practices existed in the fifth century B.C.E., before the time of Plato. Greek sophists, especially Protagoras and Gorgias, are credited with the earliest formulations of rhetoric, of arising in conjunction with the formulation of their political, rationalistic, and humanistic views. Other factors facilitating the conceptualization of Greek rhetoric prior to Plato are the production of written texts, a growing awareness of social and political needs, and the teaching of rhetoric as *techné.*(art, handbook) According to Schiappa, until Plato coined the term *rhêtorikê* in the fourth century B.C.E., rhetoric had not been conceptualized or treated as a separate discipline.[1]

The revised version of Greek rhetorical history suggests that the history of rhetoric does not necessarily begin with a well-defined, clearly demarcated disciplinary term such as *rhetoric*. Rather, rhetorical experiences, ideas, and sensibilities typically occur long before the conceptualization and codification of rhetoric. Oftentimes, in fact, rhetorical themes are embedded in texts which do not treat rhetoric as an explicit topic of discussion. In the case of Chinese rhetoric, for example, implicit rhetorical practices are contained in literary and historical texts. Ancient Chinese rhetorical theories, with the exception of those expounded by the Later Mohists, are embedded in works of ethics, epistemology, and statecraft. While the origins of Greek rhetoric are marked by the emergence of the word *rhêtorikê*, with and by its specific application to political and educational arenas, the origin of Chinese rhetoric cannot be pinpointed with such precision. There is, in fact, no single unified signifier, equivalent to the term *rhetoric*, in Chinese texts. This does not mean, however, that rhetoric did not exist in ancient China. In fact, the ancient Chinese had a well-developed sense of the power and impact of language in their social, political, and individual lives. Moreover, in the Chinese context, there are many terms whose meanings centered around language, speech, persuasion, and argumentation that have played a significant role in the formulation of the Chinese rhetorical experience. Consequently, the goal of this study is to make explicit certain rhetorical themes which have remained implicit in classical Chinese texts on history, ethics, politics, and epistemology. This explication will be made through a close examination of social and cultural contexts; identification of terms associated with language art, rational thinking, persuasion, and argumentation; as well as a careful scrutiny and analysis of rhetorical experience and conceptualization embedded in classical Chinese texts.

In the study of Western rhetoric, scholars typically attempt a clear definition of rhetorical terms. Such an approach may not be applicable to the study of Chinese rhetoric, however, since, to my knowledge, no such clearly phrased definitions are present in any of the Chinese texts. A more appropriate strategy is to identify contextual rhetorical meanings held by the Chinese. This is because, as Robert Scott has observed, "any definition of rhetoric that is taken as once-and-for-all is apt to be gravely misleading" (1973, 95). Scott asserts that "people generally have a sense of rhetoric." Furthermore, "this sense or feeling, which precedes any definition of rhetoric, is immediately rooted in experience" (82). Since people experience the world from various angles, no unified definition of rhetoric emerges. However, each culture will have a general sense of rhetoric based upon the culture's experiences with speech and language. According to Scott, the people of any given cultural setting will tend to have an embedded sense of rhetoric which pertains to that particular context. The task of a rhetorical scholar, then, is to remain open to the universal sense of rhetoric, as well as to the transformative power of a particular culture on the practice of rhetoric.

Indeed, the ancient Chinese appear to have had their own well-developed sense of rhetoric, revealed morphologically throughout primary Chinese texts in the following frequently used terms: *yan* 言 (language, speech); *ci* 辭 (mode of speech, artistic expressions); *jian* 諫 (advising, persuasion);

shui 說 (persuasion)/*shuo* 說 (explanation); *ming* 名 (naming); and *bian* 辯 (distinction, disputation, argumentation). Semantically, these terms often overlap in meaning, yet each term also serves a particular function in contextualizing and conceptualizing speech and persuasive discourse. For example, *shui* is associated with face-to-face persuasion while *ming* deals with the use of symbols in social and epistemological contexts. While each of the terms indicates some level of synchronic understanding and diachronic explanation regarding the ancient Chinese rhetorical experience, some terms follow an evolutionary process reflecting attempts on the part of the ancient Chinese consciously to transform rhetorical activities and events into theory and conceptualization.

While in most cases in the texts under consideration the terms *ci*, *jian*, *shui*, and *shuo* are used to refer to oral and written rhetorical practices, the term *yan* is used in reference to both rhetorical experiences and conceptualizations, while *ming* and *bian* are used more frequently as conceptual terms in theorizing and philosophizing language and speech. *Ming* literally means names and titles but conceptually means rational thinking or the use of language in relation to the representation of reality, law enforcement, social and political control, epistemology, and the transformation of cultural values. Given these various nuances of meaning, the standard translation of ming by contemporary Chinese scholars as "logic" is, in my opinion, inadequate. The term *bian*, encompassing to varying degrees the textual and contextual meanings of the other terms, may be perceived as a linchpin of Chinese theories of speech, persuasion, and argumentation. As such, it is used in general discussions of the use of language, modes of inquiry, rational thinking, and persuasion and argumentation in social and intellectual contexts.

While I do not intend to impose Western notions of rhetoric upon the Chinese experience, I do consider it useful to identify universally shared and yet culturally specific vocabulary and concepts, in the interest of promoting rhetorical studies cross-culturally, given the fact that misunderstanding often results from ignorance of otherness in cross-cultural rhetorical experience and conceptualization. In this regard, I will argue that the Western study of rhetoric is comparable to the Chinese *Ming Bian Xue* 名辯學, literally translated as "the Study of Naming (*Ming*) and Argumentation (*Bian*)," while it conceptually encompasses the study of language art, logic, persuasion, and argumentation. The domains of *ming* and *bian* at times overlap in the ancient Chinese texts, but each also has its own distinctive function, with *ming* aiming to seek truth and justice and *bian* concerning the art of discourse and persuasion. I will further argue that *ming* is in some sense similar to the Greek notion of *logos*, in that both are concerned with issues of language and epistemology, while *bian* shares some common ground with the Greek word *rhêtorikê*, in that both refer to argumentation, rationality, and the artistic use of language. *Ming* is not the perfect equivalent to *logos*, however, nor is *bian* the perfect equivalent to *rhêtorikê*. As the meaning of terms is always culturally specific, ancient Chinese and Greek thinkers would necessarily have attached their own linguistic and cultural understanding to such terms. Therefore, attempting to find exact cross-cultural correlations and linkages is futile.

Although ming bian was not a formalized discipline in ancient China by Western standards, notions of ming bian were expounded, developed, and directly applied to language usage, modes of argumentation, and methods of persuasion. As primary texts are introduced and analyzed, a consistent pattern or system of ming bian will emerge. What is more, grammatical and contextual similarities and differences between Chinese ming bian and Greek rhêtorikê will become apparent as comparisons are made between the two cultures and among respective thinkers. To help the reader with the transition in the use of terms in various linguistic and cultural contexts, I will use the phrase *Chinese rhetoric* initially in this project in reference to ancient Chinese speech patterns and conceptualizations of persuasion and argumentation, gradually replacing *rhetoric* with original Chinese terms, although at times I may also use English and Chinese terms interchangeably with qualification.

No system of rhetoric is born or develops in a vacuum. The meaning and interpretation of a people's rhetoric are always derived from and influenced by its social, political, and philosophical contexts. Ancient Chinese rhetorical theories and practices are reflections of, and functional responses to, cultural patterns and crises of ancient China. When analyses of such theories and practices are placed in their proper context, as will be done in this book, a portrait of ancient Chinese rhetoric can finally emerge.

Like the ancient Greeks before the fourth century B.C.E., the ancient Chinese had various rhetorical experiences, ranging from mythology to rationality, from orality to literacy, dating back to the Xia dynasty (approximately twenty-first century B.C.E). Moreover, like Greek thinkers from the fifth to third century B.C.E., ancient Chinese thinkers conceptualized the Chinese experience with language and discourse in moral, rational, dialectical, and psychological terms. Likewise, Chinese rhetorical sensibilities were called forth by social and cultural demands, and stabilized and perpetuated through increased literacy and the production of written texts. However, political structures and cultural forces in ancient China called for different rhetorical expressions and practices than those of ancient Greece, though, rhetorically speaking, some common ground does exist between the two cultures. The Chinese conceptualization of rhetoric reveals much about Chinese cosmology, epistemology, cultural values, and social demands.

From the Xia to Shang dynasties (approximately twenty-first to eleventh century B.C.E), the Chinese rhetorical experience was characterized by mythological and ritualistic communication in the form of the oral transmission of legends, along with rites of ancestor worship and divinations. Oral poetry was also a common means of communication for exchanging information and cultivating aesthetic pleasure. Ritualistic communication, often accompanied by music and performance, transmitted and perpetuated Chinese cultural values characterized by an emphasis on morality, order, and hierarchy. With increasing concern for human affairs, military expediencies, and the moral conduct of the rulers, persuasion between officials and kings, as well as between rulers and the masses, became a significant rhetorical activity. The most popular and effective persuasive appeals were made in reference to *tian ming* 天命, or the "Mandate of Heaven," which oversaw and controlled human affairs and possessed the authority to grant rewards and impose punishment according to the moral conduct of the rulers.

By the time of the Zhou dynasty (approximately eleventh to sixth century B.C.E.), an orderly society with an aristocratic ruling class had been well established. The widespread dissemination of *Zhou Li* 周禮 (the Rites of Zhou) played an essential role in strengthening cultural values, ensuring moral conduct, and reinforcing the social order. With increased literacy and the production of written texts, various forms of oral communication, including persuasive discourse in political and ritualistic settings, were documented and described. Awareness of the power and impact of language thus increased, while the rhetorical appeals expanded into the realm of morality and rationality.

By the time Chinese history had entered the arena of the Spring-Autumn and Warring States period (722–221 B.C.E.), dramatic social change had taken place, characterized by the decline of the aristocracy and the upward mobility of the lower-middle class, endless wars among autonomous states, social chaos, and a crisis in cultural values. Power struggles among the individual states and military expediency demanded skilled advisers and political consultants. Persuasive encounters between political consultants and the ruler were at the center of rhetorical activity. In response to political and social exigencies, the key players of those times proposed various recipes for restoring order and reconstructing Chinese society and culture. A central topic of discussion was the use of language and the impact of persuasion and argumentation in shaping and reshaping human thought and action. A relatively free environment for the expression of ideas promoted intellectual debates among the differing schools of thought, which in turn stimulated the formulation and conceptualization of language and persuasive discourse.

Ancient Chinese rhetorical experiences, as will be revealed through the examination and analysis of selected literary, historical, and philosophical texts, resulted in rich and varied persuasive and artistic expressions. Moral appeals made in reference to the Mandate of Heaven, the moral examples of sage kings, and prescribed humanistic principles, along with the psychological model of rewards and punishment, were the central features of ritualistic, interpersonal, and political communication. Rationality was played out both in abstract and logical arenas, as well as through metaphor, analogy, and historical examples, while emotional appeals were expressed primarily through rhetorical actions in the context of trusting relationships. As the ancient Chinese society moved from idealism to pragmatism, from freedom of expression to centralized and mechanistic means of control, utilitarian appeals became increasingly prevalent. The direct and straightforward pattern of communication previously perceived and practiced had become indirect and evasive, with its purpose more oriented toward manipulation than moral perfection.

Ancient Chinese rhetorical perspectives were not monolithic. Different schools of thoughts and individual thinkers emphasized different aspects of language, persuasion, and argumentation. The School of Ming represented by Deng Xi, Hui Shi, and Gong-sun Long was primarily concerned with issues of probability, relativism, and classification under the general umbrella of epistemology and social justice. Their views on ming bian were subsequently borrowed and developed by the Later Mohists. The School of Confucianism, represented by Confucius, Mencius, and Xunzi, concentrated on issues of morality, in particular the moral impact of speech and moral character of the speaker on the cultivation and transformation of ethical behavior and social order. Mozi, the founder of the School of Mohism, while sharing certain Confucian views regarding moral communication, attempted to develop a rational system of bian, which was in turn systemized and elaborated by the Later Mohists. The Daoists, Laozi and Zhuangzi, proposed an antirational and transcendental mode of philosophical and rhetorical inquiry, emphasizing the paradoxical and aesthetic nature of communication. Finally, Han Feizi, the Legalist, approached language, persuasion, and argumentation with a focus on strengthening centralized political power and offered acute insight into human psychology in persuasion. Through intimate and subtle interactions among these various schools and thinkers, in the criticism and responses to one another, the notions of yan, ming, and bian developed and expanded. In the articulation of their respective philosophical and rhetorical views, these ancient Chinese thinkers demonstrated their mastery of the art of Chinese rhetoric in oral persuasion as well as in their writings, where an array of rhetorical devices were employed, ranging from the metaphorical, anecdotal, analogical, and paradoxical to examples of chain reasoning, classification, and inferences.

The developmental path of philosophical and rhetorical perspectives in ancient China can be compared to a spiral composed of layers of connected and yet independent circles, each circle representing a school of thought with its own internal unity and consistency. Within this context, however, each thinker made his own unique contribution while maintaining his own philosophical identity. Such continuity and yet divergence of thought was achieved through the critical and interpretive interplay of thinkers both within and between the various schools of thought. In general, while a growing sophistication is evident in the understanding and use of language, involving a certain linguistic continuity, at the same time the refinement of rhetorical concepts can also be discerned.[2]

Careful scrutiny of certain Chinese historical, literary, and philosophical texts of the fifth through third century B.C.E. offers compelling evidence for an identifiable formulation of language and persuasive discourse at the conceptual level. Primary texts under consideration in this study include *Shi Jing* 詩經 (the Book of Odes); *Shang Shu* 尚書 (the Book of History); *Zuo Zhuan* 左傳 (Zuo Commentaries); *Guo Yu* 國語 (Discourse of the States); and *Zhan Guo Ce* 戰國策 (Intrigues). Selected philosophical works are by the following authors: Deng Xi 鄧析, Gong-sun Long 公孫龍, Confucius 孔子, Mencius 孟子, Xunzi 荀子, Laozi 老子, Zhuangzi 莊子, Mozi 墨子, the Later Mohists, and Han Feizi 韓非子.[3] Below is a chart of major texts, authors, and dates in the order to be examined in this study:

Texts	Authors/Editors	Dates (B.C.E.)
Shi Jing	anonymous	700–400
Shang Shu	anonymous	700–400
Zuo Zhuan	Zuo Qiuming	475–221
Guo Yu	Zuo Qiuming	475–221
Zhan Guo Ce	Liu Xiang	79–8
Deng Xizi	Deng Xi	546–501

Gong-sun Longzi	Gong-sun Long	325–250
Lun Yu	Kong Qiu (Confucius)	552–479
Mengzi	Meng Ke (Mencius)	390–305
Xunzi	Xun Kuan (Xunzi)	298–238
Dao De Jing	Laozi	around 500
Zhuangzi	Zhuang Zhou (Zhuangzi)	369–286
Mozi	Mo Di (Mozi)	480–420
Mo Bian	Later Mohists	300–250
Han Feizi	Han Fei	280–233

These texts and individual thinkers derive from five philosophical schools, namely: the Schools of Ming; Confucianism; Daoism; Mohism; and Legalism. In order to be included in this study, a school had to be recognized by prominent Chinese and Western historians as influential during the fifth through third century B.C.E., a watershed period in Chinese philosophical discourse. It should be noted that these philosophical schools were not consciously formulated by the founding generation of thinkers, but rather by historians of the Han dynasty (206 B.C.E. to 220 C.E.).[4] What is more, the term *philosophy* did not originate with the Chinese themselves but was, rather, a translated English term to parallel with the study of Chinese ethics, logic, epistemology, and political science.[5] At any rate, texts under consideration are classical works of ancient China which record and describe persuasive activities, as well as addressing issues of ontology, epistemology, ethics, logic, language, and argumentation. More importantly, these texts, like the canonized texts of ancient Greece, defined and shaped the cultural and rhetorical traditions of China in subsequent years.

My interpretation of the meaning of Chinese rhetorical theories and practices will be based on the primary Chinese texts. However, certain secondary materials will also be considered in order to provide further information and shed light on contextual meanings. Three categories of secondary materials are used. The first group is comprised of texts produced during approximately the same time period as the primary texts. They are: *Da Xue* 大學 (Great Learning); *Zhong Yong* 中庸 (The Doctrine of the Mean); *Yi Jing* 易經 (Canon of Changes); *Liezi* 列子 (Liezi); *Sunzi* 孫子 (Sunzi); *Zhou Li* 周禮 (The Rites of Zhou); *Lu Shi Chun Qiu* 呂氏春秋 (Spring and Autumn of Mr. Lu); *Shi Ji* 史記 (Records of the Historian); *Han Shu* 漢書 (the Book of Han); *Shuo Yuan* 說苑 (the Garden of Talks), and *Huai Nanzi* 淮南子 (Huai Nanzi). The second group of secondary materials is made up of descriptive works of Chinese philosophy and logic authored by modern Chinese scholars. Finally, the third category derives from Western communication scholars and sinologists in the fields of Chinese culture, philosophy, history, and language. While gathering information and gleaning insights from these latter two groups, I remain aware that biases and misconceptions may be embedded or explicitly stated in the scholarship.

Translation is considered the core of hermeneutics, as it is only through translation—whereby linguistic, grammatical, conceptual, and cultural knowledge are compared and negotiated—that the meanings of ancient texts can be deciphered, interpreted, and understood by readers across time and space. In the modern era translations of the Bible; Russian, French, and English literature; and Western scientific theories made possible worldwide communication and the sharing of human creativity and achievements in the humanities and sciences.

Translation in the traditional sense refers to the reproduction of the original meaning of a text by a translator who has competence in two languages. The guiding principle for the translator is fidelity or faithfulness to the original text. Yan Fu 嚴復, a well-known Chinese translator and translation theorist, articulated the following principles of translation: faithfulness, comprehensibility, and elegance (Huxley, 1923 Preface). Faithfulness, in his view, refers to accuracy in relation to the original meaning of the text. Comprehensibility refers to the appropriate use of language. Elegance concerns the stylistic and artistic choice of words. Of these three principles, faithfulness is considered of utmost concern to the translator, even at the expense of expressiveness and elegance. In Walter Benjamin's (1969) opinion, however, this emphasis on fidelity is no longer "serviceable." He argues for a revised theory of translation based upon the notion that translation is a process of interpretation rather than a mere reproduction of the original meaning. Accordingly, translation is not a one-to-one correspondence or mere substitution of words and sentences from one language into another. Therefore, a translator should be primarily concerned with "appropriation" as opposed to fidelity.

Interestingly enough, while Yan Fu advocated faithfulness as the guiding principle of translation, in his own translation of Thomas Huxley's *Evolution and Ethics* he made accommodations to Chinese thought patterns, added his own creative interpretations, and omitted foreign terms which were offensive or unknown to Chinese readers (Xiao 1995). Another feature of Yan Fu's translation, according to Benjamin Schwartz (1964), is his deliberate use of classical Chinese language in conveying Western concepts and categories to appeal to the style-conscious Chinese literati. Judging from this and other examples, a work of translation ultimately reveals the translator's own perspective, intention, and skill in bridging two worldviews through his or her conscious choice of words. Indeed, the role of the translator is not simply that of a matchmaker of symbols from two different linguistic systems, but also that of a mediator, making sense of that which was previously alien and unintelligible through the medium of language and the convergence of two worlds. Achieving such a goal requires not only competence in both languages and familiarity with the subject matter at hand, but also sensitivity to the cultures of both the original author and the audience of the translation. A truly literal translation is impossible since, in the words of Susan Bassnett-McGuire, "The interlingual translation is bound to reflect the translator's own creative interpretation of the source language text" (1980, 80).

In his book *Western Approaches to Eastern Philosophy*, Troy Organ (1975, 12–13) highlights two assumptions he believes to be false regarding a scholar's competence in the study of Eastern culture. The first mistaken assumption, in his opinion, is that an Eastern philosopher is better qualified than his or her Western counterpart to interpret Eastern philosophy to the West; the second is that a scholar whose native language is the same as that of the original text is better qualified than a non-native speaker to interpret that text. David Hall and Roger Ames (1987) argue, similarly, that it is unrealistic to expect a scholar to possess both sinological and philosophical skills. While I agree to some extent with these arguments, I am generally of the opinion that a Western scholar with both linguistic competence in the target culture and training in both Western and Eastern thoughts is better qualified to interpret and translate Eastern texts than an Eastern scholar with little knowledge of Western thought and language. In other words, a bilingual and bicultural person is better prepared to translate and interpret the nuances of cross-cultural meanings in any given text and, therefore, more able to create a "fusion of horizons"(Gadamer, 1989). Instead of arguing for reduced scholarly expectations for those who engage in research requiring linguistic competence in a target culture, we should encourage a high degree of scholarly proficiency in a second or even third language in cross-cultural studies. In this way, such competence could not only serve as a research tool but also fulfill the more ambitious goal of true cross-cultural understanding. For this project my bilingual background enables me to translate and verify meanings embedded in ancient Chinese texts into the English language, while my bicultural experience makes me more aware of cultural and textual nuances in the subject matter before me.

Primary texts under consideration are read in their original classical Chinese language. The characters of classical Chinese still retain their features of pictography, self-explanation, ideography, pictophonetics, synonymy, and phonetic loaning as identified in modern Chinese. The Chinese language does not have grammatical features of number, case, gender, and inflections as do most Western languages. Although the word order or syntactical structure between English and modern Chinese is similar, classical Chinese often places the object before the verb. Furthermore, parts of speech are often used interchangeably. Another feature of classical Chinese is that one character can be used as a subject, verb, or object. Because of these features, the meanings in classical Chinese are highly abbreviated and contextual. Most primary Chinese texts under consideration in this study were reprinted and published in the 1990s in mainland China. Each version consists of the original text in classical Chinese as well as the translation in modern Chinese by Chinese experts of classical language. To ensure authenticity, I rely only upon the original meanings of the text in classical Chinese and I consult with the translated version when in doubt. Moreover, with the exception of certain well-established names in the English language, such as Confucius and Mencius, I use the pinyin system for the romanization of Chinese characters, as the system is relatively more economical than the Wade-Giles system and has been widely accepted in the field of sinology. To avoid confusion I place the original, unsimplified characters next to pinyin when they are first introduced, for the benefit of native Chinese readers and those who can read Chinese.[6]

A number of the selected texts are available in English translations. However, I will exercise caution when using such translations, especially those done by pioneer sinologists. This is because, as David Hall and Roger Ames point out, early sinologists often approached the translation of classical Chinese texts with a "rather naive, often theologically inspired agenda" (1987, 2). If, in my judgment, the English translation is faithful to the original and stylistically acceptable, I will use the available translation. If, however, the translation is inadequate, I will revise and formulate my own translations. For certain primary and secondary texts where there are no adequate translations available, I will offer my own translations, including Chinese characters whenever appropriate, so that bilingual readers of Chinese and English can verify the original meanings. Throughout this project, unless otherwise indicated, the translations are my own. However, when the meaning is ambiguous, the accuracy of my translations will be checked by collaboration with other Chinese scholars who possess competence in both languages.[7]

This project consists of ten chapters. Chapter 1 begins with a review and discussion of hermeneutical and multicultural principles that can guide us in interpreting, translating, and understanding texts, followed by a critique of the study of Chinese rhetoric by scholars from China and the United

States. Chapter 2 reviews the political transition and cultural forces of the pre-Qin period (before 221 B.C.E.) in ancient China, which provided the context for the different modes of communication and rhetorical practices. Chapter 3 identifies key terms and their linguistic meanings in the texts under consideration. The purpose of this identification and analysis is to reveal the original rhetorical meanings of Chinese texts as well as to demonstrate an evolution of vocabulary concerning speech and persuasive discourse. Chapter 4 introduces and analyzes rhetorical features and persuasive styles in five selected historical and literary texts. Patterns of persuasion and modes of rhetorical expressions will be identified in this chapter. Chapters 5 through 9 examine philosophical views and rhetorical perspectives articulated by individual thinkers from five major philosophical schools of ancient China. Chapter 10 builds a bridge between classical Chinese rhetoric and contemporary Chinese culture and communication patterns, summarizes main features of classical Chinese and classical Greek rhetorics, and discusses implications for a multicultural rhetoric.

CHAPTER 1

Perceptions and Methodology in the Study of Classical Chinese Rhetoric

In the past few decades attempts have been made by various Western communication scholars to introduce, explain, and explore classical Chinese rhetoric (Crump 1964; Garrett 1993a, 1993b; Jensen 1987, 1992; Kroll 1985–87). Though such preliminary studies are a valuable and informative step in the right direction, they are generally somewhat limited in their understanding of this ancient tradition. In order to assume a more authentic understanding on the subject, I will review current Western and Chinese scholarship in the field of classical Chinese rhetoric. In particular, I will identify and critique certain methodological problems related to research. In order to set the stage for these considerations, I will begin this chapter with a discussion of various modes of inquiry used in the interpretation and understanding of other cultures and cross-cultural texts.

Modes of Inquiry in Cross-Cultural Understandings

Orientalism and Occidentalism

In his thought-provoking book *Orientalism*, Edward Said claims that much of Western intellectual discourse on Eastern cultures suffers from Orientalism, defined as: "a style of thought based upon an ontological and epistemological distinction made between 'the Orient' and 'the Occident'" (1979, 2). According to Said, this Orient/Occident distinction derives from a Western projection of political dominance and academic authority in relation to the Orient. Furthermore, Oriental methodology employed in the study of the Orient reflects the problems of essentialism, dogmatism, and ethnocentrism, which tend to produce distorted and inaccurate views of non-Western people, ideas, and traditions. Though Said offers a brilliant critique of Western discourse on the Orient, suggesting that Orientalism projects a narrow view of Oriental cultures that has helped perpetuate racism and cultural stereotypes, he stops short of prescribing alternative ways of understanding non-Western cultures. He does, however, call for "an intellectual way of handling methodological problems" (110) in order to avoid the degeneration of knowledge, enlarge a discipline's claims, and celebrate human values.

Serious Western study of Chinese thought and culture did not take place until the sixteenth and seventeenth centuries with the arrival of European missionaries.[1] Among them, Matteo Ricci, the first Westerner to translate Confucian works into Latin, made the greatest contribution toward introducing early Chinese thought to the West.[2] His journals, entitled *On the Propagation of Christianity Among the Chinese,* which were published in Latin, Italian, German, French, and Spanish, described the Chinese as extremely industrious and exemplary in manners and conduct. What is more, Ricci praised the Chinese for their progress and achievement in medicine, science, and technology and determined that Confucian and Christian doctrines were compatible (He and He 1985). Up to this point Western intellectuals had generally regarded China as a refined and enlightened civilization. In fact, the Western Enlightenment in Europe was informed in part by Chinese thought. For example, German philosopher Gottfried Wilhelm Leibniz (1646–1716) and French thinker Marie Arouet de Voltaire (1694–1778) had studied and been influenced by Confucianism. Both had a high regard for Chinese culture and civilization and considered China a model for the West in its moral philosophy, ontology, and epistemology (Leibniz 1977; Shen 1985).

The image of a civilized and prosperous China dissolved in the nineteenth century, however, as Westerners came to regard China as a weak, backward, and filthy country. According to Bernal (1987), this change in perspective coincided with the British Opium War on China (1840–1842) and rising racism in Europe. The stereotypical "Chinaman" was portrayed by Westerners as lazy, undesirable looking, and cruel. Early Chinese immigrants to the United States became objects of ridicule and stereotyping. For example, according to the Yellow Peril propaganda of the nineteenth century: "He [the Chinaman] talked 'funny' and was fond of eating a strange delicacy.... He became the neighborhood's Fu Manchu—the spooky crook, the bad guy, associated with murder and the darkness of night" (Takaki 1989, 241). Similarly, editors and malicious political cartoonists of the time ridiculed the Chinese as "cultural inferiors, physically grotesque, morally depraved, and carriers of the deadliest disease" (Choy, Choy, and Hom 1994, 102).[3] During this period a clear case for Western superiority and Oriental inferiority was made. China and Chinese culture were portrayed in negative and undesirable terms in Western discourse.

In the twentieth century, due to Western academic and political interests in East Asia, Western knowledge of China and Chinese culture has increased. Unfortunately, however, intellectual discourse regarding China and its relationship to the West has fallen into the dualistic and reductionist categories characteristic of Orientalism. In much of the scholarship that introduces Chinese philosophy, religion, and culture to the West, China is portrayed as a strange, different, and peculiar Other, while Occidental culture is viewed as normative. For example, Max Weber wrote that Western cultural phenomena lie "in a line of development having universal significance and value" (1976, 13). Clearly, Western scholars of this century still labor under the assumption that Western culture is at the core of universal values, civilization, and progress. Eastern culture, in contrast, is viewed as subordinate and inferior.

Orientalism has adversely affected Western perceptions of Chinese speech behavior, communication styles, and culture. In studies comparing Chinese language systems, thought patterns, and cultural characteristics with those of the West, Western scholars have systematically dichotomized and polarized Oriental and Occidental cultures. For example, the Chinese language is classified as an "isolating language" within the Western framework of historical linguistics. It is considered linguistically inferior and located outside the historical and developmental parameters of Western civilization (Becker 1986; Bernal 1987). Only European languages are deemed capable of producing scientific thought, while the Chinese language, symbolized by ideographic characters, is said to be limited in function to the mere representation of immediate experience. A language system such as that of the Chinese, according to Filmer S. C. Northrop (1944; 1946, 316), produces intuitive thought patterns which are unsystematic and disorderly. By contrast, Western languages, categorized as "postulational" or "logical," are considered relatively systematic and orderly.[4] The notion that Oriental thought processes are intuitive while Western ways of thinking are scientific and rational has, unfortunately, been widely accepted in Western academic circles.

To this day, anthropologists and communication scholars continue to superimpose dualistic and polarized categories of analysis upon Chinese cultural patterns and communication behaviors. Chinese culture as a whole is classified as "collectivistic" and "high context," while Western culture is viewed as "individualistic" and "low-context" (Gudykunst and Kim 1984; Hall 1976; Hofstede 1980; Hui and Triandis 1986). With regard to communication behaviors, Eastern cultures are said to: value silence; deprecate speech and avoid conflict; be more interested in relational messages; and use indirect modes of communication. Western cultures, on the other hand, are said to: value verbal exchange, in particular speech and argumentation; be more interested in utilitarian messages; and employ direct modes of communication (Scollon and Scollon 1995; Ting-Toomey 1988). Though, to some degree, these dichotomies are helpful in making assumptions and predictions of Eastern and Western cultures and communication, they also perpetuate simplistic views regarding both Western and Chinese language, culture, and communication. Furthermore, the portrayal of Chinese culture as wholly "other" has resulted in misunderstandings toward China in Sino-American relations and foreign policy (Fairbank 1974).

Western perceptions of Chinese rhetoric are, by and large, defined by the limits of Orientalism. Rhetoric is regarded as an invention of the West: Athens is considered the cradle of world civilization, with the ancient Greeks the founders of rhetorical discourse. Just as the claim is made that the Chinese language is incapable of producing science, it is also asserted that no non-Western culture, including that of the Chinese, is capable of producing rhetoric. In fact, in a well-studied text on the history of rhetoric, one prominent Western scholar explicitly denies the existence of any non-Western rhetorical traditions, stating that: "There is no evidence of an interest in rhetoric in the ancient civilizations of Babylon or Egypt, for instance, neither Africa nor Asia has to this day produced a rhetoric" (Murphy 1983, 3). As this example illustrates, rhetoric is viewed as the exclusive property of the West. Consequently, U.S. college textbooks on the history of rhetoric are limited almost exclusively to consideration of Western rhetorical traditions. Even *Rhetorica,* a journal whose expressed focus is the history of rhetoric, publishes few articles on Eastern rhetoric. It is not surprising, given this state of affairs, that Eastern rhetoric, in general, and Chinese rhetoric, in particular, remain unfamiliar subjects to many rhetorical scholars. Furthermore, non-Western rhetorical traditions are treated as either incorrigible or inferior. For example, "Current Western understandings of Confucius," according to Hall and Ames, "are the consequence of the mostly unconscious importation of philosophical and theological assumptions into primary translations that have served to introduce Confucius' thinking to the West" (1987, 7–8). These assumptions, which have seriously distorted the perceptions of Confucius's thinking, are associated with the mainstream of the Anglo-European classical tradition.

If Orientalism is closely associated with and caused by Eurocentrism, the same essentialistic, dogmatic, and ethnocentric methodology can also be identified in Occidentalism, which is associated with and caused by Sinocentrism. Chinese perceptions of Westerners have in the past been negative. For example, the Chinese described Europeans and Americans as having "dazzling white flesh, high noses, and red hair," referring to them as "foreign devils," "big nose," or "barbarians" (Teng and Fairbank 1954, 20).[5] The Chinese emperor regarded himself as the Son of Heaven and thus the ruler of all humankind. As described by Ssu-yu Teng and John Fairbank in *China's Response to the West*, their collaboration on the practice of trade in the early nineteenth century, foreign rulers who wished to contact or trade with the Chinese Empire were first required "to enroll as tributaries, accept investiture, send envoys to perform the kotow (three kneelings and nine prostrations) before the Son of Heaven, and otherwise obey the regulations for tributary intercourse" (18–19). In a blatantly condescending letter sent by Emperor Qian Long to King George III in 1793, Qian-Long imposed the Chinese tributary framework upon Western nations: "the virtue and prestige of the Celestial Dynasty having spread far and wide, the kings of the myriad nations come by land and sea with all sorts of precious things. Consequently there is nothing we lack, as your principal envoy and others have themselves observed. We have never set much store on strange or ingenious objects, nor do we need any more of your country's manufactures . . ." (19). This example reveals an attitude of ethnocentrism on the part of the Chinese emperor. Even though in the seventeenth century the European Jesuits informed the Chinese that they were not at the center of the world, the ancient Chinese continued to regard themselves as the most civilized nation on earth. The Chinese characters for China mean "middle kingdom" or "country in the center."

Western religious traditions and ideas were also met with great suspicion and opposition when first introduced into China. Chinese scholars generally denounced Christianity. In addition, they attacked the Western-designed calendar, clock, cannon, and map for not adhering to Chinese standards, claiming that Western science had, in fact, originated in China (Teng and Fairbank 1954, 14–15). Although appreciation for Western science has since increased and twentieth-century Western philosophy and ideas have made their way into China, Western people, ideas, and cultures are still largely viewed as the Other and perceived with suspicion and stereotyping. For example, Chinese textbooks only teach schoolchildren that the foreign devils bullied the Chinese people and looted their motherland. The contributions made by "foreign devils" to Chinese development of science and technology are largely ignored. In addition, some Chinese intellectuals still regard Chinese culture as superior to Western culture.

For a better understanding between peoples and cultures, it is necessary to critique and evaluate discourse which has until now been subject to the limitations of Orientalism, on the one hand, and Occidentalism, on the other. Both Eastern and Western scholars need to challenge their own biases and assumptions of Eastern and Western cultures. Both need to learn from each other, not only in terms of subject matter but also in efforts to construct appropriate modes of inquiry.

Hermeneutics

Strictly speaking, this project engages hermeneutics in the translation and interpretation of classical Chinese texts for the purpose of understanding classical Chinese rhetoric. In general terms, hermeneutics, from the Greek *hermêneia*, meaning "interpretation," is a discipline concerned with the interpretation of historical texts. The discipline originated with the interpretation of canonical texts across cultures, for example, the Buddhist Pali Canon, the Bible, the Qur'an, the Greek Classics, and Confucian and Daoist works. Clearly, hermeneutics involves linguistic translation along with the contextualization of historical, cultural, and social conditions relevant to the deciphering of ancient texts. In this sense, "hermeneutics belongs to the realm of opinion, or rhetoric, rather than to the realm of truth, or philosophy" (Bruns 1992, 46). Michel Foucault (1975, xvi–xvii) characterizes such interpretation as "commentary" that, at its best, transmits and restates seemingly old and silent discourse in the form of comprehensible contemporary language.

Hermeneutical theory was developed by a group of German philosophers. Friedrich Schleiermacher (1768–1834), the father of modern hermeneutics, first framed the discipline as "the art of understanding." Such understanding, according to Schleiermacher, goes beyond simply making sense of an original text. Most essentially, it is a reconstructive process undertaken by the interpreter. This is accomplished by "reexperiencing the mental processes of the text's author" (Palmer 1969, 86). For Schleiermacher, true understanding is contextual, taking place in a circle known as the hermeneutical circle, the area of shared understanding between the speaker and the hearer. In order to complete the hermeneutical circle, the speaker and hearer must share both the language and subject of a discourse.

Following Schleiermacher, Wilhelm Dilthey (1833–1911) regarded hermeneutics as a process of reconstructing and reexperiencing the author's world. He approached hermeneutics as a methodology concerned with epistemology, conceptualizing and recovering historical consciousness, and understanding the author's inner world and sociohistorical life. Understanding, for Dilthey, is not a cognitive function of the mind, but a reexperiencing of the world as lived and experienced by the original author. Such understanding opens the interpreter to the world of an individual and a culture, in addition to promoting understanding of one's own environment and culture. The central concern of hermeneutics for Dilthey is the notion of "historicality," which defines humans as dependent upon the particulars of history for self-understanding. More importantly, for Dilthey, "history is ultimately a series of worldviews, and we have no firm and fixed standards of judgment for seeing the superiority of one worldview over another" (Palmer 1969, 117). In other words, meaning is historically and culturally relative, being in relation to specific cultural contexts and the perspective of the interpreter.

While Dilthey provided the notion of historicality, Martin Heidegger proposed a hermeneutical theory of self-understanding related to process and outcome. For Heidegger (1962), interpretation is never a presuppositionless process. Rather, it is rooted in a prestructure which holds an imprint of already established ideological preconceptions. That is, interpretation does not take place in an ideological vacuum but is subject to the preconceptions of the interpreter who sees things through certain ideational lenses, revealed in his or her choice of and approach to the texts. Hermeneutics, in Heidegger's view, is the ontological and phenomenological structure of understanding. Accordingly, the skewed interpretation of texts is unavoidable.

Perhaps the most well known thinker in the development of hermeneutical theory is Hans-Georg Gadamer, who defines the realm of hermeneutics as philosophy that encompasses the dimension of dialectics and the whole human experience of the universal world. Gadamer agrees with Heidegger that interpretation begins with preconceptions. Furthermore, any one, in his opinion, who tries to understand a text is, in fact, projecting his or her own perspective and judgment. However, Gadamer points out, "the important thing is to be aware of one's own bias so that the text can present itself in all its otherness and thus assert its own truth against one's own fore-meanings" (1989, 269). To advance the knowledge of a discipline, according to Gadamer, new and rival projects must emerge to provoke questions and make new inquiries. "This constant process of new projects constitutes the movement of understanding and interpretation" (267). The task of hermeneutics, then, is not simply reconstruction or restoration, but the integration of competing perspectives. Though still addressing himself primarily to the elite discourse within the European mode of inquiry, Gadamer notes, "the keys to understanding are not manipulation and control but participation and openness, not knowledge but experience, not methodology, but dialectic" (in Palmer 1969, 215). Hermeneutics, for Gadamer, is a philosophical inquiry and comprehensive understanding of human experience in historical, linguistic, and dialectical domains.

In any event, scholarship on hermeneutics has illuminated our understanding of the art of translation and interpretation. From Schleiermacher to Gadamer, hermeneutics has evolved from a tool for understanding canonical texts to a mode of inquiry that recognizes universal and particular experience. It acknowledges the interpreter's competence and subjectivity in the reconstruction of the original texts, as well as celebrating universal values and the fulfillment of human experience. Basically, two trends can be discerned in the hermeneutical theories described above: 1) historical hermeneutics, represented by Schleiermacher and Dilthey, which focuses on a reconstruction of meaning approximating the intended meaning of the original author for the original audience; and 2) scriptural hermeneutics, articulated by Heidegger and Gadamer, which is more interested in appropriating the original meaning for a modern audience and relating it to contemporary questions. Historical hermeneutics is, in my opinion, helpful in recovering the original meaning of the text, while scriptural hermeneutics allows critical assessment of the relevance of the text to us today. Michael LaFargue argues that historical and scriptural hermeneutics cannot be truly set apart as the historical hermeneutics itself has embodied these two functions. In his words, "First, historical hermeneutics can help us critically evaluate traditional ideas by tracing these ideas to the originating experiences that gave rise to them." Secondly, "it makes possible a fully explicit, rational, public discussion concerning the contemporary relevance of any given classic" (1994, 8–9). Given the above description, historical hermeneutics includes both descriptive and interpretative function of the original meaning and an engagement with critical and evaluative method for contemporary significance. In the case of classical Chinese rhetoric, the historical hermeneutics is employed to identify the rhetorical experience and conceptualizations of the ancient Chinese in response to the social context and cultural forces in which they lived. At the same time, this tradition is made explicit and intellectually apprehensible through the examination of primary texts and comparison with classical Greek rhetoric. Moreover, the recovery of this tradition illuminates both our understanding of contemporary rhetoric and our understanding of Chinese communication behavior.

Anthropological Approaches

Hermeneutical questions are also much debated in the field of anthropology and cultural studies where issues of cross-cultural understanding and interpretation are of utmost concern. One view espoused in these disciplines, similar to scriptural hermeneutics, is that the interpreter makes sense of the foreign culture based on his or her own knowledge, perspective, and contemporary stand. Clifford Geertz calls such an approach an "actor orientation," meaning that, for example, "descriptions of Berber, Jewish, or French culture must be cast in terms of the constructions we imagine Berbers, Jews, or Frenchmen to place upon what they live through, the formulae they use to define what happens to them" (1973, 15). In other words, according to Geertz, "we began with our own interpretation of what our informants are up to, or think they are up to, and then systematize this" (15). This means the interpreter's own cultural assumptions, values, and concerns are used as the framework and basis for understanding and interpreting other cultures. For Geertz, the primary challenge in interpreting other cultures is not to describe and discover cultural meaning in its texts and contexts, but to analyze and evaluate such meanings against the interpreter's own value system and cultural orientation. In his words, "Cultural analysis is (or should be) guessing at meaning, assessing the guesses, and drawing explanatory conclusions from better guesses, not discovering the continent of meaning and mapping out its bodiless landscape" (15). However, because of the Western domination and colonization of intellectual discourse since the nineteenth century, European students generally "interpreted other societies in terms derived from European culture, very often at the cost of extreme distortion, and frequently also in an unflattering light" (Taylor 1985, 124). Similarly, biased descriptions and distortions of Western people and culture can be found in Chinese texts such as the 1996 bestseller in China *China Can Say No*.[6] Clearly, the hermeneutical studies, both Eastern and Western, have not been value-free. Cultures are classified as good or bad, inferior or desirable, primitive or civilized. Scholars from dominant cultures are, thus, invited to criticize and correct nondominant cultures. Such practices should be understood as expressions of superiority and ethnocentrism rather than as genuine attempts at scholarly enquiry. Taylor argues that "the values of one culture are frequently not replicable in another; we can find nothing exactly corresponding to them" (1985, 120). On a related note, James Clifford, a cultural anthropologist, contends that the evaluative approach to cross-cultural interpretation reinforces dichotomizing and essentializing modes of thought. He suggests that "all dichotomizing concepts should probably be held in suspicion, whether they be the West-rest (Third World) split or developed-undeveloped, modern-premodern." We should therefore "attempt to think of cultures not as organically unified or traditionally continuous but rather as a negotiated, present process" (1988, 273).

An alternative approach to cross-cultural interpretation advocated by Peter Winch in his essay "Understanding a Primitive Society" is to interpret the culture on its own terms, adopting the view and language of the target culture, and describing situational and contextual meanings specific to the culture. In Winch's study of the African Azande culture, for example, he discovered that the criteria of rationality commonly shared by Western society cannot be applied to the Azande practice of consulting oracles. He suggests that we seek "a way of looking at things which goes beyond our previous way in that it has in some way taken account of and incorporated the other way that members of S have of looking at things" (1964, 317). In the case of classical Chinese rhetoric, Western conceptions of rhetoric should not be used as criteria for the interpretation and conclusion of Chinese rhetoric. A truly authentic meaning of Chinese rhetoric can only be generated by the examination of how the ancient Chinese perceived their world and addressed their problems through the Chinese rhetorical experience and concepts.

When an interpreter explains the texts of other cultures, he or she introduces different cultural norms and ways of doing things to the reader of the target language. In this way other possibilities for making sense of the world and human life are normalized. Thus, hermeneutical experience is, in effect, intercultural experience, through which one learns to appreciate other cultures while increasing one's own self-understanding. Being a native Chinese, I study my own culture in this case; however, in doing this research, I am also engaged in cross-cultural learning. After all, the ancient Chinese culture in many ways is a different culture from today's. Moreover, I present and introduce Chinese rhetorical experience and concepts to Western readers through English language, which in and of itself is a cross-cultural experience and construction. The fulfillment of hermeneutics is the illumination and enlightenment of human experience through cross-cultural interpretation and understanding, whether of texts, specifically, or cultures, in general. According to Winch, "What we may learn by studying other cultures are not merely possibilities of different ways of doing things.... More importantly we may learn different possibilities of making sense of human life, different ideas about the possible importance that the carrying out of certain activities may take on for a man, trying to contemplate the sense of his life as a whole" (1964, 312). The study of Chinese rhetoric is an attempt to capture and analyze rhetorical possibilities as they made sense for the ancient Chinese and may provide insights for non-Chinese readers.

Multiculturalism

Canon building becomes a central issue in academic discourse. In the field of rhetorical studies what has been canonized is Greek rhetoric. Such canonization has political implications, for as Toni Morrison contends, "Canon building is Empire building. Canon defense is national-defense, Canon debate, whatever the terrain, nature and range (of criticism, of history, of the history of knowledge, of the definition of language, the universality of aesthetic principles, the sociology of art, the humanistic imagination), is the clash of cultures" (1989, 8). In the West canon building in rhetoric, art, and literature amounts to the production and perpetuation of European presumptions, along with attempts made to universalize them. This approach is seriously flawed in that non-Western ideas are made to fit into Western disciplinary and intellectual categories.

In the late twentieth century ever-expanding awareness of the importance of multiculturalism and commitment to cultural diversity has resisted and challenged the monocultural and ethnocentric practice of canon building. Multiculturalism, according to Peter Caws, is "the enrichment of the self through acquaintance with and cultivation of what is found to be the most rewarding in all the human products and practices with which one comes in contact" (1994, 372). In the words of David Goldberg, a multicultural mode of inquiry "explores the assertive foundations of disciplines, scrutinizing the boundaries of subjects, conceived as agents and disciplines" (1994, 2). In other words, multiculturalism challenges, resists, and critically evaluates canon building and hegemony in academic discourse.

Caws makes a good connection between multiculturalism and hermeneutics. For him, the hermeneutical experience is one of identity transformation for the interpreter. In the process of interpreting a foreign text, one is engaged in interactions with others and with the world at large. In Caws's words, movement toward a multicultural identity makes possible "the enlargement of individual horizons"(1994, 382). In his article "Identity: Cultural, Transcultural, and Multicultural," Caws concludes that "the challenge to anyone who seeks to work in these directions is to be at once informed about the world, accepting of the stranger, and open to the new—to be, in short, an individual with an identity unconstrained by cultural particularity or prejudice" (1994, 386).[7] From ancient times to the present, a number of scholars have dedicated their lives to the task of translating and interpreting the works of cultures other than their own. Some have embraced cultures that are "originally alien to them and have made elements of these cultures chosen aspects of their identities" (Caws 1994, 384). Such multicultural experience promotes creativity, transformation, and, ultimately, enlightenment.

The notion of multiculturalism has elevated the hermeneutical enterprise from the interpretation of canonical texts to the discovery of multicultural rhetorical meanings and a critique of the dominant discourse in rhetorical studies. As LaFargue argues,

Hermeneutics could become an important tool for intercultural understanding, and a crucial first step in critical evaluation of the various cultural traditions of the world. But it can only do this if it ceases to be understood primarily as a means of colonizing traditional texts, bringing them under the hegemony of the worldview and values of either the conservative or the radical interpreter. . . . If we dropped the idea of a canon, hermeneutics could become a truly universal science and art, applying the same principles to all human discourse whatsoever." (1994, 42–43)

Here LaFargue suggests a construction and engagement of multicultural hermeneutics, which can be defined as an essential ingredient in scrutinizing and assessing already canonized texts as well as an essential tool for discovering and claiming value and legitimacy for works of philosophy or literature from nondominant cultures. It is an instrument to promote cross-cultural understanding and the reduction of ethnocentrism. It aims to create a pluralistic, diverse, and multiversioned world experience and reflections of the experience, and, more importantly, to accept and appreciate our kaleidoscopic world through the introduction and analysis of multicultural texts. The study of Chinese rhetoric is intended as a challenge to existing and accepted canons of rhetorical history by applying the standard of multicultural hermeneutics.

Traditional hermeneutical methods, and approach to the study of non-Western texts, have unfortunately furthered the cause of Orientalism. Multicultural hermeneutics calls for an end to the tendency of seeing ideas, traditions, and people from other cultures as wholly "other" and a development of an attitude of appreciation for perceived cultural differences. While the whole project employs and aims to achieve multicultural hermeneutics in general, the next section, in particular, is a critique of Western perceptions of Chinese rhetoric that exemplify the influence of Orientalism.

Western Perceptions of Classical Chinese Rhetoric

Western scholars have identified four themes common to ancient Chinese rhetoric. First, they have identified and classified a number of ancient Chinese persuasive practitioners. Second, they have analyzed some primary texts with literary and aesthetic interests. Third, they have described modes of argumentation found in ancient Chinese texts. And fourth, they have identified in a broad sense characteristic patterns of ancient Chinese speech and communication. All these studies are helpful and show a genuine effort and interest by Western scholars in understanding this ancient tradition. While such studies provided a starting point for an understanding of ancient Chinese rhetoric, they are limited in their breadth and depth.

The first area of research is focused on the identification and recognition of Chinese rhetorical practice through the naming of various persuaders and their rhetorical activities in general terms. For example, James Crump and John Dreher offer the following description of *you shui* 游說 (traveling persuaders) in fourth-century-B.C.E. China: "Adept in persuasion, quick of wit, owing no allegiance to anything beyond their own aggrandizement, these men traveled the empire professing loyalty to first this prince, then that, turning one against the other with cleverly turned argument. While admittedly interested only in their own fortunes, these You-shwei [*you shui*] have had far-reaching effects on history..." (1951, 16).

The term *you shui* is often used interchangeably with *bian shi* 辯士 or *bian zhe* 辯者.[8] Both terms refer to debators and persuasive practitioners in ancient China. The word shi in ancient Chinese refers to learned and skilled men who "began to be known more for their rhetoric than for their philosophy" (Crump 1964, 8). They were said to be constantly acting as envoys and always using the talent of persuasion. In Crump's opinion, the best English translation for the Chinese word *shi* is the word *rhetor* (9). In his book *Intrigues: Studies of Chan-kuo Ts'e* Crump offers a general description of rhetorical practice during the Warring States period, making the point that the persuasive skills demonstrated by these shi very much resemble those of sophists in ancient Greece.

A more extensive review of ancient Chinese speech patterns and rhetorical activities is provided by Robert Oliver in his landmark book *Communication and Culture in Ancient India and China*. Oliver (1971, 84) identifies three types of rhetoricians in ancient China: 1) talkers of books or storytellers; 2) professional mediators of disputes at the feudal courts; and 3) diplomatic agents. In fact, the most influential group of ancient Chinese rhetors not included in this list is made up of prominent philosophers and thinkers who acted as you shui for political consultation for the rulers and bian shi in debates over issues of moral, epistemological, and social concern in the fifth through third century B.C.E. As J. L. Kroll observes, "Disputation took place both between philosophical schools and within a single tradition. These debates were held in different settings, either in private circumstances (sometimes through an intermediary) and 'in the lanes,' that is in public" (1985–87, 121).

These limited accounts of ancient Chinese rhetorical practices, however incomplete, demonstrate that China did have a tradition of oral persuasive discourse, called for by the need to address social, cultural, and philosophical questions and, for some, by the desire for personal gains. This line of research has challenged the erroneous assertion that China lacked a rhetorical tradition and has promoted scholarly interests in the study of Chinese rhetoric. Unfortunately, however, understanding of Chinese rhetoric remains very general, lacking substantial supporting evidence and specific descriptions in cultural contexts. Serious attention has not yet been paid to rhetorical theories associated with varied philosophical orientations in their cultural and historical contexts. In an effort to begin to rectify this situation, later chapters of this project aim to expand our knowledge and understanding of Chinese rhetoric through an extensive identification and analysis of rhetorical activities engaged in by bian shi and you shui.

The second area of research examines ceremonial speeches, aesthetic rhapsodies, and narratives in selected primary and translated Chinese literary and historical works (Crawford 1963; Egan 1977; Hart 1984; Lu 1994; Saussy 1993; Watson 1962). These studies provide rich data on Chinese rhetorical practice and are helpful attempts toward conceptualizing Chinese rhetoric. However, they are limited in their overemphasis on literary and aesthetic criticism and their interest in written language at the expense of oral speech. Consequently, such studies offer useful information on Chinese language and stylistic writing but fail to identify theories of rhetoric and communication and to offer specific explanations of the cultural and philosophical orientation that affect rhetorical practice.

The third category of research on Chinese rhetoric characterizes modes of argumentation and persuasive strategies of ancient Chinese rhetoricians. In the early studies on logic and reasoning of the ancient Chinese, analogic reasoning and chain-reasoning are identified as the two distinctive modes of thinking (Bodde 1983; Cikoski 1975). To continue these efforts, Garrett (1983) delineates four primary modes of argumentation: 1) argument by authority; 2) argument by a deductive chain; 3) argument from consequence; and 4) argument by comparisons. Jensen (1992) agrees with Garrett that the ancient Chinese used strategies of argumentation by authority, analogy, and examples but finds them generally lacking in the area of deductive reasoning process in their argument.[9] Kroll offers more specific categories of argumentation and persuasion employed by the ancient Chinese: "inference by analogy"; "thesis and antithesis"; "paradox and dilemmas"; "comparing things and joining objects of the same kind"; and "the method of [discussing] advantages and disadvantages." In Kroll's (1985–87) opinion, these methods are primarily forms of indirect argumentation and persuasion which were most commonly found in preimperial and imperial diplomatic practices.

This group of scholarship has contributed to the study of classical Chinese rhetoric by classifying and analyzing Chinese rhetorical practices, specifically in the area of argumentation. Nevertheless, the focus is placed on specific modes of argumentation rather than providing cultural and textual analysis for the engagement of such modes. More importantly, these studies emphasize the ways in which Chinese modes of argumentation differ from Western modes, at the expense of examining the similarities between the two. In addition, they tend to treat Chinese rhetoric as a monolithic tradition rather than reflecting the varied philosophical perspectives of a given time period. A serious attempt to conceptualize classical Chinese rhetoric requires a more comprehensive examination of cultural contexts, as well as historical, literary, and philosophical works.

The fourth category of research reflects a certain orientalistic tendency to conceptualize Chinese rhetoric and communication. In general, Chinese rhetoric is said to be characterized by an emphasis on harmony, deprecation of speeches, and lack of logic. Such perceptions may derive from Western scholars' "prestructural" (Heidegger 1962) and "action orientation" (Geetze 1973) approaches to the study of non-Western cultures. Instead of letting the text "assert its own truth against one's own fore-meaning" or dialectically questioning the conventional interpretations of Chinese texts, various ethnocentric assumptions are made and Western categories of intellectual discourse are superimposed upon Chinese culture and philosophy. Such an orientation is excusable in these early stages of cross-cultural explorations; however, it tends to produce and perpetuate stereotypes of Chinese culture and communication. In order to clarify various misconceptions of Chinese rhetoric made by Western scholars and to pursue the goals of multicultural hermeneutics, it is necessary to evaluate and critique Western perceptions and myths of Chinese rhetoric.

Myth #1: Chinese Rhetoric Is Characterized by Harmony

Western scholars believe the purpose of Chinese rhetoric is to achieve harmony. As Jensen notes, "a central value of East Asian cultures is the desire for harmony, oneness with nature and with other human beings—with all of life" (1987, 223). This desire for harmony is not limited in scope to ancient Chinese culture but is also the goal in modern China. Whether under socialist and communist influence, as in the People's Republic of China, or within the context of democratic and capitalist concerns, as in Taiwan, the traditional respect for authority, unity, and harmony is still maintained by those of Chinese heritage (Kincaid 1987).

As harmony is believed to be the primary cultural value of ancient and contemporary China, it is, likewise, regarded as the overriding concern of Chinese rhetoric. In comparing communication goals, East and West, Donald Cushman and Lawrence Kincaid note that "an Eastern perspective emphasizes selflessness and submission to central authority as an institutional means for achieving unity and harmony between man and nature as the principle goal of communication" (1987, 9). Oliver shares this view of the function of Chinese communication, asserting that "the primary function of discourse is not to enhance the welfare of the individual speaker or listener but to promote harmony" (1971, 261). Unlike a Greek orator who imposes his will on his audience, "the role of the speaker is much less emphasized in the rhetoric of India or China, where harmony rather than victory is often the goal" (Kennedy 1980, 10).

Clearly, such generalizations about Chinese rhetoric as a means to maintain and promote social harmony contain a kernel of truth. However, they do not reflect the complex and varied nature of Chinese culture. China has a recorded history of three thousand years, and throughout this long time span Chinese cultural values are represented by different schools of thought at different times in history. When Western scholars overgeneralize about Chinese rhetoric, they are often unclear as to the time period and school of thought under consideration as well as the social context in which the rhetoric of harmony is initiated and emphasized. In fact, ancient Chinese history is a mosaic of ideological, philosophical, and cultural diversity. For example, historians of the period of Spring-Autumn and Warring States 春秋戰國 (722–481 B.C.E.) recorded intense conflicts between and within ancient Chinese states and philosophical schools. Clearly, conflict, wars, and dissent were not absent in ancient Chinese culture and tradition. Speech patterns at the time may demonstrate more characteristics of confrontation and conflict than harmony.

It cannot be overstated that such generalizations regarding Chinese rhetoric are based on the Western assumptions of Chinese culture rather than on a close examination and interpretation of rhetorical texts and contexts. Moreover, such studies seem to lack clear criteria for determining what constitutes harmonious rhetoric. Hence, we are told that harmony is emphasized in China, but we are not told how harmony is achieved and maintained in the rhetorical sense. If harmony is achieved by submission to authority, as Kincaid, Oliver, and Jensen contend, is it true harmony or harmony at the expense of truth and individuality? If the latter, should we call it harmony or conflict in disguise? These questions should be researched more thoroughly before generalizations are made regarding Chinese rhetoric.

Myth #2: Speech in China Is Deprecated

Western scholars contend that Chinese rhetoric is not systematized and conceptualized because the Chinese deprecate speech and denounce eloquence. According to Oliver, in ancient China "loud talk and abusive language were considered poor behavior" (1971, 98). Conversely, slow talk and silence are valued in Chinese society. Jensen concludes that eloquence, argumentation, and speaking in general are deprecated in China, as they are associated with very negative connotations such as "shallowness, superficiality, untrustworthy cleverness, pretentiousness, pride, hypocrisy, and flattery" (1987, 221).

This is not a complete picture of Chinese rhetoric. In fact, a close examination of selected literary, historical, and philosophical works would demonstrate that speech in ancient China was highly valued and encouraged. Speakers enjoyed impressive reputations and played important roles in politics and education. They were considered wise men or social elites and enjoyed a high level of trust and respectability. Argumentation and debates were common among philosophers and bian shi. Debates occurred over moral and epistemological issues as well as over military strategies and foreign policies. Numerous examples of vigorous debates and persuasive speeches can be found in recorded and re-created texts produced between 500 and 200 B.C.E. Some of these speeches will be examined in chapter 4. It is fair to say that Chinese philosophers valued speech as much as the ancient Greeks and that they were eloquent speakers and rhetoricians. As Wing-tsit Chan records: "Few have shut themselves up in an ivory tower to write long treaties on philosophy or any theoretical subject. . . . the teachings of Confucius, Lao Tzu [Laozi], and others are found in conversations" (1967, 17). In Confucius's works, in particular his *Analects*, a strong emphasis on critical thinking and self-expression through questions and answers can be discerned that is, in some sense, similar to Socratic dialogue.

The literal translation of *speech* in Chinese is *yan* 言. The ancient Chinese often made distinction between different kinds of yan, such as *chang yan* 昌言 (beautiful speech) and *shi yan* 食言 (hypercritical speech) (SS, 26–27, 59).[10] Confucius taught his students to practice *xin yan* 信言 (trustworthy speech) and disliked *qiao yan* 巧言 (clever speech) (LY 13.20.134; 15.6.158; 15.27.160; 17.17.178). Mencius discussed and advocated *shan yan* 善言 (good speech) and *ren yan* 仁言 (benevolent speech) (M 14b.32.244; 13a.14.307). The criticism of speech was often targeted at those clever and hypercritical speeches that were considered manipulative and demoralizing. As Confucius said in his *Analects*, "I dislike men who argue with glib tongues" (LY 11.25.114). Clearly, ancient Chinese philosophers did condemn false or flowery speeches; however, they did so without condemning rhetoric in general. A careful reading of original philosophical texts will lead us to the conclusion that what is deprecated by ancient Chinese philosophers is not speech in general but rather glib speakers or speakers with flowery and empty words. Even in today's China, eloquent speakers who use embellishment and flowery words in their speeches are judged as glib, boastful, shallow, and untrustworthy. Those who speak with substance, wisdom, appropriateness, and humor are highly appreciated and respected. Generalizations made by Western scholars regarding the Chinese attitude toward speech fail to account for situation and social context, audience, and the manner of speech. Such generalizations are based on superficial and segmented interpretations of Chinese philosophical works as well as on Western perceptions of the role and function of speech and argumentation in ancient Chinese culture.

Myth #3: Chinese Rhetoric Is Not Interested in Logic

In the Western rhetorical tradition, rhetoric is clearly identified and closely related to logic. Western scholars are generally of the opinion that speeches in ancient China do not have the component of logic. Alfred Forke concludes in his study "The Chinese Sophists" that "The Chinese mind has never risen above these rudiments and developed a complete system of logic" (1901/2), 5). Subsequent scholars have, to their detriment, followed the lead of Northrop (1946), who held that the Chinese were "intuitive" and could not use Western logic. Echoing Forke's and Northrop's claims, Oliver writes, "the ancient East has not been much interested in logic, which necessarily correlated unlike elements, nor has it favored either definition or classification as aids to clear thought" (1971, 10). The reason for this, in Oliver's view, is "precisely because intuitive insight was considered to be the superior means of perceiving truth. Asian rhetoric, therefore, did not presume logical argument but the explication of self-evident propositions" (259). On a related note, Carl Becker (1986) attributes the so-called lack of logic in Eastern cultures to "the inabilities to make fine distinctions and abstractions" and "lack of logical rules and constraints" (84) inherent in the Chinese language.

The ancient Chinese may not have formulated a theory of logic resembling the Aristotelian logical system; however, examples of persuasion and argumentation by definition, analogy, and deduction abound in ancient Chinese texts. A case can be made, therefore, that the ancient Chinese were masters of their own "logic." In fact, the Chinese Mingjia (School of Ming) is well known among Chinese thinkers for its theory of logic and rational thinking. What is more, the School of Mohism is credited with the formulation of a logical system of speech and argumentation, as will be demonstrated in chapter 7; while intuition, rooted primarily in Daoism, is an important mode of inquiry in China. Other schools of thought, including Confucianism, have also manifested strong rationalistic orientations.

Arguing against the position that the Chinese lack an interest in logic, Chung-ying Cheng claims, "there is nothing in Chinese language which prevents the Chinese mind from developing logical thinking or formulating logical principles" (1969, 336). Similarly, Garrett concludes in her dissertation on Chinese Mohist logic that "self-conscious restriction [on the part of the Later Mohists] to deduction in all areas, including 'disputation' and ethical decision-making, was surely due, as in the Western case, to the striking success of hypothetico-deductive reasoning in demonstrating causal relations for their problems in physics, optics, and mechanics" (1983, 341). Furthermore, Chinese logic is discussed and employed in the works of Xunzi, Mozi, and even Confucius. For example, Ernest Richard Hughes argues that the Confucian concept of *ren* 仁 (benevolence) usually understood in moralistic terms, is essentially a deductively formulated theory, a syllogism: "Man can live well in society: we men of Lu State and its neighbors are men: therefore, we must be socially minded, i.e., man-to-man-ly (*Jen*)" (1967, 97). Similarly, in studying Xunzi's theory of argumentation, Antonio S. Cua points out: "A careful examination of some passages in other essays also suggests an awareness of the distinction between deductive, inductive, and analogical inferences" (1983, 867). Indeed, the Chinese system of logic does not replicate the Greek logical system; however, to claim that China has not produced a logical system is to succumb to the faulty logic of Orientalism.

Clearly, the ancient Chinese practiced rhetoric, utilized logic, and engaged in argumentation. If Western rhetorical scholars are truly to understand Chinese rhetoric, they will need to study it on its own terms, with an analysis rooted in ancient Chinese cultural texts and context. Currently the distorting influence of Orientalism is apparent in Western studies of Chinese rhetoric. Given the unfortunate fact that Chinese rhetoric is judged and evaluated by Western standards of rhetoric, it is perceived as radically Other. The same problem exists in the study of Chinese philosophy. Troy Organ (1975) notes that Western philosophers generally attempt to superimpose Western philosophical categories upon Eastern concepts without considering the difference between the two cultures. Such an approach leads to an oversimplification of Eastern philosophy, supporting the ethnocentric assumption that Eastern philosophy is inferior to Western philosophy. This state of affairs can best be understood through an analysis of how Orientalism affects Western research methodologies.

Western Approach to the Study of Chinese Rhetoric

Ancient Chinese rhetoric deserves careful analysis, yet it must be studied in its own context and on its own terms. Analytical research methodologies reveal information about the particular elements of a rhetorical system but may, in the process, produce an incomplete account of the whole. Conversely, contextual research reveals much about rhetorical systems as a whole but may obscure accounts of particular elements of those systems. Both modes of inquiry, analytical and contextual, are necessary for a full understanding of any given rhetorical system. As Western scholars are trained in European modes of inquiry, which emphasize analysis and taxonomy, they face imposing challenges in choosing appropriate modes of inquiry for the study of rhetoric cross-culturally. Such challenges are rooted in the Western tendency to separate, compartmentalize, and polarize (Kincaid 1987).

Geoffrey Ernest Richard Lloyd has brought out the fact that Greek speculative thought is characterized by polarities. In his words, "The attempt to classify, or otherwise account for, other things in terms of pairs of opposites is a feature of a great many theories and explanations which appear in various branches of early Greek philosophy and medicine" (1966, 26). Such early Greek thought patterns and mode of inquiry have formed the basis of Western academic research. Western rhetoric, conventionally believed to have been codified as early as 467 B.C.E. by Corax and Tisias, has long been regarded as a discipline unto itself, though attempts were made to incorporate rhetoric into the fields of ethics, politics, and education.[11] Furthermore, Western communication theories have tended to focus on one aspect of analysis rather than on connecting discrete aspects to other related elements. In other words, Western study of rhetoric and communication has been primarily analytical, to the detriment of holistic understanding. Kincaid urges scholars of intercultural communication to avoid polarities, noting that "the part and whole ultimately cannot be separated. One way to say this is that there is no part and whole but rather one part/whole. Each 'one' defines the other, and indeed is the other" (1987, 332). Western scholars have made generalizations about ancient Chinese rhetoric on the basis of decontextualized analysis. Consequently, they have tended to overlook the cultural mosaics (the whole) out of which Chinese rhetorical practices emerge.

Although some Western scholars are seemingly aware of the intermingling of Chinese rhetoric with Chinese philosophy, language, and culture, they nonetheless tend to be guided by an analytical approach, employing the disciplinary framework of Western rhetoric in their search for a Chinese rhetoric. In order to recover ancient Chinese rhetoric, Western scholars will need to have some knowledge of the Chinese language as well as an in-depth understanding of Chinese habits of mind. An examination of the Western literature on Chinese rhetoric reveals two primary problems with the existing research: 1) an overemphasis on analytical and definitional mode of inquiry; and 2) a dependency on translations.

An Overemphasis on Analytical and Definitional Mode of Inquiry

Western habits of mind have revealed much useful knowledge about the universe, but an overemphasis on analysis greatly limits the vision of the Western scholar. Kincaid observes that Western analytical and conceptual approaches to the study of non-Western cultures have created obstacles to the study of communication. In his words, "One of the major obstacles of the general system approach to communication has always been the lack of an appropriate research methodology to study social phenomena holistically. It is conceptually obvious to Western scholars that there is indeed a whole to which the parts studied correspond, but the entire analytical and conceptual apparatus itself has always acted as an obstacle to a clear understanding of this insight" (1987, 332).

In Asia, particularly in China, thought and speech patterns tend toward the holistic and contextualized. The ancient Chinese culture was a highly contextualized constellation of political intrigue, art, and philosophical expression within which ideas and concepts were not explicitly codified or systematized. Consequently, rhetoric was never officially codified as a separate discipline by Chinese scholars. This is not because rhetoric is perceived as unimportant. On the contrary, as Jensen observes: "[Rhetoric] was so important that it was intertwined with, inseparable from philosophy, religion, ethics, psychology, politics, and social relations" (1987, 219).

Western scholars tend to study Chinese rhetoric through an Occidental lens, looking for explicit theories, concepts, and statements about rhetoric in the works of Chinese philosophers rather than locating implicit senses and meanings of rhetoric in the contexts of Chinese philosophy, history, and society. The works of Jensen and Oliver illustrate this Western tendency to compartmentalize and categorize. For example, Jensen (1987) identifies six points of emphasis common to Daoist rhetoric, listing them in the following order: speech deprecation, argument condemnation, denouncement of knowledge, avoidance of critical thinking, respect for authority, and emphasis on ethics. This listing is accurate and helpful but lacks an account of relevant context in which these characteristics occur. Basically, Jensen's interpretation of the characteristics of Daoist rhetoric is derived from segments of works by Laozi and Zhuangzi and by reading the texts literally. Furthermore, his conclusions are reached by a mode of inquiry characterized by categorization and analysis. Jensen's analysis would have been more complete if he had first accounted for the metaphorical and paradoxical nature of Daoism.

The Daoist perspective on rhetoric is rooted in its philosophical orientation: namely *wu wei* 無爲, meaning to speak and act without artificiality and superficiality. Both Laozi and Zhuangzi condemned "glib tongues" and "flowery speeches," claiming such behavior did not conform to the essence of the Dao 道 (the Way). Furthermore, since Daoist writings are paradoxical and metaphorical in nature, the utterances of Laozi and Zhuangzi should not be taken literally. Jensen's literal reading of Daoism, along with his Western tendency to search for explicit meaning, may have led him to the conclusion that Daoism condemns speech and argumentation.

To his credit, Oliver appears to be sensitive to the paradoxical and contextual nature of Dao. He notes, "For of one thing Lao Tzu [Laozi] was certain: to break truth into separable fragments is to destroy it. Nothing has meaning except in context—and context is all-inclusive" (1971, 245). Yet Oliver's treatment of Daoist rhetoric fails to connect clearly Daoism with rhetoric, perpetuating the vision of rhetoric as a separate entity. Consequently, he is left to conclude that the "rhetorical implications of Daoism" are vague and mystical (240–45). Given the Western preference for clarity and explicitness, Oliver's conclusions imply a certain rhetoric deficit within Daoism.

Another unfortunate habit of inquiry in the Western study of rhetoric is the search for definitions and equivalence. Western scholars of Chinese rhetoric typically seek to find Western equivalents for certain Chinese terms. Key terms, such as *rhetoric, sophist,* and *logic,* are not clearly compared with Chinese terms or adequately contextualized.

While the word *rhetoric* was defined by Aristotle as "the faculty of observing in any given case the available means of persuasion" (*Rhetoric* 1355b27), no exact equivalent for the word exists in the Chinese language. A number of related words, however, are used in classical Chinese texts to capture and conceptualize persuasive behaviors and speech theories, and these will be discussed in chapter 3. In most studies of Chinese speech and persuasive discourse, the English translation of the Greek word for rhetoric is used to describe Chinese speech. This practice may obscure the textual and cultural meanings of ancient Chinese discourse. Western scholars seem generally unaware of the danger of failing to give serious consideration to original Chinese terms relating to the notion of rhetoric. Their assumptions about the meaning and scope of rhetoric lead them to the conclusion that China has no rhetorical tradition or that such a tradition is completely unlike Western rhetoric.

Sophist is another word that causes confusion in the study of Chinese rhetoric. Again, no direct translation, conveying the Greek sense of the word, exists in the Chinese language.[12] Without an equivalent for the word *sophist,* Western rhetorical scholars have tended to assume that ancient China has no tradition of sophistry. In his book *Les fondements philosophiques de la rhétorique chez les sophistes grecs et chez les sophistes chinois* (1985), Jean-Paul Reding claims that China has no tradition of sophistry because there is no counterpart in Chinese texts that contains the meaning of the Greek sophistry. However, a group of people engaged in similar activities as the Greek sophists did exist in ancient China: they were known as *Mingjia* 名家, the School of Ming.[13] The two groups shared some common interests and engaged in similar sophistic activities. Nevertheless, I do not mean to imply that Mingjia are the equivalent of sophists, for the two groups also differ in many ways called upon by the different social and cultural conditions they lived in.

The term *logic* has also been problematic in Chinese rhetorical studies. In the Western tradition, *logic* generally refers to the formal logical system set by Aristotle, which entails deductive and inductive reasoning processes. In the Chinese language, the direct translation for *logic* is *luo ji* 邏輯, a transliteration of the English word *logic*, defined as "the law of reasoning" in the Chinese dictionary. This definition is broader than its Western counterpart, in that it may include other forms of reasoning, such as analogical reasoning processes. The term *logic* may not carry all the connotated meanings of the Chinese *luo ji*. The term *luo ji* is never used in classical Chinese texts. However, Chinese words associated with the classical Greek meaning of *logos* do exist. They are *tui* 推 (inference); *gu* 故 (cause and because); *li* 理 (reason, principles used as basis for classification); and *lei* 類 (classification). The fact that such terms are unfamiliar to many Western scholars may have contributed to Oliver's assertion that China lacks a logical rhetorical tradition.

The problem of applying English terms to the analysis of Chinese concepts is not unique to the field of rhetorical studies. As Hall and Ames observe, "To settle upon an English equivalent for each major concept and then pursue the analysis through the equivalent rather than the original term is unquestionably the most problematic methodological pitfall of Western interpretation of Chinese philosophy" (1987, 41). This is true for the simple reason that an English equivalent may not accurately capture depth and nuances of the original concept.

A Dependency on Translation

The second obstacle encountered by Western scholars in their study of Chinese rhetoric is the problem of translation. As many Western scholars do not read or understand the Chinese language, they turn to translations for an understanding of Chinese rhetoric. Anyone who attempts to translate and interpret Chinese classical texts is confronting a difficult challenge and therefore deserves respect. A true sense of fidelity may never be reached in translation, since in many ways translation is an interpretation and re-creation by the translator of the author's original meaning. Nevertheless, when the translation is done by a word-for-word or literal technique without considering or providing cultural and linguistic contexts to help gain the authentic meaning, anyone reading the translation is likely to be led to an incomplete or weak understanding of the original meaning. Moreover, when a scholar depends on such translations and verification with the original texts is impossible, he or she runs the risk of misinterpreting and drawing inaccurate conclusions of the original meanings. This is especially the case with the translation and interpretation of Daoist texts.

In both Jensen's and Oliver's works, Laozi's *Dao De Jing* 道德經 is quoted as a primary support for their understanding of Daoist rhetoric. For example, Jensen appropriates the following translation of Laozi by Lin Yutang: "A good man does not argue; he who argues is not a good man." The Chinese reads as follows: *shan zhe bu bian, bian zhe bu shan* 善者不辯, 辯者不善. In this verse the word "argue" is the literal translation of the Chinese word *bian* 辯. By reading this literal translation, one is easily led to believe that Laozi condemns rhetoric or separates rhetoric from ethics, while the contextual meaning for *bian* here does not simply mean "argue." A careful reading of *Dao De Jing* suggests that the term *bian* embodies the meanings "embellishment of words," "making distinctions," and "disputing for a particular position." From Laozi's philosophical and rhetorical perspective, a person engaging in such bian activities lacks moral substance and is unable to bridge, harmonize, and transcend different points of view. When *bian* is literally translated as "argue," the connotative and contextual meanings of the word are lost. By taking the translation at its face value, it is easy to conclude that speech and argumentation are deprecated and condemned in the Daoist treatment of Chinese rhetoric.

When translation is not faithful to the original, a scholar who depends on such translation runs even greater risk of drawing inaccurate conclusions. For example, Oliver asserts that "*Tao-Teh-Ching* [Dao De Jing] seemingly renounces rhetoric and even communication itself" (1971, 238). He supports this assertion by quoting the translation as follows: "In much talk there is weariness. It is best to keep silent." The original Chinese is *Yan duo shu qiong, bu ru shou zhong* 言多數窮, 不如守中. In this version the Chinese word *shou zhong* 守中 is mistranslated as "keep silent." A more accurate translation would be "to maintain moderation." Therefore, the translation should read: "Too much talk creates emptiness; it is better to maintain moderation." This revised translation is based on an understanding of the linguistic meaning and philosophical context of Daoism. In the linguistic sense, the classical meaning of *shou* 守 is "keep" or "maintaining," while the classical meaning of *zhong* 中 is "middle" or "appropriateness." In the philosophical sense, the central idea of Daoism is to maintain balance and appropriateness. Overreacting or talking too much will lead to the opposite effect. The translation of *shou zhong* as "keeping silent" may have resulted from the translator's preconceptions about Eastern speech patterns. In any case, the translation of *shou zhong* as "keeping silent" as opposed to "maintaining appropriateness" obviously leads to a very different understanding of Daoist rhetoric. Laozi suggests we maintain appropriateness, similar to the Greek notion of *kairos*, in the adaptation of rhetorical situations.

The above examples illustrate the point that when key words or sentences are mistranslated or taken out of context, scholars are led to unfounded or inaccurate conclusions about Chinese rhetoric. Unfortunately, non-Chinese speaking readers and researchers are subject to such problems when working with translations. Consequently, they are likely to conclude that Laozi condemned all forms of rhetoric, speech, and argumentation, while overlooking the embedded meaning in the *Dao De Jing* regarding appropriateness and artistic choice in speech and argumentation. The same problem occurs with translations of texts from other cultures. For example, it occurred with non-Greek-speaking readers with regard to the translation of Aristotle's definition of rhetoric in his *Rhetoric* (Conley 1979).

The first generation of rhetorical scholars has called the attention of Western rhetorical scholars to the rhetorical practices of the ancient Chinese, and their works provide historians of rhetoric with a useful beginning. The second generation will need to develop modes of inquiry designed to account for the religious, philosophical, and rhetorical configurations of ancient Chinese culture. Such scholars will need to broaden their modes of inquiry, as well as developing a certain cautious skepticism when citing secondary sources or translations. Ideally, a scholar can avoid the problem of faulty translation if he or she reads both the language of the translation and the language of the original text.

Treatment of Chinese Rhetoric by Chinese Scholars

Although the first attempt by the Chinese to explore foreign land can be traced back to 138 B.C.E., most imported cultures and religious traditions were assimilated into the Chinese culture.[14] Serious study of European culture, thought, and philosophy did not begin until the late nineteenth century and early twentieth century when a group of Western-educated intellectuals began to introduce modern Western ideas and philosophy through the translation of texts and propagation of scientific thought.[15] These intellectuals compared traditional Chinese cultural values to modern Western science and technology, concluding that Chinese culture was spiritually oriented while Western culture was scientifically oriented.

Such comparisons polarized the two cultures. The controversy over the future of China centered on whether it should integrate traditional Chinese values with those of the West or simply adopt Western scientific methods and ways of thinking. Hu Shi 胡適, the American-trained historian of Chinese philosophy who was strongly influenced by the thinking of John Dewey and Thomas Huxley, advocated the adoption of Western scientific methods. Hu's opponents, Liang Qichao 梁啓超 and Liang Shuming 梁漱溟, who were moderates in their position of political reforms and cultural change, critically examined the strengths and weaknesses of Western culture while upholding the value of Chinese culture and tradition (Chen 1985; Kwok 1965; Schwartz 1972).

This debate over culture and tradition has also been reflected in the study of Chinese persuasive discourse and speech theory in subsequent years. In particular, two lines of research on Chinese rhetoric can be identified in modern scholarship. One line, influenced by a concern for contextual understanding, treats Chinese rhetoric as a part of Chinese philosophy.[16] The other line of research, influenced by the trend toward Western analytical and definitional modes of inquiry, has attempted to conceptualize the discipline under the original Chinese notion of *ming* 名 (naming) and the Western notion of logic (luo ji in Chinese).[17] Because of the language barrier and a general lack of scholarly exchange between China and the West, Chinese works on the study of ming have not been introduced to the West; at the same time, Chinese scholars have not fully embraced or understood the study of rhetoric in the West.

The first line of research by modern Chinese scholars recognized the roles and activities of Chinese bian shi in the historical works of Chinese philosophy. As Hou Wailu and his colleagues describe it, "In the 5th century B.C.E., it was common practice for ordinary people to discuss or talk about politics. In this kind of speech practice, the idea of *ming* (naming) and *bian* 辯 (distinction, argumentation) emerged. The School of Ming was therefore formed. The idea of *ming bian* developed in the period of *bai jia zheng ming* 百家爭鳴 (contentions of one hundred schools of thought) and became popular in the Warring State Period" (403–221 B.C.E.).[18] Hou believes that the School of Ming was primarily composed of logicians and became one of the major philosophical schools in ancient China. In Hou's works, ming and bian were not treated as separate disciplines or areas of study but as an integrated part of the Chinese philosophical tradition as a whole.

The majority of Chinese scholars seem to agree that the School of Ming was characterized by an emphasis on logic and argumentation, in both theory and practice. However, few scholars make a connection or distinction between the notions of ming and bian, being instead solely interested in group composition and the nature of group activities. As Fung described, the School of Ming "originated from men who had specialized in the art of debate, and who used their talents on behalf of clients engaged in lawsuits. Through their tricks of sophistry, we are told, they were able to turn right into wrong, and wrong into right" (1952, xxxiii). This group of individuals is often compared to Greek sophists, though, interestingly enough, the label given them by Chinese scholars was *gui bian zhe* 詭辯者 (deceitful debater), as opposed to wise man or rhetorician. Because of the negative connotations associated with this group of rhetors and the condemnation they received from Confucianists and Daoists in ancient times, they are often dismissed as "glib tongues" and "manipulators" in Chinese historical records. This line of research shares much in common with research by Western scholars on Greek sophists in that both recognize and identify rhetorical activities engaged in by a particular group of people who used words and arguments for the purpose of deception.

While the first group of Chinese scholars used the terms *bian shi, bian zhe,* and *Mingjia* interchangeably, thus mixing rhetorical activity with a school of thought, the second line of research under consideration centers on the definition of *ming,* treating Mingjia as a distinctive school of thought with the formulation of philosophical inquiry and speech theories. Although the discussion of ming originates with Confucius's notion of *zheng ming* 正名 (the rectification of names) and was developed by subsequent thinkers such as Mozi and Xunzi, the term is primarily associated with both Mingjia and the School of Mohism, referring to the discussion of logic, argumentation, and metaphysics.[19] According to Zhang, "*ming* refers not only to argumentation, but to a theory of expressing thoughts and confirming truth. It is the method of setting up an argumentation" (1982, 560). Similarly, Yu Yu (1959) contends that Mingjia was interested in logic and argumentation, identifying the following three functions of ming: 1) to discriminate things; 2) to express one's opinion; and 3) to infer truth and falsehood. These three functions of ming echo Lao's summary on the characteristics of ming as it was distinguished from other schools: "Mingjia [the School of Ming] is concerned with the question of epistemology. It has three main characteristics. First, in terms of topics, Mingjia pursues questions of logic and metaphysics instead of politics and ethics. Second, in terms of making arguments, Mingjia relies on reasoning, logic or metaphysical theory rather than historical and cultural evidence. Third, Mingjia has formulated its own theory and belongs to early metaphysics. Its practice is more of sophistry" (1984, 380). To many Chinese scholars the concept of ming is equivalent to the Western notion of logic. Thus, for example, some Chinese scholars have described their studies of the School of Ming as histories of "logic in the

Pre-Qin period" (Wen 1983; Zhou and Liu 1984). Ironically, the Chinese translation of *logic, luo ji,* is a borrowed Western term and concept, having never appeared or been used in ancient Chinese writings.

Although scholarship on Mingjia and the notion of ming by Chinese scholars offers helpful information on the group and their rhetorical interests, problems exist with such studies. As these scholars are historians of Chinese philosophy, their studies focus more on the composition and personality of the school than on attempting to codify Chinese rhetoric. Their studies are primarily interested in providing definitions of ming rather than examining rhetoric in connection with literary and philosophical works. They provide superficial discussion of logic and argumentation, and fail to offer an exploration of ethics, emotions, or worldviews as related to the use and function of rhetoric. In general, contemporary Chinese scholars are primarily interested in describing and interpreting the theories by antiquities rather than in critiquing these theories and advancing new theories. Moreover, some scholars seem unaware of the Western rhetorical tradition, giving little attention to rhetorical theories by Western philosophers. No attempts have been made to compare Chinese rhetoric with Greek rhetoric in a systematic fashion. Like their Western counterparts, Chinese scholars seem to have some difficulty with the definitions of rhetorical terms in the two languages, the approach to codifying Chinese rhetoric, and the translation from Chinese to English or vice versa. For example, translation of the ancient Chinese word *ming* as "logic" may contribute to the general confusion. For this reason we must avoid the tendency to use Western conceptual terms to describe the experiences and perceptions of non-Western cultures without careful consideration and critical examination. Using a foreign concept to replace an indigenous one is a form of cultural imperialism in which certain original meanings are lost or misinterpreted. In this case, Chinese scholars themselves employ foreign terms, rather than having them imposed.

Both Western and Chinese rhetorical scholars have made important translations, provided valuable information, and generated thought-provoking ideas in their initial studies of Chinese rhetoric or ming bian. However, such studies should be broadened and deepened. Western scholars need to acknowledge their own biases in interpreting Chinese culture and communication patterns, constantly questioning and challenging their own perceptions and opening new discoveries and findings. Chinese scholars, on the other hand, need to expand their vision of ming bian through a close examination of ancient texts featuring actual speech patterns and persuasive practices, thereby conceptualizing ming bian on Chinese terms rather than on Western ones. A comparison between Chinese and Western rhetorical traditions should be pursued in order to generate more insights for ideas of human rhetoric. Both groups of scholars have a lot to learn from cross-cultural exchange. It is important to conduct scholarly dialogue on neutral, equal, and intelligible bases and to promote intellectual conversations that result in a mutual recognition of similarities and differences in rhetorical theories and practices.

Both groups should be aware and critical of the problems of Orientalism and Occidentalism in their academic pursuits. Both should engage in multicultural hermeneutics in order to generate multicultural meanings. Such a hermeneutical orientation would not seek to canonize any particular texts, but would instead recognize and celebrate diverse human experiences and cultural knowledge through translation and interpretation of cross-cultural discourse and texts. This new understanding of rhetoric starts with an appreciation of the ways in which different cultures perceive, define, and discuss rhetoric. It begins with an understanding of the realm, role, and function of rhetorical concepts derived and addressed to cultural forces and social contexts. The next chapter reviews the cultural context and rhetorical practices in the pre-Qin period (before 221 B.C.E.), which laid the background for philosophical and rhetorical conceptualizations and formulations.

CHAPTER 2

Cultural Contexts and Rhetorical Practices of the Pre-Qin Period

In his study of Greek rhetoric before Aristotle, Richard Enos argues that the political shift toward democracy and increasing demands for power in the fifth century B.C.E. provided environment and exigencies for the formulation of Greek rhetoric. Enos criticizes the tendency of overlooking such historical contexts in the interpretation of Greek rhetoric in the current scholarship. He believes the social and political forces are vitally important ingredients in that they not only provide a grounding for the occurrence of rhetorical activities but also offer explanations of how the concept of rhetoric evolves over time (Enos 1993). Likewise, the Chinese rhetorical tradition developed over time in response to the sociopolitical and cultural dynamics and exigencies in ancient China. Moreover, like the Greek rhetorical tradition, the Chinese rhetorical tradition went through a gradual evolution of consciousness from mythical to rational modes of thought and expressions with the social and political demands and the emergence of literary works. Without knowledge of the ancient Chinese cosmology, cultural transitions, and rhetorical practices, a meaningful understanding and interpretation of Chinese rhetorical tradition cannot be reached. This chapter aims to familiarize the reader with Chinese thought pattern, value system, and forms of discourse formulated and practiced in the ancient Chinese cultural and social contexts.

In particular, this chapter will examine cultural contexts and major forms of rhetorical practices from the twenty-first century B.C.E., the beginning of the Xia 夏 dynasty to 221 B.C.E., the time of the unification of China by the emperor of the Qin 秦 dynasty, historically known as the pre-Qin period. Although the project will focus primarily on the fifth to third century B.C.E., what transpired prior to this period in ancient Chinese history greatly influenced the subsequent thinking and speech patterns. An examination of Chinese culture during this period will help us understand its rhetorical tradition, both in terms of its development over time and significance at a particular historical moment.

This historical and cultural review will unfold in chronological order. In particular, I will examine ancient Chinese cultural values and types of communication in the Xia and Shang 商 dynasties (approximately twenty-first to eleventh century B.C.E.) viewed through the lens of Chinese mythology, divination, and ancestor worship. I will then identify three general types of communication: poetry, speeches, and government decrees in the Zhou 周 dynasty (approximately eleventh–eighth century B.C.E.). Finally, I will move to a review of the vigorous Chun Qiu Zhan Guo 春秋戰國 (the Spring-Autumn and Warring States) period (eighth–third century B.C.E.). As in Greece in the fifth through fourth century B.C.E., this period was the golden age in Chinese history with regard to the production of literary and historical texts as well as the formulation of philosophical and rhetorical theories. Selected literary, historical, and philosophical texts produced in this time period will be introduced and analyzed throughout the rest of this book. Thus, an understanding of the cultural dynamics, communication practices, and various worldviews characteristic of the pre-Qin period is crucial to our understanding of the Chinese rhetorical tradition as a whole. The purpose of this chapter is to situate classical Chinese rhetorical theories and practices in their cultural contexts in order, ultimately, to arrive at the deepest possible understanding of such theories and practices.

The Xia Dynasty

Historians generally divide Chinese history into ancient (twenty-first century B.C.E.–1840 C.E.) and modern (1840–present) periods. The Xia dynasty (approximately twenty-first to sixteenth century B.C.E.), established by a legendary cultural hero by the name of Yu 禹, is believed to be the first Chinese dynasty. While some Western historians have doubts about its existence, speculating that its history was a mere reconstruction and fabrication by the later texts, Chinese historians seemed unanimously to agree that the Xia dynasty did exist. Although archaeological efforts have failed to provide written materials dating to the Xia dynasty, based on the description of the Xia dynasty given in the pre-Qin texts, they suggest that Xia possessed basic forms of agriculture and animal husbandry. There could also have been institutionalized slavery during this time, with a clear class division between the rich and the poor, indicated by the quantity and value of sacrificial items buried with the dead (Sun 1987; Zhang Chuanxi 1991). For example, *Shang Shu* (the Book of Documents) has documented some segments of Xia military and political structures along with various official speeches. Therein the Xia ruling class is described as ferocious and ruthless toward its people; the last two Xia kings are considered the cruelest and most corrupt.[1] The Xia dynasty endured for 471 years and was replaced in the eighteenth century B.C.E. by one of the Eastern tribes, Shang, also known as Yin 殷.

Mythology

Just as mythic expression was characteristic of Greek culture from Homeric times to the fifth century B.C.E., ancient China from the Xia to Shang dynasties (twenty-first to eleventh century B.C.E.) was preoccupied with its belief in myth and spirituality. Although our knowledge on the historical Xia is limited, much information of a mythic and legendary nature has survived to the present. Myth and legends are sacred stories created collectively in order to infuse life with meaning. In the telling and retelling of its myths and legends a culture transmits its knowledge, makes sense of its environment, and establishes its values and cosmology. China is no exception to this rule; its myths and legends establish ancestral lineage and origins, promote cultural heroes, and explore the creation of the universe.[2]

In general, Chinese myths and legends fall into three general categories. The first type of myth illustrates the relationship between human and nature, celebrating human power in conquering nature and exploring harmonious and disharmonious interactions between the two.[3] This type of mythology may explain why Chinese philosophy emphasizes concrete human relationships with nature and among themselves as opposed to the more abstract relationships between humans and divinity characteristic of Western philosophy.

The second type of mythology glorifies cultural heroes, praising their wisdom, courage, and morality. One well-known legend is *Da Yu zhi shui* 大禹治水 (Da Yu conquers the flood). Different versions of the story can be found in a number of pre-Qin and Han texts,[4] the earliest in *Shang Shu*. According to this version, during the rule of Yao 堯 and Shun 舜, a devastating flood threatened human lives and nature. King Yao ordered Gun 鯀, a tribal leader, to conquer the flood. Gun built a dam to prevent water from flooding in, but without success. Consequently, Shun, the Lord of the Xia tribe, executed Gun and ordered his son Yu 禹 to succeed where his father had failed. Yu worked hard for thirteen years—so hard, in fact, that not once during all that time did he return home, not even when passing by his house. Finally, with the assistance of new technology, Yu managed to channel the water into the sea and conquered the flood problem. In gratitude, Shun ceded Yu his throne and Yu became the first king of the Xia dynasty. This story, referred to by Derk Bodde (1961) as "the euhemerized version," instilled in the Chinese an everlasting zeal for eulogizing their leaders along with blind faith in their moral character. In this way legendary Chinese heroes were rationalized, moralized, and euhemerized. No longer were they mythical figures, but real-life heroes, used for the persuasive and didactic purpose of teaching and strengthening moral and cultural values.[5]

The third feature of Chinese mythology is the symbolic portrayal of animals in connection with legendary figures. This is especially characteristic of the Shang and Zhou dynasties, following the Xia dynasty. Animals were perceived as carrying the spirits of sage kings, ancestors, cultural heroes, and monsters. As informed by Chang, "nine out of ten among the ancient sages in Chinese legends were euhemerized versions of animal deities" (1976, 174). This feature of Chinese mythology should not be reductionistically understood as a mere personification of animals, but rather as a blurring of the lines between animals and legendary figures who were honored and empowered. It was believed that the souls of cultural heroes and ancestors never died. Instead they transformed into animals, exerting invisible power over the living. The overwhelming use of animals in mythical images and texts was prevalent in historical and literary writings of the pre-Qin period. Sacred meaning was attributed to animals, and they were used as central components and rhetorical devices in fables and anecdotes.

We have little knowledge on how such myths and legends were communicated among the common people in the Xia dynasty. It is possible that the writing system was formed during this time period. However, given the fact that we have no attested Xia texts, it is reasonable to assume that myths and legends were transmitted orally, in which case memory and repetition must have played important roles. It is generally agreed in the scholarship on oral tradition that the roles of the speaker and listener were passively to remember the story so as to tell and retell it over and over, rather than critically to pass judgment upon it (Gill 1994; Havelock 1963; Ong 1982). As the ruling class of the Xia dynasty enjoyed a sophisticated level of music and dance, it is likely that the myths and legends of the time were sung along with music and dance on ritualistic occasions (Sun 1987).

This public performing of stories through music and dance is a distinctive feature of an oral tradition. In this context, combining music and body movement with storytelling aids the process of memorization while entertaining the audience. Thereby the performer becomes a transmitter of cultural knowledge.[6]

The Shang Dynasty

Judging from archaeological evidence, the Shang dynasty, also known as the Yin dynasty (approximately sixteenth–eleventh century B.C.E.), was remarkably civilized in its economic and cultural affairs. Although archaeologists have discovered written symbols dating to the Xia dynasty, there is insufficient evidence to suggest that such symbols are forms of language used for communication. The earliest traces of China's written language called *jia gu wen* 甲骨文 (shell-bone script, due to the fact that it was inscribed on oracle bones) is believed to be from the Shang dynasty.[7] According to Chang (1980), *jia gu wen* was the language used by all members of the Shang dynasty. There is no evidence suggesting even the slightest degree of linguistic diversity during that time. Among the three thousand characters inscribed on oracle bones, approximately one thousand are still identifiable and are being used today. Despite efforts throughout history from Qin Shi Huang 秦始皇 to Mao Zedong 毛澤東 to simplify China's written language, certain characters still retain their original pictographic and ideographic forms, resembling the actual objects named.[8] At any rate, the discovery of the shell-bone scripts has revealed much about Chinese consciousness during the Shang dynasty, wherein symbols representing the objective world were created and utilized. This important discovery also provides valuable information about Shang culture and its modes of communication, characterized by ancestor worship, divination, oral poetry, and political persuasion.

Ancestor Worship

Still carrying traces of the predominantly mythic worldview characteristic of the Xia dynasty, the people of the Shang, or Yin, dynasty were known for their spiritual and religious orientation to life. Anthropological evidence suggests a general perception of human spirits as immortal and ubiquitous, as in animals, in nature, and in the deceased. Myth, according to Ernst Cassirer, "is an offspring of emotion and its emotional background imbues all its productions with its own specific color" (1944, 82). The emotional background of the Shang people was what Cassirer would refer to as "sympathetic," as opposed to theoretical and practical. This sympathetic attitude allowed for participation in the spirit world and harmonious relations with nature.

Communication with the spiritual world took the form of ancestor worship and divination. Worshiping ancestors was the core of religious and social life of the ancient Chinese. It was their belief that death imbued the departed with more spiritual power than they possessed while alive. By consulting their deceased ancestors for advice and asking for blessings and protection, the living were able to keep the lines of communication open. Ancestor worship was a structured ritualistic and symbolic practice of filial piety accompanied by music and performance. It involved the sacrifice of animals, the offering of food and wine, the burning of incense, prayers, and kow towing in order from the eldest to the youngest. The head of the family was given the highest honor, that of talking "directly" to the spirits of the ancestors.[9]

As the family expanded, the ritualistic performance of ancestor worship prescribed the roles and functions of kinship and family ties. In this way, kinship structure and hierarchy were established. In addition, since ancestor worship took place within the relatively narrow context of the family, it tended to strengthen family cohesiveness while weakening the general sense of social responsibility. As Laurence Thompson notes on this point, "The ancestral cult was the one universal religious institution, but by ensuring the exclusiveness of each tsu [ancestor] it fastened on the nation a system of closely knit in-group units, each of which claimed the major share of each individual's loyalties and efforts at the expense of a larger social consciousness" (1979, 44). A prevalent Western misconception is that China is a collectivistic society; in fact, it is collectivistic only in the context of in-groups, such as extended families and circles of friends, not in the context of society and state. Despite efforts made by Confucius to extend familial loyalties to the social context, Chinese consciousness remains fundamentally familial with a limited collective function, or what I like to call a system of extended individualism.

In addition to ancestors, the people of the Shang dynasty worshiped a supernatural being referred to as *shang di* 上帝 (High God). Unlike the Western God who is perceived as the Creator of the universe, the Chinese conception of shang di is similar to the conception of the Hebrew prophet in the Old Testament who has feelings and purpose, who oversees and controls political affairs. The will of shang di was known as *tian ming* 天命 (the Mandate of Heaven). The earliest form of the character *tian* was anthropomorphic in the shape of 𓀀 with a square on the top of "human" symbolizing an impersonal, all-powerful deity. *Ming* means destiny. According to the Mandate of Heaven, if a ruler acted morally and virtuously in governing his country and serving his people, he would be supported and assisted by Heaven. If, on the other hand, he chose evil over good, Heaven would replace him with a moral and virtuous leader. This theory of Heaven's Mandate has been used throughout Chinese history to legitimize the overthrow of allegedly unvirtuous rulers and the establishment of new regimes. One speech given by the first emperor of Shang, recorded in *Shang Shu*, exemplified this notion:

The king said, listen, my people. It is not because I dare to provoke chaos, it is because the king of Xia has committed so many crimes, the God of Heaven ordered me to punish him. Now you may say that our king does not show mercy for us; that he missed good seasons for farming in order to fight against Xia. I understand what you mean, but the king of Xia is guilty. I am fearful of the High God; I dare not act against his Will. Now you may ask what crime the King of Xia has committed. He labored and exploited Xia people so harshly that people do not respect him and refuse to cooperate with him. They ask when this sun will fall. Xia King's conduct is so ferocious that I must send a punitive expedition against him. (SS "tang shi," 58–59)

In this way the notion of Heaven's Mandate set up moral justification and a rhetorical appeal for establishing or overthrowing power: good must rule and evil must be punished.

The belief in shang di, whose divine message was conveyed through the tribal king's worship of and sacrifices to his ancestors, led to the establishment of a social hierarchy. According to David Keightley, this tribal level of ancestor worship in the quest for success in war, hunting, and agriculture "provided powerful psychological and ideological support for the political dominance of the Shang kings." Furthermore, "the king's ability to determine through divination, and influence through prayer and sacrifice, the will of the ancestral spirits legitimized the concentration of political power in his person. . . . It was the king who made fruitful harvest and victories possible by the sacrifice he offered, the rituals he performed, and the divinations he made" (1978, 212–12). The king's role as the only channel for communication with shang di gave him absolute power in the social hierarchy, similar to the roles of the pope and church fathers in the Middle Ages in Europe. Indeed, throughout Chinese history the perception has been that political leaders, kings, and emperors were in possession of some divine power and noble spirit. Consequently, such people were treated with great reverence, trust, and respect by their loyal subjects as the living God. Their lives were considered exemplary and were used as moral appeals in persuasion.

Divination

The desire to understand natural and supernatural forces, along with filial responsibility for ancestors, led the ancient Chinese to the practice of divination and its use as a form of communication with spirits. The art of divination supposedly originated in the Xia dynasty, achieving widespread popular appeal by the Shang dynasty. The practice involved burning bones to produce crack lines to be read and interpreted by the augur. Part of the ceremony involved addressing one's ancestors through the rituals of animal sacrifice and ceremonial speeches, called *zhu ci* 祝辭 (prayerful speech to gods and ghosts). The person delivering the speech was referred to as *zhu guan* 祝官, or *bu guan* 卜官. The terms of every divination, including relevant dates, requests made, and results, would be recorded on shell-bone scripts, which served as government archives. The language used for recording the event of divination, of which there were four types, was called *bu ci* 卜辭 (oracle inscriptions): 1) *qian ci* 前辭 (previous speech) for recording times and names; 2) *ming ci* 命辭 (naming speech) for recording the subject of divination; 3) *zhan ci* 占辭 (divining speech) for demonstrating the result of divination; and 4) *yan ci* 驗辭 (checking speech) for recording whether divination had any effect (Sun 1987, 660–61). Given the weighty responsibilities entailed in divination, it is reasonable to conclude that augurs and zhu guan, or the diviner, acting as a medium or spokesman for the spirits, must have possessed well-developed oral and written communication skills and a facility for interpreting signs. Such an individual must also have gained the trust and respect of the tribal ruler or head of the family. Although little is known about the lives of augurs and zhu guan, it is likely that they were the elites of society and, more importantly, the first trained "rhetoricians" in China.

Both Shang divination and ancestor worship were ritualistic performances signifying the value and meaning of Shang culture. Ritual, as defined by Ann Gill, is "a means by which oral humans make sense of their environment; a means of transforming certain aspects of experiences, creating patterns of meaning for a people" (1994, 84). Shang rituals reinforced the mythic and spiritual orientation of the times. Modes of communication of the Shang dynasty created kinship and social hierarchies which in turn prescribed codes of conduct for speech and action.

Oral Poetry

According to Eric Havelock (1982), Homeric poetry was a common form of ritualistic and political communication from the eighth through fifth century B.C.E. in Greece. Through the means of narration, repetition, performance, and rhyme and rhythm, Homeric poetry served as living and collective memory of the Greek culture and civilization. Similarly, the Shang culture was rich in its production of ballads, folk songs, and poems, whose roots can be traced to as early as the Xia dynasty. Oral poetry originated with the working class, who produced songs resembling the sounds of their work. Such poems, composed of no more than four characters with one syllable for each character, were arranged with consideration to produce rhymes and rhythms especially suited to memorization and chanting. Their contents ranged from descriptions of life experiences to expressions of feelings. Their purpose originally was to reduce fatigue and exchange information regarding work skills but gradually moved to maintain and reinforce cultural values as they were accepted by the ruling class. The oral poems then were sung and performed on ritualistic occasions, serving the functions of creating moral codes, unifying people, making aesthetic appeals, and transmitting cultural information.

In particular, the oral poetry of the Shang dynasty was an important means of communication at ceremonies of divination and ancestor worship. During these religious activities the diviner would say prayers, sing songs, and dance to music. The altar of worship became the center of ritualistic performance and cultural symbol making. Singing and dancing were the means of communication to shang di and the ancestors. The content of this type of oral poem was centered around praising tribal leaders for their heroic deeds and expressing wishes for a better life. Some oral poems inscribed on shell bones served as records of divination. For example, *yao ci* 爻辭 (Symbols of Prediction) in *Yi Jing* 易經 (the Book of Change) recorded historical events in the form of songs and poems.

A well-known collection of oral poems, produced for the purpose of divination and ancestor worship in the Shang dynasty, is *Shang Song* 商頌 (Eulogies of Shang), recorded in *Shi Jing* (the Book of Odes). Two types of songs are present in *Shang Song*: one type describes rituals and settings of worship; the other praises the heroic deeds of Shang kings. Unlike the oral poems improvised by working-class people, these poems, carefully crafted by highly educated diviners or religious seers, were indicative of the increasing aesthetic and moral consciousness of the Shang people, along with the marked division between literate and illiterate classes. In any case, oral poetry produced in the Shang dynasty served as an important means of communication among the common people, in ritualistic settings relating to the spirits of ancestors and shang di, and in transmitting Shang history to subsequent generations. In this way, the Shang tradition of oral poetry laid the foundation for the well-structured and highly artistic poems produced in the Zhou dynasty.

Political Persuasion

With the establishment of the Shang dynasty's shi guan wen hua 史官文化 (official culture), the position of shi guan 史官 (historiographer) was created. Shi guan were in charge of recording historical events, legends, and general knowledge. More specifically, their responsibilities included ji yan 記言 (recording speeches) and ji shi 記事 (recording events). The speeches recorded were those given by kings, conversations between kings and ministers, government proclamations, and requests from dukes and subordinates. Events recorded were major events occurring at the time, imperial genealogical information, and political or military actions taken by the king. *Shang Shu* is the first book in Chinese history to record both speeches and events. Although it was produced during the Zhou dynasty, its pages document various persuasive encounters between the king and ministers of the Shang dynasty.

The Shang dynasty possessed an established political structure and hierarchical system of government. Shang kings held absolute power. Below them were the *xiang* 相 (ministers) and *qing da fu* 卿大夫 (high officials) who advised the king to follow the Mandate of Heaven, act virtuously toward his people, and perform properly at ceremonies of divination and ancestor worship. Such advisory activity was called *jian* 諫 (advising). *Shang Shu* records a few such jian activities given by ministers. For example, in one situation a xiang by the name of Zhu Yi came to the king after hearing that the tribe of Zhou had taken over one of the Shang states. Zhu Yi's response to the king was as follows:

The Son of Heaven, the Will of Heaven, seems to have stopped bestowing its blessings upon us. Even wise men and the spirit of the turtle cannot tell the sign or omen. It is not the previous king who does not assist us, but your majesty who has abused power and is living a luxurious life that has offended Heaven. So Heaven will abandon us by not letting us have good harvests. Your majesty failed to understand and follow the Law of Heaven. Today your people all want you to resign. They ask why Heaven does not send down its punishment. The Mandate of Heaven will no longer shine on us. Now what are you going to do? (*SS* "xi bo kan li," 82)

On hearing this, the king of Shang asked, "Isn't my life destined to be blessed by Heaven?" Zhu Yi responded, "well, you made so many mistakes. You are lazy, sluggish, and bureaucratic. How can you ask Heaven for its blessing? Yi Shang will be destroyed. You should take charge of state affairs and make sincere efforts on behalf of your people" (83). Although this example does not reveal whether or not the king took his minister's advice, it illustrates a style of direct and confrontational persuasion employed by the ministers, as well as their boldness in speaking their minds about the king's wrongdoings. The mode of communication was direct and candid, aiming at helping the king with his moral weakness. Such discourse was clearly driven by a concern that the Mandate of Heaven be upheld in a sense of moral responsibility to the ruler and his subjects.

At this point in Chinese history, Chinese cosmology was still fundamentally spiritual and mythical in nature; the Chinese mode of communication was still largely oral, although it is possible that there was an intricate interplay between speech and writing. To summarize, four types of social and cultural discourse were employed at the time: 1) mythic discourse, used to share myths and legends among tribal members; 2) ritualistic discourse, enacted by heads of families at ceremonies honoring their ancestor; 3) spiritual discourse, conveyed through divination to shang di and ancestor spirits; and 4) political discourse, employed in the giving of advice and consultation between the kings and ministers. These four types of discourse revealed much about the ancient Chinese cosmology, cultural views, and religious practices. In addition, they offered spiritual comfort, strengthened communal bonds, expedited political concerns, and furthered ritualistic propriety in both the Xia and Shang dynasties. Since, as far as we know, no distinct group of "rhetoricians" emerged during these times, we can assume that those who utilized or facilitated the aforementioned types of discourse were most likely poets, performers, religious leaders, and high officials who were masters of oral speech and written language as well as models of cultural codes. These social elites continued to play crucial roles in defining Chinese thought pattern, modes of communication, and cultural orientations in subsequent dynasties.

The Zhou Dynasty

According to H. Homer Dubs (1951), the Shang people were conquered by tribesmen from western China in 1027 B.C.E., establishing the Zhou dynasty, which was regarded as the ideal society by Confucius in terms of its devout observation of rites and rituals, as well as for its strict adherence to prescribed *Zhou Li* 周禮 (the Rites of Zhou). Socially and economically it was a feudal society divided into several hundred vassal states. The emperor of Zhou had supreme power over these states, but each had autonomous power, had its own land, and military troops.

The Worldview

While the cultural tradition of ancestor worship and divination were preserved and practiced during the Zhou dynasty, they were no longer the only forms of communication nor the only culturally celebrated values. In fact, the domain of moral judgment switched from that of Heavenly Mandate to the realm of human-prescribed codes of conduct. Whereas in the Shang dynasty shang di was perceived as having ultimate power over human affairs and its spirit was thought to infuse and inspire Shang ancestors, the people of Zhou perceived shang di and the ancestors in separate spheres. While still believing in the notion of Heavenly Mandate, they regarded the living king, referred to as *tian zi* 天子 (the Son of Heaven), rather than dead ancestors, as the ultimate rulers of human affairs. According to this view, the king would enact the Will of Heaven through his morally responsible actions. *De* 德 (virtue) became the ultimate criterion for evaluating royal behavior, while *li* 禮 (rites) became important political and ideological means of control.

In addition to ancestor worship, Zhou people also practiced *ba gua* 八卦 (eight diagrams), a method of divination guided by *Zhou Yi* 周易 or *Yi Jing* 易經 (the Book of Change), which approached the universe from philosophical and metaphysical orientations. By means of various combinations and multiples of hexagramic symbols, representing "the processes of change inherent in the transformations, influences, confrontations, dominances, harmonizations, reconciliations, oppositions, and so on, of specific experiences" (Cheng 1987, 41), practitioners of ba gua were able to interpret experiences of cosmic, political, and human proportions. As a result, the purpose of divination greatly changed from the quest for fortune, predictions about the weather, and information concerning the outcome of military expeditions to acquiring insights into how to live a balanced life and become a moral person. Generally speaking, the shift was from reliance upon external and uncontrollable outcomes to a focus on the internal and controllable inner world of spirituality.

During the Zhou dynasty, with a shift in the mode of communication away from a primarily oral tradition toward a combination of oral and written traditions, thought patterns became more abstract and rational. Discursive styles changed from mythic and spiritual to poetic, moral, and official. Oral poetry evolved into well-structured and refined poetic expressions. Formal speeches and official decrees became popular in the arena of political persuasion and moral teaching.

Poems

The Zhou dynasty is regarded as a watershed period for the production of written texts. Major texts produced during this period were *Shi Jing* 詩經 (the Book of Odes), *Shang Shu* 尚書 (the Book of History), *Yi Jing*, and possibly *Zhou Li* 周禮 (the Rites of Zhou). Despite concern among Chinese historians and Western sinologists regarding the originality, authenticity, and dating of these texts, they continue to be used as primary resources in the study of the Zhou dynasty by both groups of scholars. *Shi Jing*, a collection of poems and songs produced from the eleventh to seventh century B.C.E., is believed to be the first text produced in the Zhou dynasty. In a manner similar to that of Homeric poems of the eighth century B.C.E. in Greece, some of the poems and songs were sung by blind musicians on public occasions involving ritual sacrifice, feasting, farming ceremonies, and meetings between ministers.

Unlike the role of the bard in ancient Greek culture, who re-created and improvised poems and songs for special occasions, Chinese performers of the Zhou dynasty were required to follow certain prescribed forms. As in ancient Greece, a person's ability to recite and compose poems was associated with great learning and nobility. The poems were written on various themes ranging from advice to the king to expressions of political intrigues and frustration, from descriptions of grant ceremonies to glorification of the dynasty. Some poems were composed by government officials in order to praise the virtues and success of the kings of Zhou, as well as to portray them as Heavenly Mandated rulers. For example, Duke Zhou, the king regent, composed a poem in his worship and sacrifice for the late King Wen of Zhou:

> Solemn and pure the ancestral temple stands.
> The princes aiding in the service move
> With reverent harmony. The numerous bands
> Of officers their rapt devotion prove.
> All these the virtues of King Wen pursue;
> And while they think of him on high in heaven,
> With grace and dignity they haste to do

The duties to them in his temple given.
Glory and honor follow Wen's great name,
And ne'er will men be weary of his fame.
(Legge 1967, 4.1.433)

King Wen of Zhou was the founder of the Zhou dynasty and laid the foundation for his son King Wu to overthrow the Shang dynasty. The purpose of the above poem was to praise his deeds and celebrate his glory; its function was similar to Homeric poems and Greek epideictic rhetoric. The poem was structured with four Chinese characters in each line, a style considered aesthetically appealing and morally inspiring. Some poems were sung by kings themselves on ritualistic occasions with the hope of eliciting hard work and cooperation from the farmers under their rulership. Some poems offered hospitality and friendship to guests or expressed a commitment to running the dynasty virtuously by following the Mandate of Heaven.

Compared to the oral poetry produced in the Xia and Shang dynasties, poems produced during the Zhou dynasty demonstrated a stronger tone of moral indoctrination as well as a preoccupation with good and evil. Although on occasions of ancestor worship and religious ceremonies poems were still sung and performed with musical accompaniment, the purpose of such performance was not to please shang di and the ancestors' spirits but to shape and reinforce culturally approved behavior through well-structured ritualistic practices. The sense of poems as cultural symbols and political means of persuasion has been established. Such practices reflected the belief on the part of Zhou's rulers that human behavior can be shaped by adherence to strictly defined rituals, and that a civilized society can be constructed through an appreciation of music and poems. By performing *li* (rites) embedded in *yue* 樂 (music) and transmitted through poems, the social hierarchy of Zhou society would be maintained and strengthened and the common people would submit to principles of moral conduct. This belief was later adopted by Confucius as his rationale for rectifying and transforming the society in which he lived.

Poems of the Zhou dynasty were produced primarily by individuals rather than as a result of collective efforts. They were not improvised randomly, as was true of oral poetry in the Shang dynasty, but composed with clear purpose and intention. The typical poet employed several techniques including *fu* 賦, a method of description, using direct and denotative language; *bi* 比, an indirect means of using metaphors; and *xing* 興, a technique used to introduce secondary information into the main subject. Such techniques made possible an extended use of metaphor, the subjects of which were animals, plants, mountains, and rivers. Although highly artistic and refined, Zhou poems retain the features of rhyme and rhythm for the purpose of chanting and memorization. Because such poems were easy to memorize, they were cited pervasively for illustrative and persuasive purposes in pre-Qin oral discourse and written texts.[10] The ability to memorize, recite, and compose poems was the indication of the well learned and culturally refined. More detailed analysis of *Shi Jing*, the representative text for Zhou poetry, will be provided in chapter 4.

Speeches

In the Zhou dynasty, with the popularity of poems as essential means of ritualistic and moral communication and demands for speeches for the purpose of political persuasion, self-consciousness in the art of discourse increased and people began to be aware of the power of words in changing human perceptions and actions. Rulers often gave speeches at public events, and ministers were frequently consulted on state affairs. On these rhetorical occasions elaborate and persuasive forms of discourse were required. Making ethical, emotional, psychological, and rational appeals, the culturally honored form of poetic expression could no longer satisfy the rhetorical need. Speeches characterized by persuasive intent and the development of ideas, which were accompanied by illustrations, became a more effective form of communication. With the establishment of an official culture and the increased use of historiographers, more speeches were being recorded.

Shang Shu includes a collection of speeches by ministers addressed to the kings of Zhou. Two kinds of speeches are present: *shi* 誓 (taking oath) and *gao* 誥 (public advising). A shi was performed by a ruler in relation to his soldiers before a war expediency in order to encourage morale. A gao was performed by the king at mass gatherings such as the celebration of a harvest. Shi is more akin to the Greek notion of deliberative speech that aims at political expedience and communal bonding, while gao is similar to the Greek notion of epideictic speech that amplifies deeds and celebrates virtue.

Gao might also be offered to the king by his ministers in order to inspire the king to follow the examples of King Wen and King Wu, who were known as wise, virtuous, and benevolent rulers. As a consequence of their exemplary rulership, it was mandated by Heaven that they be remembered throughout history. The following is a portion of the speech given by Duke Zhou to a future king of Zhou, offering advice on the proper conduct of a ruler:

O Feng, we must be clear about this. I want to advise you the ways you can execute benevolent governing and how you can invite punishment. Now people are restless. If we do not comfort and repeatedly educate them, Heaven will punish us. We cannot complain. Now, the crimes are not that serious or prevalent yet and Heaven has not heard all of them. Well, Feng, you must be cautious; do not make enemies; do not use bad strategies; do not adopt unfair measures, for they would block your sincerity. You should govern benevolently so that you can reassure the public. Remember their [common people's] kindness and virtue; be flexible in taxing them; provide them with food and clothing. When people are peaceful, Heaven will not blame or abandon you. (SS "kang gao," 127)

From this example it is apparent that during the Zhou dynasty the notion of de (virtue) has become culturally and ideologically important, offering assurance for the continuation of Heaven's Mandate as well as the maintenance of political control. Here we see the notion of the Mandate of Heaven being used as a universal principle to promote moral actions. At the same time, the notion is also used as a system of reward and punishment for rulers in regard to maintenance and decline of their regimes. Although structures varied according to different situations and audiences, most speeches in *Shang Shu* employed rational reasoning and the metaphorical use of language. More detailed analysis of the speeches in *Shang Shu*, along with three other pre-Qin texts, will be examined in chapter 4.

Zhou Li

The culture of the Zhou dynasty is known as *li yue wen hua* 禮樂文化 (the culture of rites and music). In classical Chinese *li* is defined as: "law and convention; ritual and civility; and standards of conduct" (Wang 1976, 232). The book of *Zhou Li* (the Rites of Zhou) offers detailed rules and norms for speech and action in the context of political ideology, official hierarchy, and ritualistic and proprietary pronouncements, as well as means for disseminating *li* to the common people. The text had been attributed to different authors at different times in the pre-Qin period by the scholars of *Zhou Li*. A study by Peng Lin (1991) contends that the text was produced by an unknown writer in the early Han dynasty (200 B.C.E.). In the text the Zhou dynasty was idealized and presented as an exemplary model for the integration of Confucian and Legalistic doctrines in political and governmental spheres of influence for subsequent dynasties to follow. At any rate, the text is believed to have presented a basically truthful picture of the cultural and political structure of the Zhou dynasty.

The essential purpose of *Zhou Li* was to regulate the thoughts and actions of the Zhou people by providing and enforcing certain prescribed rules of moral conduct and harmonious relations in social, official, and family life. Examples of such rules were *ba tong* 八統 (eight uniformities) and *si xing* 四

行 (four conducts). The eight uniformities, prescribed for kings, officials, and ordinary people alike, were as follows: *qin qin* 親親 (telling people to love each other); *jing gu* 敬故 (teaching people not to steal); *jin xian* 進賢 (getting virtuous people into office); *shi neng* 使能 (employing talented people); *bao yong* 保庸 (keeping ordinary people happy); *gui zun* 貴尊 (respecting noble people); *da li* 達吏 (helping the poor and assisting the needy); and *li bin* 禮賓 (being polite and using etiquette). The four conducts prescribed codes of conduct for human relations: one should practice filial piety toward one's parents, treat friends like brothers, marry outside one's family, and be faithful to friends. These guidelines were institutionalized as part of a public education program and enforced by governmental decrees.

According to Peng's (1991) research, basically two kinds of educational programs existed in the Zhou dynasty: *guo xue* 國學 (state learning) designed for the sons of dukes and aristocratic families; and *xiang xue* 鄉學 (country learning) designed for ordinary people, divided by districts and community groups. In the first month of every new year, high officials would disseminate through oral and written pronouncements the official decrees of *Zhou Li*. Local officials would visit every district and community under their jurisdiction to explain and promote the decrees in an effort to insure that every member of society received and understood the message. Once *Zhou Li* was institutionalized, unconditional acceptance and implementation were required. Those who violated *Zhou Li* were charged and punished as criminals. Freedom of speech, thought, and action were absolutely forbidden. The *Law of the Imperial Zhou*, as quoted by Wu, reads: "Death to anyone who disturbs the government by initiating reforms; death to anyone who confuses people by making lascivious noise, wearing barbaric clothes, exhibiting strange skills, and using strange utensils; death to anyone who confuses people through adherences to wrong doings, arguing for sophistry, studying unorthodox thoughts, and rebelling against authority; death to anyone who confuses people by practicing witchcraft, astrology, and fortune telling" (1984, 37). In this way, indoctrination into li was enforced and guaranteed. The motivation for speaking and acting appropriately did not come from one's own desire for human moral perfection, but rather from pressure to conform and the fear of being punished. The content of *Zhou Li* had become public discourse and social intercourse, while individual expressions and antistate opinions were being suppressed.

Zhou Li also functioned as a system for evaluating and selecting competent government officials. Any person, no matter the class, was eligible to take exams on the contents of *Zhou Li*. Examinations started at the local level and moved to the state level. After a careful screening process, only those deemed wise, intelligent, and learned were accepted as officials. *Shi* 士, a group of individuals of official rank following xiang (ministers) and qing da fu (high officials) were instrumental in communicating the ideas and ideals of *Zhou Li*. Though shi were not considered members of the aristocracy, their social status was above that of common people. Functioning as messengers between the nobility and the common people, shi were knowledgeable in war strategies, rituals, and moral doctrines. In addition, they organized and participated in religious sacrifice and other ritualistic ceremonies, and some were hired as tutors for the sons of noble families. All such communication channels enforced and reinforced the teaching of *Zhou Li* at both official and local levels. In this way, ideology and moral conduct were standardized. The pressure to conform was great due to the fear of punishment and the hope of advancing up the social ladder.

From the above account of cultural and communication patterns of the Zhou dynasty, it becomes clear that the Chinese cosmology underwent a radical change from Heaven-centered to human-centered orientation, from spiritual concerns to moral preoccupations. Such change greatly affected the modes of ancient Chinese communication. Myths and legends once transmitted by an oral tradition were replaced by written historical accounts. Oral poetry evolved into poetry with greater aesthetic appeal and moral emphasis. The practice of ancestor worship and divination were overshadowed by bureaucratic enforcement of *Zhou Li*. Various types of speech emerged in response to political, moral, and utilitarian needs. In addition to social and political factors, the emergence of written discourse and increased literacy have largely contributed to these changes in the form and purpose of communication, bringing oral discourse into a more sophisticated, structured, and abstract level. Up to this point the ancient Chinese had a fairly fluid and positive experience with various modes of discourse. In the next period, however, we begin to see more diverse formulations of speech as a result of dramatic culture changes and attempts to conceptualize speech and persuasive discourse.

Spring-Autumn and Warring States Period

After enjoying peace and prosperity for four centuries, the Zhou dynasty began to decline in central authority and military power around the year 770 B.C.E. and was finally defeated by the so-called "barbarians," i.e., those tribes not assimilated to Zhou culture. Consequently, Chinese history moved to its most chaotic and stimulating time, known as the Spring-Autumn and Warring States period. As the American historian Witold

Rodzinski writes: "At the beginning of the Spring and Autumn period (722–481 B.C.) [B.C.E.], political power was already, in fact, in the hands of the rulers of the various states, which were being transformed into separate territorial units. The Chou [Zhou] Wang [the emperor of Zhou] after 771 B.C. was increasingly powerless and his role reduced to that of an arbiter in the quarrels of his vassals and to ceremonial functions" (1979, 26). Vassal states began to engage in interstate conflicts and wars, each wanting to conquer their enemies and become the dominant power in China. Eventually the weaker states were overtaken by the stronger states. By the end of the fifth century B.C.E. the number of vassal states was reduced to seven powers and China entered the Zhan Guo 戰國 (the Warring States) period (475–221 B.C.E.).

In the Spring-Autumn and Warring States period, private ownership of land replaced feudal feoffment, commercial activities increased, and more cities emerged. These economic and social changes paved the way for social and cultural transformation. In this time period China experienced remarkable changes in all aspects of life. In Hu Shih's words, this period was "one of the most important and most glorious epochs in the history of human thought." Furthermore, "its vigor, its originality, its richness, and its far-reaching significance entitled it to a place in the history of philosophy comparable only with the place occupied by Greek philosophy from the Sophists to the Stoics" (1963, 1). Indeed, during this period many philosophical schools of thought emerged and flourished and many significant changes occurred.

Changes in Education

The changes began with the education system, which in China had been public and government-run prior to the Spring-Autumn and Warring States period. In these institutions and schools, according to Cyrus Lee, "the students were aristocrats and there were no low people. The curriculum of the schools was based on learning the *li*, which was important for the nobles but not applicable to the low people, who had neither interest nor necessity to frequent such a school" (1977, 60). Such educational system changed as a result of the changes in political structure and social system in two respects. First, private institutions emerged and flourished. Confucius was credited with bringing about this change. His greatest contributions, in Lee's opinion, were twofold: "1) He established private educational institutions, which depended financially upon the tuitions and stipends of the students and the contributions of some good benefactors; and 2) he attracted students from different walks of life, no matter [whether] they were nobles or low people, provided they wanted to learn" (61). During this time private institutions of learning opened their doors to the rich and the poor alike. Teaching methods were interactive, with free exchange between the teacher and students. Likewise, individualistic and critical thinking was encouraged, with governments, officials, kings, and princes often the targets of criticism and attack.

The second area of educational system reform was with regard to curriculum and teaching methodology. Rather than simply teaching li by rote, in the new system "a master taught his disciples his own concepts about various subjects; the disciples learned by living with, listening to, and arguing with him" (Hsu 1965, 100). Confucius was one such schoolmaster. "He devoted himself to the acquisition of what we may term a liberal arts education that included history, ethics, government administration, and literature" (100). Statecraft and rhetorical skills were important elements of Confucius's curriculum, designed to prepare students for becoming rulers and government officials. Language art was not taught separately, as in the Greek rhetorical education system, but integrated in the curriculum of classics such as well-known historical and literary texts.

The component of critical thinking in education introduced at this time resulted in profound changes in cultural values, social stratification, and interpersonal relations. Hsu explains: "The divine charisma of rulers and ruling groups [of the early Zhou dynasty] was no longer recognized, and respect for the past was replaced by attention to present expediency. The familial bond between the ruler and his ministers was replaced by a contractual relationship like that between employer and employee." Furthermore "it was believed that an able and virtuous person should be selected to carry on the business of government rather than relatives of the ruler" (1965, 174). In other words, the feudal class system and the rigid regulation of li were seriously challenged. The relationship between the ruler and the ruled became more equal than hierarchical. Ability and competence became greater determining factors to success than class background. This was the beginning of the Chinese system of meritocracy.

The Emergence of Shi

Because the new society recognized competence and knowledge over class privileges, it provided opportunities of upward mobility for the class of *shi* 士, the educated intellectual elite. The shi, Confucius among them, were no longer related primarily to the performance of religious ceremonies as in the Zhou dynasty. Rather, they began to take on more important official roles, becoming state chancellors or consultants in military and government affairs. The ongoing wars among states placed shi with military knowledge in high demand. They became experts in statecraft and persuasion. At the same time, they also played a fundamental role in shaping historical, cultural, and philosophical thought, making a lasting impact on the Chinese worldview and communication practices. They were referred to variously as *bian shi* 辯士 (disputer), *mou shi* 謀士 (consultant), *cha shi* 察士 (wise men), *wen shi* 文士 (scholar), *shui shi* 說士 (persuader), *jian shi* 諫士 (adviser), *you shi* 游士 (traveler), and *yan tang zhi shi* 言談之士 (talker). These terms are often used interchangeably in the pre-Qin writings.

Shi were also categorized by the particular activities they engaged in. In general, shi were divided into three groups. The first group, referred to as *xue shi* 學士, were scholars of various schools of thoughts, such as Confucius and Laozi, who had formulated ideas or written books addressing philosophical, metaphysical, and political questions. The second group, known as *ce shi* 策士, engaged in political persuasion using highly crafted rhetorical skills. Two well-known ce shi were Su Qin 蘇秦 and Zhang Yi 張儀. The third group, known as *fang shi* 方士, or *shu shi* 術士, were specialists in a particular field such as astronomy, agriculture, or divination. In this sense, shi was a much broader concept than the term *rhetor*, the connection made by Crump in his study of Chinese you shui (Crump 1964). Shi were not simply persuasive practitioners but intellectuals and elites of the society. They played fundamental roles in shaping the ancient Chinese worldviews, political culture, and communication patterns.

Persuasion and Argumentation

Social and cultural transformations also contributed to a diversity of philosophical thought and speech. With the decline of the Zhou dynasty, a relatively liberal and open society emerged. Freedom of speech and argumentation became commonplace. As Yu Ziliu describes:

Because this social reform had affected every social class and institution, people became liberal in their thinking. They asked questions relating to social change, and expressed their opinions from their own perspectives. The old tradition broke down. Since a new centralized government was not established yet, there was no dictatorship in cultural values and ways of thinking. Such apolitical situation made it possible for argumentation among the different schools of thoughts. Thus, a society of dukes having different ways of governing, and scholars having different ways of thinking came into being. (1985, 60)

Persuasion and argumentation were popular rhetorical activities in three settings. The first was the political realm where you shui or bian shi served as advisers to the kings, attempting to persuade them to adopt certain policies either for governing their own people or for conquering the neighboring states.[11] In addition to proponents of the School of the Vertical and Horizontal, or Zonghengjia 縱橫家, who functioned as freelance political advisers and consultants, various well-known philosophers were also actively involved in political persuasion. For example, Confucius traveled to a number of states selling his ideas of benevolence; Mozi persuaded the king of Chu to call for peace with his neighboring states; Mencius advised the king of Qi and the king of Liang to practice benevolent government; and Xunzi traveled to the states of Qi and Chu as a political consultant.

The second arena for rhetorical activities was the realm of education where intellectuals taught their students various subjects using a lecture and discussion format. The redistribution of land and division of labor in the Warring States period left many Chinese intellectuals in poverty, as they did not know how to farm or run a business. In order to make a living, most of them traveled from state to state teaching history, poetry, and ethics to young boys. Confucius, Mencius, Mozi, and Xunzi were all teachers of this kind as well as having a career of political consultants and advisers.

The third place for rhetorical activity was the *Jixia* 稷下 academy, located in the capital of the State of Qi, where philosophers of different schools often engaged one another in debates over moral, political, and epistemological issues. According to official records documented in *Shi Ji* 史記 (Records of the Historian), the king of Qi, who enjoyed the company of scholars and bian shi, first invited seventy-six da fu (high officials) to the Jixia academy to debate on political issues. The number soon increased to hundreds and finally to thousands. Unfortunately, only nineteen such da fu can be historically verified. These individuals, along with shi, were also regarded as *ke qing* 客卿 (guest) of the king. Since they lacked official positions and titles, they were free to express their ideas and even to argue with one another (SJ 337–38).

The Jixia scholars came from different schools of thought and debated an array of topics ranging from metaphysics to human nature, from economics to politics, from epistemology to language (Zhang 1991).[12] The leading scholars of the Jixia academy were Mencius (390–305 B.C.E.) and Xunzi (298–238 B.C.E.). During Mencius's time diverse ideas emerged and theories were formulated; the style of debates was relatively direct and confrontational, with each man holding to his own position. By Xunzi's time there was a tendency to integrate different schools of thoughts and debates became more cooperative and inclusive. The Jixia academy existed for over a hundred years from the fourth to third century B.C.E., making significant contributions to the formulation and development of Chinese political and philosophical thought, much like the impact of Plato's academy and Aristotelian peripatetics in the same time period in Greece.

The Spring-Autumn and Warring States period, known as *bai jia zheng ming* 百家爭鳴 (contentions of one hundred schools of thought), was characterized by free expression, critical thinking, and intellectual vigor. Among the one hundred schools in contention at the time, the most popular ones were Confucianism, Daoism, Mohism, the School of Ming, and Legalism. Each school had its own worldview and sought to convince its opponents and society as a whole that its perspective would best serve Chinese culture. Fung offers a general description of the rhetorical climate of the time, saying, "when the Confucians had advanced their argument for the preservation of the past, other philosophers, holding divergent views, were forced, if they wished to gain a following, to explain in their own turn the reasons why they consider their doctrines superior" (1952, 14).

The above evidence demonstrates that the China of the fifth through third century B.C.E. was a place of transition, mobility, and divergence in all aspects of life. Like ancient Greece during roughly the same time period, China enjoyed a flourishing civilization and much diversity of philosophical thought, giving rise to rhetorical theories and practice. Conversely, such theories and practices served to promote and perpetuate cultural and social change. The ideals of equality, ability, and individuality were recognized and celebrated. Similarly, well-developed communication skills were highly regarded in the social, political, and professional realms of the ancient Chinese.

Written Texts

The Spring-Autumn and Warring States period was the golden age in Chinese history in terms of its production of written materials. The free intellectual environment and diversity of thought characteristic of this time period provided ancient historians and philosophers with the inspiration to write, which in turn laid the foundation for subsequent literary forms, philosophical thinking, and cultural formation. These texts also proved valuable sources of information on Chinese cosmology, religious practices, and cultural and communication patterns of previous periods, namely the Xia, Shang, and Zhou dynasties.

During this period two categories of writings were produced. The first are historical texts recording war efforts, political events, and the activities of state rulers. Some representational texts, which documented the persuasive activities taking place in public and private settings, were *Zuo Zhuan*

左傳 (Zuo Commentaries), *Guo Yu* 國語 (Discourse of the States), and *Zhan Guo Ce* 戰國策 (Intrigues).[13] The second category includes philosophical works expounding on worldviews, philosophical principles, ideas for political and social reforms, and conceptualization of language and argumentation; such as the *Analects*, the *Dao De Jing*, *Mencius*, *Xunzi*, *Mozi*, *Zhuangzi*, and *Han Feizi*. Writings in the first group were executed primarily by historiographers with moral concerns and political interests. Those in the second group of writings were produced by philosophers with various concerns on morality, politics, social justice, epistemology, and language. Both groups were written in literary form characterized by an extensive use of metaphors and analogies in style to create moral, emotional, and rational appeals. Both groups also presented historical facts and euhemerized legends to create persuasive effect.

In this chapter I have identified and discussed ancient Chinese cosmology, cultural orientations, religious practices, and modes of communication from the twenty-first century to the third century B.C.E. This background information is crucial in understanding Chinese literary, historical, and philosophical texts, given that the speech theories and practices in these texts either address or make reference to this cultural background. As the project unfolds, with the introduction and examination of primary texts on rhetorical theories and practices, the classical Chinese rhetorical tradition, which has remained implicit up to this point, will be made explicit and its meaning revealed.

As the ancient Chinese experienced speech and communication at various levels, as they began to recognize the power of language and symbols in shaping their lives, and as their consciousness became increasingly moral and rational in the engagement of persuasion and argumentation, they developed various conceptual terms to describe their speech practices and theories, as exhibited in selected pre-Qin texts. With the increasing production of written texts and growing awareness of the power of symbols, these terms became acceptable and standardized for social and intellectual conversations on language, persuasion, and argumentation. The next chapter will identify such terminology in reference to different types of speech behaviors and functions of language, indicating an evolution in the Chinese conceptualization of speech and language.

CHAPTER 3

Chinese Terminology of Rhetoric

In the previous chapter I reviewed certain social contexts and cultural forces that called forth and affected various forms of communication and modes of discourse. This account revealed the ancient Chinese cosmology, cultural values, and characteristics of rhetorical practices that evolved from a hierarchical and spiritual nature to a moral and rational emphasis. In their rhetorical experience with poems and speeches, and in their reflection on the role and function of language, the ancient Chinese employed and developed a set of terms and rhetorical concepts to describe and interpret their rhetorical activities.

In his study of classical Greek rhetoric, Edward Schiappa (1992) traces the evolution of key rhetorical terms from *logos* to *rhêtorikê* and differentiates the characteristics of Greek rhetoric between the fifth and fourth centuries B.C.E. as revealed in the different linguistic meanings embedded in the two terms. Schiappa contends that in fifth-century-B.C.E. Greece, the word *logos* was used to describe a broad and holistic sense of rhetoric that showed a balance between success and truth seeking, between rational and emotional capabilities. A precise conceptualization of rhetoric did not begin until Plato's coinage of the term *rhêtorikê,* which separated rhetoric from philosophy and served as a disciplinary term for the art of persuasion. Schiappa concludes that "A relationship exists between vocabulary and understanding: the more complex the vocabulary, the more sophisticated the observed learning" (10).

Schiappa's study on key terms not only offers a revised account of the history of Greek rhetoric but also suggests a key-term approach to the study of classical rhetoric. This approach is especially useful for identifying and describing a rhetorical tradition that is implicit and embedded in historical, literary, and philosophical texts. This is because, through the identification of key rhetorical terms and the examination of the terms in original texts, both denotative and connotative meanings of rhetoric will emerge; a better understanding of rhetoric in its own specific cultural and linguistic context can be reached. Accordingly, an understanding of Chinese rhetorical tradition is incomplete without an examination of key classical Chinese terms for describing persuasive discourse and, more importantly, for conceptualizing Chinese speech behaviors.

In chapter 1 I discussed the limitations of imposing Western terms and concepts onto non-Western cultures and intellectual discourse, suggesting instead the use of original terms and concepts from the culture under consideration. In this chapter I will identify and examine six terms associated with the practice and theory of speech from selected texts. The purpose of this endeavor is not to find Chinese equivalents to Greek rhetorical terms, but to identify similarities as well as differences in the experience and conceptualization of rhetoric between the two rhetorical traditions. Likewise, the task aims not simply at discovering a grammar of speech but also at tracing a dynamic and evolutionary process in the conceptualization of speech patterns and persuasive discourse. Another goal of this chapter is to counteract the tendency of Western scholars to approach Chinese rhetorical tradition in a static and rigid manner. As was true for the Greeks, Chinese senses and conceptualizations of speech evolved naturally over time as they were developed by different thinkers and schools of thought in the course of history. Finally, the identification and discussion of key terms provide linguistic and philological evidence for the argument that the ancient Chinese practiced and conceptualized speech and persuasive discourse in their own unique way.

Studies and Translations of Key Words in Classical Greek and Chinese Rhetorics

In her book *The Contemporary Reception of Classical Rhetoric: Appropriations of Ancient Discourse*, Kathleen Welch calls for a recasting of the interpretation and promulgation of key words in the rehistoricizing of classical rhetoric. She contends that "key words provide one location for radical change in the contemporary reception of classical rhetoric." Furthermore, "they enable interpreters of diverse theoretical stances to partake of those changes" (1990, 73). By investigating key words in ancient Greek and Latin texts, rhetorical scholars can uncover complex and multiple meanings embedded therein. Unfortunately, as Welch is keenly aware, non-Greek and non-Latin readers are subject to the problem of having to rely on translated texts. For example, the Greek words *pistis* (proof) and *aretê* (virtue) in Aristotle's *Rhetoric* are problematic in translation because the contemporary understanding of *proof* and *virtue* carry different connotations than the meanings intended by the ancient Greeks. Welch is not the only scholar to have made this observation. For example, in his article "The Greekless Reader and Aristotle's Rhetoric," Thomas Conley offers a list of key terms and concepts which he claims have been mistranslated in Lane Cooper's version of Aristotle's *Rhetoric*. Conley concludes that Cooper's translation is "responsible for a number of widespread misapprehensions—even among those who cite other translations—of what Aristotle's *Rhetoric* is about and, in some instances, of what rhetoric in general is all about" (1979, 74).[1] Given the fact that a great deal of scholarship and the majority of college-level rhetoric courses are dependent on Cooper's translation of Aristotle's *Rhetoric*, this is, indeed, an alarming and sobering statement.

Similarly, the problem of mistranslation also exists in the translation of Chinese philosophical texts. Since the time of Matteo Ricci, a number of such texts have been translated into Western languages. Hall and Ames (1987) contend that the translation of key words in these texts is a particularly weak area. They conclude that, in order to correct this weakness, the translator should be guided by textual and intertextual meanings as well as an understanding of the etymological roots of Chinese terminologies. In the rhetorical field, no effort has been made to translate Chinese words for *speech* and *rhetoric*. The incorrect assumption is that the word *rhetoric* encompasses the meanings, theory, and practice of Chinese speech behavior.

Most Western scholars apply the term *rhetoric* to the ancient Chinese view of speech. This practice may have contributed to the failure of Western scholarship to identify implicit rhetorical theory and practice. Schiappa argues that "naming phenomena alters perceptions of and behavior toward that-which-has-been-named" (1992, 9). If we accept his argument, the use of the word *rhetoric* in Western studies to describe and interpret persuasive discourse in ancient China will affect one's perceptions of Chinese rhetoric. Consequently, Western rhetorical scholars will miss the diverse and connotative meanings of original Chinese terms embedded within ancient Chinese texts. Other factors contributing to this failure are ignorance and insufficient research regarding rhetorical terminology in classical Chinese.

A translation may never be truly accurate and flawless, as the process of translation involves the interpretation of meaning by a translator who necessarily relies upon his or her own language resources and cultural understandings of the original work. What is even more problematic, however, is the assumption that the translations of key words from one language to another are accurate and complete. Such an assumption will limit the reader's ability to discover the multiple and complex meanings of the rhetorical practices under consideration while increasing the likelihood of imposing one's own cultural meanings upon such a system.

Indeed, when translating a particular word, multiple and connotative meanings embedded in and surrounding the word are often lost, and the meaning of the original word is reduced to a one-to-one correspondence with the translated word. Further, the meaning becomes static and carved in stone. Obviously, an inaccurate translation would make matters even worse. To avoid such problems, Welch (1990) suggests that scholars need to return to key words in order to appropriate them more directly than having to reinterpret outdated or inaccurate translations. In line with Welch's proposal, David Timmerman (1993) has surveyed the Greek word *dialegesthai* in pre-Platonic texts and discovered Xenophone's use of the word to refer to conversations characterized by questions and answers, along with its translation by Plato, who, in Timmerman's words, "conceptualizes philosophic discussion in a new way that he [Plato] eventually signifies with the new name he gives to it, *dialektikê*" (122).

By tracing the origin, evolution, and transformation of key words in ancient Greek rhetorical texts Welch, Timmerman, and Schiappa respectively offer insights as well as a mode of inquiry into classical rhetoric cross-culturally. Similar efforts have been made by scholars of Chinese rhetoric in the search for rhetorical terminology or key words in classical Chinese texts. In her article entitled "Classical Chinese Conceptions of Argumentation and Persuasion" Mary Garrett (1993a) identifies three key words relating to Chinese argumentation: 1) *bian* (dispute, debate, argue); 2) *shuo* (argue, explain, discuss, persuade); *and* shui (discuss, persuade, convince). Garrett argues that these terms are discrete and overlapping, reflecting a Chinese understanding of rhetorical experience as relational and correlational and of thought patterns as holistic and organic. Xing Lu and David Frank, in their 1993 study, trace linguistic variations of the term *bian*, differentiating it from the term *ming* (naming) in Chinese philosophical texts. We argue that *bian* is the closest equivalent to the English word *rhetoric*.

While these two studies are helpful in understanding Chinese rhetoric on its own terms, neither offers an extensive investigation of key terms nor provides sufficient evidence from historical, literary, and philosophical works to justify the textual meanings of the terms. In addition, a number of related key words are left unidentified and unexplained, and the connection made between the Chinese term *bian* and the English term *rhetoric* may have created the impression that the two terms are completely synonymous. More serious efforts need to be made in tracing the origin, evolution, and transformation of key terms relating to Chinese speech practices and theories. This study meets the challenge of identifying, recovering, and translating key rhetorical terms from the original Chinese historical, literary, and philosophical texts. In particular, six key terms will be shown to reveal rhetorical practices and conceptualization processes by the ancient Chinese. The meaning and transformation of meaning of each term will be interpreted as it appears in selected texts.

The selection of each term is based on three criteria. First, the term must be used as a principal word in the text and context of describing or conceptualizing speech patterns and persuasive discourse. Second, the term must be used consistently in reference to speech theory and practice. Third, the term must demonstrate a synchronic understanding or diachronic explanation of speech theory and practice.[2] The six terms that meet these criteria are: *yan* 言 (speech, language); *ci* 辭 (mode of speech); *jian* 諫 (advising); *shui/shuo* 說 (persuasion, explanation); *ming* 名 (naming); and *bian* 辯 (distinction, argumentation). *Ci*, *jian*, and *shui/shuo* are used to describe rhetorical practices; *yan* is used to describe forms of speech as well as to theorize the use of language; *ming* and *bian* are used to conceptualize and theorize language, persuasion, and argumentation. In the following section I will give an account of the appearance of each term in selected texts, the textual meaning of each term, and changes of meaning in certain terms over time.

Investigation of Key Words in Chinese Classical Texts

Yan 言

Yan is the first word under examination since it appears in the earliest Chinese text, *Shi Jing* 詩經 (the Book of Odes), both as a stylistic device and a content word for oral speech and language. In the discovered shell-bone script the character is a pictograph in the shape of a human tongue 舌. In *zhuan shu* 篆書 (the seal style), used in the Zhou dynasty, it is shaped like 言 with the top part meaning "bitter" and bottom part meaning "mouth." *Yan* has both grammatical and semantic functions in *Shi Jing*, the first being its auxiliary function whereby it is used to modify verbs. Its placement in this case can be at the front, in the middle, or at the end of a verb. Some examples of *yan* as an auxiliary in the initial positions are: *yan yi qi chu* 言刈其楚 (cut wild rose), *yan mo qi ma* 言秣其馬 (feed that horse) (*SJ* 16), *yan cai qi wei* 言采其薇 (pick the wild beans) (23), and *yan nian junzi* 言念君子 (miss my husband) (252). *Yan* can be placed in the middle of a line, such as in *yi yan jia zhi* 弋言加之 (shot down the swallow) or *yi yan yin jiu* 宜言飲酒 (cut meat and drink) (174). In rare cases *yan* is placed at the end of the verb as in *du mei wu yan* 獨寐寤言 (in bed alone) (119). In these examples and in more than forty other places in *Shi Jing*, *yan* has no particular meaning, merely adding emphasis to create rhyme and rhythm. This function is important since poems at the time were sung rather than read, as was discussed in the previous chapter. Given its frequency and pervasiveness in *Shi Jing*, it is reasonable to speculate that the word sounded phonetically musical to the singers of the poems in order to help with memory and gratify an aesthetic pleasure. Although there was no record of ancient Chinese pronunciation and intonation, the sound of the word *yan* must have added more energy, beauty, and aesthetic appeal to rhythmic emphasis. In fact, in his study of archaic Chinese, W. A. C. H. Dobson (1964) proposes that *yan* occurred in *Shi Jing* as an allegro form and formed part of a grammatical series in the text.[3] *Yan* was also used to make a three-character verse into a four-character verse in order to conform to the conventional form of poetry and for easy memorization to facilitate the transmission of cultural knowledge.

As explained in the previous chapter, the cultural context of the Zhou dynasty during which most of the poems from *Shi Jing* were composed put more emphasis on political persuasion and moral teaching. Gradually the increasing demand for persuasive as opposed to artistic speech altered *yan*'s linguistic function from that of an auxiliary word to one with semantic meaning: to speak or to use language. *Yan* can function as a verb or a noun. Consider the following examples of how it is used as a verb: *yan zhi chou ye; yan zhi chang ye; yan zhi ru ye* 言之醜也; 言之長也; 言之辱也 (speak the ugliness, speak the longest, speak the shamefulness) (94); *bu yu wo yan xi* 不與我言兮 (why don't you talk to me?) (*SJ* 181); and *ke yu wu yan* 可與晤言 (talk to each other) (271). In *Xiao Ya* 小雅 (Small Elegance), another section of *Shi Jing*, whose poems were composed by upper-class aristocracy, *yan* is increasingly used as a noun to mean types of speech by attaching adjectives to it, as demonstrated in: *pi yan bu xin* 闢言不信 (don't trust principled speech); *ting yan ze da; zen yan ze tui* 聽言則答; 譖言則退 (answer the pleasant speech, withdraw from hurtful speech) (*SJ* 391); *min zhi e yan* 民之訛言 (people spread rumors) (366, 384); *qiao yan ru huang* 巧言如簧 (clever talk is like music) (400); and *wu xin chan yan* 無信讒言 (don't trust slanderous talk) (446).

From the above examples, we can see that the term *yan* gradually expanded linguistically in its function from what the Chinese grammarian would consider a *xu ci* 虛詞 (weak word) to a *shi ci* 實詞 (substantial word). Western linguists would describe such an evolution as from a functional word to a content word, referring to talks and speeches. This functional shift signifies the transformation of the ancient Chinese consciousness from spontaneity to rationality, from concreteness to abstraction, from using *yan* for aesthetic pleasure to creating impacts on human behavior called forth by the increasing demand for more sophisticated political and cultural expressions and discourse. The diachronic feature of *yan* is also illustrated by the switch from a neutral term for speech to a term describing unethical behavior, for example, as the meanings of hurting other people, manipulation of the king, clouding of reality, and preventing justice. This semantic extension indicated the increasing awareness of the power of symbols in society and politics by the ancient Chinese.

Another important text, *Shang Shu* 尚書 (the Book of History), a collection of royal speeches, narrations, and discussions, was supposedly compiled by Confucius in approximately the same time period as *Shi Jing*. Judging from its contents and style, however, the text appears to be a later production by the author of *Shi Jing*. The word *yan* in this text is no longer used as an auxiliary or to serve as an artistic device. Its meaning as talk, speech, or language is essential and substantial. Moreover, types of speech are further delineated as *jing yan* 靜言 (clever speech), *chang yan* 昌言 (beautiful speech), *shi yan* 食言 (hypocritical speech), *fu yan* 敷言 (assertive speech), *hui yan* 誨言 (remorseful speech), and *pian yan* 騙言 (deceitful speech). Furthermore, the king refers to his own speech as *zhen yan* 朕言 (king's speech) and to the speech of the common people as *zhong yan* 眾言 (mass speech) (SS, 8, 26, 59, 99, 161, 251). Given the social context and cultural orientation in the Zhou dynasty, as discussed in the previous chapter, these examples indicate that the ancient Chinese became increasingly conscious of different types of speech and that such delineations had their basis in moral judgment and ritualistic knowledge. Speech patterns indicate the extent to which one is culturally proper. A judgment regarding one's moral standing can be made on the basis of one's speech behavior.

In the historical texts of *Zuo Zhuan* 左傳 (*Zuo Commentaries*) and *Guo Yu* 國語 (*Discourse of the States*), *yan* maintains its linguistic function as both a verb and a noun referring to talks and speeches. In these texts *yan* is used to signify the initiation of dialogues and is often followed by the preposition *yu* 于 (to) and accompanied by *yue* 曰 (say); examples include *Kong Shu you yan yu Zheng Bo yue* 孔叔有言于鄭伯曰 (Kong Shu talked to Zheng Bo and said) and *Jiao Ju yan yu Chu Zi yue* 椒舉言于楚子曰 (Jiao Ju talked to Chu Zi and said) (ZZ, 315, 1250).[4] Elsewhere *yan* is also followed by a direct object referring to the content of the speech, for example *yan wei er ai zhi ye, yan peng you zhi dao* 言畏而愛之也, 言朋友之道 (speaking about fear indicates love, it is a speech of friendship) (1194). In addition, *yan* is used to mark types of speech. The following delineations are used in *Zuo Zhuan* and *Guo Yu* texts: *shi yan* 食言 (hypocritical speech), *chan yan* 讒言 (attacking speech), and *bang yan* 謗言 (condemning speech).

Historical accounts within *Zuo Zhuan* focused solely on the state of Lu (Confucius's home state), while *Guo Yu* covered a history of several different states. The cultural climate in the state of Lu emphasized the cultivation of mind through learning; *yan*, accordingly, was perceived as an essential oral and written means to express thoughts and ideas. For example, Confucius is cited as saying *yan yi zu zhi; wen yi zu yan; bu yan, shui zhi qi wen; yan zhi wu wen, xing er bu yuan* 言以足志, 文以足言, 不言, 誰知其文, 言之無文, 行而不遠 (Speech reflects your ideas expressed through refinement of language. Without speech, ideas will not be known; without the refinement of language, the desired effect cannot be achieved) (1106). In contrast, the *Guo Yu* text recorded the history of various states where free speech was suppressed and those who did not speak to the rulers' likings were punished. The climate of caution regarding speech is exemplified in the following phrases: *nai bu gan yan* 乃不敢言 (dare not speak); *wei shan ren neng shou jin yan* 唯善人能受儘言 (Only a kind person can accept candid speech) (GY 9, 99); *wu yan guo shi yi* 吾言過實矣 (I talk too much); and *he ji yi qi yan qu zui ye* 何急以其言取罪也 (Why be in a hurry to punish someone because of his speech?) (569, 628). These examples show that *yan* was understood not simply as an act of the speaker, but also as an indication of the speaker's moral state and sensitivity to the audience's (the ruler) state of mind, as well as the speaker's motives and willingness to take risks in offering direct advice or suggestions.

In sum, through identification of the function of *yan* in the four texts analyzed above, it becomes possible to discern a diachronic development in its usage. In *Shi Jing*, *yan* refers to those glib tongues who deceive the kings; in *Shang Shu*, it is a form of political speech with both negative and positive consequences; in *Zuo Zhuan*, it is connected with political ambition and cultural learning, and finally in *Guo Yu*, its use is perceived as a threat to authority.

In philosophical works, *yan* is used both as a term to describe types of speech and as a concept to discuss the general use of language. In Confucius's *Analects* the word appears over seventy times and is used not simply for its linguistic function as a noun or verb but is associated with Confucian principles such as *ren* 仁 (benevolence), *yi* 義 (righteousness), *li* 禮 (rites), *de* 德 (virtue), and *xin* 信 (trustworthiness). For example, a disciple of Confucius described Confucius's speech as *Zi Han yan li, yu ming, yu ren*

子罕言利, 與命, 與仁 (Confucius seldom talks about benefits, but instead talks about destiny and benevolence) (*LY* 9.1.88). Confucius taught his students the following: *fei li wu yan* 非禮勿言 (Do not speak in such a way that does not conform to propriety) (12.1.123), and *yan bi xin, xing bi guo* 言必信, 行必果 (One must keep one's word, and act faithfully to one's word) (13.20.134). Furthermore, Confucius believed that *you de zhe bi you yan, you yan zhe bu bi you de* 有德者必有言, 有言者不必有德 (He who is a virtuous person must speak well, but he who speaks well is not necessarily a virtuous person) (14.4.143). Thus, for Confucius, it was important to: *cha yan* 察言 (observe others' speech) (12.20.125); *zhi yan* 知言 (know one's speech) (*LY* 20.3.204); and *bu yi yan ju ren* 不以言舉人 (not promote someone based on one's speech only) (15.27.160). Confucius disliked *qiao yan* 巧言 (clever speech) and believed that a gentleman should be *wei yan wei xing* 危言危行 (be upright in speech and action) (14.3.143) in running government affairs. Similarly, one should *min yu xing er shen yu yan* 敏于行而慎于言 (be swift in action, cautious in speech) (1.14.2).

It is obvious that Confucius was keenly aware of the impact of language in guiding and revealing one's moral character. To some extent he was able to transmit this awareness into language. He managed to transform *yan* from a simple linguistic function and semantic meaning referring to talks and speeches, to a rhetorical concept referring to the use and misuse of symbols. Confucius's *Lun Yu* 論語 (the *Analects*) is often regarded by sinologists as a masterpiece on moral philosophy. A careful reading of the text, however, leads to the additional conclusion that this well-known work on moral philosophy is also a treatise on the use of speech and language. According to *Han Shu* 漢書 (the Book of Han), *Lun Yu*, the title of the text, refers to a collection of dialogues between Confucius and his disciples that was edited by his disciples. However, the direct translation of the title also means "Discussion of Language" or "the Discussion of Speeches." *Yu* 語, in classical Chinese, is a synonym for *yan*. Although it may not have been the intention of his disciples in compiling their recorded conversations, the content of these conversations strongly suggests that Confucius made an initial attempt to conceptualize and theorize Chinese speech behavior and rhetorical practices with emphasis on the ethics of the speaker. Following Confucius, Mencius 孟子 reinforced this moral conceptualization of *yan* by proposing *ren yan* 仁言 (benevolent speech), *xin yan* 信言 (faithful speech), *shan yan* 善言 (kind speech), and *zhi yan* 智言 (wise speech) in his philosophical text *Mengzi* (*M* 3a.2.60; 8b.11.180; 11a.1.251; 13a14.307).

Yan is also a frequently used key word in Daoist texts referring to speech, discourse, and, in general, language. In *Dao De Jing* 道德經 (Canon of Way and Virtue), Laozi 老子 used *gui yan* 貴言 (noble speech), *shan yan* 善言 (kind speech), *mei yan* 美言 (beautiful speech), and *xin yan* 信言 (faithful speech) (*DDJ* 17.52;27.72;62.146; DDJ81.185). Moreover, he perceived the use of *yan* as a dialectical enterprise, as revealed by the following assertions: *duo yan shu qiong, bu ru shou zhong* 多言數窮, 不如守中 (too much talk creates emptiness; it is better to maintain moderation) (5.27); *xi yan zi ran* 希言自然 (few words are natural) (23.63); and *zheng yan ruo fan* 正言若反 (words have opposite effect) (78.180). Zhuangzi 莊子 used the term *yan* to refer to a broader sense of speech and language, saying, *fu yan fei chui ye, yan zhe you yan* 夫言非吹也, 言者有言 (Speaking is not like the wind blowing, the speaker must talk with substance) (Z 2.20) and *zhi yan qu yan* 至言去言 (the best language is without language) (22.298). Here, Zhuangzi apparently holds an antispeech position rooted in his view of the dysfunctional and limiting aspects of language. That is, language can never be sufficient in naming the objective world and representing the changes in the universe. However, this does not mean that Zhuangzi values silence more than speech. For Zhuangzi, the key is to use language and silence appropriately, not excessively (359). Thus, both Laozi and Zhuangzi treat *yan* as speech, attempting to articulate a skeptical view of language.

From the above analysis of the word *yan* in selected historical, literary, and philosophical texts, a diachronic case is made for the meaning and function of the word. Its meaning has been extended from talking and speaking, as means of artistic expression, to a moral and philosophical enterprise. Its function has expanded from that of simply describing speech practices to the field of moral and dialectical inquiry.[5] Again, such evolution is called upon by the social and cultural forces, stimulated by moral concern and philosophical inquiry into the role of language.

Ci 辭

The word *ci* in modern Chinese is often associated with *xiu ci* 修辭 (modification of terms) or considered the Chinese equivalent of "rhetoric."[6] In selected classical Chinese texts, however, it has several meanings. *Ci* first appears in *Shang Shu* as a synonym for *yan*, but with an additional sense of eloquence and embellishment of written and spoken words, or as a mode of speech used for artistic effect. For example, in the phrase *tian fei shen ci* 天棐諶辭 (Heavenly assisted honest and faithful speech) and in *ru yong you ci* 汝永有辭 (you will receive words of praise) (*SS* 161), *ci* is used interchangeably with *yan* to mean different types of speech and discourse. As a synonym for *yan*, *ci* can also be perceived negatively. For example, Mencius described four types of *ci* with negative meanings: *bi ci* 詖辭 (blinding speech); *yin ci* 淫辭 (excessive speech); *xie ci* 邪辭 (twisted speech); and *dun ci* 遁辭 (quibbling speech) (*M* 3a.2.61). In *wu jian luan ci* 無僭亂辭 (do not misuse the testimony) and *wu jiang zhi ci* 無疆之辭 (endless dispute in court) (*SS* 234), *ci* stands alone representing a particular kind of legal discourse. In this sense, *ci* is a type of discourse spoken in particular situations for particular rhetorical purposes.

In *Zuo Zhuan*, *Guo Yu*, and *Zhan Guo Ce ci* is synonymous with *yan* but is also extended to mean explanation, eloquence, and poetic performance. In the following examples, *ci* means explanation: *zi ci, jun bi bian yan, wo ci, ji bi you zui* 子辭, 君必辯焉, 我辭, 姬必有罪 (if you explain to the king, he will understand, . . . If I explain to the king, Ji would be punished) (*ZZ* 298); and *qing ting qi ci, fu qi you gu* 請聽其辭, 夫其有故 (Please listen to the explanation and find out the reasons) (*GY* 651). In most cases *ci* is followed by the term *yue* 曰 (say), meaning to start an explanation. When used in this way, it is often persuasive in nature and referred to as *ci ling* 辭令 (a mode of speech) (*ZZ* 673, 679, 951, 1191). When *ci* is used with *wen* 文 (cultured and learned), it is associated with eloquence and knowledge, as in *fan cheng wen ci* 繁稱文辭 (cultured and refined language) (*ZGC* 60). In particular, *ci* is a general practice associated with *fu* 賦 (reading aloud or composition of a poem) and *xing* 興 (the style and expression of poetry); it is used to describe the exchange or improvisation of poems, as in *tong ci er dui yue* 同辭而對曰 (reply with a poem) (*ZZ* 1497).

To summarize, the general meaning of *ci* is speech, language, and discourse and in this sense its meaning overlaps with *yan*. *Ci* can also mean explanation and the artistic presentation of language, associations which are not emphasized in *yan*. In practical terms, *ci* is revealed through fluency in reciting and improvising poems, in citing the classics, and in manipulating stylistic devices. In a positive sense, *ci* refers to the refined use of language. The skillful use of *ci* indicates the ability and talent as a well-learned and cultured person in ancient China. In a negative sense, *ci* is associated with superficiality or the employment of empty words without substance. In fact, the skillful use of *ci* by bian shi and you shui won them a reputation of possessing persuasive powers as well as glib tongues in ancient China.

Jian 諫

The concept and practice of jian were needed as political expedients either for gaining more power or for self-defense. During the Spring-Autumn and Warring States period, members of the aristocracy would often hire assistants to seek advice and suggestions on state affairs and military strategies.

These assistants were referred to as *jian yi da fu* 諫議大夫 (senior consultants). They were also known as *jian shi* 諫士 (advisers), *ke qing* 客卿 (guest officials)[7], or *you shui* 游說 (traveling persuaders). Accordingly, the activity of jian (advising, persuading) prescribed a dominant-subordinate relationship between the audience (the ruler) and the speaker. The determining factor for persuasion to take place was not the persuasive ability of the speaker, but rather the moral integrity of the ruler. In other words, if the ruler chose not to be persuaded, there was nothing but his own moral integrity requiring him to do otherwise, since sanctions could not be imposed.

Jian activities are evident in *Shi Jing* and *Shang Shu*, but the word *jian* was first used in *Zuo Zhuan*. When officials made speeches to the kings or aristocracy in attempt to change attitudes or policy, such activity was introduced with the word *jian* accompanied by the word *yue*, meaning to start an episode (or a story line) of verbal exchange on a topic or event. Consider the following example: *Wu Fu jian yue* 五父諫曰 (Wu Fu advises and says) (ZZ 50).[8] Jian related activities included alerting the king to wrong or inappropriate actions of the past, advising or admonishing the king for present actions, and reminding the king of considerations for the future. The topics considered by a jian shi fell into two categories: domestic and foreign affairs. To insure effective persuasion, advisers typically made reference to *Shi Jing*, the legend of the Kings of Zhou, using analogies and metaphors. Subsequently, they analyzed the situation under examination, identifying advantages and disadvantages for the king. It must be noted that jian was not always a one-sided affair but often took the form of a dialogue and conversation with the king. It also sometimes took the form of a group activity with several advisers giving advice at the same time. Such advising was called *zhong jian* 眾諫 (mass advising).

Some wise kings would encourage people to jian them and would offer financial awards to the good jian shi for their efforts. One account in *Zhan Guo Ce* 戰國策 (Intrigues) tells the story of the king of the state of Qi who issued an order as follows: "any ministers, officials, and citizens who can directly tell me my wrongdoing will be awarded the first prize; anyone who *jian* me in written form will be awarded the second prize; anyone who gossips about me will be awarded the third prize" (ZGC 240, 288). Jian shi themselves took jian as their moral responsibility and often expressed a great sense of pride and accomplishment in their work. For example, Gong-sun Shu, a jian shi to Meng Chang Jun, told Meng that he had three sources of happiness. "The first source of happiness is that of over one hundred people, no one has dared to give you advice and attempt to persuade you except me. The second source of happiness is that my advice has been accepted, and my third source of happiness is that my advice has prevented you from wrongdoings" (288). Nevertheless, jian was also a risky activity, since if a jian shi was found disloyal or unfaithful to the king, his reputation or even his very life could be in jeopardy. In the word of Mozi, *fei shang bu jian, ci zhu xiong yan, qi zui sha* 非上不諫, 次主兇言, 其罪殺 (A minister should not gossip, but only jian to his superior, if the minister says bad things about his superior behind his back, the minister deserves the death penalty) (*Mozi* 48.309). On the other hand, if the king was not receptive to the jian shi's advice, no matter how loyal and persuasive the jian shi was, persuasion would not take place. In such a situation, Mencius offered the following advice to jian shi: *jun you da guo ze jian, fan fu zhi er bu ting, ze yi wei* 君有大過則諫, 反復之而不聽, 則易位 (if the superior has made big mistakes, he needs some jian, if the superior repeatedly refused to listen to jian, jian shi should leave his office) (*M* 10b.9.249). In sum, *jian* is a term used to describe persuasive and advisory activities employed by subordinates in attempting to persuade their superiors. This unequal and hierarchical relationship between the persuader and persuadee directly affects and largely defines the nature and dynamics of persuasion.

Shui/*shuo* 說

Shui and *shuo* share the same character but have different meanings. *Shui* is often used synonymously with *jian*. It is used frequently in *Zhan Guo Ce*. The character 說 originally appeared in *Shi Jing* to mean happiness and was pronounced as *yue*. According to Shen Xirong (1992, 26), the term is associated with the radical 兌 (pronounced as *dui*), which symbolizes the releasing of words from one's mouth and the consequent finding of happiness and contentedness.[9] Examples of such usage are common in the earlier classics, for example, *yue yu nong jiao* 說于農郊 (happy to be in the countryside) (*SJ* 121); *Xi Wan zhi er he, guo ren yue zhi* 郤宛直而和, 國人說之 (Xi Wan is candid and friendly, people are happy) (*ZZ* 1485); and *yin jiu yan yu xiang yue ye* 飲酒宴語相說也 (drinking and talking at banquet, [they] are both very content) (*GY* 90).

Persons who engaged in shui activity by traveling around and acting as political consultants to kings of various states were called *you shui* 游說 (traveling persuaders). Shui is similar to jian in its persuasive function and social context. Like the word *jian*, *shui* is used to introduce an episode of persuasive engagement between two parties and is also often accompanied by *yue* 曰 or *wei* 謂 (both meaning "to say"). Another similarity between jian and shui is that both involve dialogue between the persuader and persuadee (usually the king of the state). Also, as in the case of jian, the effect of shui depends on the moral integrity and judgment of the persuadee. When shui (what is said) was accepted and proved beneficial to the king, you shui could expect a handsome material reward. However, if the shui has been proved harmful to the king, you shui would be punished. In an essay entitled "On the Difficulty of *Shui* (Persuasion)," Han Feizi 韓非子 sympathetically summarized the subtle and complicated situation faced by you shui. He advised you shui as follows: *Gu jian shui tan lun zhi shi bu ke bu cha ai zeng zhi zhu er hou shui yan* 故諫說談論之士不可不察愛憎之主而后說焉 (Jian shi, you shui, and other speakers must observe whether the king loves you or hates you before attempting to persuade him) (*HF* 12.7.180). Linguistically, in this example, Han used *jian* and *shui* interchangeably, both meaning persuasive practice.

Even so, shui and jian differ in certain respects. Despite the fact that both jian and shui made ample use of analogies and metaphors, the emphasis on the techniques of persuasion varied. Persuasive techniques employed by jian shi relied primarily upon quotations or citations from the antiquities and classics; while the shui technique featured an analysis of advantages and disadvantages for the persuadee and his state. While jian relied on ethical appeal, shui appealed to the persuadee with utilitarian considerations and an analysis of practical benefits. The goal of jian was to give advice in order to correct the past wrongdoings of the king, while the purpose of shui was to provide a concrete plan or clever scheme regarding military and foreign affairs for the future benefit of the state. Jian was practiced primarily by jian yi da fu, a designated official whose obligation was to guide his superior away from any possible wrongdoings as well as to offer advice. A you shui, on the other hand, was not as committed as a jian shi to his superior. This was because he could serve several kings at the same time and was free to change his allegiance. Both jobs were highly skillful and professional occupations receiving much respect in ancient Chinese society; however, a you shui could be likened to a freelance political consultant, while a jian shi was more akin to an in-house political adviser.

The character 說 pronounced as *shui* is also pronounced as *shuo* to mean an idea, a thought, an expression, and an explanation—for example, in *qing wen qi shuo* 請聞其說 (please share your thoughts) (*ZGC* 82) and in *Da wang lan qi shuo* 大王覽其說 (The king accepted this idea) (251). In *Mo Bian* 墨辯 (Argumentation of Mo), *shuo* means to explain, as in *shuo, suo yi ming ye* 說, 所以明也 (*shuo* means explanation), and to argue, as in *shuo zai bian* 說在辯 (*shuo* is part of argumentation) (*Mozi* appendix 2, 7). In *Xunzi* 荀子, *shuo* is sometimes used with *bian* (argumentation) as *bian shuo* 辯說 to refer to persuasion and speech behaviors (*X* 22.272–277).

The linguistic and rhetorical function of *ci, jian,* and *shui/shuo* locates each term within the synchronic category of analysis. All three terms served particular functions in furthering speech and persuasion in ancient China, and in fact, these terms are still in use in modern China, referring to similar rhetorical uses and situations. At any rate, the meanings of *ci, jian,* and *shui/shuo* overlap among themselves as well as with the term *yan*. Each was used by the ancient Chinese to label and describe speech patterns and persuasive activities, and they appear most frequently in historical and literary texts rather than philosophical ones. Conceptualization of speech was not a concern of the writers (historiographers) of such texts. It was in response to the persuasive discourse of jian and shui, and in reflection and contemplation of the use of language and presentation of an argument, that the concepts of ming and bian emerged. The fact that these two terms appeared more frequently in philosophical texts rather than historical texts in reference to Chinese speech patterns, the use of language, and persuasive discourse indicated the emerging consciousness and serious attempts to conceptualize Chinese yan, jian, and shui/shuo by ancient Chinese philosophers.

Ming 名

Several semantic meanings for *ming* can be identified in classical Chinese texts. The term was coined by Confucius when he proposed the notion of *zheng ming* 正名 (the rectification of names). In this regard, Confucius said, *ming bu zheng, yan bu shun* 名不正,言不順 (if names are not rectified, speech will not be smooth); thus, *gu junzi zhi ming zhi bi ke yan ye* 故君子之名之必可言也 (when a gentleman uses a term, he must make sure it can be expressed appropriately) (*LY* 13.3.132). For Confucius, *ming* meant titles, names attached to one's social status, and one's kinship with others. Accordingly, the use of ming determined how one talked and related to others in one's family and in society at large. A king was a king, a minister a minister, a father a father, and a son a son. Such names and titles (ming) located the individual within a social hierarchy. For example, a teacher was always referred to as master rather than by personal name. For Confucius, ming entailed naming correctly and speaking properly for an orderly society, thus insuring the correct correspondence between social status and speech behavior. In an abstract sense, ming signified cultural code or prescribed behaviors for society and acted as means of social transformation.

In the *Dao De Jing,* Laozi referred to ming as honor, an indication of success, popularity, and achievement. He also used the term with regard to signs and symbols that assign and refer to *shi* 實: the objective world or universe. As Laozi said, *shi zhi you ming, ming yi ji you* 始制有名,名亦即有

(When there is a social system of control, there is naming) (*DDJ* 32.86). To Laozi, such a symbol system would be in a constant state of change, for as he observed, *ming, ke ming, fei chang ming* 名, 可名, 非常名 (Names, as long as they can be described, they will change) (*DDJ* 1.18). In this sense, ming (as symbols) can never truly capture the essence of reality. While Confucius recognized the power of ming in shaping human behavior and political structure, Laozi perceived the limitation of ming in preventing humans from seeing the totality of truth.

The different perceptions of *ming* 名 (naming, symbols) and its relation with *shi* 實 (object, actuality) had been the central concern of Mingjia 名家 (the School of Ming), members of which engaged in dialectical discussions and debates over issues of particularity and universality, designated through naming, explaining the issues of how such naming either promoted or hindered social justice and an understanding of the universe.

The founder of Mingjia is believed to have been Deng Xi 鄧析, who is credited with initiating the discussion of ming and shi (actuality) in the domain of political and social justice. Being well aware of the impact of language on the perception of reality, Deng Xi was concerned with *xun ming ze shi* 循名責實 (following the names and searching for reality). He defines *shi* as the ultimate truth, but held that when names and symbols are used to refer to actuality, they become the ultimate truth (*DX* 6). In other words, language has the power to alter our perceptions of reality. According to this line of reasoning, in running a government it was of utmost importance for the top officials to *xun ming yi du shi* 循名以督實 (follow the name and observe whether it corresponds to reality) (5), to assure a representation of reality by symbols as closely as possible to achieve social justice. Thus, for Deng Xi, *ming* refers to laws, regulations, and policies at the state level.

The concept of ming was further developed by Gong-sun Long 公孫龍 and the Later Mohists who assumed that ming, the use of language, affected human perception as well as our relation to reality itself. Gong-sun Long defined *ming* as *shi wei ye* 實謂也 (how language is being used) (*GSL* 96–97). Gong-sun differentiated the nominal sense or denotative meaning of language from the actual sense or connotative meaning of language, claiming that different use of ming signified different versions of reality. In *Mo Bian* (the Argumentation of Mo), supposedly authored by the Later Mohists, ming was divided into three categories: *da ming* 達名 (universal/common naming); *lei ming* 類名 (naming by categories); and *si ming* 私名 (particular/private naming) (*Mozi* appendix, 11). *Ming*, in this sense, was understood as a means of labeling to classify and categorize the objective world and its function evolved from political interests to rational interests. An understanding and articulation of *ming* involved *shuo* 說 (explanation) and *bian* 辯 (argumentation). In Xunzi's essay *Zheng Ming* 正名 (Rectification of Names), Xunzi proposed a theory of language that integrated both the Confucian view of *ming*, dealing with social and relational dimension, and the views of ming by Gong-sun and the Later Mohists, dealing with more abstract, metaphysical, and epistemological concerns (X 22. 272–277). To this day, *ming xue* 名學, the study of ming, is referred to by contemporary scholars of Chinese philosophy as the study of Chinese logic.

The meaning of *ming* evolved from a recognition of symbol use and abuse with social/political emphasis to a mode of rational inquiry involving an understanding of ontology and epistemology. This diachronic analysis of *ming,* examining conceptual meanings associated with the term, indicates an increasing recognition on the part of ancient Chinese philosophers of the power of the symbols in multiple dimensions and aspects of social and intellectual life. In particular, the Chinese self-consciousness of speech and discourse was expanded from the concrete notion of yan to the abstract and logical character of ming. Language was perceived as the art of discourse and persuasion as well as an indispensable tool to define and understand truth and reality. Such an evolving awareness led to conceptualization of speech under *ming.* However, *ming* was an abstract term involving intellectual engagement and rational thinking, and it does not embrace a broader sense and practical function of language. Our final rhetorical term entails moral, political, rational, and artistic concerns and can be regarded as the linchpin of Chinese speech and philosophy of language. This word is *bian.*

Bian 辯

In addition to its distinct meaning as argumentation, *bian* also shares two other features within classical Chinese language. The first is *tong yong* 通用 (words that sound the same are used interchangeably); the second is *jia jie* 假借 (borrowing a word with the same sound to mean something different). In selected texts, *bian* 辯 (argumentation) is used interchangeably with *bian* 辨 (distinction, classification), an example of *tong yong,* and means at times *bian* 變 (to make changes), an example of *jia jie. Bian* was first used to distinguish and differentiate objects and things in the classical texts. Examples of such usage are: *Ming gui jian, bian deng lie* 明貴賤, 辨等列 (differentiate the noble and base class) (ZZ 43); and *bu neng bian shu mai* 不能辨菽麥 (cannot distinguish between beans and wheats) (907). The ability to make distinctions became a crucial element of persuasion, as *jian shi* and *you shui* were asked to identify clearly for the ruler the advantages and disadvantages of certain courses of action. Similarly, such ability was an essential element of philosophical debates, as *bian shi* were called upon to define and classify key concepts clearly, as well as to provide relevant examples for their assertions and arguments. In a sense, *bian* was a rudimentary expression of a Chinese rational process of reasoning, although the ancient Chinese did not provide an explicit map of the thinking process.

Accordingly, *bian*, understood as distinction and classification, had an important place in philosophical texts. For example, Confucius twice used the term *bian huo* 辨惑 (to clarify confusion) (*LY* 12.10.124; 12.21.126). Mozi 墨子 discussed distinctions in the following ways: *hei bai zhi bian* 黑白之辨 (the distinction between black and white); *gan ku zhi bian* 甘苦之辯 (the distinction between sweetness and bitterness); and *zhao xi zhi bian* 朝夕之辯 (the distinction between morning and night) (*Mozi* 17a.88; 30b.181). Moreover, *bian* was also used to refer to distinctions in social status, truth and falsehoods: for example, *bian mo da yu fen* 辨莫大于分 (clear about the difference [in social status]) in *Xunzi* (X 5.40); *shi fei li hai zhi bian* 是非利害之辨 (the distinction between the right and wrong, the benefits and harmfulness) in *Mozi* (*Mozi* 28a.169); and *Wu e neng zhi qi bian* 吾惡能知其辯 (how can I tell who is right and who is wrong) in *Zhuangzi* (Z 2.30). In general, *bian*'s function was to identify essential differences among things or to delineate lesser differences among things within the same general category. Such distinctions were made of the objective world and of the social and moral world. In selected texts *bian* was often used in combination with two other words: *ming* 明 (wise and intelligent), as in *ming bian* 明辨; and *cha* 察 (observation), as in *cha bian* 察辨.

An example of *jia jie* of *bian* is its meaning as 變 (to make changes and adapt to new situations). For example, Zhuangzi used *bian* to mean change and transform in *er yu liu qi zhi bian* 而禦六氣之辯 (riding with the changes of six kinds of energy) (Z1.7); Xunzi used *bian* to mean responding to a situation promptly and appropriately, as in *wu zhi er ying, shi qi er bian* 物至而應, 事起而辨 (deal with whatever happens, and handle the matter accordingly) (X 3.20).

In the social context of the Spring-Autumn and Warring States period, as described in the previous chapter, many aspects of life were in flux. It was important to understand and adapt to the changing times, especially since such changes brought with them social instability and a general lack of sense of direction. In response to this situation, the meaning of *bian* when combined with the term *zhi* 治 (control, manage) expanded to include justice, proper behavior, and the management of people, as in: *wei bian shi zhi tian jun* 維辯使治天均 (managing with justice and God's will) (*Mozi* 12b.52); *xiu zheng zhi bian yi* 修正治辯矣 (modified and wisely justified behavior); *zhi bian zhi ji ye* 治辯之極也 (top management and control); and *zhi bian zhi zhu ye* 治辯之主也 (king has the ultimate power to manage his people), in *Mozi* and *Xunzi* (X 4.29;8.67; 19.235). Accordingly, *bian* became synonymous with *zhi*, as the two words were used interchangeably to reinforce the same meaning of justice, management, and control for the purpose of achieving political stability.

As discussed in the previous chapter, rhetorical activities in ancient China were not limited to political consultations and persuasions but were also evident in the intellectual debates taking place in the Jixia academy and elsewhere among thinkers. For example, conflicts over worldviews intensified between Confucianists and Mohists on the issue of morality, between Mingjia and the Later Mohists on the topic of ming, and between Mencius and Xunzi on human nature. In the interest of winning over one's opponents and promoting one's philosophical views, one's ability to speak clearly and make sound arguments became of utmost importance. As a result, the word *bian* became associated with eloquence, argumentation, disputation, and debate. In fact, the ideographic feature of *bian* 辯 consists of the word *yan* 言 (speech, language) between two *xin* 辛, each standing for a prisoner in yoke. When the two *xin* combined, they made up the word *bian* 辡, originally referring to two prisoners accusing each other in court. The meaning of *xin* has also extended to mean spicy and bitterness.

Direct participation in intellectual debates by bian shi not only led to reflection upon and conceptualization of speech practices, but also facilitated a keen awareness of making distinctions and presenting good arguments. Such awareness enabled bian shi to define *bian* as argumentation, debate, and disputation. Consider the following examples. Mencius was known as *hao bian* 好辯 (one who is fond of arguing) (*M* 6b.9.141); Xunzi believed that *junzi bi bian* 君子必辯 (a gentleman must engage in argumentation) (*X* 5.41). The Later Mohists defined *bian* as *zheng bi ye, bian sheng, dang ye* 爭彼也, 辯勝, 當也 (when arguing over a topic, the winner is the one who can persuade) (*Mozi* appendix, 3). Zhuangzi advocated *wu bian* 無辯 (nonargument), claiming that arguments aimed at winning would not produce constructive results (Z 2.34). And finally, Han Feizi wrote an essay entitled *Wen Bian* 問辯 (Inquiring into Argumentation) in which he defined *bian* as a concept of argumentation.

In the philosophical texts under consideration, *bian* was most frequently used to refer to eloquence, speech, discourse, and argumentation. For example, in the *Dao De Jing* Laozi said the following: *da bian ruo ne* 大辯若訥 (the most eloquent appeared to be stuttering) (*DDJ* 45.111); and *shan zhe bu bian, bian zhe bu shan* 善者不辯, 辯者不善 (A virtuous person does not speak with high-sounding words; one who speaks with high-sounding words is not a virtuous person) (81.185). Similarly, Zhuangzi made the following assertion: *gu zhi xing shen zhe, bu yi bian shi zhi* 古之行身者, 不以辯飾知 (The ancient sages do not use eloquence as an indication of knowledge) (Z 16.203). Examples associating *bian* with eloquence, speaking with embellished and flowery words, and flamboyant stylistic devices include Xunzi's use of *ci bian* 辭辯 (artistic articulation); Han Feizi's use of *mi bian* 糜辯 (magnificent articulation); and the frequent use of *qiao bian* 巧辯 (clever articulation) throughout the selected texts.

Those who were involved in intellectual debates by the method of making clear distinctions and manner of eloquent presentations were referred as *bian shi* 辯士 or *bian zhe* 辯者 in the period of Spring-Autumn and Warring States. There were generally two groups of bian shi. One group was composed of philosophers such as Mencius and Xunzi, the Mohists, and Mingjia, whose major thinkers were Deng Xi, Gong-sun Long, and Hui Shi. They debated issues of morality, social order, ontology, and epistemology, as well as the relationship between language and reality. The second group of bian shi, which appeared frequently in *Zhan Guo Ce* and were mentioned more frequently in Han Feizi's works, were *you shui*. Two well-known you shui were Zhang Yi 張儀 and Su Qin 蘇秦. These traveling advisers persuaded the kings to adopt proposals on military strategy, foreign affairs, and personnel issues. The first group was interested in searching for truth and justice, while the second group was concerned with persuasive effect and utilitarian gains. Sometimes the distinction between the two groups was not always clear, as philosophical bian shi also participated in you shui activities. Hence, the terms *bian shi* and *you shui* were sometimes used interchangeably in references to speakers or persuaders.

Although some bian shi, such as Mingjia, and also some you shui were perceived and portrayed negatively in the context of Chinese history, the word *bian* remains as a neutral concept for argumentation. In fact, oftentimes it assumed positive connotations in philosophical texts, as it was used frequently in connection with *hui* 惠 (loving and kindness), *ming* 明 (intelligence), *zhi* 智 (wisdom), and *bo* 博 (knowledge). For example, Mozi asserted that *bian hui zhi ren, li wei tian zi* 辯惠之人, 立為天子 (a person who is virtuous and good at argumentation should be the king of the world) (*Mozi* 12b.50). Accordingly, he discussed the criteria for *ming bian zhi shuo*

明辯之說 (the principles for an intelligent argument) (28a.169). Han Feizi considered *bo bian* 博辯 (knowledgeable argumentation) and *zhi bian* 智辯 (intelligent argumentation) important qualities for effective persuasion.

Given the various meanings of *bian* discussed above, it is clear that the word has several different yet somewhat associated meanings. Not surprisingly, *Shuo Wen Jie Zi* 說文解字, the oldest Chinese dictionary, compiled in 25 CE by Xu Shen 許慎, defines the word *bian* as: 1) *bian* 辯 (argumentation and disputation); 2) *bian* 辨 (making distinctions); 3) *bian* 變 (making changes); and 4) *zhi* 治 (achieving justice and order). In the *Modern Chinese Dictionary*, the word *bian* still retains some of its classical sense, but has become more explicitly defined as argumentation or disputation. Consider the following definition: "both sides use reason and evidence to express their opinions on matters and issues, expose their opponent's weak points, and finally achieve a correct viewpoint and mutual understanding." In modern Chinese, *bian*, understood respectively as argumentation and as making distinctions, is represented by two different characters. In the former case, the character for *bian* includes the character *yan* between its two components 辯; in the latter case, *bian* is represented by a radical meaning, "to cut" between these same two components 辨.

In the works of Mozi, Xunzi, and Han Feizi, we also find *bian* being used in combination with the rhetorical terms of *yan, ci, shui/shuo,* and *ming*. For example, *yan bian* 言辯 and *ci bian* 辭辯 are used with reference to the use of language in speech and argumentation. *Bian shuo* 辯說 became a frequently combined term for speech, argumentation, and persuasion. Examples of combining rhetorical terms are especially evident in Han Feizi's work, as exemplified in the following assertions: *Qi yan duo er bu bian* 其言多而不辯 (There is much talking, but not much eloquence); *jie dao bian shuo wen ci zhi yan* 皆道辯說文辭之言 (Speak with style, eloquence, and persuasive language); and *ruo bian qi ci* 若辯其辭 (if you argue, do so with eloquence) (*HF* 32.9. 592–593). In this sense, *bian* emerges as encompassing other linguistic meanings of speech and discourse and also can be used interchangeably or in combination with other rhetorical terms.[10]

Bian is also closely related to *ming*. In the selected philosophical texts, both *ming* and *bian* are associated with speech and language usage, both implying a logical process of classifying and making distinctions. However, while *ming* deals primarily with symbolic expression and its impact on perceptions of reality, *bian* covers moral, rational, and artistic aspects of speech and argumentation. *Ming* is more frequently used to refer to a linguistic, dialectical, and epistemological dimension of language; while *bian* seems to encompass broader nuances of speech, persuasion, and argumentation related to social, cultural, political, and ethical issues. *Ming* is limited in scope to logical, metaphysical, and social concerns; while *bian* envelopes these concerns but also includes speech and argumentation in service of morality and utility. In fact, the classical understanding of *ming* faded as Mingjia lost its influence after 200 B.C.E. In contrast, the use of *bian* has expanded and is widely used to this day. The following chart summarizes the multiple meanings of each term; the dotted line indicates the process of evolution in meaning:

Key Terms of "Rhetoric" in Classical Chinese Texts

Yan: auxiliary, ——speech, talks, ——use of language (symbols)
Ci: modes of speech, types of discourse, eloquence, style
Jian: giving advice, persuasion
Shui/Shuo: persuasion/explanation, idea, thought.
Ming: naming, ——symbol using, ——rationality, epistemology
Bian: distinction, change, justice, ——eloquence, arguments, persuasion, debate, disputation, discussion

The above examination of key rhetorical terms in Chinese literary, historical, and philosophical texts reveals three characteristics of Chinese consciousness with speech, language, and discourse. First, each term has its own distinct meaning yet also overlaps with other terms. In this regard some pairs demonstrate more overlap in meaning than others, for example, *yan* and *ci; shuo* and *bian; ming* and *bian;* and *shui* and *jian*. The rhetorical function of *shuo* is to explain and instruct; however, *shuo* is also a *bian* activity requiring eloquence and clarity. *Ming* is mainly concerned with the power of symbols, yet it is through *bian* (disputation and argumentation) that symbols are infused with power. Linguistically, *bian* is shown to overlap with all but *jian* in the selected texts. The overlapping nature of classical Chinese language marks its versatility in that certain words share similar meanings and can be used somewhat interchangeably to create emphasis with artistic presentation. Further, this feature of language also reflects Chinese worldviews. As observed by Garrett (1993a), it indicates the Chinese cosmology of holism and perception of the world as interconnected and interrelated.

The second characteristic highlighted through examination of the six terms in question is their multiple and ambiguous meanings. No single term can be wholly defined by another word, whether in Chinese or in the translated English. The safest way to interpret and translate the meaning of a term is to examine it in relation to the text and cross-texts, and, ultimately, in the broader social context. One feature of classical Chinese language is its brevity, suggesting that a single term can encompass several meanings, only decipherable in context. For instance, the term *yan* can mean speech, talk, or language in general; however, in a given situation the textual meaning might be argumentation, persuasion, eloquence, or explanation. Accordingly, imposing a one-to-one correspondence or an exclusive once-for-all definition and translation on a particular term will short-circuit the process of arriving at its true contextual meaning for the Chinese rhetorical terms.

The third finding generated by this in-depth study of key words concerns their evolutionary, transitional, and at times transformational qualities. For example, the trajectory of ancient Chinese grammar of a speech theory moved from *yan* to *ming* and to *bian*. Within each term, a diachronic development in meaning and implications was also evident. *Yan* switched from an auxiliary word to a theory of speech; for Confucius, *ming* meant naming for the purpose of achieving social order, but to Mingjia and Mohists it was a notion of rationality and epistemology; *bian* broadened its meaning from making distinctions, changing, and promoting justice to include eloquence, argumentation, and persuasion. The extension and transformation of these terms suggest a progression and evolution from the practice of speech to the conceptualization of speech by various thinkers.

It is clear that the ancient Chinese formulated their speech theories and conceptualized the use of language. However, they did not make their theories and conceptualizations as explicit and systematic as the Greek rhetoric. One of the reasons for this implicit feature of Chinese rhetorical tradition may be that there is no single identifiable term clearly and specifically referring to persuasive discourse and language art as in the case of Greek *rhêtorikê*, but rather a group of terms that are overlapping and have multiple meanings. On the other hand, there seems to be a traceable line of evolution in the choice of terms in the conceptualization process of language and speech. From the exhaustive search of key terms and their usage in this chapter, it is fair to say that in ancient China the process of conceptualizing rhetoric began with *yan* as a broader sense of language, moved to *ming* with a specific notion of rationality and abstraction, and finally fixed on *bian*, which encompassed a broad sense of speech incorporating all the meanings of speech and language that had preceded the popular use of the term.

Language of Ambiguous Similarity

In his discussion of cross-cultural understanding and ethnocentricity, Charles Taylor (1985) calls for scholars of cultural studies to identify "a language of perspicuous contrast" as a linguistic means to recognize values of non-Western cultures and to integrate such values with those of a Western culture. A language of perspicuous contrast would reveal the contrasting meanings between different cultures. Although Taylor did not explain how this language of cultural contrast could be identified and operationalized, he did suggest that the idea is rooted in Gadamer's notion of a "fusion of horizon." This notion, if embraced, would reduce the tendency to treat other cultures and ideas as incorrigible and would help avoid assumptions of culture superiority. While I applaud the search for a language of perspicuous contrast, in the interest of promoting positive attitudes toward other cultures, I am concerned that the idea may also perpetuate the perception that cultural difference is absolute. This is because language tends to be the mirror through which we view our own world as well as the world of others. A language of perspicuous contrast tends to present mutually exclusive worldviews between two cultures. Consequently, the perception of difference is heightened, creating barriers and intensifying stereotypes associated with cultures.

First, an alternative approach to studying other cultures linguistically is to identify and search for what I will call "a language of ambiguous similarity." This is primarily because the human invention of language can be both culturally specific and universally similar, given our diverse and yet simultaneously universal human experiences and perceptions of the world. Second, delineating similar linguistic meanings cross-culturally often forces one to confront the problem of misinterpretation. The search for common ground is often more ambiguous than perspicuous. It is important to consider, on the one hand, the possibility that people label their worlds differently as well as to recognize culturally specific meanings in language usage. On the other hand, it is equally important to be open to the possibility that humans across cultures might perceive things in a similar fashion. This seems to be the case with certain basic moral principles of philosophy and religion. For example, the Chinese concept *de* is similar to the Greek concept *aretê*. The Christian notion of universal love has much in common with Buddhist teaching about mercy and kindness. By searching for "a language of ambiguous similarity," we may find that different cultures are not mutually incomprehensible and, further, that linguistic categories are not dualistically opposed to one another. If embraced, such assumptions could provide common ground for communication; the attitude of incorrigibility could be reduced, and cross-cultural interests could be promoted. If "a language of perspicuous contrast" could illuminate diverse ways of life as alternative possibilities to human experience, then perhaps "a language of ambiguous similarity" could decrease cultural and psychological distance, thereby increasing understanding of shared and universal human experiences.

In fact, it may be impossible to find identical words and concepts cross-culturally. However, making efforts to discover "a language of ambiguous similarity" in rhetorical and cultural studies may bring together similar or shared meanings in the conceptualization of rhetoric, illuminating ambiguity and subtle differences embedded in such similarity. With these thoughts in mind, and given the understanding of Chinese rhetorical terms discussed previously, we can see a language of ambiguous similarity between Chinese and Greek rhetorical traditions. The rhetorical terms in both Greek and Chinese language have some shared meanings as well as exhibiting the level of ambiguity and differences.

On specific terms, this research suggests that a number of key terms in ancient Chinese texts are similar in meaning to the Greek terms *logos* and "*rhêtorikê*." Yet none of the six terms under consideration is identical to the two Greek words as conceptualized by the ancient Greeks. However, a comparison of these terms with Greek rhetorical terms will exemplify "a language of ambiguous similarity." For example, the meanings of *ming, shuo,* and *bian* may be more closely related to *logos,* the word used by Greek sophists to mean forms of argumentation, discussion, questions and answers, and speeches (Schiappa 1992). The concepts of *yan* and *bian* may resemble more closely the Greek notion of "*rhêtorikê*" which included formal speech discourse and persuasion for a political purpose. Further, *rhêtorikê* and *ming bian* share more ambiguous similarities. Both *rhêtorikê* and *ming bian* refer to speech and argumentation. More specifically, *rhêtorikê* means creating change through persuasion; *ming bian* is associated with the ability to change attitudes and beliefs. *Rhêtorikê* involves the faculty of inquiry and is the counterpart of dialectics. Likewise, *ming bian* contains a process of making distinctions and categorizations. *Rhêtorikê* refers to persuasive discourse used in political and judicial situations. Similarly, *ming bian* aims at achieving social order and justice. Clearly the ancient Chinese and Greeks shared certain similar rhetorical notions and conceptualizations, including: perceptions on the role of speech in changing attitudes and behaviors; as modes of epistemological and intellectual inquiry; and ideas regarding the impact of language on moral, political, and social issues. These similarities exist within different linguistic systems, which, when viewed superficially, appear to have little in common. By juxtaposing their similarities, more commonalities between the two rhetorical systems are to be recognized.

Regarding the relationship between *rhêtorikê* and *ming bian*, it must be noted that the two are not identical. The meaning of each word emerged from within its own social, philosophical, and linguistic context. Accordingly, the Greek sense of *rhêtorikê* is more concerned with the art of persuasion, while the Chinese sense of *ming bian* seems to be more concerned with social values and social order. *Rhêtorikê* and its English translation conceptualize rhetoric as somewhat of an end in itself, while *ming bian* is more of a means to an end. Finally, *rhêtorikê* is a disciplinary term, while *ming bian* is not. In any case, the meanings associated with *rhêtorikê* and *ming bian* overlap but also differ. Future research could explore other key terms associated with speech, argumentation, and persuasion employed in both Greek and Chinese texts so that we are open to multiple meanings and rhetorical experiences. If we can recognize, understand, and incorporate key terms from different cultures into our conceptual system of rhetoric, we will have more room for developing "a language of ambiguous similarity," thereby moving closer to a "fusion of horizons" in our hermeneutical understanding of diverse rhetorical traditions.

In conclusion, I have formulated an evolutionary and often overlapping use of certain key words used by the ancient Chinese to describe and conceptualize their speech behavior and persuasive discourse. In the exploration of the key terms that reflect this ancient tradition, I argue that *yan, ci, jian,* and *shui/shuo* best capture the Chinese rhetorical activities in literary and artistic expressions and in political persuasion, while *ming bian* best captures the conceptualization of these experiences and formulation of a philosophy of language, theories of logic, argumentation, persuasive speech behavior, and artistic use of language. A more complete understanding of the rhetorical practices and conceptualization processes will be achieved by a close examination of Chinese literary, historical, and philosophical texts. This chapter has identified rhetorical meanings in linguistic context. The following chapters will trace rhetorical meanings in the intellectual, political, and philosophical contexts. In particular, the next chapter will introduce, explain, and identify rhetorical practices of the ancient Chinese through examination of five literary and historical texts, which will be followed by extensive research into the conceptualization of language and *ming bian* by various philosophers and different schools of thought in ancient China.

CHAPTER 4

Rhetorical Features in Literary and Historical Texts

It is believed that a great portion of Greek philosophical ideas and rhetorical expressions derived from the Greek literary texts, in particular from Homeric poems popularized from the eighth to fifth century B.C.E. Greece. The ancient Greek literature along with the Greek literary forms of myth, narration, and allegories facilitated the conceptualization of Greek rhetoric (Cole 1991; Enos 1993; Havelock 1982). Likewise, the Chinese conceptualization of language and ming bian was influenced and informed by the pre-Confucian poetic tradition and by literary and historical texts that described and documented various speech practices and persuasive discourse between the eighth and third centuries B.C.E. These texts serve to identify various rhetorical practices as well as providing information on social and cultural forces that called upon certain forms of rhetorical expressions. More importantly, the various approaches in the Chinese conceptualization of speech and language to be discussed in the rest of this book are addressed to rhetorical activities and situational variables described in these texts. Even certain rhetorical devices such as metaphors and analogies in the literary and historical texts continue to be employed in philosophical texts. Accordingly, an understanding of Chinese conceptualization of speech and language is not complete without a discussion of Chinese literary and historical texts. In this chapter I will introduce and examine five written texts produced during this period, namely *Shi Jing* 詩經 (the Book of Odes), *Shang Shu* 尚書 (the Book of History), *Zuo Zhuan* 左傳 (Zuo Commentaries), *Guo Yu* 國語 (Discourse of the States), and *Zhan Guo Ce* 戰國策 (Intrigues). In particular, I will identify various rhetorical features characteristic of the ancient Chinese language art and persuasive discourse.

Texts under Consideration

As discussed in chapter 2, China had a long oral tradition involving the transmission and communication of myths, legends, and ideas. However, like the ancient Greeks, the ancient Chinese gradually replaced their oral tradition with a written one. The emergence of written discourse stabilized the use of language as well as modes of rhetorical expressions. Archaeological evidence dates the earliest written texts to the Shang dynasty. In addition, pre-Confucian texts such as *Shang Shu* and *Shi Jing* record events and speeches dating to the Xia, Shang, and Zhou dynasties. However, given the highly refined use of language, it is likely that the events recorded and speeches documented in these texts are reconstructed in a much later date.

By 221 B.C.E. the emperor of Qin, credited with uniting China for the first time, was also notorious for burning books of classics. It is believed that the pre-Qin texts available to us today were transcribed onto paper in the standardized script around the second century B.C.E. from the original writings on bamboo and wooden tablets (Karlgren 1949). This poses serious questions as to the originality and authenticity of such texts, since it is possible that during the transcription process some of the original meaning was lost and the translators' interpretations added. The texts to be introduced and analyzed in the following pages were supposedly written during the pre-Qin period, but they are not in the true sense original versions.

Historians and literary critics generally agree that *Shi Jing* and *Shang Shu* were written during the Zhou dynasty and edited by Confucius during the Spring-Autumn period (722–481 B.C.E.). The remaining three texts, which are historical and narrative accounts of real people and events dating the pre-Qin period, were produced during the Warring States period (475–221 B.C.E.). I consider them important rhetorical texts as they contain a large collection of public and private speeches employing a variety of rhetorical means and appeals of historical and cultural significance. They also indicate the increasing awareness of human thought and the process to express their thought, solve problems, and direct actions by the use of speech and discourse. More importantly, they offer evidence of concerns addressed by ancient Chinese philosophers in their conceptualization of Chinese rhetorical theories.

Shi Jing

Shi Jing 詩經 (the Book of Odes) was mentioned in different contexts in chapters 2 and 3. In chapter 2 *Shi Jing* was introduced as the major Zhou dynasty text signifying a cultural orientation and rhetorical emphasis on moralistic, ritualistic, and artistic appeals. In chapter 3 we discussed examples from *Shi Jing* containing the first rhetorical term yan, tracing its evolution in linguistic function and semantic meaning. In this chapter the persuasive element of *Shi Jing* will be identified and examined.

Just as, according to Kennedy, "the Homeric poems were . . . venerated almost as the bibles of the [Greek and Roman] culture" (1980, 10), *Shi Jing* is considered the foremost text among the five classical Chinese canons, the other four being *Shang Shu, Yi Jing, Chun Qiu* 春秋 (Spring and Autumn Annals), and *Li Ji* 禮記 (Records of Rituals), of the pre-Qin period (221 B.C.E.). Its place and significance can be compared to Homer's *Iliad* and *Odyssey*. It was revered for its moralistic power of persuasion in almost all the historical and philosophical works of the period, shaping ancient Chinese thought, culture, and communication, and has become widely regarded as a rhetorical means of achieving moral perfection and political significance. It has also established fundamental moral principles as well as setting up aesthetic standards for the Chinese throughout history.

As one of the oldest texts in ancient China, *Shi Jing* contains 305 poems, songs, speeches, and short epics dating from the eleventh to fifth century B.C.E. and is comprised of three sections: *Guofeng* 國風 (National Wind); *Ya* 雅 (Elegance); and *Song* 頌 (Eulogies). The *Guofeng* section and part of the *Ya* section were collected by Zhou scholars. The rest were composed by kings, dukes, and shi on the occasions of certain banquets, gatherings, and rituals. *Shi Jing* is comprised of a number of different sources communicating on a variety of occasions. For example, the *Guofeng* section was composed by common people representing the working class and their lives in the form of folk songs. The *Ya* section, composed by the aristocracy, was considered more literarily refined and standardized from a literary standpoint. Similar to the Homeric discourse, the *Song* section, whose origins can be traced to the twelfth century B.C.E., was celebratory and ceremonial in nature, particularly useful for events and rituals such as carnivals and ancestor worship. Both *Ya* and *Song* were produced for the official and ceremonial occasions of the ruling class. The entire text was believed to be completed by the sixth century B.C.E. and its final version edited by Confucius himself.

According to Richard Enos, "The songs of Homer and the odes of the rhapsodies were all directed toward praise of virtue over vice" (1993, 39). In *Shi Jing*, however, poems have two elements: *mei* 美 (to beautify), used in praise and celebration of persons, spirits, and occasions; and *ci* 刺 (to attack or criticize), referring to poems which exposed, criticized, or denounced the aristocracy and society. In addition to these two poetic elements there are two categories of form. The first narrates and describes persons and events; the second expresses emotions related to people and nature. As explained in chapter 2, the techniques of *fu, bi,* and *xing* were employed in poetic composition. Vivid metaphorical imagery was used to express both mei and ci, or the happiness and sorrow of life. Most *Guofeng* poetry was an expression of ci, taking the form of inner thoughts and feelings, while the poetry of the *Ya* and *Song* sections aimed primarily at mei and contain descriptions of events, persons, and occasions. It is important to remember that such poems, especially those of the *Ya* and *Song* sections, were sung and danced on ritualistic occasions accompanied by imperial music. The rhetorical experience was, thus, elevated by a combination of verse, music, performance, ritualistic practices, and elaborate decorations.

The *Guofeng* section centers around the daily lives of common people: for example, their enjoyment of working in the fields; their hardships in war; their feelings for loved ones; the misery of being abandoned by their husbands; the pain of separation from their spouses; their sarcasm and anger toward corrupt and parasitic nobles; their admiration for virtuous kings. A number of poems were composed by women celebrating women's beauty, virtue, and spirit of rebellion. When poems were of the ci type, that is, critical of the aristocracy, the rhetorical techniques employed were much more metaphorical and allusive; for instance, in the poems entitled *xiang shu* and *shuo shu,* respectively, the ruling class was compared to a mean and greedy rat:

> Behold a rat! Its skin has glossy sheen!
> Then mark that man's demeanor, poor and mean!
> Bearing of bearing void!—what means it? This:—
> 'Twere better death than longer life were his!
>
> Behold a rat! Its teeth can sharply bite!
> Then mark deportment careless of what's right!
> Manners thus careless of what's right declare
> 'Twere well the man himself for death prepare.
>
> Behold a rat! How small its limbs, and fine!
> Then mark the course that scorns the proper line!
> Propriety's neglect may well provoke
> A wish the man would quickly court death's stroke.
>   (Legge 56)

In *shuo shu* the author uses the metaphor of a "large rat" in reference to the ruling class that eats the crops cultivated by hard peasant labor. No longer able to tolerate being exploited by the "large rat," the peasants leave in search of a happy land. The use of metaphor to scorn, denounce, and ridicule the ruling class has clearly been an important strategy of the oppressed throughout Chinese history. When the society becomes repressive, the mode of rhetorical expression becomes allusive, subtle, and sarcastic.

The *Ya* section was further divided into two categories, *da ya* 大雅 (Big Elegance) and *xiao ya* 小雅 (Small Elegance), featuring praise and advice offered to the kings of Zhou and expressions of disillusionment on the part of *da fu* (high officials) made during various ceremonial occasions. Unlike *Guofeng*, *Ya* represented the sentiments of the aristocracy. As this portion of the poems was primarily composed or collected during the declining period of the Zhou dynasty, the tone was one of disappointment and nostalgia for the glorious past, the previous kings, along with a sense of responsibility to help the current king.

While some members of the aristocracy lamented their miseries in an allusive fashion, others were more direct in offering criticism and advice to the king, as in this portion of *ban*:

> Calamities Heaven now is sending down;
> Be not complacent, but the crisis own.
> Such movements now does angry Heaven produce;
> Be not indifferent and your trust abuse.
> If in your counsels harmony were found,
> The people's hearts in union would be bound.
> If to speak kind and gentle words you chose,
> How soon would these their restless minds compose!
>   (Legge 382–83)

Throughout the remainder of the poem, its author wants to propose a plan to save the dynasty but worries that the king will not listen. Finally, using the previous king as a moral example for listening and adopting the ideas of others, the author urges the present king to practice virtue so that Heaven will protect the kingdom from decline.

Instead of blaming the king, some officials attributed the problems to "glib tongues" who, they believed, had deceived and misguided him. In the sections of *qiao yan* and *xiang bo*, for example, the poets condemned those speakers who had distorted the truth, clouding the mind of the king with their *qiao yan* 巧言 (clever speech), *zen yan* 譖言 (accusing speech), and *chan yan* 讒言 (slandering speech). They advised the king to make a sound judgment regarding such speech and to listen to the words of previous kings for guidance with his own speech and conduct. The previous kings of Zhou were highly praised for their moral principles, virtuous acts, and heroic success. In *xia wu* it is written:

> Kings die in Chou [Zhou], and others rise,
> And in their footsteps tread.
> Three had there been, and all were wise;
> Ta, Chi, and Wen were all in heaven,
> When Wu to follow them was given.
> (Legge 353–54)

The rest of the poem praised King Wu for fulfilling his filial duty and, thus, being blessed by Heaven. Another poem, *wen wang you sheng,* praised King Wen of Zhou for his achievement in building a strong military and securing a peaceful life for his people. In *jia yue* King Cheng was praised for his pursuit of virtue as well as for the love he displayed to his subjects. As a result, his throne was blessed by Heaven. A few pieces in the *Ya* section, such as in *zheng min, gong liu, huang niao,* and *shao zhi hua,* were written in epic form, describing the glorious history of the Zhou dynasty along with the heroic deeds of the previous kings listed in chronological order.

The practice of glorifying and eulogizing previous kings was even more prevalent in the *Song* section of *Shi Jing*. Poems and songs were composed and sung at ceremonies honoring the ancestors; in practice, the current king would pay homage to previous kings, praying for blessing and protection while thanking them for a good harvest. In this context, a *shi* 尸 (ancestor's spirit) would enact the role of the spirit of the previous king while a zhu guan or augur would talk to the current king on behalf of the shi. The king would then praise and celebrate the virtues and accomplishments of the previous kings, perceived as sages and models of moral conduct. Praising such men functioned as a rhetorical device of the current kings: establishing a moral image and strengthening the reign. Each successor of the previous ruler would eulogize the glorious deeds and moral principles of their predecessor in order to win the trust of the ruled and secure the power position.

The *Song* section also included songs and speeches delivered by the king to his people, ministers, dukes, and regional lords at various religious ceremonies, gatherings, and banquets. Songs such as *zhen lu* and *you ke* express the same royal appreciation for honorable, devoted, and successful lords along with promises of future wealth and security for the lords' descendants. Songs such as *jing zhi* and *xiao bi,* portraying the king as a noble, virtuous, and moral ruler, were sung by the king himself expressing his determination to ward off evil and self-corruption as well as his sincerity in seeking wise counsel from his ministers and officials.

The rhetorical features of *Shi Jing* have had a great impact on Chinese cultural views and communication styles in several areas. First, the text has emphasized the moral and ethical dimension of human life, especially regarding the conduct of the ruler. *De* (virtue), which is praised and celebrated, is associated with the securing of power. A virtuous regime will be blessed by Heaven, will be protected by previous kings, and will win the support of the people. This emphasis on de is reinforced by the celebration of spiritual and ritualistic values. De is exemplified through songs celebrating the achievements of previous kings and through epideictic speeches given at ceremonies involving ancestor worship. Further, such ceremonies embody the practice of *li* (rites), enhancing the legitimacy and perpetuating the favorable image of the dynasty. In Chinese history, it is a common practice that a current ruler legitimizes his rule and reinforces his political power by constantly recalling, celebrating, and praising the deeds, achievements, and heroic acts of his predecessors.

Another rhetorical feature of *Shi Jing* is its persuasive intent, direct and indirect targeting of the ruling class by common people as well as by ministers and officials. Poems of this nature are generally called *jian shi* 諫詩 (poems of advice), as they serve to remind the king of his wrongdoings and persuade him to practice de and benevolence. In jian shi the poet employs the notion of tian ming (the Mandate of Heaven), enumerating the shortcomings of the previous dynasty along with the virtuous words and deeds of their own ancestors. This rhetorical technique, which combines moral appeal and causal relations, became more prevalent in other pre-Qin texts, giving rise to the Chinese tradition of *shi yan zhi* 詩言志 (using poems to express one's will and idea). In this way, poetry became a political means of expression in both public and private spheres.

The last rhetorical feature of *Shi Jing* is its naturalistic and aesthetic use of metaphor in the celebration of joyful events and feelings (mei), as well as the cryptic and suggestive ridicule of the ruling class (ci). *Shi Jing*'s primarily metaphorical images are of animals, plants, and other natural elements. In fact, it is calculated that the book contains one hundred types of herbs, fifty-four varieties of plants, thirty-eight kinds of birds, twenty-seven kinds of animals, and forty-one types of fish and insects (Zhao 1993, 301). Such pervasive use of metaphorical images laid the foundation for an analogical mode of thinking in other pre-Qin historical and philosophical texts. In the historical and literary texts produced after *Shi Jing*, the metaphorical use of naturalistic images to provoke various emotional states became increasingly common.

At any rate, like Homer's *Iliad* and *Odyssey*, *Shi Jing* covered a variety of topics including war, heroic deeds, ceremonial occasions, and personality conflicts. In addition, similar to Homeric poems, *Shi Jing* emphasized moral themes and was used to transmit moral teaching to subsequent generations. As with Homeric poems, *Shi Jing* employed a variety of rhetorical means and techniques in the use of language, serving the political function of persuasion as well as the artistic function of evoking pleasure. Despite these commonalities, there are also many differences between *Shi Jing* and Homeric poems: for example, Homeric poems were created on the side of the aristocrats, while *Shi Jing* was composed by aristocrats as well as common people; *Shi Jing* was primarily interested in the expression of feelings, while Homeric poems were more concerned with actual deeds; the poetic form of *Shi Jing* was short verses, while the poetic form of Homeric poems was the long epic; the language of *Shi Jing* was more ambiguous and subtle, while the language of Homeric poems was relatively concrete and explicit. These differences in content and style reflected cultural differences in rhetorical choice and aesthetic sensibilities. While both Homeric poems and *Shi Jing* revealed a convoluted and circular thought pattern, the ancient Greeks seemed to place value more on overt actions of characters through an elaborate coverage of events, while the ancient Chinese appeared to place more emphasis on internal feelings expressed in the moment or in episodic fashion.

Shang Shu

Shang Shu 尚書 (the Book of History) is believed to be the first and oldest historical Chinese text, recording historical events, speeches, discussions, pronouncements, and persuasive activities dating back to the Xia dynasty. The character *shang* 尚 in classical Chinese means "long time ago," while *shu* means "book." Thus *Shang Shu* is a book of history. The book, also referred to as *Shu Jing* 書經 (the Book of Documents), is believed to have been written in the middle and late Zhou period by unknown historiographers and edited by Confucius.

Three forms of speech or rhetorical activity can be identified in *Shang Shu*. The first consisted of *shi* 誓 (taking oath) and *gao* 誥 (advising), referring to imperial speeches delivered at various formal occasions, for example, before going to battle or at religious ceremonies and official meetings. The purpose of these speeches was to enhance morale, heighten respect and trust for the kingdom, and indoctrinate moral principles. Most likely such speeches, reflecting a variety of moods and often punctuated with exclamatory words and phrases, were delivered orally without written scripts and recorded later by historiographers.[1]

The second kind of rhetorical activity involved personal encounters between the king and his ministers. Typically, a minister would offer advice and attempt to persuade the king on state affairs. Interactions between jian shi (advisers) and the king were generally friendly and egalitarian. Zhou rulers were apparently receptive, willing to listen to different opinions and even direct criticism, while jian shi were quite free in expressing their thoughts and direct in giving advice and criticism.[2]

The third category of rhetorical activity involved group discussions between the king and his ministers. Topics of discussion centered around issues of moral self-refinement, confidence and trust building with respect to one's subjects, and virtuous speech and conduct on the part of the ruling elite. At such meetings the king would invite his ministers to speak freely and share their thoughts in a manner of mutual exchange. Discussion would be accompanied by the reading of poems and the playing of music.[3]

Upon a careful scrutiny of the text, five rhetorical characteristics can be identified in *Shang Shu*. The first characteristic is the use of tian ming (the Mandate of Heaven) as a universal principle to justify an action. The notion of tian ming derived from ancient Chinese cosmology that can be dated possibly to the Shang dynasty and was subsequently used as a rhetorical device in ancient Chinese persuasive discourse. The chapter titles *gan shi* and *tang shi* refer to speeches addressed to soldiers on the eve of battle by the king of Xia and the king of Tang, respectively. Such speeches began with the argument that the enemy had violated Heaven's Will by committing crimes against the people and thus deserved to be punished. The declaration of war was, therefore, mandated by Heaven, making war a just and moral act. In this case, tian ming served as the major premise or universal principle in the deductive reasoning process.

A speech given by Duke Zhou (a top minister and adviser of the Zhou dynasty) used the same appeal but personalized Heaven by connecting it to the deceased king. The purpose of the speech was to persuade the reluctant lords to join him in putting down a "rebellion of barbarians." In the oration Duke Zhou claimed to have consulted Heaven on the matter, using a big turtle left by King Wen as a means of divination. The resulting signs were fortuitous, leading him to conclude that the action of putting down the rebellion was not only Heaven's Will but also a fulfillment of King Wen's legacy (*SS* "*da gao*" 116–17). Since King Wen, the founding father of the Zhou dynasty, was an idolized figure known for his virtue and accomplishment, this endorsement was significant. Although he was dead, his spirit continued to influence the living. In this way Zhou rulers connected the mysteries of Heaven with concrete and tangible past rulers. To follow King Wen was to follow the Will of Heaven as well as to show one's loyalty and dedication to the rulership of Zhou. In this context, acting against King Wen's will was morally wrong and required punishment.[4]

The second rhetorical strategy identifiable in *Shang Shu* is the use of historical examples and an emphasis on learning from the past, similar to the inductive reasoning process. In general, deduction was the more privileged strategy, given the fact that even when induction was used, it was only for the sake of explaining and justifying deduction. That is, inductive examples were used to verify existing principles rather than to generate new knowledge. For example, in one speech Duke Zhou instructed the king on how to persuade the people of Zhou to stop drinking alcohol. The king's speech was presented in three parts: 1) the duke established his argument, citing King Wen's assertion that alcohol consumption should be forbidden everywhere and at all times except during state sacrifices to the ancestors; 2) examples were given of previous kings who established and maintained their rule through alcohol abstinence, and of one king, of the Shang dynasty, who lost his dynasty and support of Heaven due to his indulgence in alcohol; 3) the threat of capital punishment was made against those officials who continued to drink (*SS* "*jiu gao*" 133–37).

Elsewhere, examples were given without reference to moral principles, through enthymemic persuasion and utilitarian appeal. For example, on one occasion Duke Zhou advised the king not to indulge in self-enjoyment, using extended examples from the historical past such as stories of how Gao Zhong and Zu Jia were loved by their people, ruling forty-nine and thirty-three years respectively because of their empathy for people and restrained lifestyles. A counterexample was also given of certain kings of the Shang dynasty who indulged in hedonistic habits, thereby failing to understand the hardships of their people. Consequently, their rulerships were a mere three or four years in duration. Examples in contrast that led to more positive outcomes created powerful enthymemes of self-persuasion. Significantly, the examples given were not hypothetical but were cited as historically factual. In this way the speaker appealed to the king's desire to maintain his rule through moral persuasion.

The third rhetorical characteristic of *Shang Shu* is its psychological appeal of rewards and punishment. Such speeches may not be considered complete by contemporary communication standards, but a pattern can be discerned nonetheless. That is, they either started with a universal appeal of tian ming, or with historical examples, or in some cases with a combination of both the appeals of Tian Ming and historical examples. Examples requiring action or advocacy were always followed by appeals for rewards and punishment. Typical rewards for loyal service to the king included imperial requests on behalf of the target audience for ancestral blessings and protection, the promise of material awards, and assurance that one's descendants would be cared for. Typical punishment included making slaves of the target audience or invoking ancestral punishment, executions, and capital punishment. Sometimes, as in the case of *pan geng*, a speech by the king of Shang attempting to persuade his subjects to relocate to another capital city, the reward and punishment model was employed at the beginning, repeated and elaborated in the middle, and reinforced at the end. This particular speech was interwoven with a deductive appeal to the virtues of past kings.

The fourth rhetorical feature in *Shang Shu* is the application of moral codes to political and advisory functions. While all such speeches served some political purpose, certain ones are more explicit in stating their political agendas, advocating general principles to follow, and recommending policies requiring immediate response or action. These speeches usually took the form of advisory discussions between the king and his ministers. Such discussion often involved formulating a set of criteria for the selection of officials and definitions of virtue and a virtuous person. For example, two important criteria, virtue and speech patterns, were discussed. The following virtues were established as criteria for judging a virtuous person: magnanimous and steadfast; soft and outstanding; cautious and respectful; talented and humble; obedient and principled; honest and warm; simple and fair; upright and sound; and strong and proper (*SS* 26). Regarding the speech patterns of officials, it was determined that *chan shui* 讒說 (deceitful talk) should be punished. However, if an official had good ideas for the kingdom, his speech should be *na yan* 納言 (adopted for use).

In the section entitled *hong fan,* one of the king's ministers, Qi Zi, outlined various guiding principles and policies regarding the laws of nature, selection of officials, use of language, divination, governmental affairs, and law enforcement. He advised the king of Zhou that there were five basic elements: water, fire, wood, metal, and earth, and that each played a part in the function of the universe. Qi suggested that the king pay attention to the corresponding five areas in his quest for personal perfection. The five areas were listed as follows: "respectful appearance; fair and just speech; clear observation; open eyes and mind; and contemplation" (*SS* 99). Qi concluded his speech by outlining five kinds of happiness: longevity, wealth, health, virtue, and good death, and six kinds of misfortune: early death, poor health, misery, destitution, evil, and weakness (100–101). Here the speaker connected the physical, moral, and spiritual entities, presenting a holistic worldview of the cosmos. The components of happiness parallel Aristotle's discussion of living well and doing well, which includes good looks, good health, good family, and performing virtuous actions (*Nicomachean Ethics* 1099b1.). In terms of rhetorical technique, as is evident from the summary above, Qi was fond of using numbers to list and develop his argument. In general, numerical categories have been a popular device for illustrating and simplifying complex and abstract ideas in the Chinese rhetorical tradition.

These deliberations on what made up the universe and how to live a good life indicated the Chinese conceptualization of cosmos and moral principles that guided the ancient Chinese speech behavior and nature of discourse. The role of the minister or adviser in these situations was like that of a teacher, philosopher, and parent ruled into one, guiding the king in state affairs, self-improvement, and moral conduct. A portion of a speech given by Duke Zhou to the young king illustrates this point:

My Feng, you must reflect on your actions. Now the people of Yin-Shang watch you sincerely following King Wen, making efforts and adopting ideas which will benefit Yin people. You go to the region of Yin seeking for good ways to protect common people. You must give deep thought to the teachings of the elderly Yin people regarding how to understand what is in the minds of the people. In addition, you should study the will and doctrines of ancient sages regarding how to keep common people happy. Your heart should be more magnanimous than the sky, guiding you with the virtue of harmony, and constantly accomplish the Mandate of the Kingdom. (*SS* "kang gao" 126)

As correctly summarized by Burton Watson, *Shang Shu* "is profoundly moral and rational, characteristic of the best in Confucian thought. By making the virtue of the ruler prior to, and the cause of, spiritual sanction, rather than the other way around, as in other concepts of kingship in the ancient world, it [*Shang Shu*] places a heavy moral responsibility upon his shoulders" (1962, 30–31).

The last rhetorical feature of *Shang Shu* is its use of metaphors and analogies (often an extended use of metaphors). Specifically, in *Shang Shu* metaphors are used to explain an idea or symbolize an action. In a few cases metaphors involving animals and nature are used to symbolize an event or describe a person. For example, women's words are compared to a rooster's morning crow, while soldiers' bravery is compared to tigers and bears (SS "*mu shi*" 92); succeeding and carrying out the mission of a previous king is symbolized by new branches growing from a tree ("*pan geng*" 64). In *luo gao* Duke Zhou advises the king to emulate the glowing embers of a fire that lasts forever, rather than the beginnings of a fire, which burns for only a short while (161).

Because *Shang Shu* was written in prose, it allowed a more extended use of analogies in development of an argument than did *Shi Jing*. In one speech, for example, Duke Zhou uses the analogy of a good father and bad son to describe his role as a regent to the son of the late king: "When the father wants to build a house and has an idea, his son does not want to dig the foundation, let alone build the house. When the father cultivates a previously barren field, his son does not want to sow, let alone harvest. The father might say, what if my descendants abandon my kingdom, then I cannot finish the great mission of King Wen" (SS "*da gao*" 117). In another example, Duke Zhou uses a series of analogies in advising the king to be lenient and benevolent to the people of Yin captured by Zhou:

I think it is like farming; after working hard to open up the barren field and sowing the seeds, one should think about managing the field, building fences, and digging trenches. It is like building a house, after working hard to build the wall, one should think about finishing painting and roofing. It is like making wooden objects, after working hard to take off the bark, one should think about how to color and decorate it.... Heaven has given the people and land of China to the previous king, today's kings must practice benevolent government to please and teach the blind people of Yin-Shang, and to finish the mission of the previous king. Well, if you rule people this way, the kingdom will be carried out for a thousand years. ("*zi cai*" 144)

These analogies also functioned as inductive reasoning devices, whereby the person being persuaded is invited to draw conclusions from the analogies provided, and served as buffers in starting a speech and preparing the audience for a gradual process of self-persuasion. The use of metaphors and analogies continued to be a main rhetorical strategy for indirect persuasion in other pre-Qin texts.

Being the first historical text comprised of political speeches on public situations and private encounters and written in the form of prose, *Shang Shu* employed a variety of rhetorical techniques rooted in Chinese cosmology, cultural views, and thought patterns dating from the Xia to Zhou dynasties. Though dramatic changes had taken place in the Spring-Autumn and Warring States period, the rhetorical techniques of deduction and induction, moral appeal, utilitarian appeal, and the use of metaphor and analogy continued to characterize Chinese persuasive practices in the remaining three historical texts to be examined.

Zuo Zhuan and Guo Yu

Two other important historical texts were produced in the pre-Qin period: *Zuo Zhuan* 左傳 (Zuo Commentaries) and *Guo Yu* 國語 (Discourse of the States). Because these texts were written during roughly the same time period, purportedly by the same author and using similar rhetorical techniques of persuasive discourse, I group them together for the purpose of examination and analysis. *Zuo Zhuan* is regarded as the first detailed account of the political lives and rhetorical activities of twelve lords of the state of Lu (today's Shan Dong Province). The book, which is organized in chronological order, is believed to have derived from an oral history of Lu written by disciples of Confucius during the Spring-Autumn period (722–468 B.C.E.). Another name for *Zuo Zhuan* is *Zuo Shi Chun Qiu* 左氏春秋. *Chun Qiu* 春秋 refers to the annals that briefly recorded major historical events of the *Chun Qiu* (Spring-Autumn) period such as the deaths of influential people and natural disasters. *Zuo Zhuan* further explains these events on a corresponding time line with *Chun Qiu*. According to Si-Ma Qian, the author of *Shi Ji* (Records of the Historian), *Zuo Zhuan* was written by Zuo Qiu Ming 左丘明, an official from the state of Lu.

Guo Yu is regarded as a companion piece to *Zuo Zhuan* in that it records the history of eight states in the pre-Qin period through its documentation of various conversations involving historical figures. This historical document is believed to have been written by officials from different states during the Spring-Autumn period and compiled by the same author as *Zuo Zhuan*. Thus, it can be surmised that neither *Zuo Zhuan* nor *Guo Yu* was written by a single author but is rather a collective effort. Both texts, believed to have been completed by the Warring States period (475–221 B.C.E.), were required reading for government officials in ancient China. Some stories and sayings are still popular in contemporary China, and descriptions of statecraft, human relations, and rhetorical techniques have had a lasting impact on Chinese culture and communication.

The two texts are not only similar in their descriptions of Chinese political persuasion of the same time period, but they are also similar in that both offered personal and political advice to the rulers in response to the social and political instability, cultural crisis, and moral decline of the times. More importantly, both texts focus primarily on the hierarchical nature of Chinese communication patterns between the ruler and his ministers. Such hierarchical positioning prescribed certain inherent limitations, complicating the process of persuasion by placing the persuader in a cautious and defensive position vis-à-vis the persuadee (the ruler) and giving the latter a decided advantage. The ruler was less receptive to jian shi's advice than he was to the persuasive style of *Shang Shu*.

The rhetorical activities documented in these two texts range from private conversations between kings and ministers, parents and children, and wives and husbands to imperial speeches addressing the public and long deliberations on the part of advisers or ministers on topics such as statecraft, military strategies, sagely virtue, and benevolent government. A great number of these conversations and public speeches are rhetorical in nature, aimed at persuading the audience whether private or public, an individual or a group. The rhetorical strategies employed will be discussed under the following five categories: the appeal of moral and cultural values; the use of historical and current examples; analysis of advantages and disadvantages; emotional appeal; and metaphorical language.

(1) The Appeal of Moral and Cultural Values. As the Spring-Autumn period was a time of transition, certain traditional values continued to play an important role in people's lives. Although the religious practices of divination and ancestor worship had lost their predominant role in political life, tian ming (the Mandate of Heaven) was still considered to be the ultimate power in regulating political ideology and action. However, the meaning and understanding of tian ming had been transformed from its religious and mythical sense to a moral and pragmatic concept. Specifically, a king or a duke was given Heaven's Mandate if he conducted himself morally, exhibiting an ability to correct his own wrongdoings. Such moral conduct included personal qualities such as: virtue and benevolence in state affairs; fair treatment of one's subject; careful selection of officials; a willingness to heed and adopt the advice of one's ministers; modest and respectful relations with others; faithful and righteous service to one's people; the practice of filial piety to one's parents; and a plain and frugal lifestyle. This moral criteria for kings and officials functioned as the most powerful rhetorical means of persuasion in both *Zuo Zhuan* and *Guo Yu*.

A vivid account in *Zuo Zhuan* tells the story of Prince Chong Er of Jin's treatment by the kings of other states when in exile. When in the state of Chu, a minister pleaded with King Cheng of Chu to kill him, to which the king replied: "Prince Jin (Chong Er) has ambition and is living a frugal life; he is eloquent in speech and proper in conduct. His followers are respectful and modest, loyal and devoted. The present king has no one close to him and is disliked by people in and out of the state . . . I am afraid, Prince Jin will be the future king. If Heaven wants him to prosper, who dares to eliminate him. Those who violate the Will of Heaven will be punished" (ZZ "*Xigong*" year 23, 409). The king of Chu's belief in Heaven's Mandate, along with his articulation of that belief, persuaded himself and his minister to release the prince.

According to another account in *Guo Yu*, King Li of Jin was killed by his officials. Consequently, King Cheng of Lu asked his ministers who should be blamed, to which Li Ge replied that King Li should be blamed: because he did not practice benevolent government, he deserved to die. Citing the examples of other vicious kings in history who were either killed or sent into exile, Li Ge concluded that if a king was not virtuous and benevolent, he would ruin himself and his kingdom (GY "*Luyu shang*" 5,188). In another account, a former minister refused to save the life of King Zhao, for he believed it was the king's fault that the state was defeated. Upon the king's return from battle, his former minister called upon him, but the king at first refused to see him. The minister sent the king a message advising him that his defeat by the state of Wu was the result of his desire for revenge and asking whether the king had corrected his wrongdoings and become a virtuous ruler. If the king refused to see the minister, implying that he still held a grudge and had learned no lessons from the past, he would certainly lose his kingdom again ("*Chuyuxia*" 4, 650–51). The king eventually agreed to meet with the minister, proving himself capable of learning lessons from the past.

In *Zuo Zhuan* we read how Shi La advised Duke Zhuang not to spoil the duke's son but to teach him to be a virtuous person (ZZ "*Yingong*" year 3, 31). In *Guo Yu* we encounter the anecdote of Nei Liang Fu openly criticizing the king for granting his favor to a greedy duke who hoarded his money at the expense of his people. Nei Liang Fu warned the king that if the duke were promoted, the state of Zhou would decline. Unfortunately, the king refused to listen, and Nei Liang Fu's prediction proved prophetic (GY "*Zhouyu shang*" 4, 13–14). These cases illustrate the point that negative consequences follow from immoral and unvirtuous acts. Not only were virtue and benevolence culturally valued, they provided a convincing cause-and-effect argument for the moral conduct.

In some sections of *Zuo Zhuan* and *Guo Yu*, the cultural values of filial piety and plain living were used in the making of rhetorical appeals. For example, *Zuo Zhuan* contains the story of a battlefield negotiation between the states of Qi and Jin on the subject of hostages. Duke Qin of Qi demands the return of Xiao Tong Shu Zhi, the mother of King Jin, as a gesture of surrender. Bian Mei Ren of the state of Jin replies, "Xiao is the mother of our king. . . . *the Book of Odes* asserts that the virtue of a filial son is endless and that the practice of filial piety should be shared by all people. Violating this value by holding the king's mother hostage implies that you have refused to accept this fact" (ZZ "Chenggong" year 2, 797). Interestingly enough, this is an example of a moral appeal made through the rational process of categorization and inference.

Several conversations contained in *Guo Yu* celebrate plain living, considering it a virtue as well as an important quality for success. Decadence, on the other hand, would lead to a loss of support of the people and Heaven, ultimately resulting in the downfall of the kingdom. Two such speeches employing this type of moral appeal were made by women: one by a mother who advised her son to follow the examples of sages and wise kings, being frugal and living a life like the common people, so as not to lose touch with reality; the other by a wife who persuaded her husband to leave a comfortable life in the state of Qi in order to fulfill his ambition of becoming the king of Jin. In the latter case, the wife cited a poem from *Shi Jing* suggesting that living a comfortable life would weaken one's motivation to achieve anything (GY "Luyu xia" 13, 218–19, "Jinyu si" 2, 364–65). Subsequently, the husband left Qi, becoming one of the most powerful and respectful kings of the Spring-Autumn period.

(2) The Use of Historical and Current Examples. Historical and current examples were a powerful means of persuasion in these two texts. The ancient Chinese had great respect for history. In fact, even myths and legends were treated as historical facts, and cultural heroes such as Yao, Shui, Yu, and Kings Wen and Wu of Zhou were frequently cited as moral examples. For the ancient Chinese, there was no separation between morality and wisdom: a virtuous king was also considered wise in his judgment and governing of state affairs. As previously stated, the wise conduct of previous kings provided inspiration for the current kings; likewise, unwise kings who ruined their kingdoms provided important lessons of deterrence for the current kings. The closer the figures and events were in time, and the more familiar they were to the audience, the stronger the persuasive impact.

For example, as recorded in *Zuo Zhuan* in 494 B.C.E., the state of Yue was defeated by the state of Wu. Yue professed a desire to make peace with Wu, but Wu Yuan, the minister of Wu, doubted the sincerity of such claims, suspecting that Yue was simply trying to buy time in order to rebuild and eventually mount an attack on Wu. In trying to persuade the king of Wu against making peace with Yue, Wu Yuan used the historical example of an ancient king of Guo. The king killed the minister of Xia but allowed the minister's pregnant wife to escape. Subsequently, the child was born, grew up, established himself as a lord, and finally defeated the king of Guo (ZZ "*Aigong*" year 1, 1605–06). This example suggests that the king of Wu should defeat the state of Yue instead of making peace with them, for the same reason that Yue would fight back when they became strong. Unfortunately, the king of Wu chose not to heed his minister's advice and was eventually defeated by Yue. Another example of persuasion made by reference to past conduct is found in *Guo Yu*. According to the account, a minster of Jin, after witnessing the virtuous conduct of a field laborer who was sending meals to his wife and treating her respectfully, recommended the laborer be employed by King Wen of Jin. Because the man's father had committed a crime, the king initially rejected the minister's recommendation, to which the minister replied: "In history, Yao executed Gun, but gave the office to Gun's son; in another familiar example the king of Qi employed Guan Zhong who once was his enemy." By this argument, the king was persuaded to employ the field laborer as an officer (*GY* "*Jinyu wu*" 11, 435).

Arguments and persuasive tactics illustrated by these historical examples engaged the audience in an inductive reasoning process. However, this rational appeal was ineffective on those rulers who refused to listen to advice either out of a lack of respect for the adviser or out of an overriding ambition to pursue individual goals. According to documented accounts, those kings who engaged in rational thinking and exhibited strong moral values, listening to the advice of their ministers, would avoid disasters and succeed in their causes. Conversely, those who refused to learn from the past experienced the decline and eventually defeat of their kingdoms.

(3) Analysis of Advantages and Disadvantages. Accounts of jian shi in *Zuo Zhuan* and *Guo Yu* portray them as knowledgeable and skillful persuaders and advisers. As the states were constantly fighting against each other for land and manpower, knowledge of potential allies and enemies and accurate predictions of who would rise and who would fall became crucial. Equally important was the knowledge of elements and conditions contributing to the success or failure of each battle or confrontation between the states, as well as the knowledge of certain decisions and actions which would bring long-and short-term gains and harm. In addition to other rhetorical strategies provided, ministers and officials, or jian shi, would analyze political and military situations, the moral state of the king, the competence of the advisers, and the morale of the people, offering the king a scenario of possible outcomes in the event that certain actions were taken.

In advising the king of Wu not to make peace with the state of Yue and not to attack the state of Qi, the minister Shen Xu offered the following analysis to the king: "Yue has clever and brave ministers and officers to help the king of Yue. . . . The king of Yue keeps his word and takes care of his people. People from all over the place like to be ruled by him. They have good harvest every year and their country is getting prosperous." Shen regarded the growth of Yue as a potential threat to Wu, asserting that Yue's true intention was not to make peace, but to retaliate and conquer Wu. By the same token, Shen advised the king of Wu: "You exploited the people of Wu with harsh labor. We lost all our crops because of natural disasters. There is a famine every year. [If the people of Wu had the options of being ruled by the king of Yue], they would leave us." Shen concluded that once the state of Wu was sufficiently demoralized Yue would attack, but the king of Wu refused to listen. A few years later Wu was defeated by Yue just as Shen had predicted. Disappointed and afraid of being captured by Yue, Shen committed suicide (GY "Wuyu san" 676–77, "Wuyu si" 681–82).

Sometimes persuasion by jian shi took the form of appeals to possible loss and gains from the enemy's perspective. For example, a story in *Zuo Zhuan* documents an instance in which the state of Zheng was surrounded by the states of Jin and Qin. King Wen of Zheng then sent his minister Zhu Zhi Wu to negotiate with Duke Mu of Qin. Zhu said to the duke:

Zheng is now being attacked by Qin and Jin. We know our state will be wiped out. But defeating Zheng may not benefit you. Defeating Zheng will help your neighbor to increase their land, but will not help you to increase your own. If you leave Zheng as the host of the East, we will assist your officers when they pass by Zheng. Your interests will be protected. On the other hand, if you help Jin to put down Zheng this time, Jin will expand their territory to the West. Then, they will get land from Qin. You will be helping Jin to harm Qin, your own state. Please think twice before you attack Zheng. (ZZ "Xigong" year 30, 480–81)

In this case, Zhu appealed to the duke's concern for the future of Qin by analyzing the long-term pluses and minuses to Qin of joining Jin to attack Zheng. The approach was so effective that the duke of Qin was persuaded to withdraw his troops. Like the rhetorical appeal to historical examples, the analysis of advantages and disadvantages appeals to the audience's faculty of reasoning as well as his ability to make wise comparisons and judgments. In addition, what is being played upon here is the audience's fear of losing along with his desire for power and utilitarian gains.

(4) Emotional Appeals. The Chinese concepts of *qing* 情 (feeling) and *xin* 心 (heart) are used to express and describe emotions. Feeling is believed to come from heart. In addition to verbal expressions along with nonverbal cues, Chinese emotions as persuasive appeals are also expressed through

the degree of attachment between the persuader and audience as well as by acting upon an exigent situation. In *Zuo Zhuan* and *Guo Yu* a person's qing was thought bound to his or her state of origin and relationship with the king. Thus, a feeling for the state and loyalty to the state ruler were expected. Two types of emotional appeal were proven effective in the two texts under consideration: the verbal expression of remorse for one's actions and a determination to make amends; and crying and howling.

Unlike Western rhetoric, which was often suspicious of an emotional appeal on the grounds that it smacked of manipulation, the ancient Chinese regarded the expression of emotions as an indication of one's loyalty, sincerity, and willingness to sacrifice to the state. Such appeals were therefore considered worthy of applause and appreciation. For example, in a verbal exchange between the king of Yue and his people regarding the question of whether they should attack Wu, the king said, "We were defeated by Wu before; that was all my fault. A person like me does not know what shame is, so please do not fight with Wu." Although the king's real intent was to attack Wu, he effectively used apology and modesty to provoke sympathetic sentiments from his people. Upon hearing the king's apology, the people of Yue responded, "[we] love our king in the same way we love our parents. Just as a son wants to take revenge on behalf of his parents, ministers want to take revenge on behalf of their king. No one would fail to do his best. Therefore, we demand to fight against Wu." The king then called for a united spirit in the war against Wu (*GY* "*Yueyu shang*" 712–13).

The second means of persuasion mentioned above, crying and howling, is referred to as *ku jian* 哭諫 (crying persuasion). *Zuo Zhuan* gives an account of a minister who attempted to persuade the king not to attack the state of Jin. The king did not heed his advice. The troops returned from battle in defeat to the spectacle of their king dressed in white, crying and wailing for the loss of lives and apologizing for not listening to his minister's advice (*ZZ* "*Xigong*" year 23, 488–501). The soldiers were very moved and forgave the king. According to another touching account in *Zuo Zhuan*, Shen Bao Xu appealed to the king of Qi for help in rescuing his state by crying and wailing for seven days and seven nights. Impressed by the man's heartfelt patriotism, the king of Qin was finally moved to send troops to help ("*Dinggong*" year 4, 1547–48). This rhetorical technique has been used in other well-known Chinese literary texts, such as *San Guo Yan Yi* 三國演義 (Three Kingdoms), and *Shui Hu* 水滸 (The Out-Laws), concerning the interaction between kings and ministers or officials.

(5) Metaphorical Language. Most scholars agree that *Zuo Zhuan* and *Guo Yu* are pseudohistorical texts containing semifictitious accounts of

events and figures in the Spring-Autumn period. The literary and artistic style of these texts, however, was not for the purpose of aesthetic embellishment but rather for persuasive and rhetorical effect. The texts are primarily comprised of metaphors, proverbs, and poems from *Shi Jing*, in combination with historical and current examples of moral and utilitarian appeals, illustrating, elaborating, and reinforcing an argument.

In attempting to persuade the king of Chu to be a benevolent ruler, Ji Shi cited two poems from *Shi Jing*. The first implied that only a few people could be kind all the time; if the king was one of these rare few, the state would be saved. The second poem indicated that royal mistakes were acceptable as long as the king knew how to correct and promptly remedy them ("*Xuangong*" year 2, 657). In another example, when asked for a definition of *he* 和 (harmony), Yan Zi replied with an analogy: *he* is like cooking meat; it needs water, fire, vinegar, soy sauce, salt, plum for flavor, and firewood to cook. Furthermore, the cook must blend all the ingredients well and adjust the flavor by adding ingredients or water ("*Zhaogong*" year 20, 1419). Yan then applied this analogy to the relationship between the king and his minister, advocating an adjustment and blending of each other's ideas in their interactions and communication. This analogy implied a mutual and interdependent influence between the king and the minister and the significance of maintaining a harmonious relationship between the two.

In another example, a tree was used metaphorically to symbolize the root of trouble or disaster. When the king of Jin sought advice on the problems the state was facing, Yan Bi, the minister replied, "The root of trouble is like the growth of a tree. The more branches and leaves growing in the tree, the deeper and thicker the root of the tree will be, so it is difficult to stop the growth. If the shaft of an ax can be lengthened and the ax is used to chop off the branches and leaves and dig out the root, the problems will be eased for a while" (GY "*Jinyu ba*" 1, 506). Similarly, in advising the king of Wu to learn from the past, Shen Xu used the metaphor of mirror, saying "my big king, why not use others as a mirror to reflect yourself. Do not use water as a mirror, because water can only reflect your shadow, while a person as a mirror can clearly reflect your effectiveness and the achievement of your cause" ("*Wuyu san*" 676). A fluency in the use of poems and metaphors indicated that the speaker was a learned and eloquent person possessing a high level of literacy and conventional wisdom. This quality added to one's credibility. However, the use of poems and metaphors was only persuasive to the extent that the ruler was willing and possessed moral competence in making sound judgments.

Both *Zuo Zhuan* and *Guo Yu* contain examples of unusual circumstances that function as living metaphors arising spontaneously. For example, according to an account in *Zuo Zhuan*, a duke of Zheng placed his own mother under house arrest for the charge of conspiracy, swearing that he would never see her again unless and until they met in the netherworld. Thereafter, Yin Kao Shu, an officer, came bearing presents to see the duke and was invited to stay for dinner. At dinner Ying put aside his meat, saying "I have a mother who has never tasted the meat from a royal family. Please let me take the meat home for her," to which the duke replied sadly, "you have a mother to send food to, I don't even have a mother." Upon hearing the duke's story and after having assured himself of the duke's sincere regret and desire to see his mother, the officer suggested digging a tunnel connecting the duke to where his mother was kept so that they could visit with one another. The duke followed the officer's advice and by so doing made it possible to honor his filial duty to his mother while saving face with his loyal subjects, whom he had formally promised he would not see his mother. The story ends with a poem from *Shi Jing* praising filial piety, implying that the duke should fulfill his filial responsibilities despite his mother's actions (ZZ "Yingong" year 1, 14–16). The reader is left with admiration for the clever officer who helped turn a hopeless and embarrassing situation into a happy ending for all concerned.

In another account, the king of Jin had just returned to his kingdom in exile, when his former doorkeeper paid him a call. A messenger informed the doorkeeper that the king could not meet with him because he was washing his hair, to which the doorkeeper replied, "When washing hair, the head is in an upside down position so the king cannot think right. No wonder he does not want to see me." He then argued that although he had stayed instead of accompanying the king into exile, he had been guarding the state for the king. Furthermore, "a king should not make enemies among the common people, nor cause people to fear him." When the messenger relayed this message to the king, he immediately relented, agreeing to meet with the doorkeeper ("*Xigong*" year 24, 415–16).

An account in *Guo Yu* offers another example of this type of living metaphor. According to the story, two officials wanted to persuade Xian Zi, a high official, not to accept a bribe in a court case. Instead of making a verbal argument, however, they arranged a meal with Xian. At the meal the two officials sighed three times. When Xian asked why, they explained that they were base and greedy people: When the meal was first brought to the table, they feared they would not have enough, so they sighed; in the middle of the meal, they sighed when it occurred to them that the host would see to it that they had enough to eat; they sighed a third time at the end of the meal when they realized that they had misjudged Xian by projecting their own greedy motives upon him. On hearing this, Xian understood that they regarded him as *junzi* (gentleman) who should not be interested in material gains. Feeling honored and also fearing of losing face, Xian refused the bribe (*GY* "*Jinyu jiu*" 6, 556). The use of this type of metaphor requires metic intelligence from both the speaker and the audience.[5] It requires great skill on the part of the speaker, who must direct the audience to the connection between the immediate situation and the topic implied. More important, it requires competence and wisdom on the part of the audience, who must read beyond the immediate situation and superficial exchange on seemingly unimportant and unrelated matters in order to be enlightened. Such communication techniques are used frequently in the *koan* (dialogues) between zen masters and their disciples.

The above five rhetorical strategies are employed throughout *Zuo Zhuan* and *Guo Yu*. Some stories employed predominantly one or two strategies, but most stories used a combination of all five, illustrating the point that the ancient Chinese rhetorical tradition is characterized by moral, rational, emotional, and psychological appeals with an emphasis on moral character of the speaker and the combination of wisdom and eloquence.

From the above examples, we can conclude that the jian shi in ancient China were very much respected. They were the wise men, the loyal officials, morally obligated to advise and assist the kings. The sad fact, however, was that because of the inherently unequal relationship between the jian shi and the ruler, no matter how virtuous and eloquent a jian shi, it was up to the ruler and his moral integrity to decide whether or not the advice was accepted. The irony was that the ruler was morally idealized with no mechanism for self-control except the moral standard itself. Whenever a ruler erred in his judgment, the results were disastrous and the price high. Moreover, because the jian shi would face danger or severe punishment if his words were considered offensive, disrespectful, or useless, he was inclined to employ an indirect mode of persuasion and compelled to use tactics, psychological appeals, and cunning intelligence rather than direct criticism or open confrontation.

Zhan Guo Ce

After the decline of the Zhou dynasty, ruled by China's aristocracy, China was divided into many vassal states. Subsequently, wars broke out among these states over land and political power, with seven of them finally emerging as autonomous states with kings of their own. The wars continued, however, as each state wanted to unite China under its own rule. *Zhan Guo*

Ce 戰國策 (Intrigues) was written against this political background. Surprisingly, however, it is not a book regarding the details of wars and battles, but rather is known for its skillful use of persuasion. As Lisa Raphals correctly describes, "the skills of the councillor as politician and rhetor are central to the strategies of the Warring States. The ostensible concern of the text may be strategy, but its real issue is rhetoric and persuasion: verbal warfare" (1992, 17).[6]

Accordingly, kings were more interested in winning a war by the skillful use of rhetorical strategies than by military invasion. Sunzi 孫子, the author of *Sunzi Bing Fa* 孫子兵法 (The Art of War), a well-known Chinese classic on war strategies, argued that the determining factor in winning a war was neither the physical strength nor military power, but the ability to persuade the enemy with moral and intellectual appeals.[7] The leaders of the seven states understood the logic of political dominance through "verbal warfare." Consequently, they were receptive to you shui who traveled from state to state attempting to persuade the rulers to adopt their ideas and strategic plans. Among these you shui, one group, represented by Su Qin, advocated *he zong* 合縱 (uniting vertically), while the other group, headed by Zhang Yi, advocated *lian heng* 連橫 (connecting horizontally).[8] The final purpose of he zong is to unite all the weaker states to fight the strongest state, while the purpose of lian heng is to defeat the weaker states by the strongest state. In this context, the term *zong heng* (vertical and horizontal) refers to two different military strategies. *Zongheng Jia* (the School of Zong Heng) was comprised of you shui who used their persuasive skills to change the minds and direct the actions of rulers in fulfilling their proposed plans. Although the exact number of you shui engaged in this manner at the time is unknown and no written records of their works remain, we know that you shui were educated men who traveled from state to state acting as advisers to the king of each state in political, military, and foreign affairs.

Zhan Guo Ce is thought to have been written by many unknown authors but compiled and edited by Liu Xiang 劉向 (79–8 B.C.E.). Eleven men and their lives from the text were documented by Si-Ma Qian in his *Shi Ji* 史記 (Records of the Historian), the first complete book of Chinese history that documented biographies of prominent men in the pre-Qin period. *Zhan Guo Ce* is no doubt a valuable rhetorical text in the Chinese history, as it recorded approximately five hundred persuasive speeches of you shui involving long and short deliberations.

While the central concern of both *Zuo Zhuan* and *Guo Yu* was the morality of the ruler and his benevolent practice of government, *Zhan Guo Ce* was a more complex book in its themes and impacts. The text, on one hand, celebrated Chinese values and heroism. Through its stories about ministers and kings, themes such as honor, benevolence, loyalty, and faithfulness were praised and appreciated. On the other hand, the text also provided a number of examples of utilitarianism, self-interest, and individualism demonstrated by you shui. The central theme of the speeches and dialogues contained in *Zuo Zhuan* and *Guo Yu* centered around rituals, government, and human relationships, while the central theme of *Zhan Guo Ce* involved a discussion of military strategies and foreign affairs. There was also an obvious difference between the role of jian shi as described in *Zuo Zhuan* and *Guo Yu* and that of you shui as described in *Zhan Guo Ce*. Whereas jian shi came from aristocratic backgrounds and were loyal to the rulers and patriotic to their states, you shui were traveling persuaders, who offered their advisory services to rulers in exchange for money and other material gains. Typically, they came from humble backgrounds and were not affiliated with or committed to any particular states or kings.

Most scholars would agree that *Zhan Guo Ce*, written in the form of prose and anecdotes, is a classic work as well as a masterpiece in its use of language. Unlike the language of *Zuo Zhuan* and *Guo Yu*, which is relatively formal, refined, and indirect, the language of *Zhan Guo Ce* is colorful, vivid, and direct. The rhetorical strategies employed in *Zuo Zhuan* and *Guo Yu* are also present in *Zhan Guo Ce*; however, some employed in *Zhan Guo Ce*, such as psychological and instrumental appeals, deductive and inductive reasoning, and use of metaphors, are more sophisticated and crafted than those in the other two texts. In the following pages I will explore each of these three prominent features, summarizing the general pattern and structure of persuasive speech found in *Zhan Guo Ce*.

(1) Psychological and Instrumental Appeals. As the context for a you shui's persuasive activity was the hierarchical king/adviser relationship, a you shui faced an unbalanced power relationship with his audience. The you shui's credibility and persuasive skills were thus crucial to successful persuasion. Unlike the Greek sophist Gorgias, who was known for his use of direct emotional appeals to arouse feelings and manipulate the public, Chinese you shui attempted to persuade kings by appealing to their desires, values, and motives indirectly in both public and private settings. They understood, as Han Feizi noted, that a successful persuasion "is to beautify what the ruler feels proud and cover what he feels shameful" (HF 12.4.174). A great deal of such embellishment was similar to face-saving strategies. Flattery and the practice of praising the ruler for his morality and wisdom were the typical forms of embellishing pride and obliterating shame. More

specifically, this was accomplished by not mentioning weakness and pretending not to be aware of the ruler's true motive.

For example, when Su Qin, a well-known you shui, talked to the king, he would start the conversation by praising the king for his wise, moral, and intelligent qualities, after which he would describe the state as rich in resources and strong in military power. In one instance, at the beginning of Su Qin's talk with the king of Zhao, he pleased the king by saying "People and ministers in the world all admire your majesty's kindness and justice.... The state of Zhao is the most powerful state" (ZGC "Zhaoce er" 1, 528–29). Such praise acted as a lubricant in the process of persuasion, as it affirmed the ruler's honor and pride and was therefore likely to put him in a receptive frame of mind, as well as increase the likelihood of the development of mutual trust.

According to another account, in his attempt to persuade the king of Qin to adopt his plan of lian heng, Zhang Yi, a famous you shui in the Zhan Guo period, first compared the Qin state with other states in economic, moral, and military capacity, concluding that Qin was the strongest and most powerful state. Zhang then pointed out two occasions when Qin could have defeated other states and become politically dominant but failed to do so, attributing this failure to the incompetence of the ministers. Zhang then advised the king on an opportunity for military conquest, offering historical examples to show how the small number of Qin troops could win over larger numbers. Zhang further explained that Qin had met all the conditions for winning, such as high soldier morale, adequate storage of food, and favorable geographic positioning (ZGC "Qince yi" 5, 70–78). In this speech Zhang manipulated the audience's feelings of desire, pride, regret, and fear. He praised the king and the state to enhance the king's pride; described opportunities missed and opportunities yet to come, playing upon the king's sense of regret and hope; and spelled out various military strategies in order to eliminate fear and build confidence in his audience. At times, his psychological appeals, designed to eliminate suspicion and build trust, were stated in terms of loyalty and admiration for the ruler ("Qince er" 1 & 2, 96, 101).

Motivated by the self-interested desire for profit, you shui employed utilitarian appeals in persuading their audiences. In speeches they made to the kings of the various states, for example, they would spell out the material gains, in terms of land, beautiful women, horses, food, and clothing. The ruler could expect benefits he would gain by adopting the proposed plan. Such appeal was effective not only with respect to the ruler but also with respect to warriors and other you shui. In helping King He of Zhou prevent Jing Cui from participating in the war against Zhou for the state of Qin, Zhao Lei advised the king to say the following to Jing: "Your rank of nobility and your official position have reached a top level; even if Qin wins the war, you will not get promoted any higher. If Qin doesn't win, you will get the death penalty. You should go to help Yi Yan battle for the state of Han. This way, Qin is afraid that you will attack them. They will send you treasures to bribe you. Han will also appreciate your help and send you all their treasures" (4). Jing did accordingly and received treasures from both states as predicted. In *Zuo Zhuan* and *Guo Yu* such behavior, motivated by a desire for material gain, would have been condemned. In *Zhan Guo Ce*, on the other hand, such behavior was encouraged, rewarded, and celebrated. In fact, cultural heroes and sage kings were often cited not for their moral practice of government but for their ability to exploit a situation for their own gains ("*Qince san*" 1, 126–27). In their persuasive discourse, you shui would maximize the benefits of adopting their strategies, thereby making them so tempting to the audience that they could not resist. Some such plans were devious, clever manipulations of the situation.

(2) Deductive and Inductive Reasoning. Many of the oral and written speeches contained in *Zhan Guo Ce* combined deductive and inductive processes. Deductive elements were typically presented in the form of proverbs, wise sayings, abstract notions, or citations from classics. These elements, couched in succinct and catchy phrases or summed up in brief abstract sayings, were often used at the beginning of the speech to introduce the argument, in the middle of the speech to reinforce the argument, or as a transition to a new topic. By this time, tian ming was no longer a universal principle with wide appeal. The cultural values of benevolence, ritual, propriety, loyalty, and filial piety were no longer essential means of persuasion as they had been in *Zuo Zhuan* and *Guo Yu*. The notions of utilitarianism and fair play were used more frequently as universal appeals.

Even on those rare occasions when the cultural values of morality and virtue were employed, their practical consequences and the notion of fair play were emphasized. For example, in a letter to King Zhao of Qin, Fan Ju wrote:

I heard that a wise ruler's principle of government is that those who have merits should be given reward. Those who are competent should be given an official position. Those who have more merits should have more fortunes, higher rank of nobility, and manage more people. Accordingly, those who have no competence would not dare to take any office and those who are competent will not be unnoticed. If you think my ideas are applicable, I hope you use them to help with your political measures. If you do not think my ideas are useful, there is no use to keep me. The proverb says that an average ruler rewards the person he likes best and punishes the person he hates most. A wise ruler awards those who have merits and punishes those who have committed crimes. ("*Qince san*" 8, 134)

In the above example Fan articulated the general principle of fairness as the main criterion for virtuous leadership. He then invited the king to agree with him by presenting him with contrasting options for how he might be perceived. To further the persuasive effect, Fan provided specific examples and vivid metaphors, concluding the speech with expressions of humility and admiration for the king's absolute authority. Upon reading the letter, the king was so impressed that he immediately hired Fan as the top adviser to the state of Qin.

In *Zhan Guo Ce*, as in *Shang Shu*, induction was used to explain and reinforce deduction. In some cases options were explored through a well-informed analysis of advantages and disadvantages for the state. Here you shui were at their best, demonstrating their knowledge of geography, history, and military strategy, as well as of the political, social, and economic conditions of other states and personal information about their rulers, even concerning their marital and kin relations. When presented in a logical, sequential manner, such concrete information could provide substantial evidence and compelling argument for the proposed course of action.

For example, to illustrate his point that a humble birth could be very useful for the king, Yao Jia advised the king of Qin:

High Duke Lu Wang was once kicked out by his wife when he was in the state of Qi. He was only a butcher when in Chao Ge. He was a minister deserted by Zi Lian. He was a servant in JiJin. But eventually King Wen of Zhou untied the world with his assistance. Guan Zhong used to be a small retailer, living in degradation in NanYan. He was a prisoner in the state of Lu. But king Heng of Qi gained the power over other dukes with his help. Bai Li Xi used to be a beggar in the state of Yu, but he made all other states come to worship him. Duke Wen of Jin used pirates of Zhongshang to conquer the state of Chu. These four people all had shameful pasts, but they were all employed by wise rulers, knowing that they could help with the kingdom. ("*Qince wu*" 8, 217)

These real examples would have been familiar to the king since they were either contemporary events or part of recent history. The speaker's job was to link them together in order to construct a more convincing argument.

(3) The Use of Metaphors. The use of metaphorical and analogical reasoning has been a recurring rhetorical technique in all five texts under consideration in this chapter. However, such usage varies from text to text.

In *Shi Jing,* for example, metaphor was a means of artistic expression used to *mei* (beatify, praise) or *ci* (attack, criticize) the rulers with a single word or short phrases. In *Shang Shu* metaphor was extended to analogy for the purpose of persuasion. In *Zuo Zhuan* and *Guo Yu,* while analogy remained a feature of extended metaphor, the source of metaphor was enriched through reference to the classics of *Shi Jing* and enacted through immediate situations. In *Zhan Guo Ce* the use of metaphor reached its climax and maturity with the figurative use of language in the form of allegories, fables, and proverbs. (It is recorded that about seventy fables were used in *Zhan Guo Ce.*) Metaphorical persuasion was exemplified in two forms in *Zhan Guo Ce:* through the presentation of a complete story in the form of a fable, parable, legend, or allegory; and through a witty or popular saying in the form of a proverb, epigram, or aphorism. Most of its stories and sayings were drawn from classical Chinese literature, history, philosophy, and conventional wisdom. This varied use of metaphor appealed to the audience's general knowledge of the universe as well as to specific cultural, religious, and physical landmarks of ancient China. Three types of metaphors were most prevalent in *Zhan Guo Ce:* animal metaphors, tree metaphors, and weapon metaphors. Each is linked to a variety of topics determined by the situation.

A. Animal Metaphors. Animal metaphors are the most commonly used; examples of personified creatures are tigers, dogs, snakes, monkeys, fish, horses, foxes, rabbits, dragonflies, swans, siskins, and other birds. In some cases the antics of these animals involve a complete story line from beginning to end. For instance, in trying to prevent the king of Qi from doing battle with the state of Wei, Chun Yu-kun recounted the fable of a race between the fastest running dog and the most shrewd rabbit. In this account the dog chased the rabbit around a mountain three times and across five additional hills. By the end, both the dog and rabbit died of exhaustion. Consequently, the hunter effortlessly captured both (*"Qice san"* 11, 291–92). The story persuaded the king to stay calm and let other states fight with one another. In this way, when other states were weakened from too much fighting, the king could declare war on them and victory would be easily achieved.

At other times animals are used metaphorically according to their instincts and specific qualities in connection with the human condition and limitations. For example, in advising the king of Qi on the assignment of his ministers, Lu Lian said the following: "When monkeys leave the forest and live in water, they are no match for fish and turtles; a horse is not as good as a fox in climbing rocks.... If Cao Mo [a warrior] laid down his sword and worked in the field, he would never be as good as a farmer" ("*Qice san*" 8, 286). Elsewhere Yin Hou, the prime minister of the state of Qin, described the situation faced by the state with a metaphor involving dogs. He said to the king: "Look at your dogs; they look fine right now, but if you throw a piece of bone to them, all the dogs will fight" ("*Qince san*" 13, 153–54). He then identified the dog nature with human nature by saying that both were utilitarian and selfish, and he advised the king to bribe other kings by appealing to their greedy human nature. In this way the king would make friends instead of enemies.

B. Tree Metaphors. Another frequently employed rhetorical device in *Zhan Guo Ce* is the tree metaphor. As with animal metaphors, the tree is typically personified and acts as a character in fables and parables. For example, Su Qin opened a speech to the king of Qin with the following story of a tree: "I saw two trees when I passed *Zhu* Mountain. One was wailing for her companion; the other one was crying. I asked them why they were crying. One tree answered: 'I have grown into a tall tree, but I am very old. What I feel sad about is that people measure me and carve on me.' Another tree said 'What I feel sad about is the saw people used to drill into me'" ("*Zhaoce yi*" 12, 513–14). Su Qin used this fable to appeal to the king's morality, persuading him not to act like the saw that would make people miserable. In some persuasive speeches in *Zhan Guo Ce*, the qualities of a tree were used to describe the situation faced by a state. Ying Hou advised the king of Qin, "When a tree is overborne with fruits, the branches will be broken; when branches are broken, the heart of the tree will be affected" ("*Qince san*" 10, 148–49). He used this epigram as a vehicle for expressing his belief that the ministers of the state had overpowered the king and would bring the state harm in the future.

C. Weapon Metaphors. The third type of metaphor concerns the use of weapons, primarily in the telling of legends. Swords and arrows were the main weapons used in the Warring States period and thus were the most familiar objects. In one account Su Li told the story of a man who was very accurate in shooting arrows but exhausted himself by taking practice shots at leaves before the real battle started. When the time came to shoot the enemy, he could not even pull his bow open ("*Xizhouce*" 6, 40–41). The metaphor was used to advise the king of Zhou not to waste energy on unnecessary activities. In another account Ci Ko-Bu told the king the story of an ancient king who was unaware of the value of the sword his wife had bought for him. When someone offered ten thousand grams of gold to buy the sword, the king's wife refused to sell it. Thus the appreciation value of the sword remained unknown. Prior to her death the king's wife regretted the decision not to sell the sword and told her son to sell it so that its value would be made known ("*Xizhouce*" 9, 44). Ci Ko-Bu used this legend to persuade the king that he must make his successor's virtue known to the public in order to gain their acceptance and appreciation of the new state leader.

Compared to the speeches in *Shang Shu, Zuo Zhuan,* and *Guo Yu,* speeches in *Zhan Guo Ce* are generally longer in deliberation and more fully developed. Most seem to have been written and carefully thought out before being presented. Although the speeches contained in *Zhan Guo Ce* vary in structure and order of rhetorical techniques, in general most fall into a pattern of development consisting of six parts. The first part is an introduction of the topic along with a statement of the general principles under consideration. These principles are not limited to the realm of morality but also include considerations of practical wisdom and common sense, typically expressed through balanced phrasing for artistic effect. The general principles that laid the groundwork for the argument to follow were then applied to the current situation or problem at hand. In cases when a line is drawn between good and evil, or wise and stupid individuals or actions, what follows can be flattering words or direct and indirect criticism of the audience. The third phase of the speech reinforces its general principles, further probing the topic by its use of proverbs, historical examples, fables, analogies, or citations from classical canons. In some cases fables, analogies, or stories are fully applied to the analysis of the situation or problem. The fourth phase is the major portion or body of the speech, delineating detailed information concerning the political, economic, and military situation facing the state and the ruler. The argument presented in this portion is sometimes developed in numerical order with specific information involving exact numbers of men, horses, or other military capabilities, functioning very much like the statistical analysis of today's social science research. Phase five could be considered part of phase four in that the speaker spells out the advantages and disadvantages to the ruler of adopting or not adopting the proposed scheme, plan, or strategy. Finally, the speaker typically expresses some degree of humility, pleading with the ruler to consider the proposed plan of action. The following is a portion of a sample speech given to King Zhao of Qin by Huang Xie, a *you shui,* persuading the king to give up his plan of attacking the state of Chu and turn his attention to more immediate danger. This portion illustrates the fourth and fifth phases of a typical persuasive speech in *Zhan Guo Ce:*

Now Your Majesty only regrets that you did not have the chance to wipe out the State of Chu, but Your Majesty should know the disappearance of the State of Chu will only benefit the State of Wei. I am very much worried about Your Majesty's decision. *The Book of Odes* says, "No matter how far you can go with one step, it is still undesirable to make long journeys." According to this line of reasoning, our distant neighbor Chu is our friend while our close neighboring states are our enemies. *The Book of Odes* says, "We should be aware of other people's ulterior motives. No matter how cunning a hare is, it cannot escape from a hound." Now Your Majesty takes the State of Han and Wei as friends. This is like the king of Wu taking Fuchai as his friend. As the saying goes, we should never underestimate our enemy or let a chance pass by. I am afraid that behind their humble language, the State of Han and Wei are hiding ulterior motives. Actually, they just want to take advantage of us. Why do I say so? Because we are their enemies and we have killed their fathers and brothers. For centuries, their states were invaded by us, their societies were destroyed by us, their temples were burnt down by us, their people were butchered by us. Corpses are lying everywhere, their people are becoming captives. There is famine everywhere in their states, even the ghosts have no where to find food, let alone the people. Many families are leaving their homes and become slaves in other states. Therefore I believe, the States of Han and Wei continue to be our number one hidden danger. It is not wise to invade the State of Chu right now. If we go to invade the State of Chu, we have to go through the territories of the State of Han and Wei. I can imagine, as long as Your Majesty goes through their territory, Your Majesty will never be able to come back. This would be like giving our troops to our enemies as presents. But if Your Majesty does not go through their territories, Your Majesty has no other way but to launch attacks on Suiyan and Yourang. But these two poor regions are full of rivers, floods, and forests. They don't grow any crops. Even if Your Majesty were to occupy these places, they do not mean anything to us. If we do things like that, Your Majesty will have to take the blame for wiping out the State of Chu, and in the meantime, have nothing concrete to gain. ("*Qince si*" 9, 187–88)

In this chapter I have identified various rhetorical strategies and techniques employed by jian shi and you shui in their persuasive practices as recorded and described in the five ancient Chinese texts examined. The evidence indicates a rhetorical tradition rich in artistic expression and political persuasion at various levels of communication. It also reveals a clear evolution in the field of Chinese rhetorical thought and practices. In general, rhetorical practices developed from mere expressions of feelings and thoughts in *Shi Jing* to a moral emphasis in *Shang Shu*, extended to moral and rational appeals in *Zuo Zhuan* and *Guo Yu*, and included the element of psychology in *Zhan Guo Ce*. The rhetorical focus also switched from speech itself in *Shi Jing* and *Shang Shu*, to the speaker in *Zuo Zhuan* and *Guo Yu*, and finally to the audience in *Zhan Guo Ce*. Simultaneously, the rich and diverse rhetorical experiences of the pre-Qin period stimulated ancient

Chinese philosophers and provided them with references in their conceptualization of language, persuasion, and argumentation. In the remaining chapters, 5 through 9, of this project, I will introduce philosophical writings, analyzing the texts with particular attention to individual thinkers, their guiding philosophical principles, their rhetorical perspectives, and their formulations of language, persuasion, and argumentation. We will begin with Mingjia, or the School of Ming.

CHAPTER 5

Conceptualization of Ming Bian: The School of Ming

In the last chapter I described persuasive activities and identified rhetorical characteristics of ancient China through an examination of five Chinese literary and historical texts. The rhetorical characteristics described in the previous chapter appear not to have resulted from a conscious formulation of rhetorical theory. However, as the ancient Chinese reflected upon their attempts at communication in political and interpersonal settings, they began to formulate theories explaining the power of symbols and speech. In effect, they moved from the rhetorical experience itself to a conceptualization of the experience. The question is how did the ancient Chinese perceive and conceptualize language and speech? Furthermore, how was such theories related to their philosophical views? Finally, how do Chinese bian shi and Greek sophists or philosophers compare in their views of rhetoric? These are the questions which will be addressed in this and subsequent chapters.

In this chapter through chapter 9 I will attempt to describe and synthesize theories of speech formulated by individual Chinese philosophers from five major schools of thought that emerged during the Spring-Autumn and Warring States period, namely Mingjia, or the School of Ming; Confucianism; Mohism; Daoism; and Legalism. Within the same school of thought, while thinkers share fundamentally the same philosophy, they may differ in their approach to the particular problems they addressed. For the sake of continuity and convenience, I will group thinkers belonging to the same school together while cautioning the reader to keep in mind that the thinkers within any given school may not necessarily share one another's philosophical and rhetorical views. In particular, this chapter will introduce theories of ming bian formulated by Mingjia 名家, or the School of Ming.

The Origin of *Ming* and Mingjia

As was mentioned in the previous chapter, Chinese bian shi included government officials (shi, da fu, and qing) whose duty was to assist the king, *ke qing* (guest) who were invited by the king, and *you shui* (traveling persuader) with no state affiliation, who advised the king on moral, governmental, and military issues. Some bian shi also engaged in intellectual activities and offered ideological insights to the king. The Jixia Academy of the state of Qi attracted many such bian shi. Of diverse origins and with differing philosophical views, these men gave lectures, mentored disciples, and wrote books. Most importantly, they freely debated political, metaphysical, and philosophical issues. Compared with the persuasive practices described in *Zuo Zhuan*, *Guo Yu*, and *Zhan Guo Ce*, the debates among intellectual bian shi were generally more theoretically oriented, thought provoking, and intellectually stimulating. It was in the course of these debates that various theories and schools of thought were challenged and exchanged. Among the different schools that emerged at this time, one group known as Mingjia, or the School of Ming, was interested in the function of language in political settings as well as in rational thinking.

Ming was first conceptualized by two important thinkers: Deng Xi (546–501 B.C.E.), believed to be the founder of Mingjia; and Confucius (552–479 B.C.E.), the father of Confucianism. Deng Xi first used the term *ming* in political and legalistic context in reference to words and concepts. He was concerned primarily with the correspondence between *ming* (words, names) as prescribed laws, and *shi* 實 (actuality) as the practice of laws. The name Deng Xi is often connected to *Xing Ming Jia* 形名家 (the School of Forms and Names), populated primarily by politicians from the School of Legalism. They advocated that a reward be given to those whose description (names) of a person matched his or her deeds (forms), while a punishment should be issued when description and deed did not match. For Legalists, the term *xing*, represented by the character 刑, also referred to a penalty, while the term *ming* referred to types of criminal behavior and the corresponding punishment. In the section entitled *Qince* in *Zhan Guo Ce*, members of Xing Ming Jia advise the king of Qin to observe the correspondence between naming and actuality when determining rewards or punishment. In this context, *ming* is used in conjunction with *xing* to refer to legalistic means of control.[1]

For Confucius, a contemporary of Deng Xi, ming functioned as a social code for establishing hierarchical, social, and human relations. For example, kings, fathers, and husbands must act with benevolent authority when relating to ministers, sons, and wives, respectively. In this context, Confucius taught that ming (names, titles, codes) must correspond to shi (actuality, one's position and actions). Subsequently, this notion of ming was further developed by Xunzi and challenged by Mozi, gradually evolving into a political and rationalistic concept. In this sense, Confucius addressed the issue of ming in social and cultural contexts, while Deng Xi conceptualized it in political and legal arenas.

The name Mingjia was first coined by Han scholars in reference to a group of pre-Qin thinkers known as *bian zhe*, or *cha shi* 察士 (wise men). Best known for their eloquence and high level of abstraction in presenting theories of language, each Mingjia had his own particular concerns and perceived the role and function of language in his own way. What all Mingjia had in common was a concern for the relationship between ming and shi in addressing the problems of cultural transition, including changes in values and power struggles taking place at the deep structure of society. In many ways Mingjia resembled the Greek sophists, innovative thinkers who were typically scorned and condemned by later philosophers. As is the case with Greek sophists, there is little information available regarding their lives and works, and their contributions to Chinese philosophy and language are not fully and fairly recognized.

Having a reputation similar to the Greek sophists', Mingjia were generally held in low regard by their contemporaries as well as by scholars of subsequent years. For example, Zhuangzi described them as follows: "clouding people's minds, changing their views, winning over others by eloquence" (Z 33.468). The rhetorical practices of Mingjia were typically regarded as flippant, fancy, and deceptive. In fact, it was not until the modern period that Chinese scholars began to regard Mingjia as logicians and dialecticians. Their highly rational and paradoxical arguments were then recognized as theories of ontology and epistemology derived from interactions with individuals from other schools of thought.

As discussed in chapter 2, *ming* was the first term used in the pre-Qin period that encompassed the meaning of logic, speech, and argumentation. The exact number of Mingjia is unknown. *Han Shu* mentioned the names of seven Mingjia. Three of them remain prominent and notorious in Chinese history: Deng Xi 鄧析; Hui Shi 惠施; and Gong-sun Long 公孫龍. Like the Greek sophists, these three Mingjia held no unified rhetorical perspective and unfortunately left little of their own writings. As a result, much of what is known of their character and thought was drawn from secondary sources. For the sake of convenience, the following table lists their names, life spans, primary texts, and major theories, each of which will then be discussed in some detail.

Prominent Ancient Chinese Mingjia

Name	Life Span (B.C.E.)	Primary Texts	Major Theory
Deng Xi	(546–501)	Deng Xizi	Probability
Hui Shi	(380–320)	Fragments in Zhuangzi	Relativism
Gong-sun Long	(328–295)	Gong-Sun Longzi	Classification

Deng Xi

Social Context and Personal Background

Deng Xi could be regarded as the Protagoras (490–400 B.C.E.) of China, though his life began fifty years earlier. Deng Xi is the first person who codified Chinese speech, defining the realm, function, and purpose of *ming* and *bian*. By Deng Xi's time (the Spring-Autumn period), much social upheaval had already occurred. An elitist form of government had been gradually replaced with a meritocracy. Traditional cultural values and rhetorical practices characterized by rigid conformity to li (rites) had been challenged, though the ruling class had actively resisted such changes. In the midst of this cultural clash, Deng Xi emerged as a liberal thinker advocating that human behavior be regulated by laws and arguing that truth resides in the power of persuasive speech rather than in prescribed codes of moral conduct.

Being an innovative thinker and antitraditionalist, Deng Xi made every attempt to challenge the validity of li as practiced in the Zhou dynasty and to create an environment conducive to the free exchange of opinions and ideas. Although he held the official position of *da fu* (high official) for the state of Zhen, Deng Xi was actively involved in *xing ming zhi bian* 形名之辯 (argument over forms and names) with other Zhen intellectuals, well known for their *li kou zhi ci* 利口之辭 (sharp-tongued speech). Xunzi described Deng Xi and his followers as men who "do not model previous kings and do not conform to ritual and moral principles, but are fond of bizarre doctrines and like to play with unusual propositions" (X 6.50). Indeed, Deng Xi advocated the rational use of speech to interpret reality and guide one's actions as opposed to prescribed moralistic rules and standards. He was also the first thinker in Chinese history to perceive the significance of language in the articulation and implementation of laws, recognizing the impact of political discourse in guiding and controlling people's behavior. Deng Xi carved his views on judicial issues on *zhu xing* 竹刑 (bamboo slips) and hung them on the walls, sometimes giving impromptu speeches to people passing by (Yu 1985, 43). Deng Xi's ideas and methods must have seemed novel and refreshing to some, while others no doubt considered him quite strange and threatening. The Chinese political discourse had been deliberated by kings and ministers in court settings in the domains of administration and state affairs. There had never been a practice and appreciation of individual expressions or voice against authority. Deng Xi certainly acted as an exception.

We have no clear information regarding the content of Deng Xi's speeches. However, it is possible that they centered around antitraditionalist views and the promotion of rational thinking by legal as opposed to moral means. According to an account by *Lu Shi Chun Qiu* 呂氏春秋 (approximately 239 B.C.E.), Deng Xi made every effort to counter the suppression of ideas and opinions imposed by the rulers of Zhen: "When Zi Chan, the minister of Zhen, ordered people to stop expressing their opinions by publicly posting them, Deng Xi would deliver the posters in person. When Zi Chan ordered a stop to the delivery of the posters, Deng would try other means to send them out. Zi Chan had endless orders; Deng Xi had endless ways of combating the orders" (*LSCQ* 18.302).[2] It is perhaps because of this daring defiance of authority that Deng Xi became known as a bian zhe rather than a Legalist.

Deng Xi's views on language and argumentation resemble the relativist views of the Greek sophists, particularly Protagoras. Deng Xi was well known for his ability to argue "from right to wrong and from wrong to right" as well as for having "no fixed standard of what is right and what is wrong" (*LSCQ* 18.302). As the practice of law in ancient China required the accuser and the accused to present their own cases and the judgment was based on the persuasiveness of their presentations, Deng Xi's competence in jurisprudence and skill at making "a weaker case stronger" attracted a lot of people hoping to learn the art of winning a lawsuit. He could easily twist an argument around, and "what he wished to win was always won; and whom he desired to punish was always punished." Just as Protagoras was the first of the Greek rhetoricians to charge pupils a fee for the privilege of studying rhetoric with him, Deng Xi's "consulting business" became so successful that he began to charge a coat for a big legal case and a pair of pants for a small one. As more and more people began coming to him for advice, he received enough clothes to make him a rich man (18.302).

Deng's liberal doctrines and rhetorical practice had threatened the rulers of his time. Worried that Deng Xi's doctrines and rhetorical skills would cause internal conflicts and instability in the state, Zi Chan, the minister of Zhen, charged Deng Xi with "deceiving and agitating the masses." Subsequently, he was put to death and his dead body chopped into pieces (18.303), a much worse punishment than a persecution possibly received by Protagoras.[3]

A Theory of Bian

Despite a short life and violent premature death, Deng Xi was considered the founder of Mingjia in *Han Shu* 漢書 (the Book of Han), authored by Ban Gu 班固 (32–92 C.E.). From the time of Deng Xi forward, though some were produced, most works of ming were subsequently lost to history. Only two short essays by Deng Xi and six chapters by Gong-sun Long remain. The essays by Deng Xi attempted to conceptualize *ming bian*, proposed the notion of dual possibilities, and discussed *ming shi* relations in the context of political control and the practice of law.

In Deng Xi's theoretical work, he made a distinction between *da bian* 大辯 (big arguments) and *xiao bian* 小辯 (small arguments), two types of bian differing in content and purpose. Big arguments, according to Deng, included arguments on social and environmental issues for the well-being of the community, while small arguments referred to disputes and arguments over superficial issues for personal gain. In the latter case, people verbally attacked each other and failed to address the real issues. Deng Xi clearly favored big arguments without specifying how such arguments could be made from a rhetorical standpoint. Given his general disdain for traditional values, it is more likely that Deng Xi would suggest a rational approach with a utilitarian and practical emphasis as opposed to an appeal to ethics and morality.

For Deng, the task of bian, similar to the Greek concept of kairos, was to make use of a situation and to know what was in the mind of the listener. Deng reasoned that some you shui were not respected and their words not heeded because they had failed to adapt to a situation and to understand the audience. He emphasized the art of tailoring one's speech to one's audience, saying: "When speaking to a wise person, talk about science. When speaking to an expert, use logic and make the idea clear. When speaking to a *bian zhe*, talk with substance. When speaking to an aristocratic, talk about power. When speaking to a rich person, talk about wealth. When speaking to a poor person, talk about benefits. When speaking to a courageous person, talk about bravery. When speaking to a stupid person, use persuasion" (*DXZ" zhuan ci pian"* 6).[4] According to Deng, in order to adapt to one's audience, one must cultivate *san shu* 三術 (three strategies, or three arts) of speaking: (1) carefully observing the situation; (2) understanding different perspectives; and (3) learning all the wisdom in the world ("*zhuan ci pian*" 7). In his view, a good bian zhe should be able to "make distinctions without causing harm and examine both sides of the issue without causing disorder" ("*wu hou pian*" 5). Although we do not have evidence on how Deng Xi elaborated upon these strategies, clearly he attempted to conceptualize *bian* as the art of speaking wisely, effectively, and appropriately.

Dual Possibilities and Dual Interpretations

Deng Xi has been characterized as "the most famous lawyer of ancient times" (Fung 1952, 195). While the word "lawyer" may be misleading to Western readers, Deng Xi indeed occupied himself with lawsuits as well as with teaching people how to win legal cases,[5] employing rhetorical devices referred to as *liang ke* 兩可 (dual possibilities) and *liang shuo* 兩說 (dual interpretations). Much like Protagoras, Deng held that one should carefully examine both sides of an issue before proceeding to an argument, believing that seemingly opposing views can also be related and affect one another. This theory was illustrated by an anecdote in *Lu Shi Chun Qiu:* "Some rich person from the state of Zhen drowned himself. Someone got his corpse. The rich man's family pleaded to ransom the corpse back. The person who got it asked for a lot of money. The rich man's family told Deng Xi about this. Deng Xi said, 'Don't worry. That person has nowhere to sell the corpse except to you.' The person who had the corpse also asked Deng Xi for advice. Deng Xi said, 'Don't worry. Nobody would buy this corpse except this family" (*LSCQ* 18.302). In this case, though the rich man's family and the person who found the corpse had different motives and goals, they are closely related to one another. Since no one but the rich man's family would want his corpse, if they are not willing to pay a high ransom, the seller will have to lower his asking price. On the other hand, if the seller does not want to sell the corpse at a low price, the buyer will have to offer a better deal in order to get it. This example is reminiscent of the use of the probability argument in making a case in ancient Greece.

Indeed, for Deng Xi, bian was a tool for making a case in defense of oneself through a thorough understanding and examination of the motives and interests of one's opponents. Like Protagoras, Deng Xi believed that "humans are the measure of all things." For him, the human faculty of reasoning, rather than divine intervention or moral appeals, established the truth of the matter. Furthermore, truth could be found on either side of an issue if the argument was logically convincing and well presented. This perspective on bian is parallel and similar to the technical and sophistic traditions of classical Greek rhetoric. However, Protagoras's strategy of "arguing from both sides" differs from Deng Xi's "dual possibilities" in that while the former strategy points out differences in human perception, the latter directs one's attention to utilitarian motives and outcomes. Both, however, suggest a practical epistemology and functional way of knowing.

Relationship between Ming and Shi

For Deng Xi, in addition to the identification and understanding of various motives and perspectives in making a strong case, another important factor concerned the correspondence between *ming* (naming), broadly conceived as language, theory, symbols, laws, orders, and concepts, and *shi* (actuality). Consequently, he examined the role of naming in causing disagreements and confusion in the practice of government and implementation of laws. According to Deng Xi, a wise king should "follow names and observe actuality; examine laws and establish authority" (*DXZ* "*wu hou pian*" 4). In other words, one must understand the use of names and their correspondence to actuality; legal and political language must be tested in the practice of law and politics. In this context, "positions cannot be surpassed; official titles cannot be misused. Officials have their own responsibilities and perform them according to their names and titles. The superior follows the names and inspects if they correspond to actuality; the subordinate carries the orders and puts them into practice" (5). In this respect, Deng Xi's view on ming mingles with Confucius's notion of ming in terms of establishing and retaining social hierarchy. In other respects Deng Xi's political theory closely resembles the Legalistic view of government.

Deng Xi's theory of naming intersects with Confucius's concept of naming to the extent that both stressed the function of names in shaping and transforming actuality. However, the theories of these men differ in their definitions of *ming*. *Ming* for Deng Xi consisted of laws, political discourse of decree and pronouncement, and political means of control. *Ming* for Confucius was made up of a set of cultural norms and rules prescribed by the social elites and observed by members of society. Accordingly, their formulations of *ming* were addressed to different contexts and prescribed different mechanisms of performance. Specifically, Deng Xi addressed the political context and placed responsibility on the ruler to supervise the correspondence between names and reality, whereas Confucius responded to the cultural context and relied upon shared cultural norms to sustain the correspondence between names and actuality.

Since only two short essays by Deng Xi have survived intact, our understanding of his views on *ming* and *bian* is necessarily limited. However, it is known that the notions discussed above laid the foundation for subsequent Mingjia and Mohists in their attempts to further develop and conceptualize Chinese ming bian. Reding (1985) indicates that Deng Xi is the principle source of Hui Shi's relativistic view (490).

In Deng Xi's view, *ming* was an abstract notion, including concepts and theories generated by language that only made sense when related to actuality, the objective world. Though well aware of the significance of language in constructing reality and communicating thoughts and ideas, Deng apparently adopted different theories for different purposes depending on his own rhetorical need. For example, when his goal was to challenge the status quo and provoke change, he deliberately separated names from actuality, calling for a redefinition of names, which thus, in the ruler's eyes, generated confusion and instability among the masses. Conversely, when he spoke from the perspective of the ruling class, he insisted on a close correspondence between names and actuality in order to avoid confusion and chaos. In general, as Deng Xi would agree, an understanding of the relationship between names and actuality is an understanding of ontology and epistemology, as well as of dialectics in relation to argumentation, debates, and linguistic impact. However, the speakers' political motives and interests ultimately determine how the relationship between name and actuality is manipulated in order to achieve the desired goal.

In his formulation of Chinese *ming bian*, Deng Xi seemed to make a distinction of the two notions. For Deng Xi, *bian* was a form of communication addressing political, ethical, and cultural issues. *Ming*, on the other hand, involved the specific use of language in political contexts to affect or change others' thoughts and behavior. *Bian* involved classification as well as the ability to adapt to changes and argue dialectically from both sides. *Ming* came into play only when the relationship between names and reality was made. In sum, both concepts called upon skill of manipulation in the interest of achieving one's political aims.

Hui Shi

Social Context and Personal Background

Approximately 150 years after Deng Xi's untimely death, a Mingjia named Hui Shi became well known for his bian activity as well as for his philosophical views. As A. C. Graham notes, "everything recorded of him [Hui

Shi] suggests that he was unique among the early thinkers for his breadth of talents and interests, a true Renaissance man" (1989, 76). His reputation as an eloquent speaker can be compared to that of the Greek sophist Gorgias (approximately 480–375 B.C.E.), with whom he also shared relativistic philosophical views.

Hui Shi faced somewhat different social problems than Deng Xi, living as he did during the Warring States period. You shui were in high demand as rulers sought the best advice regarding self-defense or attacks on other states. In general, weak states were defeated while strong states grew more aggressive in their attempts to conquer other states. Political persuasion at the interpersonal level between the ruler and you shui took various forms, with Confucianists advocating benevolent government, Mohists pleading for universal love, and Legalists placing emphasis on control and practical gains.

Being a learned scholar and eloquent speaker, Hui Shi was actively involved in the you shui activity. Limited evidence we have suggests that his rhetorical style was charming and engaging. In his lifetime he was a minister under King Hui of Wei, and he traveled to several other states where he was involved in persuasive activities. During this time he met Zhuangzi, and the two became close intellectual friends. Hui Shi was a political opponent of Zhang Yi 張儀, who was among the most famous you shui in the Warring States period. Though there are no surviving records of his speeches, in *Zhuangzi* Hui Shi is described as "a knowledgeable man who has many devices and has written books that can fill five carriages" (Z 33.466). Though clearly an exaggeration, this statement indicates the onetime existence of texts authored by him. His rhetorical activities, philosophical views, and contributions to the general theory of ming bian can be traced from classical texts such as *Zhuangzi, Xunzi, Han Feizi, Zhan Guo Ce, Lu Shi Shun Qiu,* and *Shuo Yuan* 說苑 (The Garden of Talks).

Although in most of these texts Hui Shi was portrayed negatively, their authors all acknowledged his skills as a learned and eloquent speaker. In Zhuangzi's words, "Hui Shih regarded himself the most eloquent speaker in the world." In response to a challenge to explain the universe, "he [Hui Shi] provided an answer without showing modesty and without stopping to think. He explained the sources of everything in the universe. With many rhetorical devices, he never stopped talking" (Z 33.468). Even Xunzi, who bitterly criticized Hui Shi for being unethical and worthless in his practice and theory of bian, was forced to admit that Hui Shi was an excellent bian zhe capable of casting a spell over the audience (X 6.50). After Hui Shi's death, Zhuangzi lamented the fact that he had lost an opponent in argument, a partner in conversation, and a good friend (Z 24.330).

Philosophical Views

In addition to his experiences as a you shui and bian zhe, Hui Shi was also a philosopher. His philosophical views were introduced in the form of ten propositions in a fragment in chapter 33 of *Zhuangzi*, indicating the influence of Deng Xi, Mozi, and Zhuangzi. It is difficult to give an accurate interpretation of these ten propositions without an explanation by Hui Shi himself. Although they cannot be understood as a direct formulation of Chinese ming bian, there is much implied that can lead us to a more profound understanding of ming bian. For example, among these ten propositions, six of which are presented metaphorically, some explore the notions of relativism and constant change, while others show a tendency to embrace the notions of unity and interrelatedness.

(1) Oneness. For Hui Shi, the universe was made up of two components: *da yi* 大一 (large unity, or oneness), which is generative, all-encompassing, and universal, like the ultimate Dao; and *xiao yi* 小一 (small unity), the individual units generated by and closely connected to da yi. *Yi* 一 (oneness) is an ancient Chinese philosophical concept referring to the final source of the universe in the work of Laozi and to general principles in human conduct in the writings of Confucius. Hui Shi was the first to formulate the notion of yi into categories of largeness and smallness, proposing two cosmological worlds, somewhat like the modern dichotomy between macrocosmic and microcosmic worlds.

According to Hui Shi, this dichotomous perception of the world is neutralized by the unity residing in things. Furthermore, degrees of similarity and differences vary. Similarities and differences between things of big unity and things of small unity are referred to as *xiao tong yi* 小同异 (small similarities and differences). Entities of big unity and those of small unity belong to the same category but with different degrees of differences. For example, horse and sheep both belong to the species of animal and thus share a bigger unity than white horse and black horse since the unity of the two lies in the fact that they both belong to the category of horse. Thus, a juxtaposition between horses (small unity) and animals (big unity) is an example of "small similarities and differences." For Aristotle, a comparison of the two elements would be the relationship between species and kind. Hui Shi was interested in how things were interrelated, while Aristotle was concerned with how things were logically separated.

For Hui Shi, everything is connected and shares similarities from the universal perspective. At the same time, each thing has its own idiosyncrasy and from the individualistic perspective is different. According to Hui Shi, the phenomenon of all things in the universe being similar and different at the same time is *da tong yi* 大同异 (large similarities and differences). An example of this would be that human beings share certain similar physical features and values, but each human being is a unique individual in his or her own ways. By this conceptual scheme, Hui Shi suggests a mode of inquiry that both classifies and connects the things in the universe at the same time. In the end, he exulted that, loving all the things in the universe as all things in the world are ultimately and intimately connected, the spirit of love infuses relative differences with its unifying essence (Z 33.466).

The mode of inquiry that embraces both the rational approach of classification and the analogical approach of making connections has significant implications for the argumentation process in which categories are sorted out, differences and similarities compared, and connections made. This process requires mutual efforts in communication and a dialectical search for interrelatedness even among opposing elements. Finally, and most importantly, it requires the moral and emotional devotion of love.

(2) Relativism. Perhaps influenced by Deng Xi's notion of "dual possibilities" passed down through Zhuangzi, Hui Shi exhibited an obvious inclination toward relativism as revealed in the fragments cited in *Zhuangzi*. For example, therein Hui Shi claimed, "Heaven is as low as earth; mountains and marshes have the same height"; "the south has no limit and yet has a limit"; "One goes to Yue today and arrived there yesterday"; and "I know the center of the world: it is in the north of Yen and south of Yue" (Z 33.466). These propositions convey the central idea of the mutual interpenetration of the ultimate and the relative. That is, the world is relative and in constant change. Nothing is static or absolute. People have different senses of the world's center, different notions of their physical boundaries, different readings of time, and different perceptions of high and low, all because we come from different vantage points and therefore see things differently. Distinctions are human-made. There is no completely objective reality outside of our individual perceptions of reality. Likewise, there are no true opposites, since everything is related and affected by everything else. Similar to Deng Xi's notion of "dual possibilities," Hui Shi's relativism dwells in probabilities rather than in certainties. The South has no limit and yet has a limit, and the center of the world can be anywhere depending upon one's point of view. Similarities and differences are created by human beings in our particularity and expressed through language. In other

words, humans are the measure of things. In reality, there is no absolute right or wrong. When the notion of relativism is applied to argumentation, there are no real winners or losers; both sides contain some truth and some falsehood. Whatever truth there may be in any given argument, it is only relative and can always be counterargued. Thus, it is important to examine and understand an argument from an opponent's perspective.

(3) Dialectical Change. The third implication drawn from Hui Shi's propositions is the notion of change. Similar to the Greek philosopher Heraclitus's worldview, Hui Shi held that all things are in the process of change. Change for Hui Shi, however, occurs not only in the intended direction, but also in its opposite direction. In his own words, "When the sun is at noon, it is already setting; When there is life, there is already death (Z 33.466). In other words, as things reach their apex in one direction, they begin to move in the opposite direction, producing the opposite effect. For example, when in our happiest state, a tragedy may be on its way. When trying hard to please everyone, we may end up only infuriating them. For this reason, Hui Shi claimed, "linked rings can be separated," suggesting that nothing is absolutely in a state of equilibrium. Whatever is temporarily balanced can become unbalanced and disturbed. The opposite can always happen. Thus, one should avoid going to extremes and be mindful of the side effects of things being overstated or overdone, while at the same time preparing for change.[6] For Hui Shi, things are in the process of becoming and transforming. The world is unknown, uncertain, and unending. Therefore a skillful argument is made in the realm of the probable as well as in the process of becoming.

Rhetorical Approach

One area highlighted in discussing Hui Shi's rhetorical skill was his use of metaphor and analogy. He not only used metaphor and analogy in making a philosophical argument, as demonstrated in the above propositions, but he also used metaphor and analogy in his own practice of bian and shui. He was so skilled at using analogies, in fact, that when asked if he could stop using analogy, he replied with another analogy, as illustrated in *Shuo Yuan*:

The king of Wei summoned Hui Shi and said to him, "Please be direct when you discuss something and do not use analogies." Hui Shi replied, "If someone does not know what a catapult looks like, he asks 'What is the shape of catapult?' If you reply, 'A catapult looks like a catapult,' can he understand you?" The king said, "no." Hui Shi then said, "If we change to another method telling the person that the shape of a catapult is like a bow and bowstring made of bamboo, do you think the person will understand?" The king said, "yes." (*SY* 11.8.471)

Clearly, Hui Shi shared Aristotle's theory of metaphor, considering reasoning an impossibility if one failed to make an association between the familiar and unfamiliar.[7]

Hui Shi referred to the use of metaphor and analogy in persuasion as *pi* 譬, defined as "using what people know to convey and explain what people do not know." Furthermore, he asserted, "People learn new knowledge from the connection between the known and the unknown" (*SY* 11.8.471). Although metaphorical and analogical reasoning had been a prominent feature of Chinese persuasion prior to Hui Shi's time, he was the first to conceptualize it. His definition of *pi* is close to the definition of *metaphor* given by Aristotle: "giving the thing a name that belongs to something else. . . ." However, Aristotle was more interested in choice of metaphors that belonged to the same category, as he continued, "the transference being either from genus to species, or from species to genus, or from species to species . . ." (*Poetics* 1457b7),[8] while Hui Shi, based on his assumption that all things in the universe share a unity of similarities and differences, made his choice of metaphor in terms of association and connection in both linear and lateral manners. There is no doubt that metaphor is a universal practice of language and analogical reasoning, a gift possessed by humans across cultures. However, the choice and implied meanings of metaphor and analogy may differ from culture to culture. The understanding of philosophical metaphors such as Hui Shi's propositions also requires a good understanding of the text and context in which the metaphor is used or implied.[9]

Ironically, it is perhaps because of Hui Shi's negative reputation and numerous political enemies that few effective speeches were attributed to him. In fact, he was often portrayed as ineffective and unwelcome by his audience. According to one such account, King Hui of Wei once pretended that he would cede the throne to Hui Shi. Wanting to prove himself a virtuous man comparable to certain sage kings, Hui Shi feigned disinterest. The king was so offended that he forced Hui Shi to leave office. Meanwhile, Hui Shi was slandered by his colleagues as a parasite who had not done much good for the state of Wei in his role as the minister and was accused of being arrogant and aggressive in his attempts at persuasion (*LSCQ* 18.309–10). A story in *Han Feizi* documents Hui Shi's failure to persuade the king of Wei to stop fighting with the states of Qi and Chu (*HF* 30.485). In addition, *Zhan Guo Ce* records an instance in which Zhang Yi drove Hui

Shi out of the state of Wei, after which he traveled to the state of Chu but was rejected by the king of that state (ZGC "*Chuce san*" 6, 440). These stories may be nothing more than deliberate attempts by Hui Shi's political enemies to defame him. However, if true, they indicate that Hui Shi was active and well traveled, engaging in persuasive activities far and wide.

Because of the unfortunate lack of written materials authored by Hui Shi, it is impossible to tell if his formulation of ming bian had much in common with Deng Xi's, or even if his views on Chinese persuasion and argumentation were innovative. In *Zhuangzi* fragments of dialogue, speech, and writings are attributed to Hui Shi, and it is from these fragments that a system of epistemological and dialectical thinking can be discerned. One such dialogue between Zhuangzi and Hui Shi illustrates Hui's tendency toward characterization and definition. Hui Shi said to Zhuangzi, "Can a human have no feelings?" Zhuangzi: "Yes." Hui Shi: "If a person has no feelings, can you still call the person a human?" Zhuangzi: "Heaven granted a person a face; nature gave him a human body why can't you call him a human?" Hui Shi: "If you called him a human, how can he have no feelings?" Zhuangzi: "The feelings you are talking about is not what I mean by feelings. When I talk about having no feelings, I mean that one should not make judgment of right and wrong based on one's likes and hatred, which will do no good to one's physical health. One should follow things spontaneously and do not act artificially in one's life." Hui Shi: "If the person does not act artificially, how can he keep his human body?" Zhuangzi: "The Way of Heaven gave the person a face; nature gave him a human body. One should not harm one's health by feelings of likes or hatred. Now you exhaust your spirit and energy, moan against the tree, thinking hard. Heaven bestowed you a human body while you still adhere to and advocate the doctrines of hardness, whiteness, stones, and 'White horse is not a horse'" (Z 5.74–75).[10]

This dialogue reveals much about Hui Shi. First, he considered human feelings the substantive element that makes up a human. A human is not just a physical body, but an emotional and spiritual being capable of making judgments and manipulating situations. Second, without reaching an agreement on what constitutes a human being, Hui Shi successfully led Zhuangzi to clarify what was meant by "feelings" and to provide examples for further explanation. The dialogue was pursued in a rational manner similar to Socratic dialogue: issues of definition, classification, and exemplification are seen as means to ends in the eager pursuit of new knowledge. This rational approach should be attributed to Hui Shi rather than to Zhuangzi, as the rest of the writing in *Zhuangzi* is characterized by fantasy and a metaphorical orientation. Third, Zhuangzi's criticism of Hui Shi at the end of the dialogue is indicative of the disagreement between the two men over worldviews and rhetorical approaches. We are left with the impression that Hui Shi was confrontational, emotional, articulate, and contemplative in advocating a rational way of thinking and was seriously and actively involved in arguing for a clear demarcation of positions. Zhuangzi proposed a nonjudgmental state of mind, free of attachment to feelings; he advocated not a state of rationality, but one of mythical receptivity.

Like Gorgias in ancient Greece, Hui Shi's image from the standpoint of history is rather negative. In any case, from the limited information we have about him, it is clear that Hui Shi deserves a place as one of the major thinkers in ancient China for having made a significant contribution to the Chinese formulation of ontology and epistemology as well as implications on speech and persuasion.

Gong-sun Long

Social Context and Personal Background

Gong-sun Long is the third prominent Mingjia of the Warring States period. About fifty years younger than Hui Shi. He lived toward the end of this period at a time when the people had long suffered from ills of wars and were demanding peace. A great advocate of peace, Gong-sun traveled to many states attempting to persuade their kings to end the wars. During this transitional time many schools of thought and individual thinkers emerged. They proposed their theories ranging from politics to human nature, from ontology to epistemology. In addition to the Jixia Academy, where scholars openly debated their positions, written works of philosophy and other subjects were produced and disseminated. During this watershed period in Chinese thought, Gong-sun, who was not a member of the Jixia Academy, nonetheless must have been influenced by their scholarship on the issue of ming bian. He continued to argue for propositions such as "a white horse is not a horse" and the "separation between hardness and whiteness," first proposed by the Jixia scholars. In his lifetime he served as a minister and consultant to his brother King Hui of the state of Zhao. He was an active you shui on political issues and an eloquent debater of his own doctrines. Gong-sun spent most of his lifetime in the state of Zhao giving lectures and mentoring his disciples.

In *Zhuangzi*, Zhuangzi introduces Gong-sun through Gong-sun's own autobiographical account: "When I was young I studied the Way of the previous kings. When I grew up, I began to understand the conduct of benevolence and righteousness. I could reconcile difference and sameness of things, distinguish hardness and whiteness of objects, and argue from wrong to right, from the impossible to the possible. I could combat one hundred schools of thought and beat all the speakers by my eloquence" (Z 17.217). This self-description indicates that Gong-sun had studied the philosophies of Confucius, Laozi, and the Mohists; he had also been influenced by Deng Xi and Hui Shi's sophistic approach to argumentation.

Historical evidence suggests that Gong-sun was a more successful *you shui* than Hui Shi. *Lu Shi Chun Qiu* documents a series of meetings between Gong-sun, the king of Yan, and the king of Zhao, in which he successfully persuaded them to cease warring against other states (*LSCQ* 18.292, 313). Gong-sun was also an honored guest of Duke Pinyuan of Zhao, who, according to *Records of the Historian*, often consulted him for advice. In one account, Gong-sun persuaded the duke not to accept a fiefdom granted to him by the king of Zhao by appealing to his morality and identifying the harmful consequences of such an act (Si-Ma "*Fan Sui Cai Zhe liezhuan*" 358).

According to another story, the states of Zhao and Qin once signed a treaty agreeing to helping one another whenever the need arose. Soon after, when Qin launched a war against the state of Wei, Zhao decided to enter the war as an ally to Wei against Qin. The king of Qin was angry, accusing the king of Zhao of not honoring the terms of their treaty. Duke Pinyuan of Zhao enlisted the aid of Gong-sun, asking for advice on how to respond to Qin. Gong-sun replied, "You could send an envoy to the state of Qin accusing them of not honoring the treaty. You could argue that the state of Zhao wants to ally itself to the state of Wei. According to the terms of our treaty, the state of Qin must come to the aid of the state of Zhao in protecting Wei" (*LSCQ* 18.305). Here Gong-sun uses Deng Xi's "dual possibilities" approach to argument and Hui Shi's notion of relativism to turn the argument around, presenting the situation in favor of Zhao.

Perhaps it was through Gong-sun's advocacy of peace as well as his observation of intellectual debates of his time that he sensed the need for clear and consistent communication and began to focus his attention on formulating a philosophy of language. The Jixia scholars and Later Mohists, Gong-sun's contemporaries who were attracted to abstract argumentation and interested in the question of language, were possible influences in this regard. Most likely, Gong-sun's rhetorical theories emerged as a reflection of his own experiences with speech as well as in response to other scholars.

Gong-sun was a well-known *bian shi* in his own time. Indeed, the first chapter of the text *Gong-sun Longzi*, introducing his background and theory of ming, states: "Gong-sun Long was an eloquent *bian zhe* in the Warring States period. He was dissatisfied with debates on the relationships between names and actualities, he used his intelligence and talent to expound his theory that a white horse was not a horse and whiteness and solidity were two separate elements. . . . He wished to disseminate his arguments and to teach people his theories in order to reduce the confusion between names and actualities" (*GSL* "*jifu*" 1).[11] It is believed that Gong-sun wrote fourteen essays during in his lifetime; however, only six remain, and evidence suggests that much of the content of these remaining texts was edited by his disciples.

The surviving text attributed to him and described by A. C. Graham as "the most puzzling composition in the philosophical literature of China" (1955, 282), is highly abstract and logically oriented with particular emphasis on the relationship between ming and bian, or language and logical thinking. They contain three basic components: an exploration of the impact of naming; an examination of the correspondence between names and actuality; and a discussion of various modes of classification. Each of these components is discussed in Chinese terms of *zhi wu* 指物 (pointing to objects), or the use of reference or concepts; *ming shi* 名實 (naming and actuality); and *fen lei* 分類 (classification, division). I will examine each of these elements and their implications for Chinese ming bian in the following text.

The Impact of Naming

Like the ancient Greek and Indian philosophers, the ancient Chinese were interested in the role and function of language. However, they were not so much concerned with the origin of language, their interest being more akin to the epistemological questions raised by Greek sophists: "What is the role of language in shaping our understanding of reality?" "Is language sufficient or inadequate in representing reality or the objective world?"[12] Gong-sun Long, in particular, shared with Greek sophists the same concern and similar views on language.

The Chinese term *zhi* means "figure" when used as a noun, or "to point" when used as a verb. Gong-sun used this word to mean to "signify," to "refer to," or to "designate" certain *wu* (materials, objects, persons, or events) through the use of terms, concepts, and ideas constructed by language. For him, we know the world through words and concepts. Furthermore, our language serves to signify, highlight, and illuminate separate and discrete objects and events. In Gong-sun's words, "If the world (physical entities) has no concepts to refer to and signify, we cannot call or name anything" (*GSL* "*zhiwu lun*" 52). If we cannot name things, we cannot have an understanding of things. This notion assumes that the physical world is an unorganized and indeterminate field. We know the world through our subjective perceptions constructed by language. The function of *zhi*, as Chung-ying Cheng and Richard H. Swain (1970) point out, is to single out and make us pay attention to certain aspects of things and perceptions in this indeterminate field. Clearly, Gong-sun was fully aware of the role of language in naming and constructing our world and worldviews.

Since, according to Gong-sun, the objective world is made known through names and concepts, one is likely to commit the fallacy that the objective world equals the conceptual world. Gong-sun reminds his readers that concepts are not, in fact, the objective world. The real world is made up of objective reality that can never be fully apprehended. Thus, the conceptual world and the objective world cannot be taken as the same. In his words, "*Zhi* (concepts) have never existed in natural form, but *wu* (materials, objects) existed in their natural form. One cannot equate what has never existed with what has already existed. Objects are not the equivalent of concepts" (GSL "*zhiwu lun*" 54). Further, Gong-sun argued that names are neither equal to nor the same as one another when used in reference to the same objects. The Greek sophist Antiphon seemed to share a similar view with Gong-sun, as he was quoted as saying "When a man says a single thing there is no corresponding single meaning" that can be known or represented by *logos* (Guthrie 1969, 202). A sophistic view of language is clearly made in Plato's *Cratylus:* that *logos* signifies things, but a thing cannot be signified by one word only. While both Gong-sun and Greek sophists held a skeptical view of language, Greek sophists were more concerned with "correctness of names," debating between "whether the names of things had an inherent, or natural fitness or were merely conventional signs and symbols" (205). Gong-sun, on the other hand, was more interested in "rectification of names," making sure that the use of names does not misrepresent reality and mislead the human perceptions of reality.[13]

Correspondence between Names and Actuality

The correspondence between words and things, in the Chinese context of ming and shi, was also the concern of the Greek philosophers. While both the ancient Greek and Chinese rhetoricians were aware of the impact and power of logos or ming, respectively, they took different approaches in formulating the relationship between words and reality or in the regulation of the use of language. The Greeks recognized the impact of social conventions and other variables in the use of logos, acknowledging that many versions of reality could be created through the use of logos.[14] The Chinese, on the other hand, insisted on one definite version in the correspondence between ming and shi so as to avoid the number of interpretations of actuality. Another difference between the two groups on the relationship between names and reality, as Reding (1985) points out, is that the Greek sophists were interested in the adequacy and inadequacy of words in representing reality, while the Chinese Mingjia were concerned with re-creating a system of complex designations in adapting to the changing reality (492).

It must be noted that although Gong-sun approached ming and shi from an epistemological perspective, he was nonetheless forced to address the issue in reference to the social context in which he lived. In Gong-sun's time, after years of war, a strong desire for unity and stability arose among the ruling class. The role of ming in promoting relative truths and diverse views was identified as a source of confusion, separation, and instability. Political and social problems were caused by incorrect match and detachment between names and actuality. On the contrary, the role of ming serving as a mechanism of control by corresponding closely to one version of reality (shi) was desired and in demand. Furthermore, as he was employed as a you shui, Gong-sun couched his arguments for peace in language designed to appeal to the ruling elite. Accordingly, in his writings Gong-sun advised the ruler to observe and oversee the correspondence between names and actuality. If the correspondence was weak, nonexistent, or "skewed," the rectification of names should be imposed by executive measures. In this sense, ming was not understood as a means of generating different opinions, but as a way to facilitate agreements by unifying perceptions of reality.

To do so, according to Gong-sun, the ruler must make sure that each shi have its own distinctive, corresponding ming. For him, the task of eliminating confusion entailed making sure that "the name of an object matches the actuality." In the political context, designations of things, titles, and tasks (ming) must reflect the administrative functions and performances (shi). If, on the other hand, "the name does not represent actuality, the name cannot be used" (*GSL "mingshi lun"* 150). This is because if designations and their functions do not match, or if more than one function is generated by one designation, people will be confused by the use of language and will develop a misunderstanding of their perception of the reality.

In this regard, Gong-sun's philosophy of language resembled that of Plato in the sense that both acknowledged the impact of language on human perceptions and actions and both attempted to limit its misuse. However, the two thinkers differ in the solution to the problem of language. While Gong-sun proposed social control of names in the hand of the ruler, Plato sought to rationalize the use of language as the task of a philosopher. For

Gong-sun, accordingly, the challenge was to locate an ultimate source of authority, someone in the position to decide what names should be used to represent reality, someone with power to affect the general understanding of reality by proposing various usages of names. As implied by Gong-sun, it was not the intellectuals or the common people who would wield this kind of power, but the rulers of the state. For this reason, throughout Chinese history, freedom of expression on the part of intellectuals has always been suppressed and "corrected" by the ruling elites, who employed the political means of control to insure that language usage matched their version of reality.

Gong-sun's theory of ming shi had practical application with regard to argumentation during his lifetime, providing criteria for determining whether certain words used in persuasive discourse corresponded to the legitimate version of reality. His theory also generated expectations of the speaker, who must be skilled at the manipulation of language as well as at flattering the ruler while creating the impression that a close correspondence existed between names and reality, as defined by the ruler. Nevertheless, Gong-sun fell into the same self-contradictory position as Deng Xi. On one hand, he advocated the correspondence between ming and shi in the interest of the ruler in order to insure stability, clarity, and political control. On the other hand, he recognized the role of names, concepts, and language in molding and creating reality from an intellectual point of view.

Mode of Classification

While Deng Xi and Hui Shi are sometimes compared to Protagoras and Gorgias, respectively, Gong-sun is compared to Aristotle for his rational orientation. Through his you shui activities for the sake of peace as well as his involvement in intellectual debates, he must have sensed the importance of clarity, consistency, and logical thinking in presenting an argument. Contrary to Hui Shi's belief that everything in the world is interrelated and interconnected, Gong-sun believed that the world is made up of separate entities, independent from one other. According to this view, an inability to distinguish these separate entities through the use of language leads to confusion and false classification.

Gong-sun encapsulated his theory with the famous statement "a white horse is not a horse," explaining that "the concept of horse refers to the shape and image of a horse. Whiteness is a concept regarding color. The concept of color is different from the concept of shapes and images. Therefore, a white horse is not a horse" ("*baima lun*" 18). In other words, the phrase "white horse" only tells the color of the horse, not the shape of the horse, since shape and color are two separate entities. Furthermore, a white horse, like a yellow or black horse, is only a kind of horse. All horses belong to the same species, but conceptually they should not be confused with one another. The claim that "a white horse is not a horse" is an attempt to argue for the correct usage of names by requiring that concepts associated with horses match or correspond to their actual characteristics and idiosyncrasies. For Gong-sun, the word *horse* reveals the essence of the horse, encompassing the general characteristics of horses as a species. "A white horse" pronounces itself with the distinctiveness of color, subdividing the horse species. The subdivision of a species is not the same as the species itself.

The Greek sophists had a similar discussion on the problem of logos in representing composite substance. According to W. K. C. Guthrie (1969), certain Greek sophists had pointed out that there was a lack of distinction between essential and accidental predications among things and a confusion between proper and common names in the use of logos. They proposed "one, and only one, proper logos for each thing" to solve the problem and insisted on saying "a man is man and good is good" as opposed to saying "a man is good" (Guthrie 1969, 214–15), as each has its own distinctive meanings and connotations. As Gong-sun claimed that "a white horse is not a horse," Simplicius argued that a white Socrates and Socrates involved different attributes and thus must be distinguished in names. In general, Gong-sun's theory of classification echoes the Greek sophists' position that "things having a different *logos* were different, and that different things were divided from each other, and so thought to prove that everything is divided from itself . . ." (quoted in Guthrie 1969, 217).

Gong-sun's distinction between horse and white horse is similar to the distinction made by Aristotle regarding secondary (universal) substance and primary (particular) substance: "When things have only a name in common and the definition of being which corresponds to the name is different" (*Categories* 1a1), the former category can cover the latter, but the latter category cannot cover the former. In this sense, Gong-sun shared with Aristotle the notion of classification by substance, even within the same species and kind. For both, the term used to refer to a thing should delineate the specific nature of the substance.

Gong-sun believed that people constantly make distinctions among things without being conscious of the fact that they are doing so, offering the following example from the life of Confucius: "I heard that the king of Chu lost his bow while he was hunting. His subordinates wanted to get it back but the king said to his subordinates, 'The bow lost by Chu people will be found by Chu people.' When Confucius heard this, he commented,

'The king of Chu is a king of benevolence, but is not complete in his practice of benevolence.' He could have said, 'the lost bow will be found by people, rather than by the people of Chu'" (*GSL "fuji"* 4). Since, in this case, Confucius made a distinction between people in general and the people of Chu, Gong-Sun concluded that Confucius would likely agree that "a white horse is not a horse" even though not consciously adopting a similar mode of classification and division.

In the chapter "On Hard and White" Gong-sun made the same statement using a different metaphor, in this case that of a solid, white stone: Questioner: "Can we consider solidity, whiteness, and stone three separate elements?" Gong-sun: "No." Questioner: "Can we consider them two separate elements?" Gong-sun: "Yes." Questioner: "Why?" Gong-sun: "This is because, when facing a stone, we cannot see its solidity, but only its white color. When we touch the stone, we feel solidity but cannot feel white color. Thus, only two elements can be identified in the stone" (112). Gong-sun further explained that in a stone its quality of solidity and its white color are two separate components. That people see these two components as one is a fallacy, for in reality they are separate. Gong-sun's ontological view was that everything in the world is separate by nature, having its own individual characteristics. People artificially integrate and unify things instead of discerning their individual differences.

For Gong-sun, it was misleading and inaccurate to give a single name to an object that possessed a combination of elements. To do so was to mismatch ming and shi, thus causing unnecessary confusion. Here, Gong-sun introduced the concept of particularity, that is, the notion that any given entity could be composed of many separate elements. Failure to discern the particularity of things could lead to ambiguity and unclarity. This process of discernment, as Hu Shih contends, logically "means the shifting of emphasis from universals to particulars, probably resulting in giving more emphasis on induction than the earlier Neo-Mohists [the Later Mohists] had done" (1963, 124).

Gong-sun also believed that things in the world should be divided and classified according to their kind. In his chapter "On Universal Change" he asserted that oxen, goats, and horses possess some similar characteristics and therefore belong to the same category, while chickens, oxen, and goats cannot be classified in the same group. Things belonging to the same category integrate and assimilate with one another, rather than expelling or denying one another. Gong-sun was particularly interested in the changing nature of things as individual elements of the same or similar categories combine with one another.

Unlike Confucianists, who placed great emphasis on morality and ethics as strategies for inducing human and social change, Gong-sun was primarily concerned with the question of ontology and epistemology. He dichotomized the world into polarized categories of *zhi* (reference) and *wu* (materials), *ming* (concepts) and *shi* (actuality). His epistemology was similar to that of Aristotle in that both believed humans gain their knowledge of the world by first separating things into kinds and species and then classifying them according to similarities and differences. Such are the rudimentary precepts of scientific inquiry as applied to the field of rhetoric. Thus, it is too sweeping a generalization to claim that China lacked a tradition of rational thinking characterized by classification and separation, or scientific reasoning. In fact, Joseph Needham argues that *Gong-sun Longzi* had reached the apex of ancient Chinese philosophy with his dialogues resembling the Platonic style, comparing the Chinese Mingjia to the Greek philosophers Eleatics and Peripatetics. Needham concludes, "when one takes into account the enormous gaps known to exist in the ranks of the ancient Chinese writings which have come down to us, one is left with the impression that there was little to choose between ancient European and ancient Chinese philosophy so far as the foundations of scientific thought were concerned . . ." (1956, 203).

Unfortunately, to this day, few Western rhetorical scholars have any knowledge of Gong-sun Long's contribution to scientific thought. Even Chinese scholars have generally failed to recognize and appreciate his work. While his contemporaries condemned him for spreading "strange doctrines" and "bizarre sayings," modern Chinese scholars tend to dismiss him as a logician who was interested in abstraction and fond of arguments over metaphysical issues. Others criticize him for overlooking the notions of unity and complexity, lacking a complete and substantial logical system, and serving the interests of the ruling class.[15] While these criticisms carry some truth, the contributions made by Gong-sun to metaphysical, scientific, and rhetorical inquiry cannot be ignored.

If Deng Xi planted the seeds of relativism and ming bian, they were cultivated and brought to fruition by Hui Shi and Gong-sun Long, respectively. Hui Shi emphasized the theories concerning relativism and constant change, while Gong-sun articulated the logic of ming bian through classification and categorization. All three Mingjia had placed faith in language as an efficient tool of social control and intellectual inquiry. For Hui Shi, there was no fixed version of reality and thus the meaning of names was infinite and in a constant state of flux. For Gong-sun, establishing a system of designation and classification was to exert control over the changing reality that would also result in an important means of knowing. In general, Chinese Mingjia conceptualized ming bian through a careful analysis of logical, linguistic, and abstract elements of language in relation to politics, ontology, and epistemology. Through this process they established a worldview and a mode of inquiry for generations of Chinese thinkers to follow.

A Comparison between Chinese Mingjia and Greek Sophists

In the Western literature on ancient Greek rhetoric, a sophist is commonly defined as "a wise, learned man," "a master of thinking and speaking," a "professional teacher," or a "successful politician."[16] Broadly speaking, Greek sophists were known for their interest in the concepts of probability, kairos, and aesthetic pleasure. There is no direct Chinese translation of *sophist*. The English-Chinese dictionary defines a sophist as "a person having a glib tongue and a fondness for argument"; however, this definition does not encompass the contextual meaning of the term. While some scholars have attempted to equate Chinese Mingjia with the Greek sophists (Crump 1964; Forke 1901/02; Fung 1952; Graham 1989; Hu 1963; Kroll 1985–87), and the two groups do share some similarities in their philosophical and rhetorical views, they are also distinctive groups in their own cultural contexts.

Indeed, the Greek sophists and Chinese Mingjia were two distinct groups of rhetorical thinkers and practitioners. They lived in the same historical period and faced some similar and some very different cultural and political conditions and transitions. Although there is no clear evidence of contact between the two groups historically, they share certain similarities in worldviews and rhetorical perspectives. As Crump observes, "Kung-sun Lung-tzu [Gong-sun Long], Hui Shi, the Neo-Mohists, and the members of the Academy at Chi-hsia [Jixia] gate resemble so greatly the 'eristic' side of the Greek sophistic [rhetoric]" (1964, 99). Such similarities can also be extended to their philosophical views, as well as to their respective contributions to rhetorical theory and practice. For example, both groups held that "humans are the measure of all things," basing this judgment on the rational capacities of human beings as opposed to their spiritual or divine powers. Second, both groups embraced the concept of probability, and though epistemologically views varied among Mingjia themselves, both groups recognized the power of language in representing and shaping reality. Deng Xi and Hui Shi's relativism finds echoes in the works of Gorgias and Protagoras, while Gong-sun Long has much in common with Aristotle. Third, both groups provided political service for their societies by engaging in persuasive activities while slighting issues of ethics and morality, for which they were criticized by philosophers from other schools of thought.

Both Chinese Mingjia and Greek sophists were intelligent professionals, selling their knowledge and wisdom for material gain. Both groups traveled around the country or neighboring states. Both groups were made up of eloquent speakers whose intention was to impress and persuade their audiences through the embellishment of language. In addition, Chinese Mingjia used rhetorical techniques similar to those employed by Greek sophists, such as examples and metaphors, inductive and deductive reasoning, and audience psychology. Further, Chinese Mingjia were involved in a variety of rhetorical activities, ranging from debates on the notions of metaphysics, epistemology, and language, to political counseling of the kings. Greek sophists expounded on issues of language, were active members of Greek politics, and contributed to the codification of Greek rhetoric (Schiappa 1992). Similar to Greek sophists, Chinese Mingjia were also innovative thinkers and masters of the art of argumentation and persuasion, and their work contributed to the formulation of theories of language and Chinese political thought.

While the two groups share certain similarities, caution must be taken in equating one group with the other. This is because the identification of Chinese Mingjia with sophists tends to obscure our understanding of Mingjia, giving rise to at least two problems. First, in general, when Western scholars assign English equivalents to their analyses of Chinese rhetorical concepts, they tend to impose a Western context onto Chinese rhetorical theory and practice, overlooking the unique characteristics of the ancient Chinese experience. More specifically, by equating Chinese Mingjia with the Greek sophists, scholars have come to regard Mingjia as the only sophistic thinkers among the ancient Chinese, when, in fact, the Later Mohists, scholars in the Jixia Academy, Zhuangzi, and certain you shui also engaged in rhetorical activities and offered rhetorical perspectives of a sophistic nature.

In fact, significant differences also existed between Greek sophists and Chinese Mingjia. For instance, while the Greek sophists practiced rhetoric primarily in public situations, persuading their audiences by arousing passion through emotional appeals and a grand rhetorical style, Chinese Mingjia debated and persuaded their audiences mostly in private settings through psychological and rational appeals using examples and analogies. Greek sophists were professional teachers; rhetoric was considered a discipline and taught through a curriculum designed to prepare young boys for political life in Athens. Chinese Mingjia were political councillors as well as intellectuals who wrote and practiced ming and bian. The Greek sophistic tradition flourished and has been thoroughly integrated into Western political culture, surviving to the present, while Chinese Mingjia was officially rejected, losing its influence during the Han dynasty (beginning in 206 B.C.E.). Reding summarizes that while the Chinese Mingjia lost their influence on philosophy and society by their sophistic mode of inquiry, the Greek sophists continued to influence the consciousness of Western philosophy and engendered positivism, pragmatism, and skepticism and offered an open society in the West (1985, 499). Clearly, the rhetorical contribution of each group must be examined in its own social, cultural, and philosophical context. The philosophical perspectives and rhetorical strategies of these "eloquent speakers" were diverse and culture-specific. One undeniable fact, however, is that at the same moments in human history, Chinese Mingjia and Greek sophists crafted the art of speaking, provided fresh ontological and epistemological worldviews, and illuminated the arena of human thought and communication.

CHAPTER 6

Conceptualization of Yan and Ming Bian
The School of Confucianism

Confucianism, founded by Confucius, is represented in the works of the *Analects, Mencius,* and *Xunzi,* all of which were completed before 221 B.C.E. The Chinese word *ru* 儒, translated in the West as Confucianism, originally meant "teacher."[1] Since Confucius himself was considered a ru, the texts he used were known as *ru shu* 儒書 (ru books), his moral philosophy was referred to as *ru xue* 儒學 (the study of ru, or Confucianism), and his disciples and followers were known as *Rujia* 儒家 (Confucianists).

It must be remembered that Confucianism enjoyed no particular status or prestige in its early years. In fact, it was only one of several competing schools of thought during the Spring-Autumn and Warring States period. However, Emperor Han Wu 漢武帝 (156–87 B.C.E.) institutionalized Confucianism as a state philosophy and cultural ideology. Subsequently, Confucian teachings became the canonized texts for the education and training of government officials in ancient China. Later, during the South Song 南宋 dynasty (1127–1279), Confucian texts were reinterpreted by Neo-Confucianists, who integrated Buddhist and Daoist methods of self-realization into Confucianism. Along with Buddhism and Daoism, Confucianism significantly influenced the formulation of Chinese modes of thinking and ways of life. Confucianism came under attack by Western-educated Chinese scholars early in this century and subsequently in the 1960s and 1970s by Mao Zedong's ideological campaign and red guards during the Cultural Revolution. As a result, Confucianism has lost its place as a state ideology and Confucian texts are no longer taught to schoolchildren in mainland China. Although Confucian philosophy is still studied by Chinese scholars and its cultural influence is generally evident, recent studies indicate an erosion of Confucian values in social relations and communication behaviors.[2]

In this chapter I will provide an account of the philosophical orientations and rhetorical perspectives of the three most influential Confucianists in the pre-Qin period (before 221 B.C.E.): Confucius 孔子, Mencius 孟子, and Xunzi 荀子. Though not contemporaries, these three men shared a humanistic rhetorical perspective embedded in their works on ethical and political themes. Each also offered unique rhetorical insights. For example, Confucius emphasized the rectification of names and demonstrated an interest in the moral and aesthetic use of language. Mencius, on the other hand, held a critical view of types of immoral speech, focusing on the affective aspect of argumentation. Finally, Xunzi developed Confucius's notion of rectification of names and conceptualized ming bian with a rational emphasis on language, persuasion, and argumentation. In the following pages I will examine and analyze their respective views on the concepts of *yan* 言, *ming* 名, and *bian* 辯. For convenience, the following chart gives information on the three thinkers by their life span, major works, philosophical views, and major rhetorical contributions:

Confucian Philosophy and Rhetoric

Names/Dates	Texts	Philosophical Views	Rhetorical Perspectives
Confucius 551–479 B.C.E.	Lun Yu (Analects)	Ren (benevolence) Li (rites, propriety) Zhong Yong (the Mean)	Rectification of names Moral & aesthetic appeals
Mencius 390–305 B.C.E.	Mengzi (Mencius)	Good human nature	Moral & affective appeals Sincerity & qi (energy) Understanding types of language
Xunzi 298–238 B.C.E.	Xunzi	Evil human nature	Rectification of names Moral & rational *ming bian*

Confucius

Social Context and Personal Background

As the founder of Confucianism and one of the earliest Chinese philosophers, Confucius established fundamental touchstones for all subsequent philosophical and rhetorical inquiries throughout Chinese history.

Confucius lived during the transition between the Zhou dynasty and the Spring-Autumn period, a time characterized by uncertainty and disorder. The ruling aristocracy of the Zhou dynasty, along with its established social hierarchy and cultural norms, was in a state of decline. Traditional *Zhou Li* (Rites of Zhou) was regularly denounced by the emerging class of landowners; however, a new value system had not yet been established. Simultaneously, wars broke out among small kingdoms over land and political power. In this context, Confucius witnessed the moral corruption of government officials as well as a lack of direction concerning social and human development. With his aristocratic background and traditional values, Confucius cherished the ritual practices and orderly world of the Zhou dynasty. It is not surprising, then, that he longed for the restoration and reconstruction of an orderly, humanistic society under prescribed moral principles and cultural norms.

Given the general chaos of the times, there was great need for the service of political consultants and moral teachers. The class of shi was therefore in great demand, enjoying opportunities for upward mobility and freedom of thought and expression. Much concerned about the problems of cultural degradation and social anarchy, Confucius involved himself in political you shui, starting his career as an educator, an official for the state of Lu, and eventually becoming a moral philosopher.

According to *Shi Ji* (Records of the Historian), Confucius was born into a noble family in the time of decline of the State of Song, living most of his life in the state of Lu. In his youth Confucius lived a plain life and was often destitute. He traveled for fourteen years to various kingdoms, engaging in you shui activities and hoping to fulfill his political ambitions and actualize his ideas of government. Occasionally Confucius proved a skillful you shui in his persuasive activities vis-à-vis state rulers. *Shi Ji* documents instances when Confucius successfully advised Duke Jin of Qi, Duke Ling of Wei, Duke Ai of Lu, and Duke Ding of Lu on issues of government, rituals, and military strategies.[3]

Politically disillusioned and hoping to fulfill his political ideology through education, Confucius started his teaching career at the age of thirty, teaching poetry, music, language art, history, and ethics. According to *Shi Ji*, over the years Confucius taught over three thousand students, seventy-two of whom became highly skilled at *liu yi* (the six arts). Confucius was well respected by his students, who considered him a man of profound knowledge, wisdom, modesty, and persistence. In his lifetime Confucius held a number of minor offices for the state of Lu. The highest positions he ever achieved were minister of justice and acting minister for Duke Di of

Lu. Although Confucius never fulfilled his political ambition, his contribution to Chinese culture and education was significant. As Yu-Lan Fung notes: "Confucius was the first man in China to make teaching his profession, and thus popularize culture and education. It was he who opened the way for the many travelling scholars and philosophers of succeeding centuries. It was also he who inaugurated, or at least developed, that class of gentleman in ancient China who was neither farmer, artisan, merchant nor actual official, but was professional teacher and potential official" (1952, 48). Confucius was also credited with compiling the classic works produced before and during his time. In his later years he compiled the six classical canons known as *Shi Jing* (the Book of Odes), *Shang Shu* (the Book of History), *Yi Jing* (the Book of Change), *Yue Jing* (the Book of Music), *Li Ji* (Records of Rituals), and *Chun Qiu* (the Spring-Autumn Annuals). Confucius's philosophical principles were mostly recorded in dialogues with his disciples, who compiled them in the *Analects* 論語. In addition, some of his views are recorded in *Shi Ji*, *Da Xue* (the Great Learning), *Zhong Yong* (the Doctrine of Mean), and *Yi Jing*.

Philosophical Views

Confucian philosophical views are essentially moralistic and humanistic in nature. Indeed, though Confucius's moral philosophy was formulated in the political and cultural contexts in which he lived and must therefore be interpreted contextually and historically, at the same time, his work has universal implications that can benefit humankind as a whole, even in today's world. As Robert Oliver notes, "Confucius himself had a message for his own time that remains ever fresh. Its philosophical and rhetorical significance has been influential all through the East and has a value that should not be overlooked for the different cultures of the rest of the world" (1971, 121). In general, three Confucian principles are essential to his moral philosophy and directly affected his rhetorical perspectives: *ren* (benevolence), *li* (rites), and *zhong yong* (the Mean, the Middle Way). I will illustrate each principle in the following.

(1) Ren. Out of his desire to reconstruct the social and moral order, Confucius developed the concept of *ren* 仁, defining it eighty-seven times in the *Analects*. According to Chinese historian Guo Moruo, the word *ren* is semantically connected to its homonym *ren* 人 (people), which prior to the Spring-Autumn period was used to refer to the ruling class (1959, 75). Thus, it is commonly believed by both Chinese and Western scholars that the doctrine of ren is addressed to the ruling elite of society, not to ordinary people, and to men, not women. In fact, Confucius equated women with

xiaoren 小人 (base people) and referred to common people as *min* 民 (masses).

Ren is the fundamental principle of Confucian philosophy, prescribing for the social elite an ideal way of achieving moral perfection. *Ren*, as variously defined in the *Analects*, means benevolence, sincerity, goodness, gentility, and love. According to Chung-Ying Cheng (1971), ren is the central preoccupation of Confucian ethics and means "moral life at its best" or, alternatively, "moral excellence." Confucius regarded ren as the ability of men (not including women) to make moral judgments and perform moral acts. He wrote: "It is only the benevolent man who is capable of liking or disliking other men. If a man sets his heart on benevolence, he will be free from evil" (Lau 4.4.72).[4] For Confucius, ren could be achieved through the cultivation of knowledge and self-examination. Though Confucius was a learned man, he never lectured on subjects he did not know well. He instructed his students not to "talk of policies when you are not in the position of making them" (*LY* 8.14.80), but to listen and observe with discrimination and modesty. He claimed that "when walking with two other men, one of them must be my teacher" (Lau 7.22.69).

Confucius did not expect everyone to achieve ren. He divided the society into *junzi* 君子 (gentlemen class) and *xiaoren* 小人 (base people). In his view, junzi were superior to xiaoren in their moral sensibilities, psychological state, and ability to relate to authority. In his words, "The gentleman [junzi] understands what is moral. The small man [xiaoren] understands what is profitable" (Lau 4.16.74). "The gentleman is easy of mind, while the small man is always full of anxiety" (7.37.91). In other words, junzi is a cultivated and virtuous individual who values spiritual life, despises money, loves learning, respects authority, and strives for moral perfection. By contrast, xiaoren, the base person, only thinks of how to gain practical benefits, is occupied with trivial things, and shows no respect for authority. Strictly speaking, China has never had a class system determined by birth; however, people are morally judged and classified according to junzi and xiaoren criteria set up by Confucius. In Lin Yu-tang's opinion, "the charm of Confucius was very much like the charm of Socrates." The concept of *junzi* is "very similar to Plato's philosopher king" (1938, 23–24).[5] The notion of *ren*, then, aims at reconstructing a moral and humanistic society composed of and facilitated by junzi, the noble or gentle class of social elites.

(2) *Li*. While *ren* may be seen as potentiality and competence which directs and determines a person's moral conduct, *li* 禮, translated as rites, rituals, propriety, and codes of conducts, is the actualization of one's moral attributes. One definition of *ren* given by Confucius is "to return to the

observance of the rites [li] through overcoming the self" (Lau 12.1.112). Thus, if ren is the ideal goal of life and an abstract notion of morality, li is the means to achieve the goal, providing concrete criteria and standards of behavior. Put differently, if ren is the goal of speech and communication, li serves as the means to facilitate and actualize that goal. Li can be understood as self-monitored and controlled verbal and nonverbal behavior proper and appropriate to norms of filial piety, ancestor worship, and official ceremonies, exhibited through listening, speaking, singing, dancing, and performing the rites and rituals. For example, when his disciple Yan Yuan asked the master how to perform li, Confucius replied, "do not look unless it is in accordance with the rites; do not listen unless it is in accordance with the rites; do not speak unless it is in accordance with the rites; do not move unless it is in accordance with the rites" (Lau 12.1.112) Clearly, li is an essential element of Confucius's teaching. As summarized by Herbert Fingarette, "Characteristic of Confucius' teaching is the use of the language and imagery of *Li* as a medium within which to talk about the entire body of the *mores*, or more precisely, of the authentic tradition and reasonable conventions of society. Confucius taught that the ability to act according to *Li* and the will to submit to *Li* are essential to that perfect and peculiarly human virtue or power which can be man's" (1972, 6–7). It must be noted that the purpose of advocating and adhering to li, for Confucius, was to restore traditional values, namely those of the Zhou dynasty.

(3) *Zhong Yong*. Another important element of Confucian philosophy is the doctrine of *zhong yong* 中庸 (the Mean or Middle Way), an ontological and moral concept which addressed the political and ideological conflicts Confucius faced during his lifetime. In explaining the doctrine, Confucius quoted the sage Yao as saying "Oh! Shun, your succession of the throne is ordained by Heaven. Hold truly to the Middle Way. The Heavenly bestowed prosperity will be terminated forever if people of the world are surrounded by poverty" (LY 20.1.203). Thus, *zhong yong* is the divine assumption of power and stability in running a government and maintaining *he* 和 (harmony) in the world. According to Confucius, Zhong yong is a virtue not easily obtained. In his words, "The Middle Way is the highest moral virtue and it has been lacking among the common people for quite a long time" (6.29.66). Zhong yong is a quality of moderation and justice. For example, "In his dealings with the world the gentleman is not invariably for or against anything. He is on the side of what is moral [appropriateness]" (Lau 4.10.73). A person who possesses the virtue of zhong yong "is generous without its costing him anything, works others hard without their complaining, has desires without being greedy, is casual without being arrogant, and is

awe-inspiring without appearing fierce" (20.2.159). Furthermore, one "is conscious of his own superiority without being contentious, and comes together with other gentlemen without forming cliques" (15.22.135).

While zhong yong is a means to achieve harmony, it does not entail compromise or simple accommodation and reconciliation of one's differences. In fact, he (harmony), defined by Confucius, does not require giving up one's position in order for agreement to be reached. As Confucius said, "The gentleman agrees with others without being an echo. The small man echoes without being in agreement" (13.23.122). Accordingly, Confucius's doctrine of zhong yong is similar to Aristotle's concept of the Golden Mean, in that one gives the best performance and generates the best result by balancing the elements and avoiding extremes. The ideal of zhong yong has become one of the hallmarks of Chinese communication behavior. Unfortunately, its real meaning is often misunderstood as a quest for harmony at the expense of individuality through an avoidance of conflict.

Rhetorical Perspectives

Confucius's rhetorical perspectives are deeply embedded in his philosophical views and strongly characterized by moral and ethical concerns for the reconstruction of an orderly society capable of moral living. In particular, such perspectives are demonstrated through his discussions of *zheng ming* 正名, the rectification of names, and *yan* 言, the role and function of speech.

(1) Zheng Ming. As mentioned earlier, Confucius lived in an age of social upheaval in which the traditional values of the Zhou dynasty were being challenged, and in a sense neglected. Through Confucius's eyes, it was a world without order in which ministers killed kings and sons murdered fathers—in short, a world of social and cultural degradation. He attributed this state of affairs to unskillful and unclear communication in the use and definition of terms, leading to unwholesome and immoral social activities. As he pointed out, "When names are not correct, speech will not be appropriate; when speech is not appropriate, tasks will not be accomplished; when tasks cannot be accomplished, rites and music will not flourish; when rites and music do not flourish, punishment will not justify the crimes; when punishment does not justify the crimes, the common people will not know where to put their hands and feet" (*LY* 13.3.132).

Confucius proposed the concept of *zheng ming* as a solution to such social problems, claiming that the first thing he would do if asked to take a position in state affairs would be to rectify names (13.10.133).[6] For Confucius, every name carried with it a concept and a behavior. If the actualities of things did not correspond to their names, social disorder would result. For example, the names and titles of rulers, ministers, parents, and children should lead to actions, i.e., the performance of duties, in accordance with the meanings these titles convey. Otherwise, society would be in chaos: "the ruler will not be like a ruler; the subject will not be like a subject; the father will not be like a father; the son will not be a son" (12.11.124). In other words, Confucius's advocacy of the rectification of names aimed to make people at different levels of social hierarchy perform according to what they ought to be.

In this regard, Confucius's concept of *zheng ming* is centered around communication with a political, social, and moral intent. The rectification of names leads to a rectification of the social order as well as of human relationship. For Confucius, the aim of zheng ming was to regulate the public order by ensuring that everyone knew his/her place and acted accordingly. In this way, "the family will be in order. As families become better ordered, the community is cleansed of many vices, and it becomes better ordered itself. Once the community is in order, the nation is in order" (Kincaid 1987, 13).

As discussed in chapter 4, the notion of *ming* was examined from political and rational perspectives by Mingjia. However, it was Confucius who first developed the notion of *zheng ming* as a framework for articulating the relationship between ming 名 (naming) and shi 實 (actuality) in social and cultural contexts. Like his contemporary Deng Xi, Confucius was keenly aware that ming represents and transforms shi. He saw the artificial separation of ming and shi as the primary cause of confusion in the conceptual world leading to immoral action. In his view, a close correspondence between ming and shi must be observed in order to assure a true representation of reality through the use of language. When ming does not refer to our conventionally shared reality, for example, when a son does not act as a son should or a minister does not perform the way he was supposed to, the person should be reprimanded and punished. What is needed is the rectification of names, a clear prescription of everyone's roles and functions in society, which should be the task of a state king or government officials to accomplish.

Confucius's concept of the rectification of names went beyond the correct use of names for maintaining the social order and establishing a hierarchy of human relations. Confucius was fully aware of the impact of ming, or language, on human perceptions and actions. For him, ming included not only words and concepts but also cultural rules and norms infused with enduring ethical and moral values. The rectification of names, then, required widespread conformity to prescribed names and norms.

What was corrected, or rectified, through the adaptation of a new set of rules and norms were culturally inappropriate beliefs and behaviors. As John Makeham explains, "Names, not actualities, were Confucius' primary concern. He did not regard names as passive labels but rather as social and hence political catalysts" (1994, 46). By developing this transformative nature of ming, Confucius articulated an ideal way of using speech and language capable of creating order out of disorder and transforming a morally corrupt society into one of ren (benevolence), li (rites), and zhong yong (the Middle Way). The notion of zheng ming prescribed a new set of social rules, a new system of organizing a culture and society. In Hu Shih's opinion, rectification of names is a task of intellectual reorganization:

Its object is, first, to make the names stand for what they ought to stand for, and then to so reorganize the social and political relations and institutions as to make them what their names indicate they ought to be. The rectification of names thus consists in making the real relationships and duties and institutions conform as far as possible to their ideal meanings which, however obscured and neglected they may now have become, can still be re-discovered and re-established by proper study and, literally "judicious" use of the names (1963, 26).

Thus, the practice of rectifying names, according to David L. Hall and Roger T. Ames, entails the use of language toward a certain realization. That is, one influences the world through the articulation of meaning, value, and purpose. In this sense, Confucius's zheng ming plays a transformative function, providing "the impetus and direction for social and political change" (1987, 273).[7]

Indeed, Confucius used the term *ming* as a means to create new political, social, and cultural discourse. Toward this end, he developed the notion of *ren* and defined and prescribed the concepts of *li* (rites), *shu* 恕 (reciprocity), *zhong* 忠 (loyalty), *xin* 信 (trustworthiness), and *yi* 義 (righteousness). His efforts to define and develop these moral terms were motivated by an overriding concern for the rectification of cultural norms and values, and ultimately by a desire to redirect people toward moral and spiritual pursuits. In this sense, Confucius's view of language was like that of the Greek sophists, especially regarding the connection between symbols and social power and cultural values. In the Confucian scheme of things, language served the function of defining meaning, shaping reality, and manipulating state affairs. Consequently, Confucius was primarily concerned with the correct use of language. In fact, he considered it "the prerequisite for correct living and even efficient government" (Steinkraus 1980, 262). For him, language served not only its nominal function, but the function of social transformation as well.

(2) *Yan.* Mary Garrett (1991) argues in her article "Asian Challenge" that the Chinese word *wen* 文 can be seen as a definition of rhetoric in that it includes all products of refined language ranging from literature to proclamations. This is true in the case of the *Analects,* in which Confucius used the term *wen* to indicate a fondness for "learning" "culture," "the classics," and "embellished words."[8] According to *Shuo Wen Jie Zi, wen* refers to totem that is spacial and inscribed rather than temporal and spoken in symbolizing the spiritual world. When discussing oral speech, eloquence, and persuasive discourse, however, Confucius chose the term *yan* 言, using it 116 times throughout the *Analects.* Although wen was an important component of his educational curriculum, Confucius seemed much more interested in yan with regard to its moral impact and persuasive effect. For Confucius, wen were the cultural products of the past in need of restoration and cherishing. The conceptualization of yan is Confucius's invention and creation, and his *Analects* is the first treatise on Chinese speech and communication.

Some scholars have argued that Confucius denounced speech, emphasizing written communication only (Choe 1985). However, a distinction must be made between speech in general and types of speech. In fact, Confucius himself was an eloquent speaker, as evidenced by his you shui activity and his teaching. He also encouraged his students to engage in verbal exchange for the purpose of learning, achieving ren, and seeking justice. He denounced those who used speech in a demoralized way to confuse the public mind and to argue only for the sake of argument. In his time, Confucius observed various you shui who, despite their eloquence, had no sense of righteousness and morality. In fact, they were motivated primarily by a desire for personal and material gain. Consequently, Confucius concluded, "It is rare, indeed, for a man with cunning words and an ingratiating face to be benevolent" (Lau 1.3.59), as "crafted speech will disturb virtue" (*LY* 15.27.160). Well aware of the impact of language on human perceptions and actions, Confucius believed that empty, flowery speech lacking in moral content would disturb the social order and lead people astray. He made such feelings clear, stating, "I detest clever talkers who overturn states and noble families" (Lau 17.18.146). Even while Confucius condemned glib-tongued, superficial speech, however, he also attempted to construct a moral and ethical perspective of speech. For Confucius, oral discourse was of value to the extent that the speaker held to a high standard of ren and acted in accordance with li.

Though Confucius offered no definition of *yan,* or speech, he argued that a good person would be well-spoken, saying, "A person of virtue is sure to speak eloquently, but a person who speaks eloquently is not necessarily virtuous" (*LY* 14.4.143). Confucius taught that one's virtue was not determined by class or nobility but by one's moral character. For him, a virtuous and moral person lived by following a creed when communicating with others: "When seeing a thing, see it with understanding. When hearing a thing, listen to it with wisdom. Keep a pleasant look. Be modest in one's conduct. Speak honestly, act cautiously. Ask when in doubt. Think of the consequences when losing one's temper. Do not allow oneself to be tempted by profit" (*LY* 21.10.169). Confucius believed that anyone who met these nine qualifications would naturally possess virtuous, moral, and benevolent speech. Furthermore, it was only through one's speech that one's true character was revealed (20.3.204). Thus, for Confucius, speech and the speaker could not be separated. They were inextricably intertwined.

In constructing a moral perspective of yan, Confucius proposed the following categories of speech: *de yan* 德言 (virtuous speech), *xin yan* 信言 (trustworthy speech), *wei yan* 危言 (upright speech), *shen yan* 慎言 (cautious speech), and *ya yan* 雅言 (correct speech). Confucius believed that a person of virtue would automatically present de yan. For him, de yan was not necessarily eloquent speech. In fact, he claimed, "A gentleman is slow in speech but quick in action" (4.24.38). Here, Confucius should not be understood to denounce eloquence. For him, virtue essentially carries with it eloquence. To be virtuous is to be eloquent. Thus, Confucius was primarily concerned with the speaker's moral character, which determines the intention and effect of a speech as opposed to its presentation and delivery. Those who excel at the presentation and delivery of a speech may actually be perceived negatively, provoking suspicion and even hostility from the audience (5.5.44). For Confucius, in the absence of a benevolent heart and virtuous actions, a facile tongue is meaningless.

A. *Xin Yan*. In the Confucian scheme of things, communication consists of the articulation and realization of norms and values. This "thinking process" as described by Hall and Ames "entails an appropriation of the cultural tradition through the interpersonal activity of learning (*hsueh* 學), and culminates in the communal activities of realizing (*chih* 知) and living up to one's word (*hsin* 信)" (1987, 83). Confucius was suspicious of those glib-tongued individuals who offered empty promises; as he explained to his students, "I used to take on trust a man's deeds after having listened to his words. Now having listened to a man's words I go on to observe his deeds" (Lau 5.10.77). On the subject of xin yan, or trustworthy speech, he preached that one should live up to one's words, saying, "A gentleman is ashamed of his word out-stripping his deed" (2.13.64). "He puts his words into action before allowing his words to follow his action" (2.13.64). For Confucius, *xin yan* meant simply to keep one's word and apply it to one's actions. Words are useless and meaningless if they do not correspond to action. Confucius insisted that "speech must be trustworthy, action must be followed through" (*LY* 13.20.123). Furthermore, it could uplift people's spirits and inspire them to acts of social responsibility. In his words, "If you are honest and trustworthy with your speech and humble and serious in your action, you will not have obstacles even in the lands of the barbarians" (15.6.158).

B. *Wei Yan, Shen Yan,* and *Ya Yan.* Confucius perceived *wei yan* (upright speech) as a reflection of benevolent government, stating, "When the politics of a government is honest and upright, the speech will be honest and upright" (14.3.143). Confucius was fully aware of the impact of language on power dynamics and politics, believing that even one word could lead a state to prosperity or ruin (13.15.134). He advised his students to practice *shen yan* (cautious speech) and avoid *shi yan* 失言 (saying the wrong words at the wrong time to the wrong audience). In his view, the virtuous person is "quick in action but cautious in speech" (1.14.2). Furthermore, the person must observe nonverbal cues and know when to speak appropriately (16.6.169). A junzi should use names clearly, accurately, carefully, and appropriately, at the same time practicing *ya yan* (correct and standard speech) centered around ethics and morality (7.18.69).

Like Aristotle, Confucius believed that the power of persuasion lay with the audience, not the speaker. The speaker's task was to understand the audience so as to adapt his/her message accordingly. In his words: "To fail to speak to the person with whom one can communicate is to lose the audience. To speak to the person with whom one cannot communicate is a waste of time. A wise person neither loses his audience nor wastes his words" (15.8.159). In short, an effective speaker must know the audience well and speak in a timely and fitting manner. A good bian shi, according to Confucius, shows love and respect to the audience. Skillful communication between people must be based on mutual agreement and understanding. Finally, one should not "impose on others what you yourself do not desire" (Lau 12.2.112).

Rhetorical Styles

As with Plato, an identifiable rhetorical paradox exists in the work of Confucius. On the one hand, he condemned those glib individuals who spoke with eloquent and flowery words lacking in moral substance. On the other hand, he stressed the need for a proper balance between *zhi* 質 (simplicity) and *wen* 文 (style). In Confucius's words, a gentleman's works should have the elements of simplicity and style (*LY* 6.18.58).[9] Similarly, in

Zuo Zhuan Confucius observes, "Speech reflects ideas expressed through a refinement of language. Without speech, ideas will not be known. Without a refinement of language, desired effects cannot be reached" (ZZ "*Xianggong*" year 25, 1106). In his view, it is enough that the language one uses gets the point across (*LY* 15.41; 12.20.125). In other words, one's speech should accurately reflect reality and be presented with the proper balance of content and style. For Confucius, the constant refinement of language and style through collective efforts leads to the production of quality texts.

According to the *Analects*, there were four components in Confucius's curriculum: *wen* 文 (language art and classical canons); *xing* 行 (practice and conducts of morality); *zhong* 忠 (loyalty); and *xin* 信 (trustworthiness). The first component, wen, is the essential element of Confucian education and language training. Confucius regarded *Shi Jing* (the Book of Odes) as the best textbook for instruction regarding the moral and artistic use of language, saying "Unless you study *Shi Jing* you will not know how to speak well" (6.13.170). Some of Confucius's disciples, such as Zai Wo and Zi Gong, were well known for their eloquence in speech (11.3.111), and Confucius himself was a master of speech and language. Confucian works such as the *Spring-Autumn Annual* and the *Analects* are revered not only for their moral significance, but also for their embellished, refined, and artistic use of language.

Confucius's concise and vivid use of language was characterized by techniques of rhythm, antithesis, alliteration, and parallelism. Typically, his words and phrases were enlightening and easy to memorize. In fact, many of his four-character phrases in the *Analects* have become popular Chinese sayings.[10] The brevity, balance, and rhythm of classical Chinese language made it eminently well suited for the creation of proverbs, which not only helped with memorization, but also, in Richard Smith's (1983) opinion, helped bridge the gap between the intellectual elites and common people in the world of Confucius. Confucius's gift in the artistic and versatile use of language is evident in three areas in the *Analects*. They are the use of definitions, feature of juxtaposition, and employment of metaphors.

(1) The Use of Definitions. In some ways similar to Greek thinkers, Confucius was fond of offering definitions, especially definitions of key moral concepts. In Confucius's ongoing dialogue with his students, he was often asked to define a concept, a term, or an idea. Thus, the text is filled with definitions, for example, of *ren* (benevolence), *li* (rites), *junzi* (gentleman), *shu* (reciprocity), *chi* 恥 (shame), *shi* 士 (scholar), *xiao* 孝 (filial piety), and *zhong yong*. Confucius's attempts at defining terms are indicative of his interest in conceptualizing and prescribing moral practices and guide-

lines, as well as engaging in rational and abstract modes of thinking. In this context, Confucius either offered abstract value-laden definitions and elaborations of the terms under consideration or simply provided concrete examples. For example, Confucius gave the following abstract definitions for the concept *ren* at various places in the *Analects:* "respectfulness, tolerance, trustworthiness in words, quickness and generosity" (Lau 17.6.143); "Love your fellow men [and women]" (12.22.116); "unbending strength, resoluteness, simplicity, and reticence" (13.27.123). When asked to define filial piety, Confucius was more concrete, saying: "observe what a man has in mind to do when his father is living, and then observe what he does when his father is dead. If, for three years, he makes no changes to his father's ways, he can be said to be a good [filial] son" (1.11.60).

Though some of Confucius's definitions began with abstract terms that were followed by more concrete explanations and examples, he followed no consistent and systematic procedure. In this sense, his approach was unlike that of the Socratic dialogue. Two possible explanations present themselves in this regard. First, in the case of commonly used concepts which were therefore familiar to his audience, such as *xiao* (filial piety) and *li* (rites), Confucius could offer more concrete terms. On the other hand, new concepts such as *ren* were moral ideals superimposed upon society. In these cases, his target audience was intellectual and educated junzi. Therefore, his definitions were more abstract and less consistent. Second, the text of the *Analects* was compiled by Confucius's students using their notes of his lectures. It is therefore not surprising that the text lacks internal consistency and coherence. At any rate, Confucius's attempts at moralizing the culture in which he lived and communicating his visions for human development through a rationalized process were similar to efforts made by Plato and Aristotle vis-à-vis ancient Greek culture.

(2) The Use of Juxtaposition. The second feature of Confucius's rhetorical style is the juxtaposition of opposites in explaining concepts. For instance, *junzi* and *xiaoren* are frequently contrasted in polarized terms in the text.[11] *Junzi* is said to behave like a noble man and is described as morally superior. *Xiaoren,* by contrast, is described as morally inferior and said to exhibit only base and selfish behavior. Another oppositional pairing is that of *he* (harmony) and *tong* 同 (blind agreement) (*LY* 13.23.135). A junzi is said to value harmony but not to agree blindly with others. He expresses his opinions, confronts difference, and attempts to reach harmony through mutual understanding. Only xiaoren are hypocritical, cowardly in the face of injustice, and motivated by narrow self-interests. Confucius also contrasted *da* 達 and *wen* 聞, defining one who possesses da as honest, selfless, observant,

analytical, and with a well-developed sense of justice. One who possesses wen, on the other hand, appears benevolent on the surface but does not act in benevolent ways (12.20.125). While these juxtapositions are value-laden, other contrasting pairs have wider applications. For example, Confucius juxtaposed *zhi* 質 (content) and *wen* 文 (style) with regard to rhetorical writing and speaking; *zheng* 政 (state affairs) and *shi* 事 (everyday routine) with regard to government practice; *yi* (righteousness) and *li* 利 (benefits) with regard to motivation; and *xue* 學 (learning) and *si* 思 (thinking) with regard to methods of learning.[12] Each term is mentioned and explained in relation to its polar opposite. Confucius may have employed this method in order to help his students memorize and internalize abstract concepts; however, by so doing he invites his audience to engage in dichotomous and polarized thinking.

Polarity and oppositional pairing are common features of Greek texts as well. Such usage may have differed from that of Chinese thinkers, however. According to G. E. R. Lloyd, modes of opposition in the pre-Platonic period were characterized by "a certain tendency to assimilate different types of opposites together, to emphasize their generic similarity (as opposites) and to ignore the specific differences between them" (1966, 169–70). By Aristotle's time, however, oppositional pairs "constitute mutually exclusive and exhaustive alternatives" (170). Generally speaking, it would appear that the Greeks juxtaposed oppositional pairs for the purpose of classification in order to promote logical thinking, while Confucius was motivated by a desire to illuminate different states of being and acting by exploring their relationship to one another.

Though Confucius failed to offer a clear formula for rational thinking, like that of Aristotle, and also did not connect rational thinking with morality, as Plato had envisioned, his rhetorical views and methods as recorded in the *Analects* convey a strong sense of rationality and polarization that must have influenced his audience. This may be why both Xunzi and Mozi emphasized rationality in their rhetorical perspectives, as both were serious students of Confucius and his written work.

(3) The Use of Metaphors. The third feature of Confucius's rhetorical style is his use of metaphors and analogies. These features are not simply treated as rhetorical devices, but as logical arguments in and of themselves, although relatively indirect. Confucius was fond of using metaphors in order to make a point or further an explanation. For example, in describing Yu's inability to take advice, Confucius said, "A piece of rotten wood cannot be carved, nor can a wall of dried dung be troweled. As far as Yu is concerned what is the use of condemning him" (Lau 5.10.77). When asked

whom he would take if leading the Three Armies into battle, Confucius replied, "I would not take with me anyone who would try to fight a tiger with his bare hands or to walk across the river and die in the process without regrets" (7.11.87). In other situations Confucius used metaphor to explain a concept or convey its deeper meaning. For example, when Confucius's disciple Zi Lu asked how to practice benevolence, Confucius replied with a metaphor: "A craftsman who wishes to practice his craft well must first sharpen his tools. You should, therefore, seek the patronage of the most distinguished counsellors and make friends with the most benevolent gentleman in the state where you happen to be staying" (15.10.133).[13] In some cases Confucius metaphorically described his subject without indicating the subject's identity, leaving his audience to read between the lines. For example, Confucius asked his disciples, "There are, are there not, young plants that fail to produce blossoms, and blossoms that fail to produce fruit?" (9.22.99). These metaphorical images may refer to those who do not succeed in life, though in their youth they seem filled with promise. In any case, Confucius employed rhetorical methods of argument and persuasion similar to the bian shi and you shui described in chapter 2. In fact, with his artistic and versatile use of language, he was certainly one of the most skilled bian shi of his time. Unlike Plato, who separated artistic expressions from rational thinking, treating the former as inferior to the latter, Confucius appears to have made a happy marriage between the two components.

In sum, Confucius's perspective of ming and yan was grounded in his philosophical beliefs relative to the culture in which he lived. For him, ming involved the proper use of language to help society function in an orderly and moral fashion. Speech was an ethical issue. Therefore, only a person with high moral standards could be a good bian shi. Furthermore, a bian shi should be well learned and culturally refined, ethical in speech and action, knowledgeable of his audience, and able to use language appropriately and artistically.

Mencius

Social Context and Personal Background

If Confucius's place in Chinese history is comparable to that of Socrates in the West, the position of Mencius is often likened to that of Plato in his political and philosophical views (Fung 1952; Richards 1991; Verwighen 1967). Indeed, Mencius, who lived about 150 years after Confucius, calibrated Confucian thought much as Plato was the interpreter of the Socratic doctrine. While Confucius lived during a period of cultural, political, and social upheaval, Mencius lived through the Warring States period when diverse cultural values were articulated and divisive power struggles had come to an end. It was a period of tension between moral choice and utilitarian gains, of debates over philosophical thoughts and political formulas for the reconstruction of society. In many ways the Confucian model of moral persuasion had failed to achieve its desired effect. More and more state kings sought practical gain at the expense of moral ideals. The overriding concern of the autonomous states was to expand their political power or survive the attacks by other states. To achieve these ends, state kings hired political consultants whose function was to offer ideas and advice for the purpose of strengthening the state for more military aggression or self-defense. For example, the king of Qin used Legalist Shang Yang 商鞅 as his counselor. Shang Yang helped the king initiate and execute a new legal system that brought growth to the economy and strengthened the military.

During the same time period, other schools of thought such as Daoism, Mohism, and Legalism began to flourish, competing on an equal basis in matters ranging from worldviews to proposed solutions to social and political problems. As one of the leading scholars of the Jixia Academy, Mencius fought a hard battle defending and selling Confucian doctrines. Considered pedantic and unrealistic by his contemporaries, Mencius's rhetorical activities are highly regarded by contemporary scholars. As Liu Wu-Chi observes: "It [the Warring States period] was indeed an age of sparkling wits, brilliant thinkers, and profound scholars; but of them all Meng K'o [Mencius] stood out as the greatest. With his winning eloquence, moral courage, and deep conviction, he championed the ethical and political doctrines of Master K'ung [Confucius], at the same time attacking with great zeal, the heterodox teachings of the other schools" (1955, 59). Similarly, Lin Yu-tang contends, "Mencius was an eloquent writer and speaker, good at debates" (1942, 273). Indeed, Mencius described himself as "understanding words" and "fond of argumentation" (M 2a.2.60; 3b.9.141). As recorded in Mengzi, in addition to arguing with his contemporaries on philosophical issues, he advised state kings to practice *ren zheng* 仁政 (benevolent government) and follow the moral principles of *li* (rites), *yi* (righteousness), and *zhi* 智 (wisdom).

Mencius's real name was Meng Ke 孟軻. Like Confucius, he was born to an aristocratic family in decline and experienced poverty as a child. A legend described his mother as moving three times in search of a good neighborhood for Mencius to grow up in. Though he never studied under Confucius, Mencius was a devout follower of Confucius and a strong advocate of his teachings, regarding him as the greatest thinker of all times. *Shi*

Ji (Records of the Historian) documents the fact that Mencius was a disciple of Zi Si 子思, Confucius's grandson. In his lifetime he traveled to a number of states promoting his political beliefs and offering advice to kings. Nonetheless, he never had the chance to participate in politics himself, and his ideas were not well accepted in the political arena. Like Confucius, Mencius became an educator attracting many disciples in his later years. As described in *Mengzi*, he was "followed by ten carriages [of disciples] and attended by a hundred men" (M 3b.4.132).

Mencius's philosophical views and rhetorical perspectives are contained in *Mengzi*, his only book. There is speculation that his students edited the book, but most Chinese scholars agree that Mencius himself was its writer or at least its chief editor. *Mengzi* is comprehensive, dealing with such subjects as metaphysics, psychology, human nature, ethics, politics, and language. In the area of speech, Mencius used the terms *yan, ci,* and *bian* to formulate his conceptions on persuasion, argumentation, and communication, respectively.

Philosophical Views

Mencius's primary contribution to Chinese intellectual tradition lies not in his interpretation of Confucius, but rather in his expansion of Confucianism. In addition to defending and elaborating upon the Confucian notion of *ren*, Mencius also expounded upon the question of human nature, in particular the issue of emotions and feelings in connection with morality.

(1) Ren. While Confucius coined the concept of *ren* as the highest standard of moral perfection, Mencius attached to it the notion of divine power, arguing that ren was the foundation for the other three human qualities, namely li (rites), zhi (wisdom), and yi (righteousness). He defined *ren* as "the highest honor bestowed by Heaven, the peaceful and spiritual abode of humankind." Furthermore, in his view, "It is unwise not choosing benevolence when there is no external force standing in the way. A person without benevolence, wisdom, understanding of rites, and a sense of righteousness is a slave" (M 2a.7.74).[14]

As the reader will recall, the notion of tian ming (the Mandate of Heaven) had been popular during the pre-Confucius period in justifying power and action. As the ancient Chinese turned their interests more toward epistemological and pragmatic issues, however, the belief in tian ming had weakened its appeal. Even so, as a cultural trace, the appeal of tian ming was never totally lost. In the face of a society lacking a clear direction and confused about values, Mencius called upon this traditional notion, connecting it with his doctrine of ren. This strategy proved powerful rhetorically in that the practice of ren was divinely justified and morally mandated. What is more, embedded in the notion of Heaven was the fear of punishment. Connecting the notion of ren with divine sanction brought this cause-effect association into play.

Moreover, by associating a supernatural being with secular affairs, Mencius implied that humans are spiritual beings capable of making moral choices. Ren, the most moral of all choices, according to Mencius, entailed following the proper path of yi and li and acting wisely (M 6a.11.267). Furthermore, zhi (wisdom), the intellectual way of speaking and acting, was said to be inseparable from ren, the moral way of speaking and acting. According to I. A. Richards (1991), the four moral principles of *Mencius* parallel Plato's description in his *Republic* of the four virtues to be pursued and celebrated, namely wisdom, courage, temperance, and justice.

(2) Human Nature. Unlike Plato, who relied upon knowledge as a means to rectify human behavior, Mencius placed his trust on human nature. For Mencius, ren and other moral qualities are not learned behavior, but rather inherent in human nature. In his words, "Benevolence, righteousness, observance of rites, and wisdom are not given to me from the outside; they are inherent in my nature" (M 6a.6.257). Mencius believed that given these virtues, human nature was innately good. What made people morally different from one another was the fact that some sought and practiced such virtues while others neglected and therefore lost them. Evil people were not evil by nature, but because they had abandoned ren and stopped cultivating and examining themselves. In other words, for Mencius a person would be considered unnatural, rather than ignorant, if the person does not attempt to save an infant who has fallen into a well. That is to say, for Mencius, the seed of goodness has been planted in everyone. However, it is the person himself or herself and the environment in which the person lives that determine whether the seed of goodness will grow. Mencius believed that "given the right nourishment there is nothing that will not grow, and deprived of it there is nothing that will not wither away" (Lau 6a.8.165).[15] In other words, humans are capable of rectifying themselves and choosing the moral path as an act of will. According to the Will of Heaven, ren must be followed; according to the laws of human nature, the ideal of ren can be achieved.

In order to realize or restore natural human goodness, according to Mencius, one must make moral choices, engage in self-examination, treat others with courtesy and respect, befriend junzi, live a plain life, listen to benevolent language and music, and keep one's word. To be worthy of the name *junzi*, one must preserve ren in his heart and follow ren in his conduct.

If Confucius's notion of *junzi* was an ideal model hardly achievable in one's life, Mencius prescribed *junzi* in a more concrete way, seemingly attainable through conscious efforts. For instance, he gave the following hypothetical example: "Suppose a person treats others in a rude manner. A true gentleman will ask himself, 'I must have been rude to this person, showing no benevolence in my behavior. Otherwise this person would not treat me this way.' When examining himself, if he finds that he has been benevolent and courteous, and yet this person is still rude, then the gentleman will ask himself again, 'I must have failed to do my best for the person'" (M 4b.28.191). The junzi continues to examine himself honestly until convinced he is not at fault, concluding that the person with whom he is dealing has a beast nature. The benevolent act in this case is to examine oneself before blaming others. Ren is achieved through introspective discipline and moral communication. These are the qualities Mencius expected of state kings in their practice of government and of you shui in their persuasive activities.

(3) *Xin*, the Affective Domain. For Mencius, ren could not be understood and achieved through cognition alone. He located ren in the affective domain, the heart, or *xin* 心, in Chinese. In his words, "benevolence is the heart of human and righteousness is their path" (M 6a.11.267). Furthermore, in Mencius's view, one's heart and human feelings of shame, respect, and justice breed virtues. In his words, "The heart of compassion pertains to benevolence, the heart of shame to dutifulness, the heart of respect to the observance of the rites, and the heart of right and wrong to wisdom" (Lau 6a.6.163). According to Mencius, an act of true benevolence is rooted in one's heart; it does not derive from external pressures or the desire for fame. True benevolence is a voluntary act entailing compassion, sympathy, and empathy. For example, in a situation where one sees a child falling into a well, one is moved not out of a desire to win the praise of others, nor yet because one dislikes the cry of the child, but because one possesses a heart of compassion (M 2a.6. 74). It is this heart of compassion, along with shame, courtesy, modesty, and a sense of right and wrong, that makes us humans with the potential to be virtuous. Accordingly, as Garrett (1993b) pointed out, the cultivation of heart through education, self-examination, and manipulation of material environment and cultural symbols is crucial to the conformity of moral principles in ancient China. With the qualities of heart in the right place, a person can develop the virtues of ren.

In the Greek tradition, Greek sophists such as Protagoras and Gorgias had also held an optimistic outlook on pathos in molding humanistic and rationalistic behavior of humans. However, in Plato's view, pathos or emotion was the cause of evil and basis of manipulation. He refused to see any positive values in cultivating emotions and condemned Greek sophists for their expression and articulation of emotions in persuasion and human affairs.[16] Furthermore, Plato demarcated feeling and thinking as two separate domains. Thinking held a superior position to feeling; emotions were considered less reliable than reason in forming judgments. For Mencius, in contrast, the heart not only feels, it also thinks and guides the behavior of a person. Just as wisdom and benevolence cannot be separated, feeling and thinking cannot be taken apart. In Mencius's view, benevolence, righteousness, propriety, and wisdom, while rooted in one's heart, also manifest in one's verbal and nonverbal behavior as well as one's physicality (M 7a.21.311). In a word, emotion, for Mencius, is inherently connected to morality and rationality as an essential component of human beings. This is why, as Garrett observes, in the Chinese tradition "both affective and cognitive functions are equally valuable and valued" (1993b, 33).

Rhetorical Perspectives

Like Confucius, Mencius never explicitly formulated a theory of language; yet he was very much aware of the impact of language. In his view, words and speech, depending upon their usage, can nourish or violate ren. In general, Mencius's rhetorical perspective consists of five components: moral speech, sincere speech, qi (energy), understanding types of language, and bian (argumentation).

(1) Moral Speech: *Shan Yan, Ren Yan, Shi Yan*. In order to create a nurturing environment where ren could flourish, Mencius proposed the practice of *shan yan* 善言 (good speech), *ren yan* 仁言 (benevolent speech), and *shi yan* 實言 (substantial speech, speech based on reality). Shan yan, according to Mencius, was simple speech, easy to understand but with far-reaching significance. It was the language of junzi, whose seemingly trivial statements were infused with virtue and wisdom. Thus, shan yan was simple in form but profound in meaning. It was the speech of morality and wisdom, not derived from high-sounding abstract notions but generated from daily living and common sense, providing worldviews, principles, and guidance for living an ethical life.

Regarding the term *ren yan*, Mencius offered no explicit definition. He did, however, argue for conformity between ren (benevolence), li (rites), and yi (righteousness). For Mencius, ren yan, when applied to the ruler, meant persuading him to practice benevolent and just government by pointing out shortcomings and inconsistencies with courtesy and respect (M 4a.1. 149–50). For ren yan to be effective, one's audience must be ren-hearted. Those who are not ren-hearted will not be moved, inspired, or persuaded by ren yan. It is futile to talk to such people (4a.8.158; 4a.10.161). In his own experience as a you shui, Mencius once refused to meet the king of Qi simply because he did not perceive him as a benevolent man. Likewise, Mencius refused to answer a question put to him by Teng Geng because he believed Teng was guilty of violating the principles of ren (2b.12.99; 7a.43.324).

Mencius developed the Confucian notion of ming by proposing the practice of shi yan (reality-based speech). Mencius argued that speech lacking in substance and disconnected from reality would be misleading and lead to misfortune. Those who used such speech should be made accountable for the blind benevolence they perpetuated (4b.17.182). For Mencius, shi yan entailed the use of language to represent and transform reality in a moral way.

(2) Sincere Speech. In Mencius's time, he had been distressed by certain you shui who employed the tactics of manipulation and deception to achieve their persuasive ends. To counter such dishonest method, Mencius proposed *cheng yan* 誠言 (sincere speech), arguing that it was the most effective, moral, and humane mode of expression to accomplish persuasion. Mencius had borrowed the concept of *cheng* 誠 from *Zhong Yong*, a text reportedly written by his teacher Zi Si, in which *cheng* was described in ontological terms as that from which the universe and social world came to being. It was also described as a virtue one must cultivate in one's life in order to attain one's true nature as a human being. When one reached *zhi cheng* 至誠 (the ultimate state of sincerity) one would automatically influence and move others through speech and action.

Since the primary purpose of shan yan, ren yan, and shi yan was to make people realize their innate human goodness, the notion of cheng yan was central to Mencius's theory of speech and persuasion. In his work Mencius highlighted the persuasive power of cheng yan, claiming, "There has never been a case when total sincerity cannot move others. Without sincerity, one cannot move others" (M 4a.12.161). Thus, for Mencius, cheng yan referred not only to sincere and honest speech, but also to an innate moral quality out of which sincere and honest speech naturally and powerfully arise in our efforts to influence one another. Therefore, his understanding of cheng yan was similar to Aristotle's notion of ethos, in that cheng yan is an indication of ethos and serves as the most effective means of persuasion. In this sense, cheng and cheng yan were both the means to an end and the end itself of communication. Indeed, when a speaker was perceived to be sincere and credible, he or she would be more likely to move the audience's heart and elevate the audience's soul to a spiritual and moral level. Mencius himself had demonstrated an engagement with cheng and cheng yan in his own rhetorical activities both in attempting to persuade the rulers to practice benevolent government and in defense of Confucianism.

(3) *Qi*. Another important concept that Mencius believed added to the effectiveness of speech was *qi* 氣. In Chinese, *qi* literally means the air filling up the universe and one's body which makes one breath. It was defined by Liezi as a single stuff pervading and cultivating all the living things in the universe (*Liezi "tianrui"*). While qi, as the driving spiritual force for the universe, forms the basic substance of the physical world, so it can create moral energy, becoming a driving force for moral conduct. It was this latter meaning about which Mencius was most concerned.

Mencius believed that a good speaker possessed qi and that good speech derived from the cultivation of qi. In this regard, he once described himself as follows: "I understand speech. I am good at cultivating my *qi*." When asked to define *qi*, he replied: "It is vast and tenacious. One must cultivate it with correct approach without harming it. It will fill the world and is embedded in righteousness and the Way. Otherwise, it will not have power. *Qi* is the accumulation of righteous acts and cannot be formulated by one or two just acts" (*M* 2a.2.60). Given these remarks, it would appear that, for Mencius, qi was the moral quality acting upon one's mind which gave power to one's speech. In Li Jianzhao's opinion, "*Qi* refers to the mind. Nourishing *qi* refers to the practice of cultivating mind, so that the mind is occupied with righteousness and morality. Speeches are powerful in the context of such a mind and powerless without it" (1981, 153).

(4) Understanding Types of Language. The understanding of speech, or *zhi yan* 知言 (knowing words), for Mencius, has two components. One is the knowledge level of the speaker and the other is the critical ability of the speaker. For Mencius, the function of a successful speech was a good grasp of knowledge in all subjects. Consequently, he advised his disciples: "Learn widely and go into what you have learned in detail so that in the end you can return to the essential" (Lau 4b.15.130). In other words, a knowledgeable person speaks clearly and concisely. More importantly, he or she is able to see both sides of an argument and provide more convincing examples.

By all accounts, Mencius was an eloquent speaker as well as a rhetorical critic. For him, understanding speech entailed more than knowing how to use language oneself; it also meant having the ability to evaluate the use of language by others critically. When Gong-sun Chou asked, "What do you mean by saying that you understand whatever words you hear?" Mencius replied: "From biased words I can see wherein the speaker is blind; from immoderate words, wherein he is ensnared; from heretical words, wherein he has strayed from the right path; from evasive words, wherein he is at his wits' end" (2a.2.78). Like Confucius, Mencius believed that a speaker's morality was revealed through his use of language. *Bi ci* 詖辭 (biased words), *yin ci* 淫辭 (immoderate words), *xie ci* 邪辭 (heretical words), and *dun ci* 遁辭 (evasive words) revealed a person's prejudice, polarization, distortion, or lack of substance, respectively. Mencius advised his students to avoid these four types of language so that they might clean up any unwholesomeness in their environment, accumulate qi, and restore their innate good-heartedness in order to practice ren.

(5) Bian. Mencius did not condemn the practice of persuasion and argumentation. In fact, he considered himself "fond of argument." In his time, Yang Zhu's 楊朱 theory of egoism and Mo Di's 墨翟 [Mozi] ideal of "mutual love" were popular doctrines competing with Confucian principles. Mencius considered such doctrines deceptive and feared they would lead people to harmful actions, saying "If the doctrine of Yang and Mo is not put down, the doctrine of Confucius will not be known, the common people will be deceived by heresies and the path of benevolence will be blocked. When the path of benevolence is blocked, it is like animals eating humans and before long humans will eat humans" (3b.9.141–142). For Mencius, bian served three purposes: 1) to defend ren, the core of Confucianism; 2) to restore human nature by rectifying their hearts and sense of justice; and 3) to argue against heresies and prevent them from spreading. As Mencius stated in this regard: "Because I am concerned with the problem. I must safeguard the way of the former sages, argue against the doctrines of Yang and Mo, and put down biased views. In this way, advocates of heresies will not become influential. . . . I want to rectify the human hearts, eliminate heresies, oppose extreme actions, and put down biased views" (3b.9.142). Indeed, Mencius was an excellent bian shi, using bian to argue against his opponent, defend Confucian principles, and teach the rulers about benevolent government. In this sense, Mencius was not much different from Aristotle, who taught that there were four purposes to rhetoric: namely, to defend truth, teach, argue from both sides of an issue, and defend oneself (*Rhetoric* 1355a25).

In the effort to persuade people to realize ren, Mencius was concerned with the relationship between the speaker and the audience. For him, communication was a cooperative effort involving both parties. If either party did not make a sincere effort, real communication was not possible. Mencius applauded Bai Lixi, who left the employ of the ruler of Yu in order to serve Duke Mu of Qin after determining that the former was incapable of listening to him, while the latter was capable of heeding his advice (M 5a.9.225–26). For those who did not practice ren, according to Mencius, communication could hardly take place. Talking about benevolence to those lacking a benevolent heart was an exercise in futility.

For Mencius, bian shi and you shui should refuse to serve any ruler deemed unworthy of their services. If one's advice in either capacity was not put into practice, he should leave no matter how well treated in other respects. Here Mencius advocated making a moral choice. Given that only a benevolent ruler could be persuaded by benevolent speech, hence benefiting the people, a good adviser should be guided by moral principles. According to Mencius, "A gentleman should never give up practicing righteousness, whether he is successful or is destitute. If he is successful, he should bring benefits to people. If he cannot fulfill his ambition, he should cultivate his spirit" (7a.9.305).[17] Judging from this and other examples, it would appear that Mencius generally held imperial advisers in higher regard than the rulers themselves. He tended to blame the rulers for negative consequences and encourage the advisers to take the higher moral ground.

Rhetorical Styles

Mencius was a great bian shi and a master of language. His rhetorical style varied from analogical to deductive reasoning, from narrative to dialogue, from definition to comparison. Four features of rhetorical style are prominently displayed in his book: metaphors and analogies, moral appeals, rational argument, and dialogues.

(1) Metaphors and Analogies. Like Confucius, Mencius valued metaphorical and analogical thinking as much as rational thinking. The text of *Mengzi* is rich in parables, metaphors, analogies, and witty sayings. The use of these devices was extensive, ranging in context from explanations of abstract notions to interpersonal encounters with state kings. For example, Mencius compared innate human goodness with the natural downward flow of water. Elsewhere, he compared the value of ren with ripe crops, used floating fish to symbolize life, and used bare feet standing still to symbolize righteousness. He also used analogy to explain to King Xiang of Liang how his people were like crops suffering from draught and were in need of being rescued by a benevolent ruler.[18] To illustrate the important point that human nature is innately good, but artificially violated, Mencius used the following analogy:

There used to be abundant trees on the Ox Mountain. Because the mountain is situated by the city, we always see people cutting trees with axes. How can the trees maintain abundant? However, day by day, trees are growing with the nourishment from the rain. It is not because there are no new shoots growing, it is because people leave cattle and sheep on the mountain, which makes the mountain bold. When people see the boldness of the mountain, they think there have never been trees growing on the mountain while they forget the true nature of the mountain. Do humans lack benevolence and righteousness in nature? They simply have lost their conscience just like trees are being chopped by axes. . . . (M 6a.8.262)

In this example, Mencius asserts the inherent goodness of humanity, arguing that due to bad influences in the external environment, we lose our hearts and turn toward evil just as the trees lose their abundance and beauty. However, like the new shoots after a morning rain, human beings can find hope in reshaping their hearts. The notion of innate human goodness was unpopular during Mencius's time, since selfish acts were common and evil seemed to prevail. Using the analogy of the trees made the notion seem more plausible and helped promote an optimistic outlook for the future.

(2) Moral Appeals. Although Mencius's arguments were predominantly characterized by an extensive use of parables, examples, and analogies that served to explain abstract concepts and provide meanings for life, scholars of Mencius have argued that his arguments also demonstrated a skillful use of deductive inference (Resnik 1968; Verwighen 1967). In my opinion, such inference was made through an integration of moral and practical appeals perhaps best demonstrated by Mencius's persuasion of state kings on the topic of *ren zheng* 仁政 (benevolent government).

In Mencius's time, state kings often gained political power by exploiting their own people. Mencius believed that such unvirtuous actions toward one's subjects would lead to the downfall of the kingdom. He argued that the three dynasties (the Xia, Shang, and Zhou dynasties) had at first prevailed by practicing benevolent government and had subsequently lost their rule by cruelty to their people. The same could be said regarding the rise and fall, survival and collapse of all other states (M 4a.3.153). In the following example, Mencius tried to convey this message to King Hui of Liang: "If you practice benevolence toward your own people by reducing penalties and taxation and by allowing them to plough deeply and weed promptly, and if your people are filial to their parents, respect their brothers, and are faithful to their words, your people can serve their fathers and elder brothers at home and their superiors at work. They can even defeat the troops of Chu armed with strong armor and sharp weapons by wooden clubs" (M 1a.5.11).

Mencius believed that those who practiced benevolent government would exert greater influence and persuasive power, have no match in facing the enemy, and win the support of the people both within and outside their own state. He observed, "When people are made to submit to force, they do not obey the rulers by heart. When people are made to submit to virtue, they will be happy and honestly obey the rulers" (2a.3.69). The concepts of ren and ren zheng provide the foundation for such examples, since, for Mencius, following ren and practicing ren zheng would lead to the stability and success of the state. With the practice of ren zheng, a state could prosper; without it, a state would decline in influence and prosperity. Therefore, the act of persuasion should be a thorough understanding of ren as well as of the relationship between cause and effect from the standpoint of moral concerns.

(3) Rational Argument. Other features of rational argument were also evident in *Mencius*. For example, in his argument with Gaozi on the topic of human nature, Mencius introduced the practice of zhi lei 知類 (knowing the category):

Gaozi: The inborn nature is human nature.

Mencius: The inborn nature is human nature. Does this mean all the things of white color are called whiteness?

Gaozi: Yes.

Mencius: So the whiteness of white feathers is the same as the whiteness of white snow and the whiteness of white snow is the same as the whiteness of white jade?

Gaozi: Yes.

Mencius: In that case, is the dog nature the same as the ox nature and is the ox nature the same as the human nature? (6a.3.253).

In this example, Mencius first establishes argument with Gaozi on the meaning of nature with respect to whiteness and then subsequently uses the same categorical procedure to generate an absurd conclusion, thereby proving that Gaozi's argument was wrong. The practice of using what is known to generate what is not known is referred to as *tui* 推 (inference) in classical Chinese. Mencius employed this rhetorical device, for example, when advising King Xuan of Qi that his pity and mercy for animals were indications of a benevolent heart, as well as when predicting, based on the evidence of the emergence of sages in history, that every five hundred years a new sage would emerge (*M* 1a.7.14–15; 7b.38.351). Another rational concept used by Mencius was *gu* 故 (cause and because). As he explained,

"People in the world talk about human nature. If they can find the causes and infer the becauses [of the human nature], they follow the basics of the natural law (4b.26.190). In this case, gu provides the basis for making predictions. Once information regarding causal relationships is known, new theories can be generated through tui. As these examples indicate, though Mencius did not offer a systematic framework of rational argument, he was clearly aware of the criteria for establishing such an argument.

(4) Dialogue. One of the more obvious rhetorical features employed by Mencius was dialogue. Whether in his persuasion, argumentation, or teaching, Mencius enjoyed the give and take of questions and answers. His approach to asking questions was similar to Plato's in that the questioner was already in possession of the answer, yet invited his partner in dialogue to define his terms and examples as a strategy for reaching common ground. The following dialogue between Mencius and the king of Liang is an example of this approach:

The king: I am very happy to be advised by you.
Mencius: Is there any difference between killing a person with a club and killing a person with a sharp knife?
The king: There is no difference.
Mencius: Is there any difference between killing people with a knife and killing people with tyranny?
The king: There is no difference.
Mencius: Now you have fat meat in your kitchen and strong horses in your stable, but your people are starving and dying in the wild. . . . (1a.4.9)

By describing the suffering of the people and relating this suffering to different degrees of neglect and violence, Mencius led the king to agree that he was actually killing his own people by his misrule. Such dialogues often ended with Mencius preaching on matters of moral obligation and practical need to his chastised and silent audience (the ruler).

In sum, similar to those of Confucius, Mencius's sense of speech and conceptualization of yan, ci, and bian were rooted in the philosophy of ren. What is more, Mencius expanded and reinforced Confucian moral doctrines through his appeals to Heaven and assertions of innate human goodness. Mencius maintained that a good bian shi should practice persuasion with sincerity. More importantly, one should cultivate one's qi, practice benevolence, observe propriety, and adhere to righteousness. Furthermore, one should be willing to sacrifice his own interests in preserving one's integrity and moral principles as well as in guarding against perversion and distortion in the use of language. By so doing, one's words would attain persuasive power and effect. Mencius demonstrated these qualities of a bian shi in his own rhetorical activities. His eloquence is best revealed through his artistic use of metaphors and analogies, good sense of rational argument, and effective style of questioning.

Xunzi

Social Context and Personal Background

Recognized as one of the three most influential thinkers in the School of Confucianism, and compared to Aristotle in the West (Fung 1952; Oliver 1971), Xunzi contributed theories of philosophy and argumentation with perhaps more impact on Chinese culture and history than any other historical figure. Xunzi, whose name was actually Xun Kuang 荀況, lived toward the end of the Warring States period. In his lifetime, he witnessed the corruption and misrule of state kings, the greed and aggression of ministers, and the vulgar manner of certain you shui whose persuasive efforts were often at the expense of morality. As recorded in the last book of *Xunzi*, possibly written by his students, "Xun Qing [Xunzi] was oppressed by a chaotic age and lived under the intimidating threat of stern punishments. On the one hand there were no worthy rulers, and on the other hand he faced the aggression of Qin. Ritual and moral principles were not observed. The transforming efforts of teaching were not brought to completion. The humane [ren] were degraded and under constraint. The whole world was lost in darkness" (Knoblock, Eulogy, 269).[19] In Xunzi's time, the disorder and anarchy in the world were much worse than in the time of Confucius. Although Xunzi shared with Confucius and Mencius a belief in certain basic moral principles, he differed from the other two thinkers in his approach to and perception of social problems. Unlike Confucius and Mencius, who proposed moral solutions to such problems and expressed faith in human nature, Xunzi advocated the imposition of external forces on individuals and society by the ruling class in order to establish a hierarchy of order. In addition, he was more realistic and even somewhat cynical in his view of human nature. Xunzi's philosophy and worldview strongly influenced his students Han Feizi 韓非子 and Li Si 李斯, who subsequently became Legalists, assisting the king of Qin with the unification of China in 221 B.C.E.

Xunzi lived in a world that valued diversity and yet at the same time evidenced a tendency to integrate various thoughts. This state of affairs required thinkers not only to articulate their own philosophical views but also to be familiar with other schools of thoughts. Consequently, according to Knoblock, "[Xunzi] was obliged to master the doctrines of the many schools, the form of argumentation, and the techniques of rhetoric at which the *Jixia* scholars excelled" (1988, 4). Indeed, Xunzi was influenced by all the schools of thought that preceded him. Though in general regarded as a Confucian, his body of work demonstrated a mixture of the Confucian, Daoist, Mohist, and Legalist ideas flourished at the time. Like Aristotle, Xunzi not only adopted valuable thoughts from his predecessors, including Mencius, but also challenged them. Of all his predecessors, the only one he seemed to hold in high regard was Confucius.

According to *Shi Ji*, Xunzi was originally from the state of Zhao. At the age of fifty he became affiliated with the Jixia Academy, and he eventually was recognized as its most eminent teacher. While in the state of Qi where the Jixia Academy was located, Xunzi three times performed the wine sacrifice, the highest honor in the ceremony of ancestor worship. It was while teaching at the Academy that he met most of his opponents, debating with them on philosophical and political issues and defending Confucianism. He often gave lectures at the Academy, and his philosophy influenced many people of his time as well as subsequent dynasties. As the object of slanderous attacks, and having failed to influence the king of Qi on important policies, Xunzi left Qi and traveled to the state of Chu. The lord of Chun Shen, the chief minister of Chu, appointed him magistrate in Lan-ling (in today's Shangdon province). After the death of Chun Shen, Xunzi was asked to leave his office. He subsequently lived in Lan-ling, teaching and writing for the rest of his years.

The text *Xunzi* consists of thirty-two books and is believed to have been written by Xunzi himself with the exception of the last five books. The text is comprehensive on the topics of morality, politics, human nature, epistemology, and speech and argumentation. Furthermore, although the notions of yan, ming, ci, bian, and shuo had been discussed elsewhere by Mingjia, Confucianists, Daoists, and Mohists preceding Xunzi, he offered the most innovative and systematic framework of speech, persuasion, and argumentation for his time.

Philosophical Views

Xunzi covered more philosophical ground than Confucius and Mencius, expressing his views on subjects ranging from morality to human nature, from politics to epistemology. For our purposes, we will discuss his views on li 禮 (rites), human nature, and Dao 道 (the Way).

(1) Li. Following Confucius and Mencius, Xunzi held a strong belief in the doctrine of ren, sharing with his two predecessors the notion that a person of ren heart would naturally possess all the human qualities and act as a moral example for the common people. According to Xunzi, a person of ren possesses the qualities of "loyalty, trustworthiness, straightforwardness, diligence, an unwillingness to cause harm or injury, and treating everyone the same" (Knoblock 13.7.203). While Confucius proposed the notions of ren and li, and Mencius was primarily interested in ren zheng (benevolent government), Xunzi emphasized the fulfillment of ren by observing li. In his words, "Humane behavior [ren] is the manifestation of love, and thus it is expressed in one's treatment of relatives. Morality [yi] is the manifestation of natural order and thus it is expressed in one's conduct. Ritual principles [li] are the manifestation of measured moderation, and thus they are expressed in the perfection of things" (27.21.212).

In Xunzi's view, li was an effective means of establishing hierarchical order as it served the function of rectifying behavior at the individual level, maintaining class distinction at the social level, assuring stability and power at the political level, and promoting sound reasoning at the rational level. At the individual level, by following the principles of li, a person would become cultured, harmony would be reached, and one's activities would be put into order. By following the principles of li, a clear class distinction could be made between nobility and baseness, between old and young, between those of wealth and those of poverty, between those of importance and those of insignificance (10.3a.122). By following the principles of li, a person was unlikely to be deceived or fooled by false doctrines (15.4.229); thus, society would be orderly with everyone knowing his/her place and acting accordingly. By following the principles of li, a state would gain its strength, authority, and power. Without the observation of li, one's action would become unreasonable, offensive, obstinate, and savage (2.2.152); likewise, a state would be weakened and ruined eventually.

For Xunzi, "ritual principles [li] are the ridgepole of the Way of Man. This being so, those who do not model themselves after ritual and are not satisfied with ritual principles are called people who lack any method or standard" (19.2d,61).[20] In other words, li is a prescribed way of moral, cultured, and civilized living and governing, and provides a cultural framework by which people make sense of their world, relate to others, and find their identities. It is for this reason that "a man without ritual will not live; . . . a nation without ritual will not be tranquil" (2.2.153). As these examples illustrate, Xunzi sought more concrete ways of cultivating a self and constructing an orderly society than did Confucius or Mencius. He taught that the observation of li should be implemented by kings and facilitated by junzi rather than through a conscious choice on the part of individual subjects desiring to perfect themselves. Xunzi's concept of li, understood in the context of tight political and social controls, was later developed by his student Han Feizi into the notion of *fa* 法 (law).

(2) Human Nature. Another area in which Xunzi differed from Confucius and Mencius was his view of human nature. For example, Xunzi was critical of Mencius for failing to make a clear distinction between "inborn nature" and "acquired nature." According to Xunzi, inborn nature is "what cannot be gained by learning and cannot be mastered by application yet is found in man." Acquired nature, on the other hand, is that which can be gained and mastered, such as ritual principles and moral duties (23.1c.152). Given the prevalence of evil in Xunzi's lifetime, it is not surprising that he concluded that "Human nature is evil; any good in humans is acquired by conscious exertion" (23.1a.150). According to Xunzi, humans are born with the desire for profit, the tendency toward greed and aggressiveness, and a habit of envy and hatred. If man's evil nature is allowed to grow and develop, society will be in disorder and class distinctions will be violated. The way to combat such evil is to be guided by the principles of li and good role models. Humankind must constantly fight against its evil nature by seeking education, proper training, and a good environment. To reinforce this point, Xunzi offers the example of Yao and Yu, who became sage kings, not because they were born with goodness, but rather because they "rose up by transforming their old selves, [and were] brought . . . to perfection through cultivation and conscious exertion . . ." (4.10.192).

(3) Dao. For Xunzi, Dao was not a mystical or metaphysical concept as envisioned by Laozi and Zhuangzi; rather it referred to correct thinking—in other words, to the sage ability to make decisions based on comprehensive knowledge and diverse perspectives. In his words, the person of a Dao mind "can perceive all within the four seas" while sitting in the house; "lives in the present" but "can put in its proper place what is remote in space and distant in time past"; and "knows their essential qualities" through "penetrating into and inspecting the myriad things" (21.5e.105). Being influenced by Daoism of his time, however, Xunzi also made a connection between the Dao and the heart (mind), claiming that to be able to absorb diverse perspectives and break away from blindness, one needs to find stillness, emptiness, and concentration in one's heart (mind). Xunzi referred to this state as "the Great Pure Understanding." For Xunzi, not everyone was capable of achieving such a heightened state. In fact, only a sage such as Confucius who was free from attachment to one side of the

truth or another was able to see the Dao. The moral duty of a junzi, then, was to defend truth by opening to more perspectives and arguing from all sides. Though a comprehensive worldview was not easy to achieve, nonetheless, Xunzi argued for the necessity of integrating diverse perspectives through open-mindedness and cooperation. Indeed, while he was at the Jixia Academy, unlike Mencius who ardently defended and argued for a Confucian position, Xunzi attempted to integrate diverse thoughts and value different perspectives.

Rhetorical Perspectives

In response to the rhetorical shortcomings of you shui and bian shi of his time, Xunzi formulated a more extensive and complete theory of ming and bian than had his predecessors. The following discussion of Xunzi's rhetorical perspective will be divided into three parts: criticism of bian shi, rectification of names, and a discussion of bian.

(1) Criticism of Bian Shi. Xunzi lived during a time when *ru* 儒 (teacher, educated people) were given the opportunity to express their thoughts freely as well as to travel freely between the various states offering advice to the kings. Xunzi divided these ru into *su ru* 俗儒 (vulgar ru) and *ya ru* 雅儒 (elegant ru). Su ru dressed casually, dogmatically repeated doctrines, blindly served their superiors, and took previous kings as models. Ya ru, on the other hand, took later kings as models, held to moral principles, were honest about what they knew and did not know, and were more original in their thinking. Xunzi further classified ru into *xiao ru* 小儒 (small ru) and *da ru* 大儒 (great ru). According to him, xiao ru were fond of learning, community oriented, cultivated, and talented. Da ru, on the other hand, had internalized knowledge and principles of rites; made judgments by categories and classification; and spoke and acted with ease, refinement, and spontaneity (8.10.79–80; 8.12.83). Unlike Confucius and Mencius, who blamed xiao ren for all evil doings, Xunzi specifically targeted su ru and xiao ru, accusing them of causing confusion and disorder through their speech. On this point he did not mince words, saying "Some men of the present generation cloak pernicious persuasion in beautiful language and present elegantly composed but treacherous doctrines and so create disorder and anarchy in the world. Such men are personally insidious and ostentatious, conceited and vulgar, yet they spread through the whole world their confused ignorance of wherein lies the distinction between right and wrong and between order and anarchy" (6.1.222–23). In this regard, Xunzi singled out Ta Xiao 它囂 and Wei Mou 魏牟 for indulging in overly emotional speech behavior; condemned Mo Di 墨翟 and Song Xing 宋鈃 for advocat-

ing frugality and utility and overlooking social status; criticized Shen Dao 慎到 and Tian Pian 田駢 for their grandiose style, lacking in substance; and attacked Hui Shi 惠施 and Deng Xi 鄧析 for their useless and absurd propositions. Finally, he blamed Confucianist Zi Si 子思 and Mencius for developing and spreading theories without a thorough understanding of their guiding principles (6.2–6; 7.223–24). In Xunzi's opinion, the above were examples of su ru who were educated, eloquent, and persuasive, yet lacking in the qualities of ya ru and da ru. Though they were good speakers, he considered them morally harmful and socially destructive. Clearly, Xunzi was in agreement with Confucius and Mencius on the point that though a good person speaks well, one who speaks well is not necessarily a good person. On the other hand, he parted company with Confucius and Mencius in his greater willingness to advance new theories at the expense of old principles, as well as in his willingness to criticize the past and his contemporaries rather than protecting traditional values.

Xunzi attacked virtually all the well-known bian shi and you shui of his time, condemning them for using treacherous and evil speech to deceive and confuse the public. At the same time, he attributed the problem to a tendency of the human mind to be blind (bi 蔽) to reality, claiming "It is the common flaw of men to be blinded by some small point of the truth and to shut their minds to [da li 大理] the Great Ordering Principles" (21.1.100).[21] This blindness meant seeing only one side of the story or being obsessed with what one believed to be true without further exploration of the matter. According to Xunzi, certain bian shi, such as Mo Di, Song Xing, and Shen Dao, were blinded by one perspective, thereby overlooking other perspectives, causing disorder in society, and preventing people from seeing the whole truth, or Dao 道 (the Way).

(2) Rectification of Names. As Xunzi lived in a time of cultural transition and philosophical disputation, there was much disagreement and confusion in the use of language. In Xunzi's opinion, speech and doctrines offered by su ru and xiao ru were examples of jian yan 奸言 (treacherous speech), e yan 惡言 (evil speech), and liu yan 流言 (rumor). Xunzi was very concerned about the situation, saying "strange propositions have sprung up, names and their realities have become confused, and the boundary between right and wrong has become unclear" (22.2a.128). Consequently, Xunzi believed that there was a strong need for the rectification of names in order to make them truly representative of reality. Unlike Confucius, whose primary concern in rectifying names was the transformation of reality, Xunzi's primary concern was with the maintenance and reinforcement of a hierarchical social order, ritual principles, and political power. He was also concerned with

the question of how shared meaning could be achieved in the communication process.

According to Xunzi, the rectification of names should be enacted through political means. A wise king should institute and supervise the correct use of names, punishing those who create their own names and thereby bring confusion to the public mind. By so doing, treacherous speech, evil speech, and odd propositions can be prevented; the political order can be maintained. Xunzi attempted to reassure his audience on this point by enumerating the positive outcomes of these measures. In his words, "Since none dare avail themselves of odd propositions to bring confusion to the correct use of names, his [the king's] people are thus united in adhering to his laws and meticulously follow their orders. When such a situation prevails, his legacy will long endure. To have one's legacy endure and one's meritorious accomplishments brought to completion is the epitome of good government. These are the results of being assiduous in seeing that agreed upon names are observed" (22.1c.128). Strictly speaking, it should be noted that Xunzi spoke for the ruling class. The rectification of names was intended to enforce the use of language under the ruler's supervision and control as well as to deprive his subjects of the right to freedom of speech.

Indeed, Xunzi was an apologist for the feudal order in which he lived, advocating a clear class distinction in society. For him, the rectification of names served the purpose of making social distinctions in official and economic status. Each title or name—such as king, minister, or farmer—carried with it a distinction of nobility or baseness, privilege or disadvantage, wealth or poverty that could not and should not be violated. According to Xunzi, dividing people socially by linguistic terms facilitated the public communication between the ruler and the masses. In his words, "When the noble and base are clear and the same and different are kept apart, conveying intention is no longer frustrated through a failure to explain, and carrying out duties no longer suffers from being hampered and obstructed. This is the purpose of having names" (22.2b.129). Here, the rectification of names served as a rational method for making social distinctions and promoting effective public communication. In this respect, Xunzi shared with Confucius a concern for morality and social stability, a distrust for less educated and economically disadvantaged people, and faith in sage kings and social elites. As A. S. Cua remarks: "In propounding his doctrine of rectification of terms, Hsun Tzu [Xunzi], like Confucius, is mainly concerned with the uniformity of human conduct under the government of a sage king or morally enlightened political authority. Rectification of terms is ultimately a matter of rectification of moral faults and misconduct and not merely a matter of avoidance of logical or linguistic errors" (1985, 1).

In my view, Cua's remark is not entirely fair to Xunzi. Xunzi did, in fact, have a logical and linguistic concern for the rectification of names and was well aware that names are given out of conventional agreement. In his words, "Names have no intrinsic object. They are bound to some reality by agreement in order to name that object. The object becomes fixed, the custom is established, and it is called the name of that object" (Knoblock 22.2g.130–31). Clearly, Xunzi was aware that language represents reality but is not reality itself. Rather, the connection between names and objects is arbitrary and customarily accepted by agreement. If names are used in an agreed upon manner, communication takes place. Otherwise misunderstandings and confusions are likely to occur. Further, Xunzi argued that certain speakers tend to commit fallacies in their arguments by taking advantage of the name agreement deliberately to confuse people, identifying three situations in which names are used to confuse the audience. The first situation involves playing with words that seemingly share similar meaning to refer to different situations; this is illustrated in the following statement made by Later Mohists: "to kill a robber is not to kill a man." Although the word *kill* is used in two places in the sentence and shares the same semantic meaning, "to kill a robber" and "to kill a man" may refer to different realities with pragmatically different meanings. In the second situation, the misuse of names involves using names that represent only a partial reality to represent the whole, such as in the statement "mountain and marshes are level," by Hui Shi. For Xunzi, Hui Shi's fallacy was that he presented the statement as the absolute truth regarding how mountains and marshes are situated, while, in fact, only in certain places are mountains and marshes at the same level. The third case involves the confusion caused by the abuse of names, for example, in the claim "a white horse is not a horse," by Gong-sun Long. The claim distorts reality by twisting the use of names, since, in reality, a white horse is a kind of horse.

Xunzi proposed five solutions to the confusion of names and objects illustrated by the above cases. First, one must be aware that some things are different in substance though they share the same name and consequently appear to be the same. There are also times, according to Xunzi, when names may appear to be different though, in reality, they are of the same substance. The second way to detect fallacy is to determine whether a statement is applicable and in accord with reality. This requires investigation or research into the case in question. The third solution proposed by Xunzi is to examine the statement against the principles of agreement between names and objects. That is, to examine the basis of agreement regarding the meaning of certain words and concepts. The fourth solution is to distinguish between the correct and incorrect use of names and then to take institutional measures to rectify incorrect ones. The final solution involves skillfully refuting, through persuasion and counterargument, those statements proposed by one's opponents (22.2h–22.3d.131–32). All these solutions with the exception of the last one were concrete suggestions made to the ruler in order to assist him in maintaining a stable government. In contrast, the last solution focused responsibility on junzi or bian shi of high morals, providing an enthymemic approach for arguing against the fallacies caused by the misuse of names. For Xunzi, such considerations and efforts to examine the use of language would further the cause of effective communication at the semantic and pragmatic level, ensuring that the ruler's policies and proclamations were understood and carried out without hindrance.

In addition to these linguistic and institutional approaches, Xunzi proposed a logical procedure for engaging in the naming process. In this regard, he classified three kinds of names: *dan ming* 單名 (single name), referring to cases where the name is sufficient to carry meaning (such as "child"); *fu ming* 復名 (compound name), referring to cases where the single name is not sufficient to carry the meaning (such as "big-child"); and *gong ming* 共名 (general name), referring to cases where single and compound names do not conflict (such as "people"). In the process of using names to refer to things, according to Xunzi,

one makes terms more general names, and from these generalized names one further [*tui* 推] generalizes until one reaches the point where there are no further generalizations to be drawn, and only then does one stop. There are other occasions when one wants to refer to things in part, so one refers to them as "birds" or "animals." "Birds" and "animals" are the names of the largest divisions of things. By extending the process, one [*tui*] draws further distinctions [*bie* 別] until there are no further distinctions to be made, and only then does one stop. (22.2f.130)

In this example, Xunzi makes the connection between language and rational thinking. In his analysis Xunzi applied elementary scientific methods of classification to the topic of communication. For example, he used the words *gong* 共 (general) and *bie* (particular) to discuss the relationship between genus (animal, bird) and species (particular animal or bird). In addition, he used the word *tui* (inference) in discussing inductive and deductive processes as well as for metaphorical and analogical thinking. Thus, while Xunzi maintained Confucius's model of zheng ming (the rectification of names), with its central concern for morality, power, order, and society, he advanced Confucius's notion to an abstract level through his focus on epistemology, logic, linguistics, and communication. Like Plato and Aristotle, Xunzi attempted to integrate rationality and morality into a cohesive worldview. Unlike Plato and Aristotle, Xunzi appeared not to have considered rationality a prerequisite for morality. Instead, for Xunzi, morality was a prerequisite for rationality. As he argued in his criticism of su ru and xiao ru, without morality, rational thinking has no place. It is one's sense of morality rather than the logical and rational process of reasoning that enables a person to distinguish between right and wrong.

(3) Bian. Xunzi was perhaps the first Chinese philosopher to offer a complete system of Chinese persuasion and argumentation, under the term *bian* 辯 (argumentation, disputation, distinction). In *Xunzi*, for example, he used the term *bian* over fifty times in reference to speech, eloquence, making distinctions, argumentation, and persuasion. In this context, Xunzi delineated three functions or purposes of bian and shuo 說 (explanation). First, they are used to explain right from wrong, connecting concepts with reality. Second, they serve the function of defining and naming for purposes of clarity and explanation. Third, they are expressions of ren and li from the heart (X 22.274).[22] Xunzi argued that junzi have a moral obligation to advocate and defend the principles of ren when encountering jian yan (treacherous speech), i.e., speech that is not modeled after sage kings and does not conform to ritual and moral principles. He repeatedly emphasized *junzi bi bian* 君子必辯 (a gentleman must argue and distinguish) (X 5.41).[23] Furthermore, he must "never grow wary of the principle of humanity, for he loves it in his innermost mind [heart], his actions find peace in it, and his joy is in discussing it" (Knoblock 5.9.210).[24]

While Confucius divided people into junzi and xiaoren on the basis of their speech and conduct, Xunzi stretched this dichotomy into three categories: sage, junzi, and xiaoren. He further identified three kinds of bian exhibited by these three groups. A sage argument was characterized by appropriateness in word choice, coherence and the use of classification in developing the argument, and flexibility in adapting to ever-changing situations. An argument presented by a junzi was characterized by clarity and coherence in developing the argument, practicality in adaptation, knowledge in all subjects, and conciseness in the use of language. The primary difference between an argument put forth by a sage and an argument put forth by a junzi was that the former required no preparation beforehand and was given spontaneously, while the latter was prepared in advance. Finally, an argument put forth by a xiaoren was characterized by embellishment, lying, a glib tongue, snobbishness, arrogance, and obnoxiousness.[26] For Xunzi, a person's character could be discerned by the content of his speech and how the speech was presented.

Xunzi maintained that the three groups also differed in their modes of argument, saying "A sage, though he speaks often, always observes the logical categories appropriate to what he discusses. A gentleman [junzi], though he speaks but seldom, always accords with the model. A petty man [xiaoren] speaks frequently but in a manner that does not adhere to the model, his thoughts drowning in the verbiage of his idle chatter even when he engages in the disciplined discourse of formal discrimination [bian]" (Knoblock 27.108.234–35). Furthermore, a good speech demonstrates a good balance of wisdom and eloquence. A bad speech exhibits artistic use of language and style but lacks an ethical foundation. A superb speech internalizes all the skills and moral principles required of a speaker.

The process of argumentation, according to Xunzi, was developed by *mingming* 命名 (naming), *qi* 期 (definition), *shuo* 說 (explanation), and *bian* 辯 (argumentation, distinction). Each stage was considered necessary in preparing for the next stage of an argument. As Xunzi explained, "It is when the object is not fully understood that it is 'named.' It is when the name still does not fully convey the meaning that it is defined. It is when the definition is not completely clear that it is explained. It is when the explanation is not fully understood that we employ dialectics [bian]" (22.3f.132). Xunzi defined *ci* 辭 as the proposition that connects different realities and expresses a coherent meaning. For him, communication takes place when propositions conform to explanations, explanations conform to heart, and heart conforms to the Way [Dao]. To make speech effective and argument persuasive, one must first have an ethical standard and the ability to enlighten and illuminate his audience. Next, one must reason by *lei* 類 (classifying) and *bie* 別 (distinguishing) and use *tui* 推 (inference) to draw conclusions. Finally, one must be able to convey meanings clearly by the use of language.

Xunzi was convinced that humans have the ability to recognize and explain the laws of the universe, as well as the relationship between things. That is to say, human beings have the ability to make logical references. This, Xunzi believed, was demonstrated in the activity of bian. In his words, "When we engage in *bian*, we should find out all the necessary means and exhaustive explanations of cause and because" (*bian ze jin gu* 辯則儘故) (X 22.274). Xunzi saw the process of making distinctions and inferences supported by examples as an effective way to present an argument. He stated, "As a general principle, what is to be prized in the presentation of a thesis is that there is consistency in the structure of the discrimination advanced to support it and that there is evidentiary support for the thesis which shows that the facts accord with the reality like the two halves of a tally" (Knoblock 23.3b.156). Elsewhere he stated more explicitly, "we should categorize and classify things; we can use one particular rule to apply to universal cases" (*yi lei xing za, yi yi xing wan* 以類行雜, 以一行萬) (*X* 9.86). Clearly, Xunzi was familiar with the process of rational reasoning through deduction and induction, although he never systematized the process as Aristotle had done. However, Xunzi's manner of presenting his own arguments in the text of *Xunzi* entailed the assertion of the universal moral principles of ren and li supported by abundant historical and hypothetical examples, as well as analogies and metaphors.

Xunzi failed to provide a clear structure for his linguistic system. His primary contributions were his conceptualization of ming and bian, featuring logic and rational argument and his articulation of standards for making distinctions, classifying, analyzing, and synthesizing moral arguments. As Cua summarizes, Xunzi set up "standards of argumentative competence. Apart from conceptual clarity, there are also requirements of logical consistency, coherence, respect for established linguistic practices, and a general accord with reasonable or rational justification" (1983, 886).

For Xunzi, bian was not mere intellectual activity; it was also moral and humane. Thus, a bian shi was no ordinary person, but a junzi, a person of high moral standard and a heart of ren. Xunzi believed that real persuasion could only take place when the speaker was a moral person. When engaging in a dialogue or attempting to persuade others, one must be sincere, honest, determined, confident, enthusiastic, and gentle. The speaker should employ methods of analogy and analysis in order to make his point understood. If he possesses the qualities of humaneness, receptivity, and knowledge of ren, he will naturally speak about ren. Consequently, his speech will be powerful and persuasive. For Xunzi, the most effective way of engaging in persuasion was through the integration of what Aristotle called ethos, pathos, and logos. According to Xunzi, to make a skillful argument, one should "introduce the topic with dignity and earnestness, dwell on it with modesty and sincerity, hold to it with firmness and strength, illustrate its meaning with parables and praiseworthy examples, elucidate its significance by making distinctions and drawing boundaries, and present it with exuberance and ardor. If you make something precious and rare, valuable and magical, your persuasion will always and invariably be well received . . ." (Knoblock 5.8.209).

Finally, Xunzi believed that a skillful argument entailed cooperation with one's audience. In his words, "He [the speaker] engages in argumentation, but not to the point of causing a quarrel. He is critical, but not to the point of provoking others. When he upholds an upright position, he is not merely interested in victory" (3.4.175). The purpose of making an argument is not to defeat others. Since the power of persuasion lies in the moral quality and cultural refinement of the speaker, when one shows sincerity and humanity, and when one's speech is refined, people will naturally be moved to his/her point of view. Those who are only interested in achieving victory over their audience will lose their audience. Likewise, Xunzi advised his readers not to argue with those who are in a contentious and quarrelsome mood (1.12.141). In his view, a good bian shi is never arrogant, verbally hurtful, or pretentious; rather, he has high moral and ethical standards and is worthy of the name *ya ru* or *da ru*.

To conclude this chapter, the three thinkers of Confucianism—Confucius, Mencius, and Xunzi—all shared a moral and humanistic view of language, persuasion, and argumentation. They were all concerned about the reconstruction of society and human development through the use of symbols. However, as they each lived in different cultural contexts involving different challenges, their rhetorical perspectives naturally had different emphases. Confucius showed more concern with the social impact of language; Mencius exhibited more interest in affective domain of persuasion; and Xunzi placed more emphasis on reason and logic. In the process of conceptualizing their senses and experiences with language, persuasion, and argumentation, the definitions of yan, ming, and bian were developed, modified, and extended by each thinker under consideration within the School of Confucianism. In this context, a sense of language, persuasion, and argumentation gradually developed from ming to bian, from morality to rationality, from individual to sociopolitical, and from abstract notions to concrete procedures and methods. From the time of Confucius to that of Xunzi, the concepts of ming bian became important elements in Chinese political, social, and cultural life. Finally, the conceptualizations of ming bian indicate much common ground between ancient Chinese and Greek thinkers on the role and function of speech as well as on the relationship between the speaker and the audience.

CHAPTER 7

Conceptualization of Ming Bian
The School of Mohism

While the School of Confucianism is well known and much studied in the West, few efforts have been made to study the School of Mohism, one of the influential schools of thought that coexisted with those of Mingjia, Confucianism, Daoism, and Legalism in the Spring-Autumn and Warring States period. This is because, first of all, Mohist texts are the most neglected among ancient Chinese texts by Chinese scholars. After the School of Mohism lost its influence in 221 B.C.E., later Han scholars did not reintroduce and interpret Mohist doctrines as they did other pre-Qin classics. The only ancient interpretive text of Mohist doctrines, *Mo Bian Zhu* 墨辯注 (the Study of Argumentation of Mohism), written by Lu Sheng 魯勝 of Western Jin 西晉 (265–316 C.E.), is also lost. It was not until the seventeenth century, when scattered interpretive and original Mohist works began to surface, that the study of Mohism was resumed and continued by a few Chinese scholars.[1] Second, no Mohist texts were translated into any Western language until the 1920s. When the Italian missionary Matteo Ricci (1552–1610) first translated Chinese classics into Latin, he did not include Mohist texts in his body of translated work. Despite the fact that such texts were translated into German by Alfred Forke and later into English in the 1920s by Yi-Pao Mei, and Joseph Needham's introduction of Mohism to Western readers in 1956 was one of the sources of Chinese science, the School of Mohism remains unpopular in the West. Although some attention has been paid to Mohist texts since A. C. Graham's translation of *Mo Bian* 墨辯 (Argumentation of Mo), or *Mojing* 墨經 (the Mohist Canon), in 1978, Mohist studies are still limited.[2]

If Confucianism is the most influential school of thought with regard to Chinese culture and political systems, Mohism is the school most resembling

Western logical, religious, and ethical systems. In the last chapter we learned that Confucianism gradually extended its rhetorical perspective from a moral concentration on the part of Confucius and Mencius to its inclusion by Xunzi of a rational dimension. The School of Mohism played a major role in this development, challenging the moral principles of Confucianism by its pragmatic and rationalized philosophy and more explicit theoretical framework of language and argumentation. As Frederick Mote observes, "Mohists became deeply involved in questions about the sources of knowledge, uses of names, and methods of inference, and always showed a preference for common-sense attitudes" (1971, 97). Furthermore, according to Hu Shih: "This [Mohism] is the only school of Chinese thought which has developed a scientific logic with both inductive and deductive methods. It has also advanced a theory of knowledge based on psychological analysis. It continued the pragmatic tradition of Moh Tih [Mozi] and developed an experimental method" (1963, 61). Indeed, the School of Mohism, especially of Later Mohism, provided within the context of Chinese philosophy a complete system of language and argumentation, comparable to the system articulated by Aristotle. Likewise, Mozi's moral philosophy of universal love comes closest to Christian teachings on the subject, leading Western missionaries to observe that "the love of God and universal love were already known to the Chinese" (Lin 1942, 785).

Although Mohism has received little attention over the centuries, its seeds are embedded in the soil of Chinese culture as well as in the minds of the Chinese people. In recent times, its vitality is more and more evident in providing explanations and guidance for contemporary Chinese communication and social behavior. Likewise, its philosophical value and contribution to a theory of bian has been increasingly recognized by Chinese and Western scholars alike.

The school of Mohism consists of two groups: Early Mohists and Later Mohists, also known as Neo-Mohists. These classifications were articulated primarily in the text of *Mozi*, which was compiled and written by Mozi's disciples. Early Mohists were primarily concerned with social, political, and religious questions, while Later Mohists were more concerned with issues of argumentation, logic, epistemology, and science. The early concerns were evident throughout *Mozi*, while the later concerns were expressed in six chapters of *Mozi* known as *Mo Bian* or *Mojing*. The analysis of Mohist rhetoric in this chapter will examine Early and Later Mohist teachings in *Mozi* and *Mo Bian*, respectively. The chapter will conclude with comparisons between the Later Mohists and Chinese Mingjia, and between the Later Mohists and Aristotle. For convenience, the following chart illustrates the works, life span, philosophical views, and rhetorical perspectives of Mozi and the Later Mohists:

Mohists' Philosophy and Rhetoric

Names/Dates	Texts	Philosophical Views	Rhetorical Perspectives
Mozi 475–390 B.C.E.	Mozi	Universal love Utilitarianism Identification with the superior	Moral *bian shi* Application & practicality of speech in society Rational *bian: lei* & *gu*
Later Mohists 250 B.C.E.	Mo Bian		Epistemological emphasis Rational, probable & contextual senses of ming Social & rational functions of *bian: lei* & *gu*

Mozi

Social Context and Personal Background

Mozi, also known as Mo Di 墨翟, lived between the time of Confucius and Mencius and was born in the state of Lu, Confucius's home state. Unlike Confucius, who came from a family of aristocracy in decline and considered himself a representative of the social elite, Mozi was a skilled carpenter who identified with the middle and lower classes of society. Both men lived during a time of social and cultural transition, although about seventy years apart, and both were concerned with the establishment of a moral and orderly society. However, because of differences in social background and in the specific challenges that each faced, their philosophical views and rhetorical perspectives took different paths.

As previously mentioned, Confucius lived during the Spring-Autumn period when observation of *li* 禮 (rites) was highly valued, ancestor worship was generally observed, and certain traditional values and the moral examples of sage kings held mass appeals. Mozi, on the other hand, lived during the early Warring States period when corrupt and exploitative rulers engaged in endless wars for more land and power, and people were motivated by a desire for utilitarian gains rather than by moral ideals. Mozi witnessed "the attack on the small states by the large ones, disturbances of the small houses by the large ones, oppression of the weak by the strong, misuse of the few by the many, deception of the simple by the cunning, disdain towards the humble by the honoured" (Mei 4.16.87).[3]

Since Confucius identified with upper-class officials and intellectual elites, his attitude toward them was relatively uncritical. Likewise, his proposition for social change was quite abstract and idealistic. Mozi, on the other hand, identified with the lower class of craftsman, traders, and artisans who were directly affected by the social and economic conditions. Consequently, his attitude toward the ruling elite was more critical, and his political ideas were relatively pragmatic, realistic, and centered around the interests and benefits of common people. Mozi openly condemned rulers for "heavily taxing the people, robbing them of their means of livelihood, in order to have their palaces covered with porches and pavilions in various designs and adorned with paintings and sculpture" (Mei 1.6.23). He spoke for the politically powerless and economically disadvantaged, advocating a government that represented the interests of the common people, an egalitarian society filled with universal love and run by virtuous and wise people.

The great demand for you shui meant opportunities for upward mobility during the Warring States period. This state of affairs enabled Mozi actively to participate in the political arena. Likewise, the environment for relatively free intellectual exchange and philosophical debate allowed Mozi to reflect upon and formulate theories of government, language, and argumentation. His view from the margins of society not only posed a threat to Confucianism but also generated more vitality and diversity in the arena of ancient Chinese thought.

As recorded in *Huai Nanzi* 淮南子, Mozi had received his education under Confucian teachers but subsequently broke with Confucianism and established his own school of philosophy, Mojia 墨家, with strict rules for its members (*HN* 21.1029). As the head of the school, Mozi, referred to as *ju zi* 巨子 (huge son),[4] exercised absolute authority and control over the lives of his members, from whom he received absolute loyalty in return. In this sense, Mozi's role was not unlike that of today's religious cult leaders. The exact size of Mozi's following is unknown; however, *Huai Nanzi* suggests that his disciples numbered from eighty to one hundred. Elsewhere, in an attempt to intimidate the king of Chu, Mozi claimed to have three hundred disciples already "armed with my implements of defence waiting on the city wall of Song for the bandits from Ch'u" (Mei 13.50.259).

Little is known about Mozi's personal life.[5] We do know that he was a *da fu* 大夫 (high official) for the state of Song, an expert in military defense, and an advocate for thrift in government expenditures. Like other philosophers of his time, Mozi was a great bian shi. He was described in the philosophical works of his time as sharp tongued, fond of disputation, and frequently hard to combat. In his own assessment, "To refute my principle with one's own principle is like throwing an egg against a boulder. The eggs in the world would be exhausted without doing any harm to the boulder" (Mei 12.47.229). Like Confucius, Mozi was also a shi; traveling widely with his disciples, he advised the various rulers of his time to pursue peace rather than war. In fact, he appeared to have been a determined peace advocate. Zhuangzi described him as the most perfect person who loves and is the savior of the world (Z 33.458–59). It is known that he once successfully persuaded the duke of Qi not to attack the state of Lu and prevented the duke of Lu from invading the state of Zheng. On another occasion, he walked ten days and nights nonstop to reach Ying, the capital of Chu, where he managed to persuade the king of Chu to drop his plan of attacking the state of Song (Mei 13.49–50.242–59).

Mozi and the Later Mohists formulated ethical, political, religious, epistemological, and rhetorical doctrines in response to the social and political conditions of their time. In the process of articulating their views, they challenged bian theories associated with the Schools of Ming, Confucianism, and Daoism. According to Yang Junguang's extensive research on Mozi and his written work, the original text of *Mozi* had seventy-one chapters; in its current form it only contains fifty-three chapters. It is speculated that certain chapters were written by Mozi himself but that the majority were written by his disciples, who cited Mozi's sayings in the text (Yang 1992). With the exception of those chapters of *Mo Bian* representing the views of the Later Mohists, the remaining chapters represent the views of Mozi and the Early Mohists.

Philosophical Views

Like other philosophers of his time, Mozi was primarily concerned with bringing peace, stability, and order to society. Toward this end, he proposed a series of intriguing notions, the two most relevant to our discussion being *jian ai* 兼愛 (universal love) and *shang tong* 尚同 (identification with the superior). While jian ai was a moral principle associated with the Will of Heaven and the deeds of cultural heroes, shang tong was more of a political expediency designed to unify the masses by ensuring official roles and functions in the hierarchical political system.

(1) Jian Ai. In his *Analects*, Confucius defined ren as "loving people." His notion of "loving," however, was selective and discriminatory depending upon one's status and relationship with others. In Confucius's view, one's duty to family and lord should take precedence over all other relationships. Mozi, on the other hand, utterly rejected the type of selective love advocated

by Confucius, considering it the primary cause of conflict between people and disorder in society. He argued: "As he loves only his own house and not the others, the minister disturbs the other houses to profit his own. As he loves only his own state and not the others, the feudal lord attacks the other states to profit his own. These instances exhaust the confusion in the world" (Mei 4.14.79).[6]

Mozi proposed the notion of jian ai, or universal love, as the ultimate solution to the problem of moral decline and social disorder. He defined universal love as "loving others as one's self" (4.14.79) and argued, "If everyone in the world will love universally; states not attacking one another; houses not disturbing one another; thieves and robbers becoming extinct; emperor and ministers, fathers and son, all being affectionate and filial—if all this comes to pass the world will be orderly" (4.14.80). While the Confucian perspective of love and benevolence holds that harmony and order can only be achieved if one speaks and acts according to social titles or ranks, Mozi's universal love promotes a social equality which transcends such hierarchy. Mozi advocated the cultivation of unconditional love for all humankind in order for a true sense of harmony and order to be achieved. As Burton Watson explains, "This [universal love] is a noble and original ideal indeed, especially when we consider the fierce strife and hatred that characterized the society of Mo Tzu's [Mozi's] time. Here at least is a man who dared to look beyond the hierarchical and geographical divisions of feudal society to a view of all mankind united in fellowship and love" (1963, 9–10). Similarly, after a careful analysis of Mozi's moral philosophy, Augustinus A. Tseu concludes that "his doctrine of universal love is similar to Christian humanitarianism in its 'raison d'etre' and also in its practice" (1965, 393).

Mozi never explicitly stated that universal love, as a moral principle, was superior to the Confucian notion of selected love, although he truly believed this to be the case. For rhetorical purposes, Mozi claimed that the principle of universal love was in accordance with tian yi 天意 (the Will of Heaven), which was "the origin of magnanimity [ren] and righteousness [yi]" and was, therefore, more "honourable and wise than the emperor" (Mei 7.27.141–42). The notion of tian yi was derived from the ancient notion of tian ming (the Mandate of Heaven), which was thought to exercise ultimate power over the secular world by rewarding or punishing human beings according to their acts. Thus, for Mozi, the Will of Heaven must be obeyed. He claimed that universal love was not his invention. Rather it was the belief and practice of sage kings; he had simply borrowed the idea from them. For example, citing the praise of King Wen in Shang Shu and the description of the oath taken by Yu and Tang therein, he claimed that these examples illustrated the theme of universal love and that he had, in fact, drawn inspiration from the tales of such heroic deeds. Clearly, Mozi invoked the power of Heaven and cultural heroes in making his moral and psychological appeals in order to combat his opponents.

Interestingly, Mozi did not expect humankind to embrace universal love out of moral idealism, as Confucianists had proposed with regard to ren. On the contrary, Mozi argued that the motivation for embracing universal love was a desire for *jiao li* 交利 or mutual benefit.[7] In other words, one was motivated to love and benefit others by a desire to receive the same in return. This was because, according to his observation, "whoever loves others is loved by others; whoever benefits others is benefited by others; whoever hates others is hated by others; whoever injures others is injured by others" (4.15.83). Furthermore, in Mozi's view, there were "those who obtained blessings because they loved and benefited the people as well as those who were visited by calamities because they hated and harmed the people" (1.4.16). In making this argument, Mozi was keenly pragmatic, pursuing the ultimate goal of profit and mutual benefit even while endorsing the principles of egalitarianism and fair play. For this reason he was condemned by Confucianists, who regarded the quest for personal gain as the immoral acts of xiaoren.

The reader should be reminded that the School of Confucianism was composed of members of the aristocracy, who, therefore, had no experience of working for money or doing business for profits. Thus, the adherents of Confucianism saw *yi* 義 (morality, righteousness) and *li* 利 (benefits, profits) as morally opposed, mutually exclusive terms. As Confucius stated, "The gentleman understands what is moral, the small man understands what is profitable" (Lau 4.16.74). The Mohist experience in crafts and trade, on the other hand, enabled members of the School of Mohism to see li (benefit and profit) as an ethical and egalitarian concept. As Oliver states, "Mo Tzu [Mozi] frankly and fully accepted what he regarded as a fundamental of human nature, that individuals will pursue what they conceive to be their own self-interest. What he sought to teach was that benefit for oneself may be found only through dedication to righteousness, expressed in universal love" (1971, 193).

(2) Shang Tong. Even though Mozi's views differed from those of Confucius and others on matters of philosophical belief, he shared with Confucianists and Legalists the same mythological beliefs regarding the ruler, or the Son of Heaven. According to this common view, the Son of Heaven possessed absolute moral virtue and impeccable judgment, which

were mandated by Heaven. He was, therefore, eminently qualified to rule, to have the final say in all conflicts among his subjects. For Mozi, the primary means of achieving social order and political stability was to ensure that the ruler's message was communicated to his people and that people's beliefs were unified under certain principles advocated by the ruler. Mozi referred to this ideal state of affairs as shang tong, or identification with superiors.

According to Mozi, shang tong was ultimately assured by a hierarchical ordering of official positions. At the top of the hierarchy was *tianzi* 天子 (the Son of Heaven, the ruler). Directly below him were *san gong* 三公 (three ministers), who oversaw the empire comprised of feudal states. Each state was run by *zhuhou* 諸侯 (feudal lords), who chose *qing* 卿 (executive officers) to supervise *xiang zhang* 鄉長 (village leaders). When a pronouncement was made by the ruler, the executive officer was responsible for passing it on to the head of the village, who then delivered it to *jia jun* 家君 (the head of each family). Finally, the head of the family (often an extended family) was responsible for ensuring that the ruler's pronouncement was understood and obeyed by every family member.

In Mozi's view, a good ruler or superior must keep the official channels of communication open to his people, allowing them to express both positive and negative opinions and to criticize the ruler's actions so that he could take the appropriate steps to reward good and punish evil, both in himself and others. This system did not entail freedom of speech, however. When a difference in opinion occurred, or when the subordinate's opinion was incompatible with the superior's, the subordinate's view should be brought in line with that of the superior. In Mozi's words: "Upon hearing good or evil one shall report it to a superior. What the superior thinks to be right all shall think to be right; what the superior thinks to be wrong all shall think to be wrong. When the superior is at fault there shall be good counsel; when the subordinates show virtue there shall be popular recommendation. To identify one's self with the superior and not to unite one's self with the subordinates—This is what deserves encouragement from above and praise from below" (Mei 3.11.56).

Mozi believed that if the ruler appointed virtuous people to positions of authority and heeded the opinions of his subjects, righteousness would be guaranteed; good communication between the ruler and the common people would be assured. For Mozi, the principle of shang tong should be employed by superiors at every level of society, from the ruler to the family. In his words, "to govern the world-empire is the same as to rule a single family clan; to command all the people in the world is the same as to order a single individual" (3.13.75). In this sense, Mozi shared the Confucian desire to establish and maintain an ordered society. Toward this end he advocated the practice of shang tong, saying "If the kings, dukes and important personages of the world now sincerely want to practise magnanimity [ren] and righteousness [yi] and be superior men, if they want to attain the way of the sage-kings on the one hand and contribute toward the benefit of the people on the other, they cannot leave the principle of Identification with the Superior unexamined and un-understood. Identification with the Superior is, indeed, the foundation of government and essence of orderliness" (3.13.77).

Rhetorical Perspectives

Although the general feature of classical Chinese rhetoric is its implicitness, that is, its embeddedness in the philosophical works of ancient times, the rhetorical views of Mozi and his followers may be considered an exception to this rule. Mozi was the first philosopher to formulate an explicit theory of language, persuasion, and argumentation. More importantly, his pioneering work laid the foundation for the Later Mohists to develop a systematic theory of bian characterized by its emphasis on logic and dialectics. In Graham's opinion, this particular interest in bian can be attributed to the cultural context in which the Mohists lived. "He (Mohist) lives in an age of rapid social transformation in which ancient authority is no longer an adequate guide to conduct." Consequently, "He has developed the moral teaching of Mo-tzu [Mozi] into an elaborate ethical system justified not by authority but by the procedures of disputation [bian] . . ." (1978, 33). Further, Garrett attributes the Mohists' reliance on bian to their social background, arguing that "as a lower-class group the Mohists could not persuade on the basis of their authority or power, and so had no recourse but to join the philosophical and political debates, with the resultant sharpening of their skills in argument" (1983, 320). In particular, Mozi was concerned with the moral state of bian shi, the practical function of speech, and was interested in the notion of bian as a system of distinction, argumentation, and disputation.

(1) Moral Bian Shi. A major emphasis in the text of *Mozi* was its criticism of unethical speakers and promotion of ethical bian shi. Like the Confucianists, Mozi disliked those glib individuals who used *chan yan* 讒言 (flattering words) to please the ruler instead of being honest and straightforward. In his words, "artful ministers are harmful to the lord and flattering subordinates are injurious to the ruler. The lord should have uncompromising ministers; the ruler should have stern subordinates. Only when counsel

is given with far-sightedness and advice administered with sternness, can the life of the state be secure and permanent" (Mei 1.1.2–3). Unlike Mencius, who would refuse to advise any rulers who were not receptive to the speech of benevolent government, for Mozi, those who assisted the ruler had the moral responsibility to advise the ruler as skillfully as possible. Failure to do so would cause the people to suffer and the state to decline, for "If the subordinates should value their positions and keep silent, the ministers near at hand would be speechless and those far away could only sigh, and the people would become bitter. When the ruler is surrounded with praise and flattery and insulated against good counsel, the country is in danger" (1.1.3). According to Mozi, the high moral standard and *xin yan* 信言 (trustworthy speech) characteristic of a bian shi were the most effective ways to counteract such danger. He claimed, "He will not be listened to who talks much but is slow in action, even though he is discerning. He will not accomplish anything who is capable but likes to boast of his feats, even though he drudges. The wise discerns all in his mind but speaks simply, and he is capable but does not boast of his deeds. . . . In speech, not quantity but ingenuity, not eloquence but insight, should be cultivated" (1.2.7–8). In keeping with this advice, members of the School of Mohism favored substance over style in both speech making and the use of language. Likewise, Mohist writings were known for their dryness and lack of grace and taste when compared with the elegant and refined style of Confucian writings.

Mozi referred to those bian shi who were "firm in morality, versed in rhetoric, and experienced in statecraft" as "the treasure of the nation and props of the state" who should be "enriched, honored, respected, and commended" (2.8.31). In his opinion, only a *bian hui zhi ren* 辯慧之人 (person of virtue and eloquence) who spoke *shan yan* 善言 (good speech) and performed *shan xing* 善行 (good act) could rightly be called the Son of Heaven (3.12.59). In giving speeches, such bian shi exhibited sagelike behavior. When silent, they were deep in thought. When speaking, they instructed and taught their audience. When acting, they aimed at concrete results (12.47.224).

(2) Criteria of Speech. For Mozi, speech and action should be guided by *biao* 表 (principle). Consequently, he delineated the following *san biao* 三表 (three principles) as criteria for judging speeches and doctrines: foundation, verifiability, and applicability. As Mozi explained, a speech should be informed by the virtues of the ancient sage-kings, verified by the senses of hearing and sight of the common people, applied through government policies, and observed by witnessing its benefits to the country and its people (9.35.183). According to Mozi, on hearing an argument one should

question its verifiability by determining the origin of the source, whether the argument is justified, and whether it is applicable. Toward this end Mozi advised studying the history for sources, surveying the lives of ordinary people for justification, and checking the application of the argument against the welfare of the state and the interests of the people. In essence, Mozi's criteria were based on the authority and experience of the past, the effects on ordinary people in the present, and the future benefits for the state and its people. Such criteria were rooted in experience and external evidence rather than in an abstract faculty of reasoning created by an internal source (the speaker). For Mozi, words and speeches were of no use if they could not be put into action for the sake of practical benefit. In his words, "Doctrines that can be translated into conduct may be taught frequently. Doctrines that cannot be translated into conduct may not be taught frequently. To talk frequently about what cannot be carried out is merely to wear out one's mouth" (11.46.217). In other words, for Mozi, truth and knowledge were determined against standards of moral justification and practical consequence.

(3) Audience Adaptation. Mozi was well aware of the importance of audience adaptation in persuasion and argumentation. If the audience was an opponent in a philosophical disputation, Mozi would attack the opponent when being attacked and soften the tone of his argument when the opponent had softened (12.48.238). However, when the audience was a superior, the situation was much more complicated. If the superior was not a wise ruler, but one preoccupied by greed and aggression, the bian shi faced a difficult challenge. As Mozi explained, "In the case of the ruler's committing violence in the state, to go and warn him will be called insolence, and to offer warning through those around him will be called meddling with counsel" (12.48.230). However, if the ruler was wise and capable of making good judgments, the bian shi should be loyal to him. More specifically, "When the superior is at fault he should wait and warn; possessing a good idea he should give counsel to the superior without revealing it to the world; he should correct irregularities and lead in goodness; he should identify himself with the superior and not ally himself with subordinates" (13.49.247–48). Mozi called for ethical bian shi to stand up and attempt to persuade the rulers and common people alike to practice virtue and universal love. In fact, he considered persuasive activity of this nature the most honorable and valuable of all activities:

> I concluded that none of these [activities] is as good as to familiarize myself with the Tao [Dao] of the ancient sage-kings, and discover their principles, and to understand the words of the sages and be clear about their expressions; and with these

to persuade the rulers and then the common people and the pedestrians. When the rulers adopt my principles their states will be orderly. When the common people and pedestrians adopt my principles their conduct will be regulated. Therefore, I think, though I do not plow and feed the hungry or weave and clothe the cold, I have greater merit than those who plow and feed, and weave and clothe. (13.49.249)

In general, Mozi's perceptions of the relationship among the speaker, speech, and audience were products of his moral/ethical concerns combined with and rooted in his philosophical principles of universal love, identification with superiors, and utilitarianism.

(4) Bian. Mozi was faced with political and humanistic views in opposition to his own, such as those of Confucianism. Since Confucius's doctrines preceded his teachings, Mozi had the burden of proof regarding whose doctrines were more practical, moral, and applicable. Given the fact that the people and culture had already accepted the moral notions of *ren* 仁 (benevolence), *Dao* 道 (path, the Way), *de* 德 (virtue), and *yi* 義 (righteousness), Mozi had to redefine these concepts, identifying the differences between his views and those of others. It was in his criticism of Confucianism and advocacy of his own doctrines that Mozi developed his system of bian (distinction, argumentation). For Mozi, bian was both morally and epistemologically significant. In this regard, he insisted, "Let those who can argue argue, let those who can expound the doctrines expound the doctrines" (11.26.213).

Mozi was the first scholar to treat bian as an important concept, though thinkers before him, such as Laozi and Confucius, had used the term sporadically. The purpose of bian, for Mozi, was to distinguish between what was beneficial and what was harmful as well as to clarify perceptual experience and conceptual understanding. He offered the following analogy:

Now, if there were a man who, upon seeing a little blackness, should say it is black, but upon seeing much, should say it is white, then we should think he could not tell the difference between black and white.... Now when a little wrong is committed people know that they should condemn it, but when such a great wrong as attacking a state is committed people do not know that they should condemn it. On the contrary, it is applauded, called righteous. Can this be said to be knowing the difference between the righteous and the unrighteous? Hence we know the gentlemen of the world are confused about the difference between righteousness and unrighteousness. (5.17.100)

In other words, if killing one person is wrong, going to another state to kill all the people there is even more wrong; therefore, to call such an act righteous is logically absurd.

When Mozi was challenged with the assertion that universal love was a difficult and unachievable ideal, he replied, "this is simply because the gentlemen of the world do not recognize [bian] what is to the benefit of the world, or understand [the cause: gu] what is its calamity" (4.15.83). The task of bian, then, was to make the *gu* 故 (cause, reason, because) known—to discover, through moral and practical considerations, the truest reasons for one's actions. To accomplish this, Mozi emphasized the importance of *zhi lei* 知類 (understanding categories of classification) and *ming gu* 明故 (knowing the cause and because). For him, actions of the same nature belonged to the same *lei* 類 (kind, category). For example, if to kill one person was to commit an act of unrighteousness, to kill ten or a hundred people was to commit the same unrighteousness except to a greater degree. Likewise, both those who steal fruit and those who steal horses cause people to suffer and thus belong to the same category of criminal (5.17.98–100). In the following account, Mozi applied the notion of lei to analogical reasoning, attempting to persuade the king of Chu not to attack the state of Song:

Suppose there is a man who, putting aside his elegant carriage, desired to steal his neighbor's shattered sedan; putting aside his embroidery and finery, desired to steal his neighbor's short jacket; putting aside his meat and grains desired to steal his neighbor's husks. What kind of a man would this be: The Lord [king of Chu] said that he must be suffering from kleptomania. Motse continued: The land of Chu amounts to five thousand lisquare while that of Song is only five hundred, this is similar to the contrast between the elegant carriage and the shattered sedan. Chu possesses Yun Meng which is full of rhinoceroses and deer. The fish, tortoises and crocodiles in the Yangtse and the Han Rivers are the richest in the empire, while Song is said to possess not even pheasants, rabbits, or foxes. This is similar to the contrast between meat and grains and husks. In Chu there are tall pines, spruces, cedars, and camphor trees, while Song has no tall trees at all. This is similar to the contrast between embroidery and finery and the short jacket. When your ministers and generals set out to attack Song, it seems to me there is the same analogy. I can see, my Lord, you will be violating righteousness to no advantage. (13.50.258)

Regarding things of a different nature, Mozi located them under different lei. For example, in defending his theory of *fei gong* 非攻 (condemnation of offensive war), he was asked, "do you condemn attacks and assault as unrighteous and not beneficial? But anciently, Yu made war on the Prince of Miao, Tang on Chieh, and King Wu on Chow. Yet these [men] are regarded as sages. What is your explanation for this?" Mozi replied, "You have not examined the terminology of my teaching [lei] and you do not understand its motive [gu]. What they did is not to be called 'attack' [gong] 攻 but 'punishment' [zhu] 誅" (5.19.110–11). Because in this case the men who made war were considered sage-kings, for Mozi, their "attack" on other states was justified. Because their targets were evil people, their actions should be referred to as punishment rather than attack. "Attack" and "punishment" were different lei (categories) with different gu (cause and because). Likewise, stealing from innocent people's houses and causing them suffering was different from stealing from a bad person's house in order to punish the bad person. The latter case is justified and may be referred to as "taking" rather than "stealing."

Another method suggested by Mozi for practicing bian was *tui* 推 (inference). In his words, "When one is not successful in making out plans then predict the future by the past and learn about the absent from what is present" (5.18.101). In response to the statement "The past can be known, the future cannot," Mozi offered the following hypothetical example: "Suppose your parents met with misfortune a hundred *li* (miles) away. And there was just the margin of a single day. If they could be reached they would live, if not they would die. There are a strong wagon and an excellent horse, and also a bad horse and a square-wheeled cart. And you are allowed to choose. Which would you take?" The response was that "the excellent horse and the strong wagon would of course make for a more speedy journey" (13.49.253). This example illustrates Mozi's point that predictions about the future can be made based on what is known and what is present. This is not strictly a case of logical inference, but rather a process of tui based on first- or secondhand experience.

As an excellent bian shi, Mozi set a good example for his disciples. He was well known for his skillful use of various modes of argumentation, ranging from deduction to induction as well as from moral to psychological appeal. Furthermore, his conceptualization of language, persuasion, and argumentation greatly influenced his disciples, the Later Mohists, in addition to Mingjia and Xunzi. Through the following analysis of *Mo Bian* (the Argumentation of Mo), the evolution of Mozi's theories of epistemology, language, and argumentation is revealed.

Later Mohists and *Mo Bian*

Mo Bian 墨辯 (the Argumentation of Mo), also known as *Mojing* 墨經 (the Mohist Canon), consists of six chapters in the text of *Mozi*.[8] Though controversy exists as to whether Mozi was the original author of *Mo Bian*,[9] it is generally believed to have been completed by a collective effort of Mozi's disciples, conventionally known as the Later Mohists 后期墨家 in the third century B.C.E., toward the end of the Warring States period. Some speculate that the text is, in fact, a compilation of Mozi's lecture notes that were passed down by his disciples. Graham describes the text as "the only surviving document of pre-Buddhist China which discusses the forms of reasoning continuously and at some length" (1964, 1). The text is often studied separately from the rest of the chapters in *Mozi* because of its emphasis on epistemology, language, argumentation, and science ranging from geometry and mechanics to optics and astronomy. It is deliberately written in the language of definitions and conceptualizations for the purpose of memorization and abstract thinking. Compared to all other pre-Qin texts, *Mo Bian* is both the most comprehensive in content and abstract in style. For our purposes, we will examine the formulations of epistemology, of ming (naming), and of bian (argumentation, distinction). Finally, a comparison will be made with Aristotle's theory of epistemology and systems of naming, logic, and argumentation.

Epistemology

While the ancient Greeks believed truth and knowledge resided in human faculties, and modern scientists saw truth and knowledge in observation and scientific experiment, Later Mohists' views of such matters integrated both perspectives. In *Mo Bian*, zhi 知 (knowledge, cognition, consciousness) is perceived as possessing four components: capability of humans, seeking, touching, and understanding.[10] It was the Later Mohists' belief that the ability to know resides inherently in humans. However, knowing must be driven by the desire or motivation to know. *Zhi* as touching and *zhi* as understanding identified two ways of knowing the world. Touching refers to knowing by sensing and experiencing the physical world, while understanding refers to knowing through the faculty of reasoning described as a cognitive process of illuminating.

The Later Mohists' notion of epistemology shares some striking similarities with Aristotle's system of knowing. In his *Metaphysics* Aristotle also identifies two sources of knowing: knowing by senses and knowing by art and reasoning. In fact, unlike his teacher Plato, who favored rational thinking at the expense of the primary senses, as source for truth and knowledge, Aristotle seemed to recognize the validity of both sources of knowing. In his words, "All men by nature desire to know. An indication of this is the delight we take in our senses"; the function of senses "makes us know and brings to light many differences between things" (*Metaphysics* 980a25). The difference between knowing by understanding (through art and reasoning) and knowing by experience is that, as Aristotle continues, "the former know the cause, but the latter do not. For men of experience know that the thing is so, but do not know why, while the others know the 'why' and the cause" (981a25). By this Aristotle did not mean to suggest that knowing by the senses or by experience was inferior to knowing by reasoning. In his words, "With a view to action, experience seems in no respect inferior to art, and we even see men of experience succeeding more than those who have theory without experience" (981a10).

Also similar to Aristotle in their epistemological views, the Later Mohists were interested in the integration of the two sources of knowing. Toward this end, in fact, they further extended these two sources of knowing into the following modes of inquiry: *wen zhi* 聞知 (knowing by hearing); *shuo zhi* 說知 (knowing by explaining); *qin zhi* 親知 (knowing by experiencing); *ming zhi* 名知 (knowing by naming); *shi zhi* 實知 (knowing by pointing to objects and actuality); *he zhi* 和知 (knowing by relating or combining); and *wei zhi* 爲知 (knowing by acting out one's will) (*MB* 81.186). For the Later Mohists, a true sense of knowing would only be derived from the integration of theory with practice as well as the combining of words and action. This parallels Aristotle's belief that one who does not actively exercise his knowledge "would be in the contradictory state of not knowing" (*Physics* 255b1).

Wen, the concept of knowing through secondhand information, or received wisdom, derived from hearing with one's ears, was apparently of particular interest to the Later Mohists. Considered a means of getting to know how other people think and feel, wen comprised *chuan wen* 傳聞 (received information) and *qin wen* 親聞 (direct participation) (*MB* 82.187–88). Through these means one could *tui zhi* 推知 (generate or infer the unknown by what is known). While the tui zhi of the Later Mohists aimed at discovering "what," Aristotle seemed more interested in the question of "why." For Aristotle, four questions were paramount in pursuing knowledge: "the fact, the reason why, if it is, what it is" (*Posterior Analytics* 89b20). Both the Later Mohists and Aristotle addressed the question of how humans gain their knowledge. Furthermore, both recognized the faculty of reasoning as an important means of discovering truth and knowledge. However, while Aristotle proposed a critical assessment of received and self-experienced knowledge as a means of gaining new knowledge, the Later Mohists emphasized the practice of inference as a means of discovering new knowledge. They were also more elaborate than Aristotle in identifying the sources of such knowledge. Finally, compared with Aristotle, the Later Mohists were more interested in the question of "because" than the question of "cause" and more keen on rational thinking than on critical evaluation of the process and purpose of inquiry. In sum, for the Later Mohists, truth and knowledge derived from a combination of sensory experience of the objective world and rational thinking, involving naming and explaining such knowledge, had significant impact on directing and influencing action.

A Formulation of Ming

One of the most significant features of ancient Chinese philosophy was the debate over the relationship between *ming* 名 (naming) and *shi* 實 (actuality). For Confucius, ming played a prescriptive and performative function in the area of social transformation, capable of redefining or changing shi. Laozi, on the other hand, utterly rejected the prescriptive and descriptive function of ming, holding out the notion of namelessness in its stead. Mingjia raised the question of the necessary correspondence between naming and actuality for political and epistemological purposes. Mozi also insisted on a close correspondence between ming and shi with a more commonsense approach relative to the idealistic concerns of Confucius and the epistemological interests of Gong-sun Long. In responding to Confucius's notion of *zheng ming* 正名 (rectification of names), Mozi criticized those Confucian junzi who could not choose to act benevolently because they did not know the meaning of benevolence; thus, their actions lacked any correspondence between the ideal of ren and the practice of ren (Mei 12.47.225). For Mozi, the notion of zheng ming was, therefore, hypocritical and unreachable.

The Later Mohists continued this debate on the relationship between ming and shi, for the first time connecting ming with *yan* 言, defined as saying, speaking, and using words to represent the objective world and emit references. As they explained, "To inform about this name is to refer to the other object. Therefore 'saying' is an emitting of something's characteristics of which any speaker is capable" (Graham 286). Thus, *ming* (naming with words, phrases, concepts, or ideas) is the use of *yan* (language) to describe, represent, and name the objective world.

The Later Mohists identified three kinds of ming: *da ming* 達名 (general or unrestricted names); *lei ming* 類名 (classified names); and *si ming* 私名 (private names). According to their explanation, "'Thing' is 'unrestricted' and object necessarily requires this name. Naming something 'horse' is 'classifying,' for 'like the object' we necessarily use this name. Naming someone 'Jack' is 'private'; this name stays confined in this object" (Graham 325). Thus, *da ming* are common names for things of a generic nature; *lei ming* are names used for things belonging to certain categories or groups; and *si ming* are the proper names designated for particular people or things.

According to the Later Mohists, names possess a threefold function: *ming* 命; *ju* 舉; and *jia* 假. *Ming* serves the nominal function of designating general names for things, such as the category of dogs without reference to a particular dog. *Ju* refers to particular names, for example, a particular dog. And *jia* refers to the borrowing of a name to express feelings or desires through an emotive tone of voice, for example, in the phrase "here dog." Such delineation of *ming* indicated Later Mohists' attempts to distinguish between the referential and emotive functions of language as well as between their abstract and concrete features.

Regarding the "use [of] names to refer to objects" (483), the Later Mohists were concerned primarily with the use of names in representing or distorting reality. If a bian shi used a name to represent a commonly agreed upon object, he stood a good chance of communicating his message. If he used a name that did not represent an object, he would send a confusing and misleading message. If names and objects are mismatched, disagreement is inevitable and consensus can hardly be reached. In Graham's opinion, the art of discourse "is concerned with the consistent naming of similar and different objects so that the names 'stay' in them throughout their duration" (1989, 147).

The Later Mohists did not simply state that ming and shi must correspond. They were aware that at times names do not fully or accurately represent an object. As explained in *Xiao Qu* 小取, "Names and objects do not necessarily go together. If this stone is white, when you break up this stone all of it is the same as the white thing, but although this stone is big, it is not the same as the big thing" (Graham 470). In other words, a big stone may be called a big thing in general as it shares the size of bigness with the big thing, but the name "big stone" is a specific name that can only be used to refer to a piece of stone that is big in a strict sense. The same can be said for the naming relationship between a white stone and a white thing. For Mohists, naming does not simply serve a nominal function; rather, it helps classify objects into specific kinds and categories. Some names are general; others are specific. For example, because a whelp is a kind of dog, it is not acceptable to say "killing the dog is not killing a whelp" (*MB* 155.264). In this example the word *whelp* is a specific word while the word *gou* 狗 (dog) is a general name. However, both belong to the same lei (category). The Later Mohists' system of ming was more helpful than that of Gong-sun Long in that the former explained the relationship between universal and particular categories of language while the latter explained only particularity.

Interestingly, Aristotle made a similar observation about the use of names; he noted, "When things have only a name in common and the definition of being which corresponds to the name is different, they are called *homonymous*. Thus, for example, both a man and a picture are animals. These have only a name in common and the definition of being which corresponds to the name is different; for if one is to say what being an animal is for each of them, one will give two distinct definitions" (*Categories* 1a1).

Like Aristotle, the Later Mohists recognized that things belonging to the same kind could be referred to by a common name. Using one name to refer to things of seemingly different substances was acceptable because the different substances were combined under one essential category and classified as lei ming. For example, in responding to Gong-sun Long's argument that "a white horse is not a horse," the Later Mohists claimed, "A white horse is a horse. To ride a white horse is to ride horses. A black horse is a horse. To ride a black horse is to ride horses. Jack is a person. To love Jack is to love people. Jill is a person. To love Jill is to love people" (Graham 485). The Later Mohists would agree with Aristotle's assertion that this was a case of two different substances sharing a common essence. This is because "a man and a white man are the same thing, as people say, so that the essence of white man and that of man would be also the same" (*Metaphysics* 1031a25). According to Aristotle, "things are said to be named 'univocally' which have both the name and the definition answering to the name in common. A man and an ox are both 'animal,' and these are univocally so named, inasmuch as not only the name, but also the definition, is the same in both cases: for if a man should state in what sense each is an animal, the statement in the one case would be identical with that in the other" (*Categories* 1a5). Clearly, both Aristotle and the Later Mohists recognized the rational function of naming with regard to categorization and classification, as well as in making distinctions between particularity and universality.

The Later Mohists were also aware that the meaning of names is relative to the user. Although names should have designated points of reference, the points of reference may be interchangeable depending on the point of view of those using the names. In their explanation, "It is admissible for the man who uses names rightly to use 'that' for this and 'this' for that. As long as his use of 'that' for that stays confined to that, and his use of 'this' for this stays confined to this, it is inadmissible to use 'that' for this. When 'this' is about to be used for that, it is likewise admissible to use 'that' for this. If 'that' and 'this' stay confined to that and this, and accepting this condition you use 'that' for this, then 'this' is likewise about to be used for that" (Graham 440–41). In other words, both *this* and *that* have designated meanings that cannot be replaced, but the definitions and points of reference of *this* and *that* are relative to the perspective of the person. To explain the nature of relativity in naming, the Later Mohists offered the following example: "Knowing that what we judge them to be neither is the place nor is in the place, nonetheless we call these places the 'North' and the 'South.' Having passed beyond them we treat the already ended as so; previously we called this place 'southern,' therefore now too we call this place 'Southern'" (400–401). In other words, one names a place south or north depending upon one's own standing in relation to the place. Aristotle expressed a similar view of the relativity of naming, which he defined as "just what they are, of or than other things, or in some other way in relation to something else" (*Categories* 5b35). Aristotle further explained, "For the same thing turns out to be at the same time both large and small since in relation to this thing it is small but in relation to another, this same thing is large" (*Categories* 5b35).

For Later Mohists, the meaning of a word was also dialectical with respect to the user as well as to context, to the extent that a word is used to refer to its opposite. In their words, "If 'beautiful' is said of this, then inherently it is this that is beautiful; if it is said of another, it is not the case that this is beautiful; and if it is not said of this the converse applies" (Graham 354). For example, the Confucian understanding of *li* as benefit and profit was considered base and selfish, while Mozi considered the same notion egalitarian and mutually beneficial. The same word can mean totally different things depending upon the speaker's perspective as well as the subjective meaning attached to the term. A name can also take on different meanings across time. In the example given by the Later Mohists, the concept of *yi* in Yao's time meant righteousness, while in the present it has come to mean *li* 利, or benefit. This is because "Yao's notion of *yi* was conceived in the ancient time. Time has changed. Today's notion of *yi* is different" (*MB* 154.262–63). Aristotle would agree with this observation. In his words, "things do not appear either the same to all men or always the same to the same man, but often have contrary appearances at the same time" (*Metaphysics* 1011a30).[11]

A Formulation of Bian

The primary contribution of the School of Mohism to Chinese culture was not its moral philosophy or theory of knowledge, but rather its formulation of language and argumentation. Though Mohists did not originate the term *bian*, they were the first explicitly to discuss it as an independent area of inquiry. According to Graham: "It is in Mo Tzu [Mozi] that we first meet the word pien [bian] 'argue out alternatives,' . . . which was to become the established term for rational discourse" (1989, 36). The term *bian* as argument cognates with the term *bian* as distinction and thus carries the meaning of distinguishing from right to wrong. Like the Greek sophists, the Later

Mohists were interested in discovering truth and falsehood through a rational engagement with debate and argumentation.

Although they did not offer a clear-cut definition of *bian*, the Later Mohists regarded *bian* as an important means of finding truth and defending justice. Such an attitude is implied in the following discussion of the purpose of *bian* in *Mo Bian*: "(1) to clarify the portions of 'is-this' and 'is-not,' to inquire into the principles of order and misrule; (2) to clarify points of sameness and difference, to discern the patterns of names and objects; (3) to set the beneficial and the harmful, to resolve confusions and doubts" (Graham 475). Clearly, for the Later Mohists, *bian* was considered a rational activity employing language and moral activity to solve political, ideological, and practical problems. The following section will be divided into two parts. Part 1 will explore the rational component of *bian*, revealed in the logical concepts of *lei* and *gu*. Part 2 will discuss its moral component and methods of *bian*.

(1) The Concepts of *Lei* and *Gu*. The concept of *lei* is crucial in the field of Chinese argumentation. Two subcategories of *lei*, *yi lei qu*, 以類取 (to accept according to the kind) and *yi lei yu* 以類予 (to propose according to the kind) (*MB* "Xiaoqu" 321) involve inductive reasoning processes. For example, when two things are of the same lei, they are put into the same category; therefore the same conclusions can be drawn when comparing one with the other. Conversely, when they belong to different lei, they are not comparable, and thus the same conclusions cannot be drawn for both. Hence, *lei* is useful in the classification process as well as in reaching conclusions by inference. However, it must be noted that the application of *lei* does not simply refer to abstract definitions and formal logical procedures. In fact, in most situations, *lei* is employed with regard to metaphorical and analogical thinking.

A related concept originating with the Later Mohists is *zhi* 止 (stop), similar to the Western notion of counterargument. An example of zhi is when someone draws a conclusion based on his/her way of classification and another person argues for a different conclusion by refuting the first person's method of classification (*MB* 101.202). Naturally, different methods of classification will result in different conclusions. As in the inductive reasoning process, a conclusion is affirmed or denied on the basis of a comparison of instances, which are selected by the criteria of *tong lei* 同類 (same category).

The Later Mohists' understanding of *ming* enabled them to classify things by *lei*, or species and kind. *Bian* was based on the ability to identify *lei* (categories of classification) and discover *gu* 故 (cause and because). For purposes of *lei*, the Later Mohists classified things into the general categories of *tong* 同 (sameness) and *yi* 异 (difference), which were then subcategorized.

Tong included the subcategories *chong tong* 重同 (identical); *ti tong* 體同 (unity); *he tong* 合同 (togetherness); and *lei tong* 類同 (of a kind). More specifically, *chong tong* referred to the practice of using two different names for the same object; *ti tong* meant being part of the greater whole; *he tong* referred to two things being in the same place; and *lei tong* referred to being the same in some respect, in that both things under consideration are related to one thing (MB 87.192). An example of the latter is: two kings are different, but both practice virtuous and benevolent governing.

Yi (difference), the second general category, included the subcategories *er* 二 (two), *bu ti* 不體 (not unity), *bu he* 不合 (not together), and *bu lei* 不類 (not of a kind). More specifically, *er* referred to two things being totally different; *bu ti* referred to two things not sharing the same structure; and *bu lei* referred to two things not belonging to the same category (MB 88.192–93). For the Later Mohists, *tong* and *yi* were not clearly delineated, since it was believed that there were times when it was difficult to treat objects as necessarily the same or different. More often than not, sameness and difference were considered relative in the interplay between "having and lacking, more and less, departing and approaching, hard and soft, dead and alive, elder and younger" (Graham 339). However, in some instances things were clearly of different kinds. For example, "someone deemed a *fu* 夫 (husband), when you link *yong* 勇 with it (*yong fu* 勇夫 'brave man') is not being deemed a husband" (352). A husband and a brave man are measured by different criteria; therefore, this is an example of *bu lei* (not belonging to the same category).

One of the Later Mohists' principles of argumentation involved "using propositions to dredge out ideas" (483), since such propositions were based on the ability to understand and correctly classifying ideas or categories. The Later Mohists emphasized the role of *lei* in proposing an argument:

The proposition is something which is engendered in accordance with the thing as it inherently is, becomes full-grown according to a pattern, and "proceeds" according to the kind. It is irresponsible to set up a proposition without being clear about what it is engendered and grows up from. Now a man cannot proceed without a road; even if he has strong thighs and arms, if he is not clear about the road it will not be long before he gets into trouble. The proposition is something which "proceeds" according to the kind; if in setting up a proposition you are not clear about the kind, you are certain to get into trouble. (480)

One way to avoid getting into trouble with the classification process is to follow *fa* 法 (standards, law, criteria). While Mozi defined the concept as a moral principle for engendering an orderly society, the Later Mohists borrowed the concept to refer to the standards used in classifying things and finding reasons (MB 71.178).[12] For them, the ability to classify was dependent upon one's ability to understand and apply *fa*. Two examples were offered to illustrate this point. According to the first example, "when some people are dark, some people are not dark. It does not mean that all people are dark. If someone is loved, someone is not loved, it means not all people deserve love. Which conclusion should you believe?" (MB 98.200). According to the second example, when we say that a thing with four legs is an animal, we cannot include all the animals. Only certain animals have four legs. It is a fallacy to call all the animals with the same name (102.202). To make a correct classification in these cases, one must understand the logical connections and disconnections between the statements so that the classification according to kind will not be confused and fallacious conclusion can be avoided. An approach to grasping *fa*, according to the Later Mohists, was to "identify the sameness, and observe if concepts or propositions are being distorted or cunningly borrowed from one to another" (97.199).

Another important logical concept proposed by Mozi and further discussed and elaborated by the Later Mohists was that of *gu* 故. "Using explanations to bring out reasons" (Graham 482) was considered the most important principle in argumentation. *Gu* was employed both to explain "causes" leading to effects and to explain "because" leading to conclusions. It can be seen as the premise for drawing inferences. For the Later Mohists, *gu* was understood as the reason as well as the result caused by the reason. According to the Later Mohists, there were two kinds of reasons: "Major reasons [da gu 大故]: having this, it will not necessarily be so: lacking this, necessarily it will not be so. Minor reasons [Xiao gu 小故]: having this, it will necessarily be so: lacking this, necessarily it will not be so" (263). An example of a major reason is eyesight, without which one cannot see and with which one can see. Minor reasons are like dots, without which a line cannot be formed but with which a line is not necessarily formed.

Various scholarly views exist concerning the interpretation of *gu*. Chang Ping-Ling argues that the Later Mohists' concept of *gu* contains a doctrine of syllogism with the major reason as the major premise and the minor reason as the minor premise (in Hu 1963). Hu Shih (1963) disagrees with this assertion, maintaining that the Later Mohists' theory of *gu*, though deductive in nature, it is not a theory of syllogism; rather, it is essentially a theory of correct prediction. Graham concurs with Hu on this point, claiming that the Later Mohist system of reasoning "has nothing to do with syllogistic demonstration" (1989, 153). In my opinion, the Later Mohist formula of minor and major reasoning is similar but not identical to syllogism.

A syllogism or deduction, defined by Aristotle, "is discourse in which, certain things being stated, something other than what is stated follows of necessity from their being so . . . no further term is required from without in order to make the consequence necessary" (*Prior Analytics* 24b20). In this sense, *da gu*, the major reason, is very much like the major premise of a syllogism: it is a statement that either affirms or denies a thing and from which a conclusion necessarily follows. The minor reason, or *xiao gu*, is a necessary condition which may or may not result in necessary consequences. In other words, a minor reason is a probable "cause and because" leading to a consequence, while a major reason assures a certain and inevitable "cause and because." According to an example offered by the Later Mohists, if there is general agreement in the statement "Robbers are people," the assertions that "loving robbers is not loving people, not loving robbers is not not loving people, killing robbers is not killing people" (Graham 487) are not logically consistent with the general agreement, though they are quite acceptable propositions. This is to say, there are times when logical reasoning does not accord with common sense regarding a particular situation.

A probability, defined by Aristotle, "is a reputable proposition: what men know to happen or not to happen, to be or not to be . . ." (*Prior Analytics* 70a1). Accordingly, major and minor reasons are indicative of two separate reasoning systems. Since they are not logically connected, they cannot form a syllogism. Major reason operates in the realm of *bi wu ran* 必無然 (certainty), while minor reason operates in the realm of *bu bi ran* 不必然 (probability). Whether a "cause and because" is considered a major or minor reason depends on the nature of *lei*. If *lei* is clearly marked, sameness or difference can be clearly distinguished, establishing a *da gu* (major reason) leading to an inevitable conclusion. If *lei* is only partially connected, a *xiao gu* (minor reason) is established leading to a probable conclusion.

Through their identification of the concepts of *lei, fa,* and *gu*, a rational system of argumentation emerged from the camp of the Later Mohists. The components of this system were *zhi lei* 知類 (knowing the kind or category), *xiao fa* 曉法 (knowing how to classify), and *ming gu* 明故 (understanding cause and because). Once these three elements were clearly laid out, *tui*, the process of inferring and generating conclusions, could properly proceed. At any rate, the concepts of *lei, fa, gu,* and *tui* were components of the Later Mohists' logical system, demonstrating their interest in rational thinking, as well as in the relationship between the certainty and probability of an argument. Though employing different terms and strategies in articulating and structuring their respective systems, the ancient Greeks and the Later Mohists shared the common goal of furthering the cause of rational thinking. As Garrett correctly concludes, "The summa [referring to *Mo Bian*] also reveals the mind-set of the formal operational thinker in its objectivity, its search for general laws, its use of the schemas, and its theory-building" (1983, 116).

(2) Moral Implication and Methods of Bian. Zhuangzi once argued that bian should not aim at finding out what is right and what is wrong, for in reality there is no right and wrong since each bian shi bases his judgment on his own perspective. Nor is a third person's judgment valid, since the arbitration is determined by the person's own perspective (Z 2.34). The Later Mohists strongly objected to Zhuangzi's attitude regarding bian. For them, bian was indispensable; its very purpose was to discover truth and whoever possessed truth was the winner. While both Confucius and Laozi advocated the notion of noncontentious argument, the Later Mohists disagreed. For them, "Pien [bian] (disputation) is contending over claims which are the converse of each other. Winning in disputation is fitting the fact." They further explained, "The things that something is called are either the same or different. In a case where they are the same, one man calling it a 'whelp' and the other man a 'dog,' or where they are different, one calling it an 'ox' and the other a 'horse,' and neither winning, [there] is a failure to engage in disputation. In 'disputation,' one says it is this and the other that it is not, and the one who fits the fact is the winner" (Graham 403). That is, winners and losers are determined by the argument that is most *dang* 當 (fitting).

According to Dale Sullivan, the notion of fittingness is a central component of the Greek notion of kairos, which is "grounded in an ontology that accepts the reality of Being" demonstrated in Pythagorism and Gorgias's use of logos (1992, 320). Similarly, for the Later Mohists, fittingness refers to the correspondence between a stated argument and the existing facts, generated through classification according to lei and the skillful use of gu. More importantly, the argument must be appropriate to the situation, as well as applicable to problem solving and sense making. In contrast with the Daoist view of bian, the Later Mohists believed that if an issue were controversial, it would not be possible for both sides of the argument to be right; one side must be right and the other side wrong. Furthermore, it was only through the presentation of a good argument that the rightness of one's views could be determined. The most effective means of persuasion, according to the Later Mohists, was to attack an argument for not fitting the facts (*MB* 95.198). Such attacks and propositions were articulated through *shuo* 說 (explaining/demonstrating), defined as "the means by which one makes plain" (Graham 317). Through shuo, lei was classified, gu was discovered, and tui was correctly accomplished.

In developing an argument, the Later Mohists proposed the following four principles for a bian shi to follow: "(a) use names to refer to objects; (b) use propositions to dredge out ideas; (c) use explanations to bring out reasons; and (d) accept according to kind, propose according to kind" (Graham 483).[13] These principles summarized the Later Mohists' conceptualization of ming bian. They also served as sequential steps in structuring and presenting an argument. These four principles share remarkable similarities with Aristotle's four means of securing a good argument: "(1) the securing of propositions; (2) the power to distinguish in how many ways an expression is used; (3) the discovery of the differences of things; (4) the investigation of likeness" (*Topics* 105a20). Numbers 1 and 2 are comparable to the Chinese concept of *ci* 辭 (expression), understood as a means to express ideas. Numbers 3 and 4 match with the notion of *lei* as means of discovering sameness and difference.

In addition to skillfully employing *ming, ci, shuo, lei,* and *gu* to win an argument, the Later Mohists further proposed the following four methods of bian: *pi* 闢 (illustration), *mou* 侔 (parallelism), *yuan* 援 (adduction), and *tui* 推 (inference) (Graham 483). *Pi* involved the use of what was known to infer what was unknown through a metaphorical use of language or analogy. *Mou* referred to the comparison of two propositions. *Yuan* involved the effort to prove to the opponent the validity and truthfulness of one's argument. *Tui* referred to using what had already been accepted by one's opponent to argue against what one's opponent seemingly opposed in order to point out the inconsistencies and contradictions in his/her claims. For example, in responding to the Daoist claim that language was perverse and misleading, the Later Mohists argued, "To say that 'all speeches are fallacious' is fallacious by itself" (*MB* 172.281). To say that something is perverse is to say that it is not acceptable. If a person's language is acceptable, then it is not perverse. Therefore, there is such a thing as acceptable language. That is, the Daoist assertion that language is perverse implies that the assertion itself is incorrect. If the sentence is correct, then it is not necessarily true that all language is perverse. This Later Mohists' criticism of the Daoist view of language was clearly meant to justify their use of bian. The familiar notion of rhetorical paradox can be identified in this criticism. As Chad Hansen points out: "The criticism of Taoists [Daoists] made by Neo-Mohists is precisely the one we should like to make of any doctrine of the inherent inadequacy or paradoxical nature of language" (1983, 123). Unlike the Greek tradition of technical rhetoric, which emphasized the systematic instruction of speech making and argument presentation, the four methods *pi, mou, yuan,* and *tui* were not used in any particular order.

Rather, they could be employed anywhere in the argument. The Later Mohist strategy for making an argument seems to lie in using all available means to defeat one's opponent rather than seeking truth through a cooperative effort.

For the Later Mohists, if the above methods were employed, one's argument would be stronger and more convincing. However, there was always the danger that such methods could lead to false analogy or false comparison, and thus to a fallacious argument. This is because, as the Later Mohists asserted:

Of things in general, if there are respects in which they are the same, it does not follow that they are altogether the same. The parallelism of propositions is valid only as far as it reaches. If something is so of them there are reasons why it is so; but though its being so of them is the same, the reasons why it is so are not necessarily the same. If we accept a claim we have reasons for accepting it; but though we are the same in accepting it, the reasons why we accept it are not necessarily the same. Therefore propositions which illustrate, parallelize, adduce and infer become different as they "proceed," become dangerous when they change direction, fail when carried too far, become detached from their base when we let them drift, so that we must on no account be careless with them, and must not use them too rigidly. Hence saying has many methods, separate kinds, different reasons, which must not be looked at only from one side. (Graham 483–84)

What the Later Mohists are saying here is that the meaning of language is different for each individual, so too for each particular situation. Truth for some people in some situations may not be truth for other people in other situations. Hence, one must be flexible and moderate when applying such methods in an argument; otherwise bias, erroneous conclusions, or false generalizations could result. As Graham argues, the Later Mohist "lays out his parallels, not in a fumbling search for the syllogism, but to show where the mutability of words in different combinations vitiates inferences, by false parallelism in the descriptions from which the inferences start" (1989, 155).

Not all persuasion and argumentation achieve their desired effects. According to the Later Mohists, there were seven possible kinds of agreement called *nuo* 諾 reached at the end of the disputation: (1) *Yi nuo* 詒諾, pretending to agree with one another but still differing in their hearts; (2) *cheng nuo* 誠諾, agreement from both mouth and heart; (3) *yuan nuo* 員諾, agreeing with the other but also adding something to the agreement; (4) *zhi nuo* 止諾, partial agreement; (5) *xiang cong nuo* 相從諾, accepting another's opinion and giving up one's own; (6) *xiang he nuo* 相合諾, a true agreement between the two sides; and (7) *wu zhi nuo* 無知諾, an attitude of noncommitment, neither agreeing with nor denying an argument (*MB* 94.196–97). The Later Mohists believed that the kind of nuo reached as the result of an argument depended upon the skill of the participants in asking and answering questions, classifying things, discovering reasons, and generating conclusions. A cheng nuo, or true sense of agreement, is difficult if not impossible to reach, given the Later Mohists' belief that in any given argument there should be a winner and a loser. The final result of an argument is one side wins and the other loses.

Comparisons with Mingjia and Aristotle

Comparison with Mingjia

Given Mozi's lower-class background and concern for the well-being of the common people, it is not surprising that he and his followers pursued the rhetorical strategies of ming bian for the purpose of establishing a new world order based on the unification of thoughts, egalitarianism, and utilitarianism. Later Mohists' views on epistemology, language, logic, and argumentation were influenced primarily by their founder Mozi and to a lesser extent by the teachings of the Chinese Mingjia. While Mozi's formulation of bian placed particular emphasis on social justice and practicality, the Later Mohists placed more emphasis on epistemological concerns. Toward this end, they incorporated Mozi's notion of *zhi lei* and *ming gu* into their logical system while specifying the location and function of these logical concepts. As already stated, they were greatly influenced by the Chinese Mingjia, primarily as opponents in disputation. As Feng notes: "It was from their criticism of the Chinese sophists [Mingjia], they [the Later Mohists] became interested in argumentation, logic, and epistemology" (1964, 405). Indeed, the Later Mohists' formulation of the concept of relativism was influenced by Hui Shi's notion of *he tong yi* 合同异 (integration of sameness and differences), while their adherence to bian as a means of discovering relative truth was influenced by Deng Xi's teachings concerning *liang ke* 兩可 (dual possibilities) and *liang shuo* 兩說 (dual interpretations). Perhaps they were mostly influenced, however, by Gong-sun Long, from whom they borrowed and developed the concept of ming, not only with regard to the classification of things belonging to the physical world but also at linguistic and abstract levels. It must be noted, in this regard, that although both schools were interested in argumentative methods, the School of Mohism never lost sight of its broader concern for social justice. In fact, the Mohists' interest in epistemological issues was motivated by the desire to further the cause of social justice and for no other reason. For them, bian was a means of discovering truth and knowledge. Mingjia, on the other hand, were more interested in the abstract level of disputation as well as in the generation of universal principles, independent of moral and social concerns. Consequently, they were much less thorough and systematic in their formulation of ming bian and of processes and methods related to persuasion and argumentation. While individual Mingjia expressed various concerns and expounded on different issues, the Later Mohists, by integrating the diverse ideas first proposed by Mingjia, seemed more unified in their thoughts. For example, in developing and formulating their logical system, they combined the notions of probability and relativism from Deng Xi and Hui Shi with the notions of logical necessity and abstraction from Gong-sun Long.

Comparison with Aristotle

As evidenced above, there are some obvious similarities between Aristotle and the Later Mohists regarding their theories on naming, lei (kind, categorization), and argumentation. However, the two differ in the formulation of their respective systems of logic. Aristotle was more interested in the relationship between and among things based on their definition and essence. Premises were based on how one element essentially and necessarily related to another and how a third perspective was automatically deduced from this relationship.[14] In other words, Aristotle's syllogism featured logical progression from premises to conclusion, and premises were related to each other as species relating to the kind. In contrast, judgment made according to the Mohist notion of lei were based not on whether two things were the same or different, but on whether an example (the minor premise) could be justified against a universal principle (the major premise), or whether the kind was part of a species.

Compared to Aristotle's syllogism, the Later Mohists' logical system involved considering variables and probable interpretations of "cause and because," as well as recognizing probable conclusions. Such conclusions often appeared illogical, though they were explainable by common sense. While directing one's attention to identification, classification, and comparison of sameness and differences on relative terms, the logical system of the Later Mohists also acknowledged the challenge, complexity, and intricacy of engagement in persuasive and argumentative tasks. Such a system allowed flexibility and applicability with regard to particular situations, while Aristotle's system prescribed necessary connections assuring more certainty than probability. In a sense, the Later Mohists emphasized "opinions," thereby providing a more dialectical perspective of argumentation. Aristotle's more "scientific" and demonstrative approach may be the hallmark of the difference between Chinese and Greek systems of logic and argumentation.

Clearly, the Mohists made a significant contribution to Chinese classical rhetoric, offering the most systematic and complete theory of ming bian. Unfortunately, they quickly lost their influence after 221 B.C.E. This loss in influence can be attributed to three reasons. First, after the unification of China in 221 B.C.E. and, in particular, after the establishment of the Han dynasty following the downfall of Qin, the social hierarchy reestablished itself, and the ruling elite reexerted its absolute authority and control over the people. The new ruling class no longer allowed the upward mobility of the lower and middle classes out of which the School of Mohism had formed. Thus, the Mohists were robbed of both the opportunity and means to ensure that their voices were heard and doctrines adopted. Second, like those of the Greek sophists, Mohist views, especially those regarding the formulation of ming bian as a means of knowing, generating truth, and achieving justice, challenged the Confucian orthodoxy that advocated reliance upon ancient models and prescribed moral principles as the basis for establishing truth and knowledge. The Mohist recognition of the human faculty of reason and sense making threatened the ruling authorities, who perceived freedom of expression and the intellectual pursuit of knowledge as the cause of social unrest and ideological confusion. Third, to reinforce central control and assure uniformity of thought, after 150 B.C.E. Dong Zhongshu 董仲舒 (179–104 B.C.E.), a scholar from the Western Han dynasty, proposed the practice of 罷黜百家, 獨尊儒術 "Doing away with the one hundred schools; Only respecting Confucianism," which was adopted by Han Wu Di 漢武帝 (140–87 B.C.E.). Confucianism established itself as the dominant ideology. Under such ideological dominance, combined with political control, society could no longer provide an environment conducive to the free exchange of diverse ideas. By the Confucian standard of morality, the Mohists' advocacy of utilitarianism was considered unethical and deceiving. Moreover, the Later Mohists were mistakenly equated with Mingjia and accused of showing a lack of concern for the morals of society by spreading "bizarre doctrines" with glib tongues. We can now reflect upon these unfortunate and unfair comparisons and judgments of the Mohists and recognize their contributions to the Chinese rhetorical tradition.

CHAPTER 8

Conceptualization of Yan and Ming Bian
The School of Daoism

In the previous chapters I discussed conceptualizations of ming bian by Mingjia, Confucianists, and Mohists, respectively. Though different aspects of ming bian were emphasized by these schools, all agreed that reality could be represented by language and that language could affect social, political, and moral conditions. A competing school of thought, known as Daoism, however, presented a view of language and ming bian completely different from all other schools.

Daoism is known to the West as a mystical philosophy attractive only to those "tired of competition, and to those resigned in the face of authoritarian administrations" (Becker 1986, 88). Western rhetorical scholars, in general, consider Daoism antagonistic toward rhetoric and rhetorical expressions. In particular, Daoists are known for deprecating speech, condemning argumentation, denouncing knowledge, and avoiding critical thinking (Jensen 1987; Oliver 1971). These perceptions are based on too literal readings of Daoist texts and on inadequate translations, complicated by the tendency of Western scholars to objectify and autotomize a discipline. Such perceptions will be challenged, however, and a new interpretation will emerge once Daoist rhetoric is placed in its proper philosophical context.

In this chapter I will use Daoist texts, namely the *Dao De Jing* 道德經 and *Zhuangzi* 莊子, to argue that Western scholarly views of Daoist rhetoric are generally incomplete, if not inaccurate. Understood in its totality, Daoism presents a worldview with metaphysical, dialectical, and rhetorical signficance that, in fact, does not condemn speech and argumentation but simply points out their limitations. In many respects, Daoism shares common ground with Greek sophistic epistemological relativism and Nietzschean aesthetic appeal. Furthermore, Daoist theories on human development have been found compatible with Maslow's humanistic perspective on the healthy personality and Kohlberg's perspective on universal justice (Ma 1990). In Lin Yu-tang's opinion, "Taoism [Daoism] is not a school of thought in China, it is a deep, fundamental trait of Chinese thinking, and of the Chinese attitude toward life and society" (1942, 625). The following chart highlights the Daoist philosophy and rhetorical perspectives:

Daoist Philosophy and Rhetoric

Names/Dates	Texts	Philosophical Views	Rhetorical Perspectives
Laozi 500 B.C.E.	Dao De Jing	Dao (the Way) & De (virtue) Nonaction, spontaneity Noncontention	Less talk Namelessness Paradox
Zhuangzi 369–286 B.C.E.	Zhuangzi	Mystical Dao De as a state of mind Nonattachment	Skepticism of language Transcendental *bian* Aesthetical appeals

Daoism was founded by Laozi, a contemporary of Confucius and Mozi, and Zhuangzi, a contemporary of Hui Shi and Mencius. Its most well known texts, *Dao De Jing* and *Zhuangzi*, were allegedly written by Laozi and Zhuangzi, respectively. This chapter will cover these two men and their works with respect to worldviews, philosophy of language, and perceptions regarding speech and argumentation. We begin with Laozi and the text of the *Dao De Jing*.

Laozi

Social Context and Personal Background

As a contemporary of Confucius, Laozi lived in the wake of the declining Zhou dynasty. The hierarchical social order and traditional cultural values were held up to public scrutiny. Society was faced with the challenge of restoring the old value system or establishing a new one. Intellectual debates and you shui activities were characterized by contention, competition, and a preoccupation with personal advantage, fame, and status. Confucius and

Mozi, acting as the vanguards of social ethics, advocated a new set of moral principles and cultural codes designed to restore social order and reshape human behavior. Laozi, on the other hand, regarded such efforts as the very cause for moral decay and social disorder. For him, dissension and contention were violations of social harmony. Likewise, the prescription and enforcement of moral principles and social structures were an artificial interpretation of spontaneous natural processes. In their place, Laozi proposed the notions of *wu wei* (nonaction, spontaneity) and *bu zheng* (noncontention), hoping to reduce the social impact on human behavior, to create space for spontaneity and creativity, and, finally, to touch the depths of human existence.

In reaction to the general climate in which he lived, as well as to Confucius's efforts to alter human behavior through moral propagation and purposeful action, Laozi argued that the principles of benevolence and rectitude should be abandoned, since the more people talked about such principles, the more corruption and hypocrisy would emerge. It was Laozi's belief that any constraints or artificiality imposed on society and human behavior were counterproductive to the natural development of things. In his words, "The more taboos there are in the empire, the poorer the people. . . . The better known the laws and edicts, the more thieves and robbers there are" (Lau 58.84–85).[1] Laozi believed that by taking no action, people would transform and rectify themselves, allowing themselves to prosper.

Little is known of Laozi's personal life and rhetorical activities. *Shi Ji* records that Laozi's real name was Li Er 李耳 and that he was also known as Lao Dan 老聃. Laozi was from the state of Chu and worked as an archivist for the Eastern Zhou dynasty. According to legend, after living in the capital of Zhou for many years and having witnessed the decline of the Zhou dynasty, Laozi was disillusioned with society and politics. The text *Dao De Jing* (Canon of Way and Virtue), also known as *Laozi* or *The Book of 5000 Words*, was written at the request of a Zhou official before Laozi left Zhou to live the life of a hermit (Si-Ma "*Laozi Hanfei liezhuan*" 314).[2] The text has eighty-one chapters and is divided into *Dao Jing* (Canon of Way) and *De Jing* (Canon of Virtue). Although only five thousand words in length, it covers a wide range of subjects. Benjamin Schwartz describes it as "a handbook of a prudential mundane life philosophy, a treatise on political strategy, an esoteric treatise on military strategy, a utopian tract, or a text which advocates 'a scientific naturalistic' attitude toward the cosmos" (1985, 192). Indeed, the Dao De Jing holds a significant place in Chinese history. It influenced the Legalist Han Feizi, whose efforts, under the employ of the emperor of Qin, helped unite China for the first time in Chinese history. Moreover, its ideas were subsequently applied to Chinese military strategies, the study of metaphysics, the Chinese conversion of Indian Buddhism, and Chinese *qi gong* 氣功 (meditation). As observed by Watson, "While the works of other ancient thinkers sank into obscurity or retained only a limited appeal, the Daoist writings, from the time they became known until the present, have constituted an indispensable part of the education of very cultured Chinese" (1962, 156). It is fair to say that Laozi's teachings, like those of Confucius, have permeated every area of Chinese life: its culture, thought patterns, and state of mind. In fact, one cannot truly understand the Chinese mind without understanding the Daoist sensibilities embodied in the *Dao De Jing*, the only Chinese classic that enjoys an equal status with Confucius's *Analects*.

The writing style of the *Dao De Jing* differs dramatically from other well-known philosophical works, such as those of Confucius and Mozi. Unlike Confucius and Mozi's style of engaging the reader in rational argument by offering an elaboration of ideas or preaching in a didactic manner, Laozi's style was witty, enigmatic, imaginative, rhythmic, and paradoxical. By employing this style, he invited the reader to feel and reflect upon his/her own experience and be awakened by the use of words. The *Dao De Jing* is an example of the use of literary style and aesthetic appeal to convey profound philosophical ideas. In this sense, it is remarkably similar to Plato's dialogues with the ancient Greeks.

Philosophical Views

The ancient Greeks and the ancient Chinese explored the question of ontology and epistemology. While ancient Greek philosophers speculated that the cosmos was made up of water, fire, air, or number, the ancient Chinese identified water, fire, wood, metal, and earth as the five basic elements of the cosmos and sources of growth (*SS "hongfan"* 98–101). In addition, the ancient Chinese further classified the natural components of Heaven and Earth into two abstract driving forces: yin (female, negative) and yang (male, positive). While the ancient Greeks dichotomized the physical and divine worlds (mind, soul), the ancient Chinese regarded yin and yang as interrelated and interdependent. The balance of yin and yang kept the physical and spiritual worlds in harmony, generating change and growth. Chinese cosmology, infused with these principles, is applied to every aspect of Chinese life. While the ancient Greeks grappled with the concepts of the One and the many, and being and becoming, the ancient Chinese explored the question of nonbeing. While Greek perceptions of the cosmos can be reduced to Plato's Form and Aristotle's science, the Chinese understanding of the universe is best summarized by the notion of *dao* (the Way), approached through *de* (virtue) and manifested in *wu wei* (nonaction, spontaneity) and *bu zheng* (noncontention).[3]

(1) Dao, the Way. In classical writings before Laozi's time, the word dao was used to mean the way, or road. The oldest version of the Chinese character *dao* 澫, which appeared on oracle bones, is comprised of three ideographs: a road 兂, a human head 旨, and a human foot 丫. According to Chang, this combination symbolized "a leader and follower united in finding their path" (1963, 25). This literal meaning of the way or path was extended in pre-Confucian texts such as *Shang Shu*, *Shi Jing*, and *Zuo Zhuan* into an abstract notion of divine force and principles of human behavior. Dao was divided into *tian dao* 天道 (the Way of Heaven) and *ren dao* 人道 (the Way of human). Confucius emphasized ren dao, prescribing moral principles to guide human behavior. Mozi employed tian dao as a rhetorical appeal in his attempts at moral persuasion, in particular, in advocating the principles of righteousness, universal love, and mutual benefits.

Laozi, on the other hand, discussed *dao* as a metaphysical and ontological concept for exploring the intricate relationship between abstract and concrete entities, as well as between the speakable and the unspeakable. In the *Dao De Jing*, *dao* is defined as the source of the universe, referred as *da* 大 (Great), for it is said to exercise absolute control over everything in the universe (25.68; 42.106). This notion of the *dao* challenged popular beliefs of the time that Heaven controlled the universe by its divine will and, conversely, that humans controlled the universe by acting in accordance with the will of Heaven. Laozi argued that neither Heaven nor humans were the controlling force of the universe. Rather the dao was above all else, directing the universe by its natural laws. The dao gives birth to life as well as to an environment conducive to physical and spiritual maturity, thereby transcending the dichotomy between *tian dao* and *ren dao* and making them into a unified whole.

A comparison of Laozi's dao with Greek philosophers Parmenides and Plato's Being and Form is instructive. According to the interpretations of Parmenides' philosophy by Western scholars, Parmenides divided the world into two parts: the physical world, characterized by plurality and change; and the intellectual world, unchanging, ungenerated and indestructible, known as One Being.[4] Influenced by Parmenides, Plato considered sensory knowledge of the physical world a deceptive and unreliable appearance, while, for him, truth and knowledge apprehended by intelligence captured the essence of entities and substance known as Form (Cornford 1939; Guthrie 1969; Ross 1951).

In contrast, Laozi's dao integrated physical and spiritual elements of the universe into one inseparable entity. Paradoxically, this dao was considered both unchanging in its essence and changing in its expression of that essence: unchanging in that its principles were enduring and encompassing with the capacity to transcend and reconcile opposites; changing in that all things were said to undergo a perpetual cyclic movement from birth to death to birth to death (25.38–39). Moreover, the dao was said to include the domains of both *you* 有 (something, being) and *wu* 無 (nothing, nonbeing). *You* was understood as the visible, formal, and limited, while *wu* was the invisible, formless, and unlimited. For Laozi, "The myriad creatures in the world are born from Something, and Something from Nothing" (Lau 40.61). That is, nonbeing/nothing is nothing other than an infinite, unmanifested vitality, possessing no limitations or distinctions. Being/something, on the other hand, is the actualization of the concealed and formless. Through naming and classification, this world of being/something is organized and made comprehensible.

(2) *De*, Virtue. Much more than an ontological and metaphysical text, the *Dao De Jing* provides wisdom and insights for an enlightened life. Its title is composed of two characters: *dao* 道 (the Way); and *de* 德 (virtue). While *dao* refers to the invisible, untouchable, and unspeakable law of nature, *de* refers to the fulfillment of the *dao* through wise speech and proper action. Scholars of the *Dao De Jing* tend to emphasize the notion of dao and overlook the notion of de, while, in fact, dao and de are intricately related and cannot be treated separately. Laozi made the following connection between dao and de: "The way [dao] gives them life; virtue [de] rears them..." (Lau 51.73). In other words, de is a natural manifestation of the dao, while dao is the potential that guides or molds the exercise of de. In this sense, the relationship between dao and de is similar to the relationship between ren (benevolence) and li (rites) proposed by Confucius. However, for Confucius, one observed ren and li through conscious effort inspired by the threat of externally imposed social sanctions, while for Laozi, de expressed itself spontaneously and from the inside out. As Laozi states, "A man of the highest virtue does not keep to virtue and that is why he has virtue. A man of the lowest virtue never strays from virtue and that is why he is without virtue" (38.57). That is, when virtue becomes internalized in a person's thought and action, he or she will not have to think about it at the conscious level.

Laozi discussed two kinds of de: *xuan de* 玄德 (mysterious virtue) and *chang de* 常德 (constant virtue). Mysterious virtue was the most profound and far-reaching of the two. It had the inner force to life but did not claim its presence (10.15). Constant virtue, on the other hand, was compared to a baby before it had lost its innocence or a block before it was carved. It was the sagely practice of nonaction by those with few desires for material life and personal gain. A person of de should understand his/her own position as well as all opposing perspectives in order to know how to act appropriately. Unlike Confucius, who regarded *ren ren* 仁人 (a benevolent person) as a person of moral superiority, Laozi's *de ren* 德人 (a person of virtue) was wise and "empty," in the sense of not being confined or restricted by a particular worldview but rather open to limitless, constantly changing possibilities of interpretation, understanding the laws of nature and able to "go with the flow." In particular, Laozi's notion of de embraced the notions of *wu wei* 無爲 (nonaction, spontaneity) and *bu zheng* 不爭 (noncontention).

(3) Wu Wei. Just as Aristotle challenged Plato on matters of philosophy and rhetoric, Laozi's Daoism was in response to his contemporaries, in particular, Confucius. While Confucius advocated a rational refinement of people and society, Laozi proposed wu wei. It was Laozi's belief that deliberately interfering with the natural order of things, rather than allowing things to run their course, would bring about the opposite effect to the one desired. Accordingly, Laozi predicted that whoever tries to impose his or her will in running an empire will only ruin the empire (29.45). At the personal level, whoever regards things as easy will meet with frequent difficulties (63.93). Similarly, by not talking about benevolence, benevolence will be gained. For example, the sage who "never attempts to be great . . . succeeds in becoming great" (63.93).

In proposing wu wei, Laozi was not advocating that people do nothing. He was concerned with achieving a kind of balance or equilibrium. For him, too much interference with natural social patterns would generate rigid patterns of response, sacrificing spontaneity at the social and individual levels. Unfortunately, in the West the principle of wu wei is often misinterpreted to mean doing nothing, while, in fact, it means to "do nothing artificially." As Chen Ku-Ying explains: "Lao Tzu [Laozi] considers that all phenomena must be allowed to develop in accord with their particular circumstances and potential, and must not be inhibited in any way by the imposition of external determinants" (1977, 17). In other words, to be in harmony with the dao, one must abolish all artificial restraints and comply with the laws of nature.

In his article "Communication East and West: Points of Departure" D. Lawrence Kincaid offers the following examples of nonactive and spontaneous communication:

When someone advises a young man or woman to act naturally and quit trying so hard to win someone's affections, they are advocating wu-wei, the principle of nonaction. In a similar manner, it is common practice for doctors to advise couples who have repeatedly failed to get pregnant to quit trying so hard for a while and see what happens. The athlete of any sport is well advised to give up trying to achieve his/her goal as he/she was taught and to simply get into the flow of the game, to visualize himself/herself performing rather than thinking about it conceptually step by step. (1987, 337)

When applied to the field of communication, these examples imply that direct and effortful persuasion may not bring about the desired effect in some situations. More often than not, failure in persuasion is caused by trying too hard to persuade. Effective persuasion may occur when one keeps silent or says as little as possible.

Unlike other skills, spontaneity is not deliberately practiced or acquired, nor does it involve a rational explanation. Paradoxically, it can only be accomplished through a kind of surrender infused with wisdom. Such wisdom involves a sensitive, intuitive, and artistic choice, rather than a formal, logical procedure. In other words, one must decide in the particular moment how best to get one's message across. As Wing-tsit Chan notes, "Taoists [Daoists] were not arguing for nihilism. Rather, they were arguing for the doctrine of self-transformation . . ." (1967, 134). In other words, the *dao* means allowing things to arise naturally, then transforming themselves from inside out.

(4) Bu Zheng. While Confucian philosophy advocated success through contention and competition, Daoist philosophy considered the opposite strategy more powerful and virtuous. Throughout the *Dao De Jing* Laozi encouraged people to dwell primarily in the realm of nonbeing, embracing the spiritual notion that noncontention is the best way to accomplish one's goals. He taught that what appears weak and soft may possess true strength, while what appears strong and aggressive may have certain inherent weaknesses. In his words, "The most submissive thing in the world can ride roughshod over the hardest in the world" (Lau 43.65). Metaphorically speaking, "Highest good is like water. Because water excels in benefiting the myriad creatures without contending with them and settles where none would like to be, it comes close to the way" (8.11). Further, According to Laozi, "The way of the sage is bountiful and does not contend" (81.117). "It

is because it does not contend that it is never at fault" (8.11). For Laozi, such noncontention is not only good for others but also for oneself, for when one is not contentious, there is nothing for others to contend with. Noncontention is not, however, passive or inactive. Instead, it is a positive action which only appears to be passive. As Chen argues:

> Lao Tzu's [Laozi] concept of "not contending" does not involve a negation of the self, nor does it imply an escape into the seclusion of some mountain retreat. Rather, it is propounded as a means for dissolving the dissention which racks human activity. It is not a display of pessimism or negativism. On the contrary, Lao Tzu urges man to "do"—this "doing" being an expression of human endeavor in accordance with what is natural. It is a willingness to "do" without seeking to appropriate the fruits of these endeavors for oneself. This spirit of duty to others ("benefitting the myriad things") and of not contending with others for achievement and reputation is both optimistic and positive. (1977, 33–34)

Accordingly, the qualities of nonaction, spontaneity, and noncontention are inherently virtuous in that they are true demonstrations of the dao. When the dao is applied to an argument, it takes on a moral quality, as it involves concern for and action on behalf of others. It is also a rhetorical strategy in that it invites one to "act" in order to realize one's potential in harmony with one's opponents or environment. In fact, the dao may well influence and carry more persuasive power than strategies involving contention and confrontation in a given situation. It is in this respect that Lin Yu-tang referred to Daoism as a philosophy of camouflage and characterized the *Dao De Jing* as a handbook for practical wisdom. In his words, "It teaches the wisdom of appearing foolish, the success of appearing to fail, the strength of weakness and the advantage of lying low, the benefit of yielding to your adversary and the futility of contention for power" (1942, 579).

Rhetorical Perspectives

Laozi's rhetorical teachings are rooted in his Daoist worldview and epistemology, the manifesting of de, or virtue, in terms of wu wei and bu zheng. His aim was to reduce the negative impact of language on human behavior. Basically, Laozi advocated *xi yan* 希言 (talking less) and *wu ming* 無名 (namelessness), attempting to awaken his audience and readers through the technique of *zheng yan ruo fan* 正言若反 (paradoxical and oxymoronic words).

(1) Xi Yan. In his study Vernon Jensen (1987) concludes that speech and argumentation are deprecated in the Daoist tradition. This might be true if we were to read Laozi's and Zhuangzi's work literally. However, as was discussed above, Laozi considered the path of nonaction, spontaneity,

and noncontention a virtuous basis for speech and argumentation. In this sense he did not condemn speech and argumentation out of hand, but only in those instances where they failed to conform to the virtues of nonaction, spontaneity, and noncontention. It was Laozi's assumption that those who employed contentious, flowery, and hollow expressions in their speech and argumentation were guilty of imposing too much artificiality upon the natural process. Such a strategy could only prove to their audience the opposite of whatever they intended to prove. Accordingly, Laozi argued, "truthful words are not beautiful; beautiful words are not truthful. Good words are not persuasive; persuasive words are not good. He who knows has no wide learning; he who has wide learning does not know" (Lau 81.117).

In the *Dao De Jing* Laozi advocated the virtuous practice of *gui yan* 貴言 (noble speech), *xin yan* 信言 (trustworthy speech), *shan yan* 善言 (good speech), *xi yan* 希言 (talking less), and *yi yan* 易言 (easy speech). Conversely, he advised against *duo yan* 多言 (talking too much). For him, a good speech was not determined by how much a person talked but by whether such talk was appropriate to the situation and substantial in meaning. The more verbose, the greater the artificiality imposed upon the natural process and the farther away the person was from the dao and de. It was for this reason that Laozi claimed, "One who knows [the dao] does not speak; one who speaks does not know [the dao]" (56.81). Ironically, though human beings invented speech, we have become victims of our own invention to the extent that words have lost their connection with the dao.

(2) Wu Ming. While in the rhetorical context Confucius proposed *zheng ming* 正名 (rectifying names), Mingjia advocated *cha ming* 察名 (observing names), Mozi and the Later Mohists emphasized *lei ming* 類名 (categorizing names), and Laozi's focus was on *wu ming* 無名 (namelessness). For Confucius, Mingjia, and the Mohists, *ming* was perceived as a means of knowing the world, establishing order, and shaping social and human behavior; thus, for them, the classification of *ming* was of utmost epistemological importance. Laozi, on the other hand, recognized the epistemological limitations of *ming*, namely, its ability to obscure and distort reality, thereby misleading human action.

Laozi's notion of namelessness was directly related to his understanding of the dao. As the dao was inclusive, mysterious, and ever changing, it followed that no names or symbols could sufficiently describe it. Consequently, for Laozi, while naming helps us function in the world, it can never fully embrace or represent the real nature of the thing, for language as a means of expression conceals as much as it reveals, distorting as well as capturing experiences and ideas. Therefore, according to Laozi, "the way is ever nameless" (32.49). Any efforts to name the dao could not possibly do it justice. In Laozi's words, "The way that can be spoken of is not the constant way; the name that can be named is not the constant name" (1.3). Hence, Laozi warned his readers, "As soon as there are names, one ought to know that it is time to stop. Knowing when to stop one can be free from danger" (32.49). This observation should not be understood as a blanket condemnation of speech but rather as an expression of concern about the abuse of language, which could lead to distorted perceptions of reality and immoral actions. As Graham explains, "The trouble [as Laozi sees it] with words is not that they do not fit at all but that they always fit imperfectly" (1989, 219).

According to Chung-ying Cheng (1977), there are two kinds of skepticism regarding language in the Western tradition: negative and positive skepticism. Negative skepticism attacks the notion that truth can be expressed through language without offering alternative insights regarding how such truth might be expressed. Such skepticism can be identified in the works of Sextus Empiricus and David Hume, for example. Positive skepticism "argues positively for higher level truth and knowledge above and over the skeptically criticized knowledge and truth" (Cheng 1977, 137). Such skepticism is evident in the work of Immanuel Kant, Rene Descartes, and Saint Augustine. With this in mind, it is useful to note that Laozi's skepticism fits the description of positive skepticism, since it aims not only at constructing a critique of language but also at elevating truth and knowledge to a higher level, namely the dao through the approach of wu ming (namelessness).

The concept of ming, like the Greek notion of logos, was consistently associated with linguistic representation and rational thinking in the context of ancient Chinese philosophy and rhetoric. By proposing the concept of wu ming (namelessness), Laozi challenged traditional notions of language, communication, and thought at their very foundations. Although other philosophers were aware of the negative impact of eloquent speeches lacking in moral substance, Laozi was the first to question the role and function of language itself from a philosophical perspective. For Laozi, to the extent that language classifies and dichotomizes reality, it interferes with the natural order of things, or the dao. Classification and bifurcation help us function in the world but in a limited and selective way primarily controlled by social elites and dominant intellectual discourse.

Laozi argued that neither logical reasoning nor sensory experience was an adequate means of expressing the dao, given their associations with the world of being and naming. For him, the dao could only be known through intuition or direct awakening of consciousness. According to Laozi, a person's state of mind is like a *xuan lan* 玄覽 (mysterious mirror) capable of direct reflection and clear knowledge of the dao. In this view, a person's failure to gain wisdom was attributed to misconceptions, metaphorically described as smudges upon the mirror, distorting one's experience of reality. To the extent one's mirror was free of smudges (free from being captivated by words), one would be able to *xuan tong* 玄通 (mysteriously comprehend) the dao (Lau 10.15; 15.21). It is fair to say that Laozi was the first Chinese thinker to discover the mode of inquiry commonly known as intuition and meditation, which laid the foundation for the smooth adaptation and assimilation of Buddhism from India.[5] Unfortunately, the intuitive process fostered by meditation is generally regarded in the West as inferior to logical thinking.

(3) *Zheng Yan Ruo Fan* (paradoxical and oxymoronic words). Laozi's philosophical and rhetorical views are conveyed not by a coherent explanation of concepts but through a deliberate twisting of normal thought patterns, including the reversal of words. This rhetorical strategy, which Laozi called *zheng yan ruo fan,* or using language in such a way that it seems paradoxical or oxymoronic, served the purpose of bridging seemingly oppositional elements and reaching a dialectical truth.

We live in an empirical world in which we perceive distinctions among things. We view our existence as divided into polar opposites such as high and low, weak and strong, black and white, right and wrong. Laozi agreed with the general notion that everything in the universe was composed of two oppositional elements. However, for him, such elements did not repel or contradict one another. Instead, they were complementary, mutually affecting one another. In fact, according to Laozi, one element could not exist without the existence of its opposite. The union of the two formed the continuous and dynamic process of the dao. In Laozi's words, "Something and Nothing produce each other; The difficult and the easy complement each other; The long and the short off-set each other; The high and the low incline towards each other; Note and sound harmonize with each other; Before and after follow each other" (Lau 2.5). This antithetical balance was also manifested in value judgments. For Laozi, people attribute certain characteristics to the good and the beautiful based on what they know as the bad and the ugly. In other words, the concepts of beauty and goodness only exist because of the existence of the concepts of ugliness and badness.

Moreover, because the movement of the dao is cyclical, all phenomena are in a state of constant interdependent flux. When the development of a phenomenon reached its extreme limit, it had also reached the point of opposing effect. In metaphorical terms, "a weapon that is strong will not vanquish; A tree that is strong will suffer the axe" (Lau 76.109). On the other hand, "The submissive and weak will overcome the hard and strong" (36.53). Likewise, in the context of speech and argumentation, verbal showing off will lead to its opposite effect: "He who shows himself is not conspicuous; He who considers himself right is not illustrious; He who brags will have no merit; He who boasts will not endure" (24.37).

To illustrate this dialectical nature of speech further, Laozi typically employed a strategy of reversal, giving negative meanings to affirmative words and phrases. Examples of such paradoxical sayings are: "Great perfection seems chipped; Great fullness seems empty; Great straightness seems bent; Great skill seems awkward; Great eloquence seems tongue-tied" (45.67). This type of paradoxical or oxymoronic use of language generated a kind of creative tension in Laozi's audience, ultimately propelling them out of conventional linguistic categories and habit of thought and into a direct, or intuitive, experience of the dao. While the Western notion of dialectics is generally associated with certain logic implications and defined as a counterpart to rhetoric, Laozi's version of dialectics is based on a profound understanding of the reality of change and changelessness that goes beyond mere logical categories.

Unlike the Western mode of inquiry, which emphasizes the affirmative, Laozi's emphasis was on the negative. For Laozi, the negative and weak were unlimited and without boundaries, while the positive and strong were limited and restricting. He believed that something seeming to be weak has inner strength (40.61). By celebrating the virtues of the seemingly weak and negative, Laozi directed our attention to the realm of nonbeing that is unlimited, integrated, and all-encompassing. Graham notes that Laozi's use of linguistic reversals to achieve this end is strikingly similar to Jacques Derrida's strategy for deconstructing the chain of opposites underlying the logocentric tradition of the West. In his words, "Both use a language which already escapes the opposition 'logic/poetry,' a language in which contradictory statements do not cancel out, because if made in the appropriate sequence of combination they set you in the true direction" (1989, 227). The direction Laozi set for us allows us to see both the light and shadow, both the visible and invisible, both the speakable and unspeakable.

Laozi's skillful use of paradox served the important rhetorical function of changing people's habitual thought patterns and leading them to see the reverse possibilities, by appealing to our intuition and deepest levels of knowing. This highlights for us the relative nature of the universe and our perceptions of reality, reminding us of the principles of change and of interdependence. In this view, nothing is fixed, eternal, or absolute. The element of negation and weakness is, in fact, the source and impetus for change. It must not, therefore, be overlooked or subordinate to the positive and the strong.

Laozi's epistemological and dialectical views were addressed to the society in which he lived and developed in response to Confucius's teachings. However, both the content and style of the *Dao De Jing* have profoundly affected the Chinese mind and culture throughout Chinese history. Moreover, despite his skepticism concerning language, Laozi proved himself a genius of the art of language.

Zhuangzi

Social Context and Personal Background

Zhuangzi's real name was Zhuang Zhou 莊周. Born in the state of Song, he was a contemporary of Hui Shi and Mencius. The record of Zhuangzi's personal life is very limited. He witnessed social chaos and moral decline resulting from the endless wars and pursuit of political power characteristic of the Warring States period. He also lived in a climate of vigorous philosophical debates over issues of morality, politics, and epistemology. Oftentimes those engaged in such debates attempted to "overwhelm the others with phrases and silence them with shouts" (Watson 24.268).[6] For Zhuangzi, such manner of speaking left no room for the art of persuasion and argumentation, proving only that the speaker was a slave of language and narrow in his worldview. In Zhuangzi's words, "They could outdo others in talking, but could not make them submit in their minds. Such were the limitations of the rhetoricians" (33.376).

In Zhuangzi's time, two views of ming were proposed as strategies of promoting social order and epistemological inquiry. One was *xing ming* 形名 (forms and names), which was proposed by Legalists and aimed at reward and punishment through the observation of laws. The other was *ming shi* 名實 (names and actualities), proposed by Mingjia and centered around the distinction between names and actualities. At the same time Confucius and Mencius propagated the principles of ren and li (rites). Although each proposed a different ideology, there was a general agreement regarding the power of symbols in shaping society and the life of the individual for the better. In contrast, Zhuangzi believed that symbols had been abused to such an extent that they had led to the formation of a hierarchical society, caused greed and fear to flourish, and encouraged people to engage in endless disputations over truth and falsehood. He criticized Hui Shi's use of language, characterizing it as "big and useless," and accused Gong-sun Long of arguing only for the sake of winning and temporary gains (1.33; 17.187). In particular, he targeted Confucius, accusing him of decking his speech out in feathers and paints, conducting his affairs with flowery phrases, mistaking side issues for the crux of the matter, and distorting his inborn nature in order to make himself a model for the people (32.357).

Zhuangzi was described by Si-Ma Qian in *Shi Ji* as a learned scholar whose philosophical principles originated with Laozi. In Zhuangzi's lifetime, his written work amounted to approximately a hundred thousand words, many of them in the form of fables and parables. He was also well known for his descriptive and eloquent style of writing (Si-Ma "*Laozi Hanfei liezhuan*" 315). Unlike other philosophers, or bian shi, who were actively involved in politics and statecraft, Zhuangzi showed little interest in social and political life. In fact, he believed that participation in politics placed certain unacceptable limits upon one's personal freedom. When invited by the king of Chu to be his minister of state, he responded with the following metaphor, "I have heard that there is a sacred tortoise in Chu that has been dead for three thousand years. The king keeps it wrapped in cloth and boxed, and stores it in the ancestral temple. Now would this tortoise rather be dead and have its bones left behind and honored? Or would it rather be alive and dragging its tail in the mud?" He then told the two officials sent by the king to go away, saying he would rather drag his tail in the mud like the tortoise than lose his freedom to work for the king (Watson 17.187–88).

Zhuangzi's cynicism toward politics was also reflected in his plain, even poor, personal life. According to one account, when visiting the king of Wei, he "put on his robe of coarse cloth with the patches on it, tied his shoes with hemp to keep them from falling apart" (20.216).[7] Although he once held a minor political position, Zhuangzi soon resigned and retreated from politics. Unlike Laozi, who became a hermit, hiding himself from the outside world, Zhuangzi traveled to various states and immersed himself in nature. In fact, his dialogues often took place by the river, in the mountain, or in the forest. "Free and Easy Wandering," as he named the first chapter of *Zhuangzi*, characterized his spirit of adventure and love for nature. Through such free and easy wanderings he formulated an aesthetic view of the world that found expression in his aesthetic use of language.

Although Zhuangzi was not considered a you shui, occasionally he engaged in persuasive activities. For example, the book of *Zhuangzi* recorded an incident in which he successfully persuaded the king of Zhao to stop sword fighting. Rather than using logical argument to make his case against sword fighting, Zhuangzi challenged the king to a sword fight. Just before the beginning of the fight, Zhuangzi explained to the king that he had three kinds of swords—the sword of the Son of Heaven, the sword of the feudal lord, and the sword of the commoner—and asked him to choose one with which to fight. The king asked Zhuangzi to explain the meaning behind each of the swords. After Zhuangzi did this, the king found himself using the sword of the commoner, which Zhuangzi described as "used by men with tousled heads and bristling beards, with slouching caps tied with plain, coarse tassels and robes cut short behind, who glare fiercely and speak with great difficulty, who slash at one another in Your Majesty's presence. Above, it lops off heads and necks; below, it splits open livers and lungs. Those who wield this sword of the commoner are no different from fighting cocks—any morning their lives may be cut off. They are of no use in the administration of the state" (30.343). On hearing this, the king reportedly gave up the sword fight and treated Zhuangzi to a good meal. In this example, Zhuangzi used psychological appeals to the king's sense of shame and honor, causing him to examine himself and the practice of sword fighting more carefully.

Though Zhuangzi was not regarded as a bian shi by his contemporaries, the book of *Zhuangzi* records his arguments with Hui Shi as well as his verbal attacks on Confucius, Mozi, and Gong-sun Long. It also records his views on matters of epistemology, speech, and argumentation, expressed through an artistic, imaginative, and often witty and sarcastic use of language. One account of Zhuangzi's writing describes it as "a string of queer beads and baubles, they roll and rattle and do no one any harm. . . . Though his words seem to be at sixes and sevens, yet among the sham and waggery there are things worth observing, for they are crammed with truth that never come to an end" (33.373). Zhuangzi's style of persuasion and argumentation was unusual for his time. Unlike other pre-Qin writers who presented themselves as moral teachers and engaged moral and rational approaches to persuasion, Zhuangzi's strategy was to shock his readers into self-realization of their own bondage, simultaneously gaining insights through the use of satire, humor, paradoxical anecdotes, and dazzling descriptions of mythical and magical figures. A literal reading of *Zhuangzi* may lead one to conclude that Zhuangzi was naive, illogical, incoherent, and oftentimes talking nonsense. A careful reading and reflection of *Zhuangzi* in the context of Zhuangzi's philosophy and wisdom leaves no room for doubt, however, that he was a sophisticated persuader, an eloquent bian shi, and a profound thinker.

While Confucianists, Mohists, and Mingjia aimed at reconstructing society and reforming human behavior through moral codes of conduct and the power of words, Zhuangzi, like Laozi before him, perceived their efforts as fetters constraining and confining a natural development of human nature. For example, Zhuangzi described the Confucian principles of benevolence and righteousness as two toes webbed together and a sixth finger which violate the inborn nature body (8.98–99). For Zhuangzi, the primary problem faced by individuals and society was not that people failed to follow the prescribed political and moral creeds, but rather that they had become slaves to the prescribed codes of conduct formulated through language and concepts. Accordingly, Zhuangzi was interested in the emancipation of the individual mind from conventionally accepted ideas and practices. His *Zhuangzi* was an exposition in content and style of this central theme and purpose. In this sense he was a deconstructionist, a critic, and a liberal thinker. In the following pages I will examine the text of *Zhuangzi*, in particular its philosophical ideas, theories of yan and bian, and aesthetic appeal.[8]

Philosophical Views

Zhuangzi shared with Laozi a similar worldview as well as an interest in issues that went beyond the obvious. However, Zhuangzi's exposition of the notions of dao and de was both more mysterious and profound than that of Laozi. The text of *Zhuangzi* was believed to have been produced some years after the *Dao De Jing*, though, strangely, Zhuangzi never mentioned the *Dao De Jing* in his writing. However, we can see in *Zhuangzi* traces of Laozi's influence in philosophical thought, especially on the notions of dao and de.[9]

(1) Dao. Zhuangzi's description of the dao was similar to that of Laozi. For him, the dao was "complete, universal, all-inclusive" (22.241). In this sense, it was the One, embracing yin and yang, subject and object, form and formless. In other words, the dao was that which unifies dualities and multiplicities, balancing as well as reconciling opposites.

Like Laozi, Zhuangzi also taught that the dao was the source and controlling force of Heaven and Earth. However, while Laozi defined the dao as both form and formlessness, changing and unchanged, Zhuangzi emphasized the formless and changing nature of the dao. In his words, "The Way has its reality and its signs but is without action or form. You can hand it down but you cannot see it" (6.81). In attempting to explain ways to reach the dao or the mind of sage, Zhuangzi employed the rhetorical strategy of pseudoconversations between Laozi and Confucius. For example, in *Zhuangzi* Laozi reportedly advises Confucius to abandon the desire for fame and give up attempts to correct others, but, more importantly, "you must fast and practice austerities, cleanse and purge your mind, wash and purify your inner spirit, destroy and do away with your knowledge" (22.238). This method of attaining the dao was later incorporated into Chinese Buddhist practices for attaining enlightenment.

For Zhuangzi, the dao could not be reached by adhering to certain principles. To purify one's mind was to forget about socially imposed principles and allow one's mind to be free from interference and the influence of external boundaries.[10] Further, Zhuangzi developed Laozi's notion of wu wei (nonaction, spontaneity), applying it in the interest of spiritual freedom rather than political gain. In this context, *wu wei* meant not being confined to principles of reason in the guidance and justification of one's actions, but rather leaving space for one's mind to roam freely, attend to the total situation, and act instinctively and spontaneously. Echoing Laozi, Zhuangzi claimed, by doing nothing, "yet there is nothing that is not done" (22.235).

To illustrate the organic spontaneity of being in harmony with the dao, Zhuangzi offered the following fable of cook Ting: "Cook Ting was cutting up an ox for Lord Wen-hui. At every touch of his hand, every heave of his shoulder, every move of his feet, every thrust of his knee—zip! zoop! He slithered the knife along with a zing, and all was in perfect rhythm, as though he were performing the dance of the Mulberry Grove or keeping time to the Ching-shou music." When asked how he reached such skill of perfection, the cook replied: "What I care about is the Way, which goes beyond skill. When I first began cutting up oxen, all I could see was the ox itself. After three years I no longer saw the whole ox. And now—now I go at it by spirit and don't look with my eyes. Perceptions and understanding have come to a stop and spirit moves where it wants. I go along with the natural makeup, strike in the big hollows, guide the knife through the big openings, and follow things as they are. So I never touch the smallest ligament or tendon, much less a main joint" (3.50–51). This anecdote skillfully explains the process and outcome of "gaining the dao," illustrating the point that a master of life is not a technician who thinks about rules and follows instructions, but an artist with a thorough understanding of the situation who acts with great ease, precision, and spontaneity.

(2) De. While Laozi discussed the dao in metaphysical terms, Zhuangzi emphasized the dao with epistemological interests revealed in his elaboration of two kinds of de: *xuan de* (mysterious virtue) a mind state needed for achieving well rounded perspectives and *chang de* (constant virtue) a human quality for gaining a virtuous mind that has no fixed form but is in perfect

harmony with all things. Zhuangzi described virtue as the ability to perceive things in a harmonious and interconnected way. Accordingly, the man of virtue was a man who "rests without thought, moves without plan. He has no use for right and wrong, beautiful and ugly" (12.137). The virtuous mind is characterized by limpidity, silence, emptiness, and inaction. Furthermore, the virtue of the sage is complete, and his spirit is unimpaired. In other words, a virtuous person lives his/her life without desire for fame and benefit, and without preference for values and judgment. Ultimately, for Zhuangzi, de was not a moral or ethical attribute, but a state of mind free of attachment to any particular perspective and, therefore, limitless.

While Confucius's ideal individual was a junzi, Zhuangzi's ideal individual was a *zhen ren* 眞人 (true person), who lived in the secular world while possessing the attitude and state of mind of the sage. For Zhuangzi, a zhen ren was utterly free from worries and fears. He "slept without dreaming and worked without care; he ate without savoring and his breath came from deep inside" (6.77–78). A zhen ren possessed forgetfulness in the sense that he was free from bias, prejudice, and attachment. His mind was in a state of perfect equilibrium, even while embodying diverse views and conflicting opinions. In other words, it was a mind of nonattachment, inclusiveness, and spiritual transcendence. For Zhuangzi, the primary obstacle to gaining such a mind was one's attachment to language and symbols. To remove this obstacle, one must deconstruct one's previous conceptual framework, creating a new way of seeing the world and living one's life in its place.

Rhetorical Perspectives

As did Laozi's, Zhuangzi's rhetorical perspective centered around his goal of attaining dao and de. Basically, he expressed a skeptical view of language combined with a transcendental vision of argumentation.

(1) Skepticism of Language. Zhuangzi proposed a more complete theory of yan (language) than had Laozi. While Laozi identified the limitations of ming in representing the all-inclusive dao at an abstract level, Zhuangzi discussed yan in more concrete terms with reference to words, speech, persuasion, and argumentation. For Zhuangzi, the dao and yan were closely related. As Hansen observed of Zhuangzi's work, in *Zhuangzi*, "almost every mention of tao [dao] is paralleled with a similar claim about language [yan]. The character tao/way is used thirteen times in the chapter [chapter 2] and eleven of those times the claim about tao is introduced, followed, or explained by a claim about yan/words: language" (1983, 37). The connection between dao and yan is crucially important because yan is considered both

an obstacle and means of access to the dao, and, as the reader will recall, the notion of the dao redefined the role and function of language.

In Zhuangzi's view, a good speaker possesses both dao and de. For him, speech should not be merely eloquent, flowery, or high-sounding expressions; rather, speech must be made meaningful. Just as in *Gorgias* and *Phaedrus*, respectively, Plato made a distinction between true and false rhetoric, Zhuangzi divided speeches into two categories: *da yan* 大言 (great words), that is, speech that aims at achieving the dao by its clear and limpid expression of language; and *xiao yan* 小言 (small words), speech that is interested in winning through embellishment.[11] While da yan paves the way for the reconciliation of opposing perspectives, xiao yan merely agitates a person into contention, artificiality, and dogma. Da yan in some ways resembles the Chan/Zen 禪 teaching of *language samadhi*, the enlightened expression of language (Zenji 1977).

For Zhuangzi, the problems of language lie not only in its potential abuse and artificiality, but in its limited functions of classification and value judgment. It was Zhuangzi's contention that some people could not attain the dao and de because their minds were clouded with distinctions and classifications formulated through the use of language. In other words, language, to the extent it functions as a dichotomizing element, is an obstacle to truth and knowledge. For instance, when "there is left, there is right, there are theories, there are debates, there are divisions, there are discriminations, there are emulations, and there are contentions" (Watson 2.44). When language is used in such a way, the different and uncompromising perceptions of reality cause conflicts and struggle such as wars and personal attacks at the social and individual levels. For Zhuangzi, the act of clinging to and being confined by the boundaries and limitations of language is characterized as *xiao zhi* 小知 (little understanding). Being aware of such boundaries and limitations and acting accordingly is referred to as *da zhi* 大知 (great understanding). Xiao zhi is a state of mind preoccupied with the desire to win an argument and the drive to distinguish right from wrong, while da zhi is a state of mind characteristically open to diverse possibilities and attempts at reconciling opposites. According to Zhuangzi, language should be used to achieve true harmony of opinions rather than to create false dichotomies and opposites. The latter use of language will not do justice to reality, which is by its very nature integrated in accordance with the dao.

For Zhuangzi, the limitation of language is evident not only in its rational function, but also in its inadequacy in representing ideas. In this regard, according to Zhuangzi, language is no more than a tool for expressing ideas that, ultimately, cannot be fully expressed through language. For this reason, it would be dangerous for people to take the meanings expressed through language for the subtle and unfixed meanings underlying them. What is more, language, especially xiao yan, creates illusions and inescapable bias, twisting one's intended meaning and distorting reality. In Zhuangzi's words, "Men of the world who value the Way all turn to books. But books are nothing more than words. Words have value; what is of value in words is meaning. Meaning has something it is pursuing, but the thing that is pursuing cannot be put into words and handed down" (13.152).

Indeed, words cannot fully represent the mind; language can never completely express ideas. Ultimately, meaning and ideas can only be transmitted directly from mind to mind. In fact, in Chinese culture, the ability to know another's mind beyond words is considered an essential element of truly artful communication, for once things are put into words, their rich, subtle, and profound meaning is lost. This direct transmission of knowledge from mind to mind is a communication principle and practice in Chan/Zen Buddhism.

As the function of language is limited, Zhuangzi suggested using it in a limited way while utilizing our minds for more profound and subtle exploration. In his words, "We can use words to talk about the coarseness of things and we can use our mind to visualize the fineness of things" (17.178). We tend to rely on language for meaning, in the process becoming dependent on it, when, in fact, the mind is more powerful than language in containing and absorbing meaning. For this reason, Zhuangzi warned us not to be trapped by words. He offered the following analogy to illustrate the limited function of language: "The fish trap exists because of the fish; once you've gotten the fish, you can forget the trap. The rabbit snare exists because of the rabbit; once you've gotten the rabbit, you can forget the snare. Words exist because of meaning; once you've gotten the meaning, you can forget the words" (26.302). Zhuangzi's words echo Ludwig Wittgenstein's advice to his readers that "when he [the reader] has used them [propositions] as steps to climb up beyond them, he must, so to speak, throw away the ladder (after he has climbed up it)" (1961, 151).[12] According to Burton Watson, the best way to understand *Zhuangzi* is "to read and reread his words until one has ceased to think of what he is saying and instead has developed an intuitive sense of the mind moving behind the words, and of the world in which it moves" (1968, 7).

Indeed, it was just this sense of the mind moving beyond the words that led Zhuangzi to propose *wu yan* 無言 (no language) and *wang yan* 忘言 (forget language) as means of freeing oneself from the captivity of language, accentuating one's attention to ideas, and allowing things to develop by their own nature. *Wu yan* and *wang yan* do not mean to abandon language altogether, but rather to be free of its limitations so as to perceive the world of unlimited possibilities. In this context, *yan* refers to language that has been tainted, biased, and artificially constrained. Using such language, "you may speak all your life long and you will never have said anything." Abandoning such language, "you will never have stopped speaking" (Watson 27.304). In this way, you will have mastered the art of silence and nonverbal communication.

Like Laozi, Zhuangzi believed that the dao can never be fully described, named, or expressed in words. Consequently, he advocated *zhi yan qu yan* 至言去言 (perfect speech is the abandonment of speech), *bu yan zhi jiao* 不言之教 (wordless teaching), and *bu yan zhi bian* 不言之辯 (dispute without words) (Z 22.298). Moreover, he praised silence as the best way to learn and communicate, saying "Eloquence is not as good as silence. The Way cannot be heard; to listen for it is not as good as plugging up your ears. This is called the Great Acquisition" (Watson 22.240). For Zhuangzi, nonverbal communication was not only more useful and essential than verbal communication, it was also the highest phenomenological level, for when things are in their perfect state, the presentation of it is nonverbal. In Zhuangzi's words, "Heaven and earth have their great beauties but do not speak of them; the four seasons have their clear-marked regularity but do not discuss it; the ten thousand things have their principles of growth but do not expound upon them" (22.236). Thus, nonverbal communication is both the means and end of communication just as nonbeing is both the source and the driving force of the universe.

While Zhuangzi condemned the use of language by Confucius and Mingjia, he also attempted to redefine the purpose, process, and manner of speech and persuasion in order to help people attain the dao. Similarly, Plato condemned the use of rhetoric by the Greek sophists yet redefined rhetoric as an art leading to the soul (*Phaedrus* 261). As a means of attaining spiritual freedom or awakening to the dao, Zhuangzi encouraged the use of *da yan* 大言 (great words), saying "If you talk in a worthy manner, you can talk all day long and all of it will pertain to the Way. But if you talk in an unworthy manner, you can talk all day long and all of it will pertain to mere things" (Watson 25.293). He proposed a Daoist process of persuasion: "go along with things and let your mind move freely. Resign yourself to what cannot be avoided and nourish what is within yourself" (2.61). Clearly, Zhuangzi advocated an open and spontaneous approach to persuasion, one requiring what John Poulakos called "discretionary powers" (1983, 42), rather than an understanding of rules. This approach was similar to the

Greek notions of kairos and *prepon*, two highly regarded artistic elements of persuasion. According to George Kennedy, kairos is the art of tailoring one's rhetorical style to one's audience, while prepon is the art of fitting one's response to the situation (1963, 67). Similarly, Zhuangzi's proposed approach to speech and persuasion cannot be learned mechanically, since it involved artistic choice as well as a gift for communication rooted in an intimate familiarity with the dao. The highest form of communication, according to Zhuangzi, was neither words nor silence but an appropriate and worthy manner such as noncontention and the practice of da yan. Since *da yan* could mean silence, as in *da yan wu yan* 大言無言 (great words are not words), or some other form of rhetorical strategy, depending upon the context, Zhuangzi was unfortunately unable to specify its content and style. It might well have been Zhuangzi's intention not to articulate the content and style of da yan, given his skeptical view of language.

Zhuangzi's view of language resembled that of the Greek sophists in the assumption that language creates infinite possibilities and versions of reality. For this reason, it can also create illusions and deceptions. This skeptical view of language is similar to that of Plato. Zhuangzi held both of the above views of language at the same time, allowing his reader to see language as a complex human entity rather than in exclusively positive or negative terms. In this sense, Zhuangzi's rhetorical views were internally consistent.

(2) Transcendental Bian. Plato defined the oration practiced by the ancient Greeks as "a knack" designed to convince the ignorant and gain gratification and pleasure (*Gorgias* 459c, 462c). Similarly, Zhuangzi perceived the function of bian (argumentation, debate, disputation), practiced by Mingjia and other bian shi of his time, as enabling debaters "to invent wily schemes and poisonous slanders" and "bewilder the understanding of common men" (Watson 10.113). He felt that in their efforts to persuade others they had been "dazzling men's minds, unsettling their views" (33.376). For both Plato and Zhuangzi, the world in which they lived was filled with illusion, deception, and confusion caused by the use of language and argumentation. However, while Plato sought a philosophical rhetoric characterized by rationality and morality, Zhuangzi attempted a redefinition of *bian* that would embrace both feelings and reasons, relative and absolute truth. Furthermore, while Plato aimed at establishing a new rhetoric based on knowledge of eternal truth, Zhuangzi pursued the mythic and inclusive dao.

According to Siao-fang Sun, "truth in the absolute sense is a concept of metaphysics, while truth in the relative sense is a concept of semantics" (1953, 138). In the Daoist scheme of things, the dao resides in both these realms, with Laozi emphasizing metaphysical concerns and Zhuangzi emphasizing semantic domains. Laozi's metaphysical dao infused Chinese culture with new ontological and cosmological insight, while Zhuangzi's semantic dao recognized the relative nature of perceptions and unavoidable differences in opinions. From the perspective of the semantic dao, no version of reality was absolutely right or wrong since linguistic meaning is not fixed and people perceive reality differently. The following dream illustrates the relative nature of human perception:

Once Chuang Chou [Zhuangzi] dreamt he was a butterfly, a butterfly flitting and fluttering around, happy with himself and doing as he pleased. He didn't know he was Chuang Chou. Suddenly he woke up and there he was, solid and unmistakable Chuang Chou. But he didn't know if he was Chuang Chou who had dreamt he was a butterfly, or a butterfly dreaming he was Chuang Chou. Between Chuang Chou and a butterfly, there must be some distinction! [Yet in the dream nondifferentiation takes place.] This is called the transformation of Things. (Watson 2.49)

In this example Zhuangzi suggested that the distinction between dreaming and waking, the imaginary and the real was blurred. Our knowledge about the world was therefore subjective, uncertain, and relative. To Zhuangzi, reality was a unified whole with different interrelated and interdependent elements, each equally valid. In his words, "Everything has its 'that,' everything has its 'this.' From the point of view of 'that' you cannot see it, but through understanding you can know it. So I say, 'that' comes out of 'this' and 'this' depends on 'that'—which is to say that 'this' and 'that' give birth to each other" (2.39). For Zhuangzi, distinctions between right and wrong can only lead to one-sided views, preventing a person from seeing both "this" and "that." Whereas the Mingjia, Mohists, and Confucianists were basically concerned about the difference between "this" and "that," Zhuangzi questioned whether between "this" and "that" any real distinctions exist. Further, Zhuangzi fully acknowledged the interrelationship of the opposites and attempted to foster a flexible attitude based on the recognition of the changing nature of subjective and objective dispositions.

Given Zhuangzi's relativistic ontological and epistemological views, and his skepticism about language in general, it is not surprising that Zhuangzi questioned the force and validity of argument. However, it cannot be overstated that it was not the art of bian that Zhuangzi opposed, but rather its limitation on classifying oppositions and its role in perpetuating oppositions. As Kuang-Ming Wu observes, "His [Zhuangzi's] opposition to opposition . . . is neither a total refusal to debate nor a complete involvement in it, but a continual allusion to the profound significance of the freedom of life, expressed in seemingly frivolous ironies, stories, and arguments" (1982, 20).

Clearly, for Zhuangzi, there was little value in bian if its aim was to win over others by distinguishing right from wrong. According to Zhuangzi, argument of this kind can lead nowhere for the simple reason that ultimately there was no such thing as truth and falsity. In Zhuangzi's words:

Suppose you and I have had an argument. If you have beaten me instead of my beating you, then are you necessarily right and am I necessarily wrong? If I have beaten you instead of your beating me, then am I necessarily right and are you necessarily wrong? Is one of us right and the other wrong? Are both of us right or are both of us wrong? If you and I don't know the answer, the other people are bound to be even more in the dark. Whom shall we get to decide what is right? (Watson 2.48)

In Zhuangzi's view, one's worldview is always limited because of his/her limited experience and the subjective meaning one gives to words in presenting an argument. Given the fact that each individual has his/her own unique illusions about the world, different opinions are inevitable. Furthermore, the clash of different perceptions can never be satisfactorily resolved if each person clings to his or her own illusions regarding truth. In Zhuangzi's words, "The common run of men all alike debate how to reach it (Dao). But those who have reached it do not debate, and those who debate have not reached it" (22.240). In Russell Goodman's interpretation, "our debates and defenses are ridiculous, and the world is not something to be proved or forgotten but to be enjoyed" (1985, 236). Here, it was debate aimed at winning and losing that Zhuangzi considered futile and ridiculous, rather than debate itself.

While identifying dualistic and entrenched argument as a cause of illusion, deception, and confusion, Zhuangzi also proposed an antidote. For him, the problem of perceptual dualism could only be resolved by reaching totality—that is, by coming to rest in that perpetual state of equilibrium known as the dao. From such an exalted vantage point all things are equally valid, including the different opinions expressed by different people. For Zhuangzi, a skillful argument should go beyond limitations and distinctions. A sage speaker, accordingly, does not quibble over right and wrong but rather attends to the total situation, synthesizing diverse views and conflicting perspectives, and thereby proceeding not in the way of dichotomy but of illumination. In Zhuangzi's words, "He too recognizes a 'this,' but a 'this' which is also 'that,' a 'that' which is also 'this.' His 'that' has both a right and a wrong in it; his 'this' too has both a right and wrong in it.

He should try to reach a state of mind in which 'this and 'that' are no long perceived as opposites; he aims at integrating opposite visions into one and harmonizing the right and wrong" (Watson 2.40–41). In other words, Zhuangzi's ideal speaker is a free person—free from limitations, illusions, and deceptions. Such freedom allows an open, inclusive, and transcendent mind capable of absorbing and harmonizing different opinions. It is the state of both/and rather than either/or. As Cheng explains, "Chuang Tzu's [Zhuangzi's] recommendation is that one should treat the opposition between the two sides as if it is not an opposition. . . . This also amounts to accepting all sides of opposition in a comprehensive framework" (1977, 145). In this way communication will be a shared, humane, and complete experience. This view is similar to Martin Buber's philosophy of the genuine dialogue in which one sees oneself not as a separate individual, but rather as a part of the "essential We" that lies in the sphere of the "between" (1958).

Zhuangzi's Aesthetic Appeal

Zhuangzi is remembered and studied not only for its profound philosophy, skepticism of language, and transcendence of argumentation, but also for its aesthetic and rhetorical appeals in the use of language. The reason for this is that, though he claimed that the dao was incommunicable (by the rational and didactic use of language), Zhuangzi nonetheless used every artistic and rhetorical device at his disposal to communicate the dao. Even while pointing out the limitations of language, he utilized the art of language to liberate his reader from attachment to language, leading him/her to an altogether new state of mind. The text of *Zhuangzi* is filled with fables, anecdotes, fantasies, analogies, aphorisms, ironies, and humor used as rhetorical and aesthetic devises for communicating Zhuangzi's relativistic and transcendent insights as well as his love for nature and preference for a plain but enlightened life. In reading *Zhuangzi*, the reader is both enlightened and entertained. Impressed by its "sheer literary brilliance," Watson observes, "His technique is seldom to argue or persuade, but to shock the reader into awareness of his own narrow conventionalism and coax him out of it with visions of the realm beyond, usually couched in the metaphor of a mystic, soaring journey through boundless space" (1962, 162). Chad Hansen characterizes Zhuangzi's "unique philosophical style" as one "that is both attractive and frustrating, both delightful and challenging to interpreters of his work" (1992, 265). Clearly, *Zhuangzi* is a masterpiece of wisdom and eloquence, and its author a master of the art of communication.

As is Nietzsche's, Zhuangzi's writing is romantic in tone, characterized by exaggeration and flights of imagination. It praises nature and celebrates individual freedom. To be sure, Zhuangzi is an accomplished craftsman of words. His poetic and aesthetic style not only entertains the reader, but also seduces him/her into surrendering all preconceived limits. According to Steve Whitson and John Poulakos, this type of aesthetic appeal "allows people to suspend willingly their disbelief and be exposed to a world other or seemingly better than the one with which they are familiar, all too familiar. That is why the rhetorical art asks not for dialectically secured truths but for linguistic images that satisfy the perceptual appetites or aesthetic cravings of audiences" (1993, 138). Once one's attachment to the all too familiar is loosened one can begin to become familiar with the previously unfamiliar dao.

Zhuangzi employed the following six rhetorical devices in making his aesthetic appeals for philosophical understanding: (1) three modes of speech; (2) paradoxical and oxymoronic sayings; (3) fables; (4) pseudo-dialogues; (5) reconstructed anecdotes; and (6) glorification of the ugly and handicapped.

(1) Three Modes of Speech. Zhuangzi employed the following three types of words or modes of speech in his writing: *yu yan* 寓言 (imputed words); *chong yan* 重言 (repeated words); and *zhi yan* 卮言 (goblet words). Imputed words were those put into the mouths of individuals who were not followers of Zhuangzi. By using this strategy, Zhuangzi could freely express himself through other persons. Repeated words were those spoken by respected and established elders, primarily Confucius and Laozi. This strategy appealed to the Chinese cultural tendency to value the elders and, in the process, also added to the credibility and persuasive effect of Zhuangzi's ideas. Goblet words were those used to present all sides of an issue, giving equal treatment to different schools of thoughts. In Zhuangzi's view, of the three strategies, imputed words were the most effective, repeated words were the second most effective, and goblet words were the least effective.[13]

It must be noted that the distinction among these strategies is often blurred in the text. For example, imputed words were often spoken by elderly individuals or by someone from a different school of thought; repeated words were often used to present different opinions; and, finally, goblet words were often spoken by the elderly or by individuals not representing any particular school of thought. Furthermore, these strategies were not employed in the sense of today's scholarly papers in the social sciences or humanities, in which evidence is presented from different sources or authoritative scholars are cited to support the argument. Rather, Zhuangzi's literary style was one of imagination, exaggeration, and creation. In the last chapter of *Zhuangzi*, a summary of Zhuangzi's style and purpose of his writing was given:

He expounded them [daoist ideas] in odd and outlandish terms, in brash and bombastic language, in unbound and unbordered phrases, abandoning himself to the times without partisanship, not looking at things from one angle only. He believed that the world was drowned in turbidity and that it was impossible to address it in sober language. So he used "goblet words" to pour out endless changes, "repeated words" to give a ring of truth, and "imputed words" to impart greater breadth. He came and went along with the pure spirit of Heaven and earth, yet he did not scold over "right" and "wrong," but lived with the age and its vulgarity. (Watson 33.373)

(2) Paradoxical and Oxymoronic Sayings. Like Laozi, Zhuangzi often used paradoxical and oxymoronic language to communicate the essence of the dao. For example, to illustrate his point that the perfect state of a thing that is beyond words and even beyond being itself cannot be expressed in overt verbalization and action, Zhuangzi said, "The Great Way is not named; Great discriminations are not spoken; Great Benevolence is not benevolent; Great Modesty is not humble; Great daring does not attack" (2.44). Likewise, in order to awaken the reader to the fact that artificiality could never accomplish one's desired effect and to direct the reader's attention to the spontaneous nature of the dao, Zhuangzi claimed, "Perfect speech is the abandonment of speech; perfect action is the abandonment of action" (22.247). In this way, as with the *Dao De Jing*, the reader was inspired to abandon conventional beliefs and to see the world in all its dialectical possibilities.

(3) Fables. Fables, primarily in the form of complete stories with vivid and detailed descriptions of characters and events, were used in *Zhuangzi* as extended metaphors. For example, in chapter 1, Zhuangzi tells the following story of a fish named Kun: "Kun is so huge I don't know how many thousand li [miles] he measures. He changes and becomes a bird whose name is Peng. The back of the Peng measures I don't know how many thousand li [miles] across and, when he rises up and flies off, his wings are like clouds all over the sky. When the sea begins to move, this bird sets off for the southern darkness, which is the Lake of Heaven." Following this account, Zhuangzi gives a vivid description of Peng's journey: After conquering a whirlwind, Peng leaps into the air and rises up ninety thousand li carried by the wind.

Subsequently, Zhuangzi describes the following reaction from a cicada and a little dove who laugh at Peng's efforts, saying, "When we make an effort and fly up, we can get as far as the elm or the sapanwood tree, but sometimes we don't make it and just fall down on the ground. Now how is anyone going to go ninety thousand li to the south!" A little quail also laughs at Peng, saying "Where does he think he's going? I give a great lead and fly up, but I never get more than ten or twelve yards before I come down fluttering among the weeds and brambles. And that's the best kind of flying anyway!" (1.27–31). On the one hand, Zhuangzi characterizes the relatively limited flying abilities of the cicada, little dove, and little quail as examples of "little understanding." Peng's ability to fly ninety thousand li, on the other hand, is viewed as an example of "great understanding." This great understanding is knowledge of the dao, which is difficult to comprehend for those of narrow vision bound by their own limitations. To help his audience comprehend dao's great mystery Zhuangzi uses the concrete metaphor of a bird who can fly ninety thousand li instead of defining the dao in abstract terms. In this fable the rhetorical effect is created through the language of exaggeration and imagination, as well as through vivid and detailed description.

In his study of the narrative rhetoric of *Zhuangzi*, William Kirkwood (1992) identifies two rhetorical means, "telling" and "showing," typically used by a narrator in revealing his/her story to the audience. In the former technique, "authors can provide insights about a narrated performance which readers may not be able to gain by reflecting on the details of the performance" (Kirkwood 1992, 15). In the latter technique, the authors "stipulate essential narrative details which preclude rival explanations for the state of mind a performance displays" (15). Kirkwood argues that Zhuangzi relied heavily on the latter technique in order to elicit a nonrational, nonjudgmental state of mind. In my opinion, however, Zhuangzi employed both telling and showing, given that in the majority of his fables he offered detailed descriptions as well as pointing out the meanings embedded in the story.

(4) Pseudodialogues. In *Zhuangzi*, though the reader will occasionally find examples of narration, explanation, and assertion, the text is primarily dialogical in nature. Such dialogues involve persuasion, discussion, exploration, and argument between real historical figures such as Confucius and Laozi, Confucius and his disciples, Zhuangzi and Hui Shi, as well as between anthropomorphic characters such as the Lord of the River and Jo of the North Sea, and Penumbra and Shadow. Zhuangzi's pseudodialogues contain both logical and aesthetical features, which serve to unfold differing perspectives, make assertions, and explore multiple dimensions of an issue. Imputed words, repeated words, and goblet words intermingle throughout

the text. Unlike Platonic dialogue, which is pursued by a rational process of definition followed by examples and verification of the definition by fitted examples, in the case of Zhuangzi's dialogue the characters either tell a story, offer advice, or utter witty sayings. Some dialogues have clear beginnings and ends, while some are incomplete. Furthermore, the purpose is not to rationalize a theory or persuade one's partner in dialogue, but simply to illustrate a point of view. Unlike Platonic dialogue in which the questioner presumes a superiority of knowledge, in Zhuangzi's dialogue the questioner is portrayed as a humble person of modest manner. In fact, he is eager to learn, seeking advice and insights from the other person. For example, in several dialogues between Confucius and Laozi, Confucius is portrayed as the humble questioner while Laozi is the wise man offering profound knowledge and wisdom of the dao. In these dialogues Confucius is criticized and ridiculed for his adherence to the moral principles of ren (benevolence) and li (rites) but also praised for his good manners, modest attitude, and willingness to learn and attain the dao. In fact, Confucius is often depicted as teaching his disciples the wisdom of wu wei for political persuasion and personal well-being. In my opinion, such dialogues are presented as models of bian in which the Confucian and Daoist doctrines are integrated and bian shi aim at learning from and joining with one another, not at defeating their opponents.[14]

(5) Reconstructed Anecdotes. In the Chinese classics prior to *Zhuangzi* anecdotes, legends, and historical examples abound as means of analogical reasoning. In *Zhuangzi*, however, historical examples are reconstructed, integrating true historical figures into exaggerated and imagined stories in their historical and cultural context. Furthermore, in other pre-Qin classics, previous rulers are often glorified as sages and used as role models for moral persuasion, while in *Zhuangzi*, though the rulers are still respected, they are not glorified. Like other rulers, these so-called sage kings are portrayed with human limitations and weaknesses. For example, the descriptions of Confucius as a learned and modest scholar are consistent with the historical Confucius. However, his meetings with Laozi and his embracing of Daoist teachings were constructed. Given Confucius's character, it is possible that he did, in fact, humble himself to Laozi. It is also possible that he made fun of himself. By presenting such possibilities, Zhuangzi's reconstructed "Confucius" was made believable. In fact, in reading Zhuangzi's account of Confucius, one is not bothered by the question of fidelity. Instead, one is fascinated by this more well rounded and interesting version of "Confucius." This technique is rhetorically effective, according to Poulakos,

because "by voicing the possible, the rhetor discloses his vision of a new world to his listeners and invites them to join him there by honoring his disclosure and by adopting his suggestions" (1983, 45). By reconstructing historical figures in new and imagined contexts, Zhuangzi was able both to enlighten and delight his readers.

It is commonly believed that the anecdotes used in other pre-Qin classics served the purpose of political persuasion, while *Zhuangzi*'s sole aim was the enlightenment of self. This is only partially true. In fact, not all Zhuangzi's anecdotes are aimed strictly at the individual. For example, in chapter 7 of *Zhuangzi*, in the course of telling six fables, he explains his political views. In one of the fables Zhuangzi's invented characters Tian Gen and Wu Ming-ren are having a conversation. Tian Gen beseeches Wu Ming-ren, "Please may I ask how to rule the world?" to which Wu Ming-ren replies "Let your mind wander in simplicity, blend your spirit with the vastness, follow along with things the way they are, and make no room for personal views—then the world will be governed" (Watson 7.94). Though seemingly offered to an individual ruler, such advice is indirectly applicable to governments and political entities. In general, Zhuangzi did not use the historically well-known sage kings as glorified models but rather created his ideal sage king who influenced the world without bragging or letting his people depend upon him. In Zhuangzi's words, "With him [the ruler] there is no promotion or praise—He lets everything find its own enjoyment. He takes his stand on what cannot be fathomed and wanders where there is nothing at all" (7.94). Such device allows the reader to look beyond traditional cultural heroes for models, as well as to hold rulers to a new standard of accordance with the dao.[15]

(6) Glorification of the Ugly and Handicapped. Just as Laozi praised the inner strength and power possessed by the seemingly weak and negative, such as water and femininity, Zhuangzi characterized the ugly, the filthy, and the physically handicapped as possessing inner qualities of beauty, wisdom, and virtue. For example, in one of his accounts a man named Wang Tai, who only had one foot, was more respected than Confucius. In another story an extremely ugly man by the name of Ai Tai-ta was very much liked and honored by the people. In Zhuangzi's words, "When men were around him, they thought only of him and couldn't break away, and when women saw him, they ran begging to their fathers and mothers, saying, 'I'd rather be this gentleman's concubine than another man's wife'" (Watson 5.72). Comically, Zhuangzi named his handicapped or ugly-looking characters by their deformed features, such as "Mr.

No-Toes," "Mr. Lame-Hunchback-No-Lips," and "Mr. Pitcher-Sized-Wen." When such characters talked to dukes and kings, however, they were favored and respected to such an extent that the rulers began to see normal men as abnormal (5.74–75).

Zhuangzi saw beauty in ugliness and completeness in physical deformity. For him, people with such apparent defects were often more complete and beautiful in their virtue and spirit than the physically normal and appealing. In this case, Zhuangzi deliberately turned about commonly held judgments regarding beauty and ugliness in order to direct people to the less obvious and neglected and to challenge unexamined value judgments.

According to Zhuangzi, a virtuous person would dwell upon one's inner beauty and wisdom rather than making judgment on the basis of outward appearance. In one touching account, a person who lost a foot told Zi Chan: "The Master and I have been friends for nineteen years and he's never once let on that he's aware I'm missing a foot." For Zhuangzi, "if virtue is preeminent, the body will be forgotten. But when men do not forget what can be forgotten, but forget what cannot be forgotten—that may be called true forgetting" (5.75). Again, Zhuangzi not only directed the reader to observe the insignificant, the neglected, and the negative, but also empowered them by glorifying their inner strengths and inner completeness. For him, the ability to see and not forget the unobvious rather than paying attention to the obvious was an indication of having attained the dao. In another example illustrating this point, an innkeeper who had two concubines, one beautiful and the other ugly, treated the ugly one as a lady of rank, while the beautiful one was treated as a servant. When asked the reason, a young boy of the inn replied, "The beautiful one is only too aware of her beauty, and so we don't think of her as beautiful. The ugly one is only too aware of her ugliness, and so we don't think of her as ugly" (20.220).

As Sonja Foss states, "Language or rhetoric is a force through which the essence of a substance or an idea becomes known or becomes 'real' to us because it halts the constant flux of the contents of consciousness by fixing a substance with a linguistic symbol" (1989, 290). Indeed, though Zhuangzi was skeptical about language, the fact remains that the aesthetic and rhetorical force of his words made the essence of the dao apprehensible to his readers. He faced a more difficult challenge than other philosophers and bian shi of his time, for his aim was not to appeal to the reader's preexisting value system, but to challenge this preexisting framework, ultimately freeing his followers and readers from all previous perceptual limitations.

Through his use of language, he presented a world of endless possibilities, spiritual freedom, and multiple perspectives.

In examining Daoist texts regarding language and ming bian, we can conclude that Daoism neither rejects nor deprecates speech. Instead, it offers an illuminating vision of speech and argumentation. Grounded in the Daoist principles of nonaction, spontaneity, and noncontention, aimed directly at transforming conventional claims and values through an aesthetic use of rhetorical devices, Laozi and Zhuangzi held out to the ancient Chinese a vision of the beauty of language, the boundlessness of mind, the wealth of rhetorical possibilities, and the artfulness of living wisely and freely.

CHAPTER 9

Conceptualization of Shui and Ming Bian by Han Feizi

We have, thus far, examined classical Chinese rhetorical theories and practices documented in historical texts and expounded by philosophers representing four schools of thought. Each rhetorical perspective is rooted in its own unique philosophical, political, and cultural context. Nonetheless, all share an appreciation for the significant role of language—in particular, persuasion and argumentation—in shaping human behavior and perception, as well as in effecting social change.

This chapter is devoted to the philosopher Han Feizi, a representative of *Fajia* 法家 (the Legalist School), one of the five major schools of thought in ancient China. While the other schools of thought were interested in government "primarily from the point of view of the people," Han distinguished himself by showing an interest in government "wholly from the view point of the ruler or the state" (Fung 1952, 312). Like his counterparts, however, Han's rhetorical perspective derived from his own unique philosophy. He viewed language, persuasion, and argumentation through the lens of political power—more specifically, in the power struggle between a ruler and his ministers. Accordingly, as observed by Roger Ames, Han's political philosophy and rhetorical perspective can be summarized as "government of the ruler, by the ruler, and for the ruler" (1983, 50).

While ancient Chinese historians identified Han Feizi as a Legalist, ideologically aligned with Daoism, modern Chinese scholars generally consider him a Legalist, described variously as a "materialist," "a synthesizer of the Legalistic thoughts in the pre-Qin period," and "an excellent pragmatic logician" (Si-Ma "*Laozi Hanfei liezhuan*" 316; Zhou and Liu 1984, 241). The term *Legalism* is problematic for sinologists, however, as it does not parallel the Western understanding and practice of law. In an effort to convey its meaning in Western terms more accurately, Western scholars have renamed Legalism in various ways. For example, H. G. Creel (1953, 140) calls Legalism "totalitarianism," as the school advocated total government control at the expense of individual freedom; Arthur Waley (1939, 151) considers the Legalists "realists," as they took a pragmatic approach to social problems (as opposed to Confucian idealists in this regard); Benjamin Schwartz (1985, 321–22) characterizes Legalists as "behaviorists" since they aimed at regulating human behavior by a system of rewards and punishments; Robert Oliver (1971, 217) regards them as "thoroughly Machiavellian," given their emphasis on power and manipulation; John Dreher and James Crump even find common ground between Legalist thinking and the central message of Hitler's *Mein Kampf,* "both in respect to its regard of the common man and in its idealization of the strength of the state" (1952, 10).

All such characterizations contain elements of truth regarding the School of Legalism and Han Feizi's political philosophy. Like other Chinese terms used in this project, the use of the term *Legalism* is an example of the language of ambiguous similarity in that the translation of the Chinese term *fa* 法 as "law" shares some similarities with the Western notion of law under the broad umbrella of social and human control. However, its meaning is also ambiguous to Western readers concerning its specific role and function in ancient China. My intention, therefore, is to provide insights regarding the essence of Legalist philosophy and its rhetorical perspective—in particular, the philosophy and rhetorical perspective of Han Feizi.

Han Feizi

Social Contexts and Personal Background

Through his writing Han Feizi (280–233 B.C.E.) responded directly to the political situation of the Warring States period (475–221 B.C.E.). The political transition spanning the fifth through third century B.C.E. gave rise to cultural diversity and the free expression of ideas, on one hand, and, on the other, the decentralization of political power, nonconformity in cultural values, and social disorder. With the decline of patriarchal society and the subsequent emergence of autonomous states, political conflicts arose and intensified among the various states, as well as between the new ruling class and the old aristocracies. Faced with the need to conquer others in order to survive, the states were pitted against one another to such an extent that even allies battled each other. The Confucian model of benevolent government held little appeal for state rulers. At the same time, however, constant political intrigue and instability both within and between states during the Warring States period forced such rulers to develop their rhetorical skills to the level of art.

Facing the common problems of moral decline, wartime calamities, and the corruption of ministers and rulers, Confucian philosophers advised the political elite to follow the sage kings of the past and practice benevolent government. Confucius, Mencius, Xunzi, and many other bian shi and you shui had employed this strategy with regard to the rulers of their respective times. Han characterized such people as "stupid scholars," however, saying that they "do not know the actual conditions of order and chaos but chatter nonsense and chant too many hackneyed old books to disturb the government of the present age" (Liao 4.14.123).[1]

In defense of such accusations, Han argued that societies of different times have different concerns. For example, "Men of remote antiquity strove to be known as moral and virtuous; those of the middle age struggled to be known as wise and resourceful; and now [current times] men fight for the reputation of being vigorous and powerful" (Liao 19.49.279). According to Han, as values and human activities change over time, the mechanism of promoting or controlling human activities should also be changed. A wise ruler should adapt to the ever-changing situations in his policy making and means of communication. For Han, therefore, the Confucian dependency on the moral example of sage kings and traditional values was naive and unrealistic. Instead, in the interest of assuring fairness, a stable government, and maximum control of the people, Han advised state enforcement of universally applied laws. This system of ruling was based upon a rational understanding of the human desire to increase one's benefits and avoid harm rather than upon a code of ethics and morality.

The political situation and shifting of power, resulting from reforms within the individual states during the Warring States period, provided Han with a unique opportunity to apply and practice his political theory. For example, as a result of the political reform enacted by Shang Yang 商鞅 (390–338 B.C.E.), a former minister of Qin, the state of Qin had grown into one of the most powerful states both economically and militarily and was anxious to conquer the other six states in order to unite China under its rule. Noting Qin's ambition and its position as an emerging hegemony, Han offered to assist the king of Qin in accelerating the process of centralization and uniformity through the practice of artful rulership. Han's assistance did not entail advice concerning military strategy. Rather, his support was limited to offering political wisdom in statecraft as a means of political control.

Han formulated his political philosophy and rhetorical perspective in reaction to the various schools of thought and individual thinkers preceding him. In this context, he was indeed an innovative thinker. For example, while Han was well aware that Confucius, Mencius, and Mozi's response to the cultural diversity, social chaos, and moral decline of the times was to advocate peace, morality, and benevolent government, relying upon education and moral persuasion of the individual as means to achieve this end, Han advocated the enforcement of governmental laws, relying upon a set of legal standards applied to all members of society en masse. Though Han was critical of various aspects of Confucianism, Mohism, and Mingjia, he borrowed ideas from these schools of thought as well as from the early Legalists, integrating them into his own worldview. For example, he appropriated the Confucian notion of li (rites), a system for moralizing cultural norms and behavior, into the notion of fa (law), a political means of control. From Daoism, he borrowed the notion of wu wei, incorporating it into his political ideology and strategy for ruling. He also shared common philosophical ground concerning shang tong (identification with the superior) and utilitarianism with Mozi. Finally, he extended the notion of fa conceptualized by the early Legalists.

Han, a student of Xunzi, was born into an aristocratic family. *Shi Ji* described him variously as "fond of the study of names and penal laws," "a stutterer," and "not good at delivering speeches, but an excellent writer" (Si-Ma "*Laozi Hanfei liezhuan*" 316). *Han Feizi*, the book ascribed to his authorship, consists of fifty-five chapters. Among them, *Nan Yan* 難言 (the Difficulty of Speaking), *Shui Nan* 說難 (On the Difficulty of Persuasion), and *Wen Bian* 問辯 (Inquiring into Argumentation) are specifically devoted to his theory of persuasion and argumentation.

Perhaps because of his speech defect, Han participated in persuasive activities primarily in written rather than oral form. For example, according to *Shi Ji*, he wrote many *jian shu* 諫書 (letters of persuasion) to the king of Han in an attempt to persuade the king to adopt his political philosophy. When the king of Han refused to listen, Han directed his efforts to the king of Qin, who was so impressed with Han's political ideas of unification that he invited Han to work for the state of Qin. When Han tried to persuade the king of Qin not to attack the state of Han (Han's home state), however, he lost favor with the king, who began to distrust his motives. In the wake of a slanderous attack by Li Si 李斯, a former classmate, Han committed suicide shortly after his arrival in Qin. Si-Ma subsequently commented upon the irony of the fact that "Hanzi [Han Feizi] wrote 'On the Difficulty of Persuasion' while he failed to protect and save his own life by persuasion"

(319).² Nevertheless, Han's ideas survived his death and were put into practice by the king of Qin in his efforts to unify China.

Philosophical Views

In the words of Guo Moruo, a modern Chinese historian, "the thought of Han Fei is rooted in Daoism, connected to Confucianism, and married to Mohism" (1959, 305). This statement is only partially correct, however, for at times Han was also uprooted from Daoism, challenged Confucianism, and was divorced from Mohism.

(1) Connection and Challenge to Confucianism. Although Han severely criticized Confucian moral ideals as a strategy for addressing political problems and reconstructing Chinese society, as a student of the Confucian philosopher Xunzi he was, nonetheless, influenced by Confucianism. In fact, in certain respects his notion of fa evolved from the Confucian notion of li 禮 (rites).

As early as the Zhou dynasty, li, in the form of government decrees, had been used as the means of organizing and controlling society. Through official channels elements of li were disseminated to every member of society. It is important to note that li did not originate with the common people but rather was formulated and enforced by the ruling class, who had the privilege of interpreting the concept. In practice, li amounted to the strict observance of cultural norms and rules imposed on the masses by the ruling class in their own interests in the context of a hierarchical and patriarchal society. The word *li* is, in fact, used interchangeably with the word *fa*, referring to the regulation of human behavior and control of society in the text of *Zhou Li* (Hou 1987, 62–63).

Hoping to reestablish the Zhou dynasty, organized and managed by the social order of li, Confucius adhered to the principle of li disseminated through moral and literary education, as well as through the rectification of names by government officials. For Confucius, li was the actualization of ren (benevolence) in state affairs and personal conduct, prescribing the criteria for achieving moral perfection for junzi and rulers. With little success in persuading the rulers to execute and observe li at the social level, Confucius devoted his efforts to education and self-cultivation at the individual level.

If for Confucius li entailed social ideals and prescribed rules of conduct for the social elites, for Xunzi it amounted to a concrete measure of social values at the social, political, and individual levels for all members of society. In Xunzi's words, "the rituals [li] contain the model for the primary social distinctions and the categories used by analogical extension for the guiding rules and ordering norms of behavior" (Knoblock 1.1.139). For Xunzi li meant maintaining class distinctions as well as social and political control. As such, it was associated with a standard of governing. Accordingly, Xunzi's emphasis was on the enforcement of li by the ruling elite and the observation of li by everyone else.

As a student of Xunzi, Han embraced his theory of li. However, for Han, although both li and fa were socially enforced methods of control, li was not sufficient in controlling people's behaviors, since it could be easily violated without fear of punishment. For Han, the social distinction between the superior and the inferior was so important that if such hierarchy collapsed, "the sovereign will lose his life and ruin his state" (Liao 17.44.229).

For example, according to Han, when the musician Kuang threw a harp at the duke of Ji for saying something that displeased him, such an act broke ministerial etiquette, violating li, and thus should have been punished by fa, or penal laws, enacted by the ruler and applied equally to every social class (Liao 15.36.149–50). Nothing short of this extreme measure could ensure the power of the state to control human behavior. It must be noted that though Han's notion of fa as the standard and measure for regulating and controlling human behavior was derived from the concept and practice of li prescribed by Confucianists, it differed from Confucian li in that fa was enforced by law, while li was aimed at cultural construction and reconstruction; fa was observed out of fear of punishment, while li was motivated by the desire for moral perfection; fa placed the power in the hands of a single ruler out of concern for the ruler's well-being, while li was concerned with the ethical well-being of the individual and society.

Han's choice of fa over li was intimately related to his view of human nature, which was, in turn, related to Xunzi's view of human nature. While Mencius believed that human nature was inherently good, emphasizing self-development as a means of fulfilling human nature, Xunzi argued that human nature was evil and could only be corrected by education and punishment at the social level. As a student of Xunzi, Han had a view of human nature that was very much affected by his master. Consequently, he held a low opinion of humanity, believing that by nature humans were motivated by the desire for power, fame, and material gains, even in the case of familial relationships. He observed that parents killed their baby girls, keeping baby boys for their own self-interests; fathers and sons resented each other for their own selfish reasons; and ministers killed kings for the sake of acquiring power. Unlike Confucius, Mencius, and Mozi, who were moral idealists, Han was pragmatic and utilitarian in his view of the motives underlying human actions.

Han interpreted human motives purely from the perspective of selfish gains, illustrating his argument with the following examples concerning various occupations:

The physician sucks patients' cuts and holds their blood in his mouth, not because he is intimate with them like a blood relation, but because he expects profits from them. Likewise, when the cartwright finishes making carriages, he wants people to be rich and noble, when the carpenter finishes making coffins, he wants people to die early. Not that the cartwright is benevolent and the carpenter is cruel, but that unless people are noble, the carriages will not sell, and unless people die, the coffins will not be bought. Thus, the carpenter's motive is not hatred for anybody but his profits are due to people's death. (5.17.147).

Clearly Han believed that in order to achieve their selfish end, humans, including rulers and their ministers, would resort to all manner of deception, trickery, and disguise. While Xunzi proposed education and law as means to rectify the evil nature of humans, Han advocated the enforcement of laws alone. In his words, "the purpose of enacting laws and decrees is to abolish selfishness. Once laws and decrees prevail, the way of selfishness collapses" (17.45.235). While Han was certainly influenced by his teacher, his views on human nature were more cynical and pessimistic. Xunzi's work is often regarded as a bridge between Confucianism and Legalism, a bridge which led Han down the path toward Legalism.

(2) Connection to and Deviation from Daoism. Chinese and Western scholars agree on the philosophical affinity between Legalism and Daoism. In this regard, Han was the first philosopher to interpret Laozi, using Laozi's notion of wu wei as the basis for his political philosophy and proposing it as the basis for artful rulership. Han's use of the notions of dao and de was different from that of Laozi, however. For example, Han expanded Laozi's definition of the dao as the source of everything in the universe into a concrete standard of right and wrong. Accordingly, a ruler must keep to the standard, making judgment about good and evil. Similarly, while for Laozi de was an "empty" and all-inclusive state of mind, Han applied the notion specifically to the statecraft of the ruler. For Han, "by virtue [de] of resting empty and reposed, he waits for the course of nature to enforce itself so that all names will be self defined and all affairs will be settled of themselves. Empty, he knows the essence of fullness: reposed, he becomes the corrector of motion" (1.5.31). In other words, the empty quality of a thing (wu wei), is an indication of its virtue (de). This does not mean the ruler allows freedom and flexibility to his subjects; rather, for Han, wu wei was understood as a mechanism for enhancing the authority of the state,

which was protected by universal laws. More specifically, it was a strategy for avoiding manipulation by clever ministers, disguising the ruler's true intentions, and warding off the biased and emotionally charged opinions of one's subjects. In other words, the final purpose of wu wei was to enable the ruler to control the masses through techniques of rulership that "were intended to prevent any insight into the ruler's personality which might interfere with the operation of the governmental machinery" (Ames 1983, 53).

Another relevant concept discussed in *Han Feizi* is *li* 理 (principles, standards).[3] For Han, while the dao is the universal law controlling everything in life, li is the concrete standard governing particular things. In his words, "principles [li] are determinants of things and everything has a unique principle. Inasmuch as everything has its unique principle and Tao [dao] disciplines the principles of all things" (Liao 6.20.192). Thus, the relationship between the dao and li is one of an absolute standard related to probable criteria. As such, it is similar to the relationship between absolute and relative truth. According to Han, there are two primary characteristics of li (principle, standard): its ability to make distinctions among things; and its ability to direct human attention to many changing and complex variables in life. When principles are not fixed, it is difficult to make judgments of right and wrong. Hence, fa should be enforced to standardize judgments just as compasses and rulers are used to draw squares and circles. Fa's limitation was that it reduced political systems of control to techniques and mechanisms at the expense of individual expressions. Its overriding purpose was to deprive the masses of their individual rights and exert more governmental power. Therefore, although theoretically Han identified himself with Daoism, in practice he violated Daoist principles that celebrated the autonomy of the individual and advocated less interference by the government.

(3) Connection and Reaction to Mohism. Mohism, unlike Confucianism, received only mild criticism in *Han Feizi*. In fact, Han was indebted to the Mohists, having borrowed many ideas from them, including: the assumption that human motivation was utilitarian; the theory that universal love was mutually beneficial; and the belief that humans were by nature profit- and benefit-seeking. In his words, "their minds are well disposed to act for each other because they cherish self-seeking motives respectively" (11.32.45). More fundamental than any ethical standard, utilitarianism was the measure and purpose of all levels of human relationship, even between parents and children, not to mention the ruler and his minister.

In addition, Mozi's notion of shang tong (identification with the superior) echoes Han's promotion of despotism, upholding the absolute right of the ruler to impose his will upon his obedient subjects. Han and Mozi also shared the belief that uniformity in thought and action assured stability and control. They differed, however, over the means of achieving this end. In the case of shang tong, the ruler stated his position demanding conformity of his subjects, while Han's notion of absolute rulership involved a system of rewards and punishment in the making, supervision, and enforcement of laws.

It should be noted that Han borrowed from Mozi the idea of rewards and punishment as a basic means of governing and a motivating force for human behavior. However, differences remain as to the origins and methods of such a system. For Mozi, one was rewarded or punished according to the Will of Heaven as a motivational means for engaging of spiritual and moral action, while Han's model was enacted by a concrete and rational system of law. Furthermore, Mozi was in complete opposition to Han in his advocacy of peace for the common good, rather than war for a powerful few. Despite such differences, Mohism laid the foundation for the development of Han Feizi's Legalistic theory. It is not an exaggeration to claim, as Vitaly Rubin does, that "the Legalists were Mo Tzu's [Mozi's] heirs" (1976, 64).

(4) Borrowing from Early Legalistic Views. Though it is difficult to pinpoint any of the early Legalists as the founder of the Legalist School, it is not difficult to locate Legalistic practice and treaties. The first recorded Legalistic practice can be traced to Zi Chan 子產 (?–522 B.C.E.), the minister of the state of Zheng (also the home state of Deng Xi). *Zuo Zhuan* documents the fact that Zi Chan drafted penal laws in protection of private property. Another legal document was written in the Warring States period by Li Kui 李悝 (455–395 B.C.E.), the minister of the state of Wei. Both documents have unfortunately been lost. What remains are *Guanzi* 管子 (Guanzi) and *Shang Jun Shu* 商君書 (The Book of Lord Shang). In *Guanzi*, fa was first conceptualized as the standard for strong rulership and government as well as the measurement of everything including moral principles of ren and li. According to *Guanzi*, there are two functions of fa: to reward the brave and punish the evil; and to distinguish between right and wrong (Rickett 1965, 90–106).[4]

The Book of Lord Shang, whose authorship is a matter of controversy, articulated the Legalistic ideology of Shang Yang in that it denied the relevance of traditional values, stressed the need for legal reform, delineated clear goals for improving the economy, and specified a system for disseminating fa.[5] The reforms enacted by Shang Yang, documented in *Shi Ji*, included the social restructuring that aimed to break up the close family ties. Family members were rewarded for reporting each others' wrongdoings to the proper authorities. Rewards were also given to those who possessed military prowess, while sanctions were imposed upon those who fought to protect their own self-interests. Rewards and punishments were also applied in the context of farming as a way of promoting agricultural productivity. The ruler promulgated the laws, which were disseminated to every member of society. Unquestioned obedience was the order of the day for the common people. Shang Yang's reform was highly successful in the narrow sense that it centralized and consolidated state power at the expense of individual freedom and free expression.

At any rate, Han's version of Legalistic philosophy crystallized the Legalistic ideas first proposed in *Guanzi* and *The Book of Lord Shang* by promoting well-defined laws, urging policies of statecraft, and denouncing traditional values. Through selective integration of the views expressed in the various schools of thought, Han developed his own Legalistic views concerning government and art of ruling, which, in turn, laid the basis and established a rationale for his rhetorical perspective on political persuasion.

Legalistic Views and Political Communication

Han Feizi's Legalistic strategy for governing involves three components that are political principles as well as important areas of political communication: *fa* 法 (penal law), *shu* 術 (political strategy), and *shi* 勢 (power position). Borrowed from his predecessors, these components were used to formulate Han's own theory and approach to political control and communication.

(1) Fa (Penal Law). The Legalists preceding Han were primarily politicians whose interest in the law was motivated by a desire to strengthen the state and maintain order. With this same goal in mind, Han emerged as a true theorist of law. As such, he was the first Legalist to give a complete treatment of law, addressing its function, effect, and application. In condemning the notion of benevolent government, Han argued that fa was the most efficient way to strengthen the state and empower the ruler and was, therefore, a superior approach to governing. Furthermore, according to Han, it served the interests of everyone, providing a stable and peaceful environment for economic growth. In his words, "the most enlightened method of governing a state is to trust measures [fa], and not men [men's cleverness]" (Liao 20.55.332). The most enlightened act of a ruler "is to unify laws instead of seeking for wise men, to solidify politics instead of yearning after faithful persons" (19.49.289).

For Han, fa was the most effective strategy for crime prevention; it "forbade extra-judicial action," "exterminated selfishness," and "executed decrees and censured inferiors." Another important feature of fa, as mentioned above, was its universal application. Unlike li (rites), which prescribed different codes of conduct for particular social groups and individuals, fa was equally applied to everyone. In Han's words, it "does not fawn on the noble; the string does not yield to the crooked. Whatever the law applies to, the wise cannot reject nor can the brave defy. Punishment for fault never skips ministers, reward for good never misses commoners." Accordingly, the function of law, in Han's view, was "to correct the faults of the high, to rebuke the vices of the low, to suppress disorders, to decide against mistakes, to subdue the arrogant, to straighten the crooked, and to unify the folkways of the masses" (2.6.44 45).

Such a system of law, with its ideal of objectivity and fairness to all, would seem to threaten intellectuals, bureaucrats, and aristocrats who enjoyed certain privileges by virtue of their social positions. However, this was not the case. In fact, it aimed at serving the despot. The law applied to everyone except the ruler whose task was to formulate the law and supervise its enforcement. Therefore, it did not serve to limit his power, but to extend and strengthen it. In discussing the defects in the Chinese system of law, Liang Chi-Chao (1873–1929), a Chinese scholar and reformer, notes, "the emperor is given full legislative authority. When the authority lies in an individual, it is clear that the emperor may rescind a law just as easily as he makes one" (1930, 131).

According to Rubin (1976), compared with the legal systems of ancient Greece and India, ancient Chinese law was devoid of moral and religious sanctions. As a result, Chinese law was culturally destructive by its ferocious aversion to intellectual and cultural values. Legalists' views, as Ames has observed, "have nothing to do with cultivation of personal life or its societal implications. Rather, their concern is effective political control, and culture is rejected as inimical to this end" (1983, 12). The notorious practice of *fen shu keng ru* 焚書坑儒 (burning books and burying intellectuals alive), enacted by Qin Shi Huang 秦始皇 (the first emperor of China, 221 B.C.E.), was an extreme example of such cultural destruction.

(2) Shu (Political Strategy). If fa was the core of Han's political philosophy, the means to actualize this philosophy, in terms of political control, was shu, often translated as methods, technique, or strategy. Han borrowed the concept of shu from Shen Bu-Hai 申不害 (385–337 B.C.E.), a former minister of the state of Han and one of the early Legalists,[6] defining it as "the means whereby to create posts according to responsibilities, hold actual services accountable according to official titles, exercise the power over life and death, and examine the officials' abilities" (Liao 17.43.212). In this sense, shu referred to the practice of statecraft or administrative ruling.

Han made the following distinction between fa and shu: "law [fa] is codified in books, kept in governmental offices, and promulgated among the hundred surnames. The tact [shu] is hidden in the bosom and useful in comparing diverse motivating factors of human conduct and in manipulating the body of officials secretly" (16.38.188). That is, while fa was written for both officials and common people and was publicly communicated, shu was a secret weapon for the ruler in overseeing the thoughts and actions of his officials. For Han, fa and shu were equally important political methods of control that should, therefore, be given equal attention by the ruler. In his words, "If the ruler is tactless, delusion will come to the superior; if the subjects and ministers are lawless, disorder will appear among the inferiors" (17.43.212). Although Han applauded Shang Yang and Shen Bu-hai for their Legalistic ideas of fa and shu, he criticized them for concentrating too narrowly on one aspect to the detriment of the other, thus failing to achieve their intended goals (17.43.213).

It was Han's assumption that the relationship between the ruler and his minister was marked by self-interests. The ruler was interested in maintaining power, while the minister was interested in gaining favor and material benefits from the ruler. Some ministers might also have had the ulterior motive of undermining the ruler. Accordingly, it was important for the ruler to exercise caution in adopting ideas advocated by his minister. It was also important for the ruler to observe if the speech of the minister matched his actions and try to ascertain the minister's real motives. Among the seven types of shu Han proposed for the ruler, the following four were directly aimed at this purpose: "comparing and inspecting all available different theories; listening to all sides of every story and holding every speaker responsible for it; inquiring into cases by manipulating different information; and inverting words and reversing tasks" (9.30.281).

The concept of shu was rooted in the notion of wu wei in that ideally the ruler should remain "quiet and empty" in order to allow different opinions to be fully expressed. Only then could the ruler determine the true motives of the minister and make a sound judgment or decision. In other words, shu was the practice of hiding one's true motives, using pretense and deception to cause one's opponent to expose his weakness to one's own advantage. A wise ruler, according to Han, should listen to the opinions of his ministers individually, after which he should call a conference to allow his ministers express their opinions collectively. In this way, he would be able to assess the consistency of their words as well as the correspondence between words and consequences. If a minister's ideas have generated positive consequences, he will be rewarded; if his ideas have proven faulty, he will be punished (18.48.260). In this way, the ruler is able to collect and utilize the wisdom of his ministers, while at the same time avoiding the pitfalls of manipulation. In this sense, the content of communication is regulated and controlled by the practice of shu.

The foregoing discussion illustrates the fact that shu is not based on an ethical standard but on interpersonal cunning. This practice has fostered a mythic and inscrutable image of the ruler who is not above using tact, pretense, and trickery, or deliberately creating scenarios that will test the minister's motive, loyalty, and wisdom. For Han, the art of statecraft entailed an understanding of complex and ever-changing human motivations and psychology, rather than abstract knowledge of government, or prescribed moral conditions.

The notion of shu epitomizes the sophisticated and complex nature of Chinese interpersonal communication. The notion was first proposed by Sunzi in his *Sunzi Bing Fa* (The Art of War). In that context *shu* referred to the ability to make use of a situation to achieve military victory through a well-thought-out plan, or *gui dao* 詭道 (crafty plot, cunning scheme), involving careful consideration and analysis of physical and psychological conditions of the enemy. According to Sunzi, the art of war entailed "understand[ing] your enemy as well as yourself. Without such understanding, every battle will meet with danger" (*Sunzi* 48). *Gui Guzi* 鬼谷子, a classical rhetorical text dated to the Warring States period, discussed shu in the following terms: *mou* 謀 (plotting); *chuai* 揣 (estimating); *mo* 摩 (figuring out); *you* 誘 (seducing); and *quan liang* 權量 (weighing advantages and disadvantages). These techniques, regarded as basic components for effective and successful persuasion, were implemented through verbal facility.[7] The notion of shu is similar to the Greek notion of *metis* and *phronesis* (practical intelligence), which, according to Lisa Raphals (1992), amounts to "metic intelligence," characterized by intimate knowledge of subtlety, indirection, and cunning in the context of interpersonal relations and political persuasion.

(3) Shi (Power Position). The notion of shi was first discussed by Shen Dao 慎到 (395–315 B.C.E.), a scholar of the Jixia Academy and an early Legalist influenced by Daoism. While fa assured imperial control through the observance of governmental laws and shu allowed the ruler to assess the motivation of his ministers, shi, the third component of Han's Legalistic philosophy, referred to the absolute authority upheld by the ruler. Han strongly believed that no matter how elaborate and detailed the penal system and no matter how cunning and cautious the ruler, if the ruler was not capable of holding a powerful position and exercising his authority, he would have no significant impact. To illustrate this point, Han offered the

following observation: "Yao [a sage king], while a commoner, could not govern three people, whereas Chieh [a ruthless ruler], being the Son of Heaven, could throw All-under-Heaven into chaos. From this I know that position and status are sufficient to rely on, and that virtue and wisdom are not worth yearning after" (Liao 17.40.199).

Han was well aware that both extremely good and extremely bad rulers were rare. In his view, the majority of rulers were, in fact, average in intelligence. What was needed in order to secure their power was legal and military might. In Han's words, "If they [average rulers] uphold the law and make use of their august position, order obtains; if they discard the law and desert their august positions, chaos prevails" (17.40.204–5). This is because only with shi can fa be enforced and shu carried out. According to Han, a ruler possesses two *bing* 柄 (handles) for controlling his ministers and maintaining his power position. One is chastisement, the means "to inflict death or torture upon culprits," and the other is commendation, the means "to bestow encouragements or rewards on men of merit" (2.7.46).

These two handles, reward and punishment, are not concerned with "behavior modification" in today's sense of the term. In fact, given his belief that human nature was essentially evil and self-seeking, Han had little confidence in the notion that human behavior could be altered through examples or education. For him, on the one hand, rewards satisfied the human desire for material gain and fame, and were thus effective means of winning the hearts of ministers and common people alike. Punishment, on the other hand, served as a forceful deterrent. Since the ruler was the only person permitted to use the two handles of reward and punishment, his ability to amass and sustain absolute power was greatly enhanced. When granting rewards, he would be the one to whom others would be most indebted; when dictating punishment, he would be the most feared. In Han's words, "As the ruler has the handles in his grip and thereby upholds his august position, what is ordered works and what is prohibited stops. The handles are regulators of life and death; the position is the means of overcoming the masses" (18.48.258). Han advised the ruler not to delegate the handles (power) of reward and punishment to his subordinates, for he believed that one's subordinates would abuse the power and use it to usurp the throne. Thus, a wise ruler should always uphold his position of power and never trust anyone.

For Han, maintaining shi was essential to the ruler and also accorded with human nature. In his words, "The people are such as would be firmly obedient to authority, but are rarely able to appreciate righteousness.... The people are by nature obedient to authority" (17.49.281–82). For Han, a weak and obedient people abided by fa, carefully selected loyal officials practiced strict adherence to shu, and authoritative rulers embraced shi—accounting for the three basic components for strengthening the government and maintaining power. As observed by Rubin, "The idea that the relations between the state and the people are antagonistic is a feature that distinguishes Legalist theory from other trends of political thought in both the East and the West" (1976, 62). Even Machiavelli, who, like Han, advised rulers of strategies for holding and manipulating power, favored a moral component, placing faith in the people as well as in the government.[8]

Rhetorical Perspectives

As mentioned above, Han's rhetorical perspective derived from his political philosophy and Legalistic views. In general, the former served as a means to achieve the latter. Regarding his rhetorical views, Han was particularly interested in the notion of ming, perceptive with respect to shui, and antagonistic toward bian.

(1) The Concept of Ming. The relationship between names and actualities was a primary concern of ancient Chinese philosophers in general. While Confucius proposed the rectification of names in the interest of social and cultural reconstruction, Gong-sun Long and the Later Mohists discussed the relationship between names and actualities in an abstract and logical fashion. Han incorporated the notion of ming shi 名實 (names and actualities) into xing ming 形名 (form and name) in the context of his Legalistic philosophy. His concept of xing ming was influenced by Shen Bu-hai, who argued that observing the correspondence between names and actuality was the basic element of shu where the ruler was concerned. Another source of influence was Deng Xi, who first proposed a close supervision of names and actualities on the part of the ruler and legalistic settings.

Han's notion of xing ming was entirely centered around his Legalistic point of view concerning fa, shu, and shi in the interest of the ruler. For Han, ming (naming) referred to language and speech, indicating unity and control in the appointment of officials and assignment of tasks over which a ruler could exercise shu through government decrees. Xing (form) referred specifically to personal qualities justifying the official title of the person, actions carried out in the context of certain promises, and proposed ideas and behaviors resulting from the enforcement of laws.

Han was fully aware of the impact of ming in creating political reality. For him, ming could either unify the collective understanding of reality or diversify it. The purpose of law, as a positive example of ming, was to unify people's thoughts to standardized views concerning political reality. Toward this end, Han applied the Confucian notion of the rectification of names. In his words, "The way to assume oneness starts from the study of terminology. When names are rectified, things will be settled; when names are distorted, things will shift around" (Liao 2.8.53). Han listed a number of examples in which naming caused a distortion of reality:

Those who are generous, sincere, genuine, faithful, and active in mind but timid in speech, are called spiritless; those who follow laws firmly and obey orders fully, are called stupid; those who revere the superior and fear punishment, are called cowardly; those who speak on the right occasions and act in the proper manner are called unworthy; and those who are not double-faced and engaged in private studies but listen to magistrates and conform to public instructions are called vulgar . . . (17.45.230–31).

Han was not concerned that the common people would misuse language in this way, but rather that the ministers and social elites, whose pronouncements were more far-reaching and authoritative, would agitate people's minds and weaken the power of the ruler. Thus, he advised the ruler to oversee the correspondence between ming and xing. That is, "he [the ruler] rectifies their names [official titles and tasks] first, then works with them, and finally makes them accomplish the tasks" (2.8.54). This could be accomplished through the examination of names and by tracing the forms (personal qualities and actual consequences).

In addition to using xing ming as a component of shu in selecting and monitoring officials so as to avoid being manipulated or usurped by cunning and wicked ministers, Han also advised the ruler to employ xing ming in determining right and wrong in the context of law enforcement. In deciding whether rewards or punishment should be given, according to Han, "he [the ruler] will decide between right and wrong according to the relation between name and fact and scrutinize words and phrases by means of comparison and verification" (2.14.120). If the names and facts do not correspond, producing the desired result, a legal sanction would be imposed. If the proposed ideas proved useful in accordance with the facts, a reward would be granted. In Han's words, "If the ruler closely accords form with name, the people will attend to their daily business. To leave this key and seek anything else is to fall into serious bewilderment" (2.8.58). Here the notion of xing ming served as a mechanism of political control, as opposed to abstract intellectual engagement.

In examining the correspondence between ming and xing, Han advised the ruler first to gather all differing opinions from ministers. Once different opinions were gathered, "he [the ruler] should estimate them in the light of their background, scrutinize them with the principles of Heaven, verify them by the course of affairs, and compare them with the sentiments of mankind. If these four demonstrations coincide with one another, then the ruler may proceed to observe deeds" (18.48.266–67). When hearing the different perspectives, the ruler should not openly express his approval or disapproval of ideas or persons, but remain tranquil and mystic. To expose further the true motives of the person and verify the deed against names, Han offered the following list of techniques for examination and comparison:

Cite the past facts and thereby check the antecedent words. Keep detectives near by the officials and thereby know their inner conditions. Send detectives afar and thereby know outer affairs. Hold to your clear knowledge and thereby inquire into obscure objects. Give ministers false encouragements and thereby extirpate their attempts to infringe on the ruler's rights. Invert your words and thereby try out the suspects. Use contradictory arguments and thereby find out the invisible culprits. Establish the system of espionage and thereby rectify the fraudulent people. Make appointments and dismissals and thereby observe the reactions of wicked officials. Speak explicitly and thereby persuade people to avoid faults. Humbly follow others' speeches and thereby discriminate between earnest men and flatterers. Get information from everybody and know things you have not yet seen. Create quarrels among adherents and partisans and thereby disperse them. (4.12.106)

In sum, Han's methods, based on cynical assumptions regarding human nature, involved observation, investigation, comparison, and testing. More specifically, they involved detailed planning and plotting as well as the implementation of deceptive and cunning strategies. Ironically, though fa was considered the ultimate mechanism for monitoring and controlling human behavior, even among government officials, rulers appear to have had little confidence in the efficacy of law with regard to official conduct, instead relying upon human wisdom and intelligence. The sad fact was that such strategies often generated mistrust and betrayal, fanning flames of vicious rumor, slander, and persecution, while strengthening the ruler's position of power.

(2) A Theory of Shui. In Han Feizi's time, the most common form of persuasion was interpersonal communication between the ruler and his adviser, usually a you shui, or a minister. The relationship between the two was often subtle and delicate. The ruler had the ultimate power and was always on guard, attempting to discern his advisers' true motives. The adviser had no power but relied on his persuasive skills and tactics in winning the ruler over to his point of view. The ruler had only to judge the credibility of an adviser and the value of his message. After many failed attempts at

persuading the king of the state of Han, Han had a clear sense of the inherent difficulties of acting as an adviser. Consequently, he developed his theory of persuasion by penetrating into the psychology of the speaker and audience in the areas of audience adaptation, trust, and listening.

A. Adapting to the Audience's Psychology. In two articles, *Nan Yan* (the Difficulty of Speaking) and *Shui Nan* (On the Difficulty of Persuasion), Han explored the difficulties in audience adaptation, suggesting strategies that ought to be mastered in order to achieve successful persuasion. For Han, persuasion was difficult, primarily because it was hard to know the psychology of one's audience and adapt one's message accordingly. In Han's words, "the difficulties in the way of persuasion lie in my knowing the heart of the persuaded in order thereby to fit my wording into it" (4.12.106). Members of an audience may have vastly different and even conflicting perceptions of a speech for reasons having little or nothing to do with the speech itself. Han used himself as an example:

Thy servant, Fei, is by no means difficult of speaking. As to why he has to hesitate in speaking: if his speeches are compliant and harmonious, magnificent and orderly, he is then regarded as ostentatious and insincere; if his speeches are sincere and courteous, straightforward and careful, he is then regarded as awkward and unsystematic; if his speeches are widely cited and subtly composed, frequently illustrated and continuously analogized, he is then regarded as empty and unpractical. . . . (1.3.23)

According to Han, because of the unbalanced power relationship between the ruler and his ministers, each side may have selfish ulterior motives that cannot be detected in speech. The primary challenge, therefore, was to discover the audience's true values, motives, and character—all of which were often concealed by pretense and deception. Any message, no matter how well conceived and delivered, would be misinterpreted if not addressed to the true motives of the audience. Han offered the following example:

If the persuaded strives after high fame while you persuade him of big profit, you will be considered low-bred, accorded mean treatment, and shunned from afar. If the persuaded strives after big profit while you persuade him of high fame, you will be considered mindless and ignorant of worldly affairs and will never be accepted. If the persuaded strives after big profit in secret but openly seeks for high fame while you persuade him of high fame, you will be accepted in name but kept distance in fact; and, if you persuade him of big profit, your word will be adopted in secret but your person will be left out openly. These points should be carefully deliberated. (4.12.106)

As the true motives of the audience are often masked by pretense and deception, going beyond the surface appearance of things becomes essential in adapting one's persuasive strategies to the audience. Ironically, Han argued that pretense and deception on the part of the ruler could enable him to penetrate the pretense and deception of his underlings. Among the seven shu Han proposed for the ruler, two directly related to pretense and deception: "the pretense of not knowing something that you already know"; and "asking a question contrary to what one really wants to know." By using such techniques, the persuader was able to "trap" members of his audience, gradually discovering their "insides," and adjusting his message accordingly.

For this reason, recognizing pretense and deception was crucial in adapting to one's audience as well as in forming one's own communication strategy. In attempting to persuade the ruler, an adviser should not speak openly about the ruler's true hidden motive. If he unskillfully discussed matters that the ruler would prefer to keep hidden, he would not only fail to persuade the ruler but would place himself in danger of losing his office or even his life. In the interest of effective and self-protective persuasion, the persuader must be very sensitive to his audience's state of mind and heart, being subtle and circuitous in presenting his message. As Garrett observes, "persuaders were urged to pander to the audience's interest and to approach emotionally distressing conclusions indirectly, through a graduated series of examples or analogies" (1993b, 28).

Successful persuasion also depended upon how successfully a persuader managed to save face for the ruler. In Han's words, "the business of the persuader is to embellish the pride and obliterate the shame of the persuaded" (Liao 4.12.108). For example, "If he makes much of his own strength, do not bring in any difficult task that impedes him. If he thinks his own decisions brave, do not point out their unlawfulness; that angers him. If he thinks his own scheme wise, do not recall his past failures which embarrass him" (4.12.109).

Helping the audience save face also served to protect and empower the speaker. An important strategy was to keep the ruler's secrets. The persuader should pretend not to be aware of the ruler's true intentions and secret plans. Such a strategy was based not only on Han's insights into the psychological nature of an audience but also on his intimate understanding of Chinese social and power relationships. If a ruler were to lose face, his moral character would be challenged and his office put in jeopardy. To maintain his sense of dignity, a ruler who had lost face would be forced to take revenge and punish the speaker. For example, as Han observed,

"Tzu-hsu schemed well but was killed by the King of Wu; Chung-ni [Confucius] taught well but was detained by the Ruler of Kuang; and Kuan I-wu was really worthy but was taken prisoner by the Ruler of Lu. Not that these three statesmen were not worthy, but that the three rulers were not intelligent" (1.3.24–25). From such anecdotal evidence, Han concluded that the determining factor in effective persuasion was neither eloquence nor loyalty but the ruler's moral state and intelligence in making judgments. Indeed, Han himself was both an eloquent and loyal adviser, but because the king of Qin failed to protest the slanderous attacks made against him, Han committed suicide. It is a shameful fact of Chinese history that many loyal and competent ministers were killed by their own superiors.

Due to this unfortunate state of affairs, Han concluded, "whoever attempts remonstration, persuasion, explanation, and discussion before the Throne, must carefully observe the sovereign's feelings of love and hate before he start persuading him" (4.12.112). In other words, knowing the psychological mind-set of the audience was essential to the art of persuasion. In the Chinese tradition, Han was the first philosopher to recognize the intricacy and subtlety in the audience's mind and to articulate strategies for penetrating into it. For Han, audience analysis and the accompanying adaptation of oneself to the psychological mind and heart of one's audience were indispensable tools in effective communication. Such adjustments should be subtle, tactful, and diplomatic, since the true motives of one's audience were often in disguise.

B. Gaining Trust. For Han, establishing trust was the most challenging and essential component in successful persuasion. Such trust was obtained not through superficial criteria such as status, but by displaying trustworthy conduct and establishing close social and affective relationships. Han divided trust into two categories: *xiao xin* 小信 (small trust) and *da xin* 大信 (big or real trust). The former was gained through everyday speech and accomplishing trivial things, which paved the way for the latter. Such a strategy was closely connected to Han's utilitarian view of human communication, as the long-term profits of big trust were made possible by the accumulation of small trusts.

For Han, successful persuasion often depended more on the speaker's relationship with the audience than on what was said. The fact that his advisers were regarded as wise men often posed a threat to the ruler. However, a good relationship between the ruler and his adviser would reduce such a threat and ensure trust. To build trust and gain the favor of the ruler, advisers sometimes had to employ unconventional strategies, such as in this historical example offered by Han: "In remote antiquity, when Tang was the sanest and I Yin the wisest of the age, though the wisest attempted to persuade the sanest, yet he was not welcomed even after seventy times of persuasion, till he had to handle pans and bowls and becomes a cook in order thereby to approach him and become familiar with him. In consequence, Tang came to know his worthiness and took him into service" (1.3.25). This example not only illustrates the importance of establishing trustworthy relationships in paving the way for persuasion, but also pinpoints the patience and humility one must sometimes exhibit in order to gain "big" trust. However, Han did recognize that the degree of inherent closeness between the parties involved was also a significant factor in determining the level of trust. Han offered the following example to illustrate this point: "There was in Sun a rich man. Once it rained and his mud fence collapsed. Thereupon his son said: 'if their fence is not immediately rebuilt, burglars might come. So also did the father of his neighbors say to him. On the evening of that day he incurred a great loss of money. Thereafter his family had high regard for his son's wisdom but suspected the father of the neighbors" (4.12.110).

Indeed, more often than not, the relationship itself dictates the degree of trust an audience will have in a speaker, which, in turn, dictates the effectiveness of persuasion. This is especially true in China, where family ties, piety, and loyalty are particularly valued. Unlike Aristotle's view that the speaker's ethos was created and established in the process of persuasion, Han's implication seems to be that ethos was determined by the relationship between the speaker and the audience, especially with regard to interpersonal communication. Once trust was established, the persuader could freely express himself vis-à-vis the ruler. In Han's words, "When your meaning is not offensive and your wording is not flippant, you are then under way to use all your wisdom and eloquence to persuade anybody. In this way you can become near and dear to him, avoid all suspicion, and exert your speech to the utmost" (4.12.109).

Another technique for gaining trust involved flattering the ruler. In order to acquire fame and material benefits, as well as to protect oneself in the hierarchical and bureaucratic system of ancient China, ministers learned the art of flattery through self-disparagement, showing obedience and loyalty, establishing a close personal relationship, and elevating the ruler's self-esteem and pride. Through these techniques, which are still prevalent in today's superior-subordinate relations in China, a minister would likely win the favor and trust of the ruler, thus paving the way to exert influence on the ruler in the future.

C. The Art of Listening. The above persuasive strategies were utilized by ministers and advisers. However, while an adviser typically formulated his message based on the ruler's state of mind, the deciding factor in such persuasive activity was the audience—in this case the ruler. In Han's view, ministers and rulers were bound together by mutual self-interests, with rulers seeking help from their ministers in order to maintain their power and ministers gaining fame and fortune as skillful advisers. As a result, the minister was rarely candid and loyal vis-à-vis the ruler. Only an enlightened ruler could detect the minister's true motives through a sound assessment of his speech, issuing appropriate rewards and punishments on that basis.

Accordingly, it was important for the ruler to *cha yan* 察言 (verify speech). Of the seven shu proposed by Han to the ruler, the last two were particularly aimed at this purpose. The sixth shu involved "manipulating different information" by inquiring into some area about which the ruler was already knowledgeable in order to uncover unknown details. The last shu involved "inverting words" by falsifying one's intention in order to cross-examine the minister's true motive (9.30.285). The practice of cha yan was so important that it could assure the position of power even if the ruler were extravagant and indulgent. Without cha yan his reign would be undermined even if "he is frugal and industrious, wears hemp clothes, and eats poor food" (17.44.226).

In addition to cha yan, a ruler should also know how to *ting yan* 聽言 (listen to speech). Han advised the ruler to apply the shu of wu wei when listening to the ministers' advice in order to elicit all points of view while at the same time ascertaining the real motives behind words. According to Han:

In general, the right way to listen to the ministers is to take what they utter as the measure of what they harvest. The ruler investigates their names so as to determine their office, and clarify their duties so as to distinguish between different varieties of work. The right way to hear different utterances is to look drunken. Never start moving your own lips and teeth before the subordinates do. The longer I keep quiet, the sooner others move their lips and teeth. As they themselves move their lips and teeth, I can thereby understand their real intentions. Right and wrong words come to the fore in such fashion, the ruler does not have to join issue with them. (2.8.56)

Furthermore, a ruler must put aside any emotional attachment to his ministers. Likewise, he should never openly show likes or dislikes, closeness or distance with regard to any of his officials. He should also never discuss the ideas proposed by wise and intelligent men with his ministers nearby.

This was to prevent wicked ministers from deceiving in order to win trust and favor by telling him what he wants to hear rather than what is good for the state.

According to Han, a ruler should avoid trusting his ministers. This was because once the ruler began to trust one of his ministers, he would likely be under the control of that person and would, therefore, stand a good chance of being deluded by the minister's ill-conceived opinions and arguments. For Han, "The lord of men in keeping ministers in service ought to know the motive and purpose of every speaker in order to hold his words responsible for an equivalent fact, and ask the non-speakers to decide between the pros and cons of the proposition so as to hold them accountable for the result of the work" (5.18.153). By so doing, ministers were encouraged to present accountable speeches rather than irresponsible opinions. As a way to guard against the deception of flattering and embellished speeches, "the intelligent sovereign, whenever he listens to any speech, would hold it to accountable for its utility, and when he observes any deed, would seek for its merit. If so, empty and obsolete learning cannot be discussed and praised and fraudulent action cannot be disguised" (18.46.247). Law should be used to promote the articulation of useful speech while preventing the formulation of empty and deceptive speech. Anyone who furthered the cause of useful speech would be rewarded with a promotion, while those who indulged in empty words would be punished by being removed from office. In selecting men for office, the ruler should not make judgments based on his personal likes and dislikes but rather on the accountability, utility, and practicality of the views expressed during the interview process.

(3) Attacks on Bian. Although Han was an expert in persuasion, he was antagonistic toward bian when he felt it indulged in empty words and theories rather than conforming to laws and bringing about concrete results. Throughout the text of *Han Feizi* Han condemned Mingjia and Mohists, attacked Confucian scholars, and even ridiculed Daoist philosophers on their practice of bian. In his view, the misuse of bian was the primary reason for disorder and confusion. Only the systematic, uniform enforcement of laws could establish and maintain order while eradicating various empty views and opinions expressed and articulated by bian shi.

Like other philosophers, Han was a bitter critic of Chinese Mingjia and Mohists. In his view, although members of both schools tended to be eloquent speakers, their speeches lacked utility from the standpoint of the ruler and the state. Accordingly, their speeches were "absurd discussions," "aimed only at contention," and "too ineffable." He criticized their theories as roundabout, exaggerating, and impractical (11.32.26–27). In Han's opinion, "words and deeds should take function and utility as mark and target" (17.41.208), and he felt that Mingjia and the Mohists failed to live up to this standard of practicality.

While both Mingjia and the Later Mohists considered probability an important feature of argumentation because of the subjective and relative nature of language and human perception, Han regarded this notion as self-contradictory, illustrating his point with the following story:

Somebody said: Once there was a man selling halberds and shields. He praised his shields for their solidity as such that nothing could penetrate them. All at once he also praised his halberd saying, "My halberds are so sharp that they can penetrate anything." In response to his words people asked, "How about using your halberds to pierce through your shields?" To this the man could not give any reply. In fact, the shields advertised to be "impenetrable" and the halberds advertised to be "absolutely penetrative" can not stand together. (17.40.203–4)

This story was a direct response to Mingjia belief that one could argue from right to wrong and wrong to right. For Han, argument based on probability only produced contradictions and confusion. He believed in authoritative truth, which, in practical terms, meant whoever has the power has the truth. In his words, "In the state of an enlightened sovereign, his orders are the most precious among the words of men and his laws are the most appropriate rules to affairs. Two different words cannot be equally precious nor can two different laws be equally appropriate" (17.41.207). The Chinese term *mao dun* 矛盾, which originated from this story, means conflict, contradictory, and embedded the meaning of things of dialectical nature.

Moreover, Han accused Confucius and Mozi, in their practice of bian, of using obsolete knowledge to disturb the minds of the current rulers. Han belligerently characterized them as "stupid scholars" who "do not know the actual conditions of order and chaos but chatter nonsense and chant too many hackneyed old books to disturb the government of the present age." What is more, he referred to Confucianists as "vermin" who plagued society and caused confusion. He expressed disappointment with "Men who quote the early kings and preach benevolence and righteousness," bemoaning the fact that such men "fill up the court, wherefore the government can not be free from disorder" (19.49.289). Thus, he advised the ruler that "those who specialize in refinement and learning, should not be employed; for if employed, they would confuse the law of the state" (19.49.285). He warned the ruler, "whoever listens to their words, will incur danger. Whoever employs their schemes, will invite confusion" (4.14.123). For Han, ideas must have practical application for the immediate situation and must be proved useful by facts. Blindly following the ancients with no regard for the specifics of current problems and ever-changing situations was misleading and deceptive to the ruler.

Han particularly targeted Confucius, arguing that his ethically based advice to the ruler was a violation of law, since, in his view, under the Confucian system men of no merit would be rewarded and guilty criminals would be absolved (16.38.178).[9] In short, Han decried the use of bian in putting forth ethical appeals. In fact, in his system, there was no place whatsoever for bian either as a means of illuminating diverse points of views or as a rational activity for distinguishing truth and falsehood. Such criteria were best prescribed and predetermined in written codes of laws. Another rationale for Han's argument was his assertion that the people of his time were more sophisticated, cunning, and selfish than the simpleminded people of ancient times. In Han's words, his contemporaries were "alert and astute and apt to preen themselves and disobey the superior" (20.51.316). Accordingly, measures of control should be more stern and severe. Moral appeals were only effective for simpleminded people.

In his chapter *wen bian* (Inquiring into Argumentation), Han attributed the misuse of bian to the ruler's lack of control and failure to set up clear criteria for speech. As previously mentioned, Han considered the ruler's pronouncements the most authoritative and his laws the most appropriate rules for governmental affairs. Accordingly, any opinions not conforming to the ruler's orders were against law. In a state where laws prevail there is no need for argumentation and disputation. This was because "stupid persons fear punishment and dare not speak, and intelligent persons find nothing to dispute" (17.41.207–8). Bian originated, according to Han, because rulers made the mistake of honoring the bian shi's wisdom, revering their speeches as eloquent and profound rather than punishing them for causing confusion and disorder. As this observation indicates, for Han, bian was not a moral or rational activity creating infinite interpretations of truth and reality; rather, as practiced by bian shi and you shui, bian posed a threat to the enforcement of laws. As Oliver rightly asserts, "The right end of persuasion in his [Han's] view was to serve neither truth nor the good of society, nor even the advantage of the speaker, but the requirements of the ruler" (1971, 220).

Han's views regarding bian were self-contradictory in nature. On one hand, he advocated suppressing bian through the enforcement of law. On the other hand, he considered bian a powerful tool for maintaining and implementing the law. It was his expressed hope that "the people, within the boundary, when practicing persuasion and eloquence, always conform to the law" (Liao 19.49.291). Although, on one hand, Han forbade the practice of bian if it did not conform to law and authority, on the other hand, he gave credit to those who spoke on behalf of the government. In his words, "If anybody, not authorized by laws and orders, attempts to cope with foreign intrigues, guard against civil disturbances, produce public benefit, or manage state affairs, his superior should heed his words and hold it accountable for an equivalent fact. If the words turn out true, he should receive a big reward" (17.41.207). In this respect, Han's intention was not to devalue bian by placing it under law and authority; instead, he saw bian as an important means of serving the ruler and governing his people. Indeed, Han valued bian to such an extent that he regarded it as one of the most important qualities in evaluating government officials. As he advised the ruler, "In general, the right way to listen to the ministers is to take what they utter as the measure of what they harvest. The ruler investigates their names (speech) so as to determine their office" (2.8.56). Accordingly, the appointment of official posts should be made "with reference to eloquence and penetration in wording, honesty and integrity in money, and knowledge of human affairs" (10.33.78). In this sense, Han's view of bian is contradictory.

Han's Rhetorical Style

As mentioned in the discussion of Han's background, though his verbal expression was marred by his stuttering, he was a good writer. Furthermore, while generally critical of bian as practiced by bian shi and you shui, he himself employed various kinds of rhetorical means in presenting his argument. In fact, among all the philosophers discussed so far, Han was the most eloquent, logical, and forceful bian shi. His primary rhetorical devices can be summarized under the following four headings: (1) metaphor and analogy; (2) anecdotes; (3) chain reasoning; and (4) application of the law of contradiction.

(1) Metaphor and Analogy. The text of *Han Feizi* is rich in metaphor and analogy. For example, Han frequently used the metaphor of the "ruler" for drawing lines and making measurements and the "compass" for making circles. These metaphors symbolize the use of laws and principles as criteria for human behaviors. Han often made the point that if a carpenter failed to use rulers and compasses in his work, he would not get things straight or round as intended. Whatever he produced would, therefore, be of poor quality. Likewise, if a state failed to articulate and enforce its laws, the people would speak and act with no clear criteria to follow, which would, in turn, cause disorder and loss of control on the part of the ruler. Such a metaphor was both appropriate and effective. Its appropriateness was due

to the fact that people of all levels were familiar with the function of rulers and compasses; thus, it was relatively easy for them to associate rulers and compasses with the role and function of laws. Though the use of metaphor was also evident and pervasive in texts by other ancient writers, Han differed from other writers in that he effectively used the same metaphor frequently and consistently throughout the text to reinforce his argument that laws were necessary in the formation and maintenance of an orderly society.

Analogy, or extended metaphor, was another rhetorical strategy employed frequently in *Han Feizi*. For example, he frequently used the analogy of the family, comparing a mother's love for her children with the notion of benevolence and a father's authority in the family with the enforcement of laws. To illustrate his point that benevolence was not as effective as laws, Han used the following analogy: "Mothers love sons with deep love, but most of the sons are spoiled, for their love is over-extended; fathers show their sons less love and teach them with light bamboos [beatings], but most of the sons turn out well, for severity is applied" (Liao 18.46.242). Furthermore, no matter how much a mother loves her child, "yet, when the child has mischievous actions, she sends him to follow the teacher; when he is badly ill, she sends him to see the physician" (18.47.254). In short, external forces or sanctions were sometimes in the best interest of the child. Similarly, for Han, state-enforced laws were necessary external aids for making people well behaved. This analogy implied that it was harsh legal penalties rather than benevolent affection that brought peace and order to a state. Laws were tough for the ultimate benefit of the people.

Han compared the ruler of a state to the head of a family. The ruler's relationship to his subjects was like that of a father to his children. In his words, "what parents desire of children is safety and prosperity in livelihood and innocence in conduct. What the ruler requires of his subjects, however, is to demand their lives in case of emergency and exhaust their energy in time of peace" (18.46.241). Thus, the role of the ruler was to protect his obedient subjects just as the role of the father was to protect his obedient children.[10]

(2) Anecdotes. Although superficially Han seemed the epitome of the boring bureaucrat bent on disseminating his Legalistic theories, he was quite resourceful and versatile in his use of anecdotes in the presentation of his arguments. Unlike Zhuangzi's anecdotes, which were drawn from myths, legend, and nature, Han's were drawn from historical facts and current affairs. This was consistent with his utilitarian and pragmatic orientation. Approximately 340 anecdotes were used in *Han Feizi*, concerning

over 100 historical figures, from ancient tribal kings to rulers of various states, from learned scholars to common people (Zhao et al., 1993, 817). These real-life human beings were portrayed with all their strengths and weaknesses, emotions, desires, and motives.

Han's anecdotes, often combined with assertions, explanations, and comments, were used to support his Legalistic views concerning absolute imperial control, deceptive human nature, and complex human psychology. In the formulation of an argument Han typically presented anecdotal evidence in one of two ways: complete and detailed anecdotes pertaining to historical facts were listed in a series to provide compelling evidence for his assertion; or, anecdotes were used as a prelude to illustrate the seriousness of a problem.[11] Subsequently, Han would identify the cause of the problem, after which he would present an analysis of the problem and propose a solution.[12] In either case, Han's anecdotes were not used simply to explain concepts or enlighten his readers. Rather, they were used for solving practical problems in the communication between the ruler and his ministers, as well as between the ruler and the common people.

(3) Chain Reasoning. As noted in chapter 1, chain reasoning, or deduction by chains, is a recognized feature of the Chinese reasoning process. This feature is prevalent in *Han Feizi*. Although Han was not the first ancient Chinese thinker to use chain reasoning, he can certainly be credited with having used this rhetorical technique to its fullest.

Chain reasoning is a type of logical inference. While in the West, Aristotle used chain reasoning to draw conclusions by generating inferences from categories, the conclusion drawn from Han's use of chain reasoning centered around cause and effect. If one begins with a particular statement and then generates from it a certain consequence, the consequence then becomes a deductive principle which generates another consequence. In other words, the effect of one thing is shown to be the cause of another. For example: to prove that those who had suffered much in the past would be better prepared to grasp current affairs, Han said the following, "Man encountered by misery feels afraid in mind. If he feels afraid in mind, his motives of conduct will become straight. If his motives of conduct are straight, his thinking processes will become careful. If his thinking processes are careful, he will attain principles of affairs" (Liao 6.20.176). No particular order or format could be obtained with regard to Han's chain of reasoning. Oftentimes, in fact, the chain was not strictly followed. Another chain might start at any time, anywhere, from any previous statement or consequence. For example, as Han continued, "If his motives of conduct are straight, he will meet no misery. If he meets no misery, he will live a life as decreed by Heaven. If he attains principles of affairs, he will accomplish meritorious works. If he can live a life as decreed by Heaven, his life will be perfect and long" (6.20.176). By applying Han's chain reasoning process, one could infer endless consequences, not necessarily by a strictly logical, linear process of cause and effect but also by randomly expanding the chain to start new connections and draw new consequences.

Chain reasoning, as practiced by Han, sometimes began with two statements and proceeded on two separate chain reasoning tracks. However, when this strategy was employed, the meaning of the two chains reinforced one another. For example, in what follows, the second chain is a metaphor for the first chain: "In general, who first has the state and then loses it, and who first has the body and then drives it to misery, cannot be called able to have possession of the state and keep the safety of the body. Indeed, who can have possession of the state, must be able to keep the Altar of the Spirits of Land and Grain in security; who can keep the safety of the body, must be able to live through the period of life as decreed by Heaven. Such a man can be called able to have possession of the state and keep the safety of the body..." (6.20.182–83). This chain reasoning continued until two conclusions were reached. The first metaphorical conclusion was that protecting one's state was like protecting one's body. The second quasi-logical conclusion was that only those who ruled the state had the real power. Comparatively speaking, while Aristotle's chain reasoning stressed abstract and categorical thinking, Han's chain reasoning emphasized concrete consequences and metaphorical connections.

(4) Application of the Law of Contradiction. Though Aristotle acknowledged the concept of relative truth, proposed by Greek sophists, he insisted that "the most indisputable of all beliefs is that contradictory statements are not at the same time true" (*Metaphysics* 1011b10). In other words, a thing cannot be true and false at the same time. Aristotle believed that we must accept the principle that "the same attribute cannot at the same time belong and not belong to the same subject and in the same aspect" (*Metaphysics* 1005b15). If an argument violated this principle, the argument would be self-contradictory. Aristotle proposed this principle to avoid logical fallacy and increase the logical consistency of an argument.

Han would be in complete agreement with Aristotle on this important point, as is exemplified vividly in his story of the man who argued that his halberds could penetrate anything and at the same time that nothing could penetrate his shields (Liao 17.40.203–4). For Han, "the shields advertised to be 'impenetrable' and the halberds advertised to be 'absolutely penetrative' cannot stand together." The salesman committed a logical fallacy, contradicting himself with his two mutually exclusive assertions. Han used this "logical principle" of self-contradiction to present his argument, saying "Similarly, worthiness employed as a form of shih [shi, power] cannot forbid anything, but shih employed as a way of government forbids everything. Now, to bring together worthiness that cannot forbid anything and shih that forbids everything is a 'halberd-and-shield' fallacy. Clearly enough, worthiness and circumstances are incompatible with each other" (17.40.204). In other words, a ruler could not hold absolute power and have people of wisdom and intelligence around him at the same time. Likewise, a state could not be ruled with benevolence and upheld by legal sanctions at the same time. Things must be one way or the other. For Han, absolute imperial power and legal sanctions were the only effective means of bringing a state into order. In this regard, Han combined logic with politics, using the law of contradiction to argue against the rhetorical perspectives of other philosophers as well as to justify his own Legalistic theory.

In this chapter I have introduced Han Feizi's Legalistic philosophy, his views on political communication, and his rhetorical theory regarding ming, shui, and bian, as concerned with political power, audience psychology, and practicality. This Legalistic view of speech and language created an ideology of despotism decried by Confucianism and other schools of thoughts. Such an ideology has done much to stifle the expression of diverse rhetorical theories. As such, it is akin to the rhetoric of the Middle Ages in the West where God was considered the only authority in the interpretation of truth. A significant difference, however, is that in the case of ancient China, the sole authority was a living god who exerted total political control over his people and was therefore capable of greater cultural, intellectual, and economic destruction. Unfortunately, Han's political and legalistic views were subsequently adopted by the king of Qin, who conquered the individual states, uniting China under a single legalistic system (221 B.C.E.). This marked the end of the Spring-Autumn and Warring States period, a period of transition and change in all aspects of Chinese life, of flourishing ideas and thoughts, of open discussion and the evolution of rhetorical sensibilities.

CHAPTER 10

Conclusions and Implications

The purposes of this project, as stated in the introductory chapter, are to uncover an implicit Chinese rhetorical tradition, to compare classical Chinese ming bian with classical Greek rhetoric formulated during the same time period, and to shed light on the scope and function of rhetoric cross-culturally. Toward this end, I have explored Chinese rhetorical practices, in particular those conceptualized as yan, shui, ming, and bian, by various ancient Chinese thinkers. I have also examined social and cultural conditions contributing to the formulation of philosophical and rhetorical views in ancient China, for, like classical Greek rhetoric, Chinese ming bian arose in response to such factors and cannot be adequately understood out of context. Moreover, the meaning of ming bian evolved as cultural and social conditions changed over time.

Guided by the principles of multicultural hermeneutics, which undercut any attempt at canon building, aiming instead at celebrating diverse human values and traditions, this project challenges Western scholarly misconceptions regarding the field of Chinese rhetoric and expands the horizons of rhetorical studies for Chinese scholars. In the process, it provides a more authentic and complete understanding of Chinese rhetorical tradition. This task is accomplished by turning to the original Chinese terminology, searching for rhetorical meaning in primary philosophical texts, and taking into account historical and cultural conditions in ancient China. By this method a rich and dynamic rhetorical tradition known as ming bian is made explicit.

My concluding remarks fall into three general categories: 1) a summary of Chinese rhetorical theories and practices during the pre-Qin period; 2) a general comparison of classical Greek rhetoric and Chinese ming bian; and 3) a discussion of the implications of contemporary Chinese communication patterns for the construction of a multicultural rhetoric.

Summary of Chinese Rhetorical Theories and Practices

From the Xia dynasty to the Warring States period, Chinese rhetorical practice took various forms, from ritualistic ceremonies to attempts at political persuasion, from poetic compositions to philosophical debates. Ancient Chinese thinkers formulated such experience in terms of ming (naming) and bian (distinction, argumentation), and to a lesser extent yan (speech, language). Though not explicitly defined, the rhetorical meanings of these terms were embedded in the philosophical texts under consideration in this study. Like the Greek notion of rhetoric, Chinese rhetorical perspectives are not monolithic but rather diverse, evolutionary, and contextual in nature.

This study has examined philosophical views and rhetorical perspectives by ten well-known thinkers and one collective group (the Later Mohists) representing five schools of thought, namely Mingjia, Confucianism, Daoism, Mohism, and Legalism. Each of the individuals selected for inclusion in this study holds a unique rhetorical perspective while borrowing from others. In general, there are four areas of emphasis characteristic of the Chinese rhetorical tradition: moral, epistemological, dialectical, and psychological.

Moral Emphasis

Long before the formulation of ming bian by Chinese thinkers, moral appeal, in the name of tian ming (the Mandate of Heaven), had been the most effective rhetorical device for regulating imperial conduct. In turn, the notion of li (rites) was developed and enforced by the rulers in order to regulate the behavior of the ruled. As demonstrated in *Shi Jing, Shang Shu, Zuo Zhuan, Guo Yu*, and *Zhan Guo Ce*, the notion of tian ming was thought to embody the highest moral principles and was thus employed as a universal appeal in moral persuasion. As the understanding of tian ming was transformed from the mystic figure of *shang di* (High God) to concrete characters of sage kings, the moral example set by the king was increasingly used as a major premise in moral persuasion. This was true throughout the pre-Qin era. Furthermore, moral persuasion was also achieved through the use of metaphorical and analogical reasoning. For example, legends, anecdotes, and parables were popular ways of explaining moral concepts or exemplifying moral deeds. In fact, they often proved to be more effective than abstract deliberations or formal, logical arguments, as they were concrete, tangible, and easy to understand.

Western scholars tend to attribute Chinese rhetorical strategies employing metaphorical and analogical reasoning to a lack of intellectual conviction and rationality (including the inability to think in logical, analytical, and abstract terms) on the part of the Chinese (Bodde 1938; Oliver 1971). This view overlooks the fact that metaphorical and analogical thinking, though not logical by Western standards of rationality, is, in fact, "logical" according to its own rhetorical standards. It is also a highly effective means of persuasion.

The works of Confucius, Mencius, and Mozi greatly emphasized moral/ethical persuasion for the purpose of maintaining peace and social order at the cultural level, and moral perfection at the individual level. More specifically, Confucius was primarily concerned with the rectification of names and restoration of traditional values in order to guarantee an orderly and harmonious society; Mencius asserted the necessity of nurturing human goodness through the cultivation of qi and the use of sincere speech; and Mozi upheld the principles of universal love and human interrelatedness in achieving a peaceful and egalitarian society.

Though differing in their understandings of virtue (as ren, dao, universal love, sincerity, or trustworthiness), as well as in their views concerning its implementation, the Chinese philosophers included in this study, with the exception of Mingjia, believed that morality was the most important characteristic of a bian shi. It was also considered the determining factor for successful persuasion since, in their view, only a moral person possessed the power to influence others. For Confucians, morality and benevolence went hand in hand. A true junzi was a moral and benevolent speaker. Eloquence did not lie in superficial technique but in the moral character of the person speaking. Such morality entailed taking into account the well-being of family, community, and society. For Mencius, a good speaker was equipped with zheng qi, a mind of righteousness and morality. Similarly, for the Daoists, only a virtuous or moral person could follow and speak dao. Mozi's teachings regarding "universal love" located moral conduct at the pinnacle of all activity, including the practice of bian. It is not surprising, then, that Mingjia were harshly criticized by these thinkers for their empty and amoral speech.

Epistemological Emphasis

Like the ancient Greeks, the ancient Chinese entertained cosmological questions and formulated their own ontology and epistemology. The cosmos of the ancient Chinese was composed of both physical and spiritual elements, which became known through symbols and symbolic performances. The earliest means of acquiring the knowledge of the world was through divination and ancestor worship. By the time of the Zhou dynasty, the Chinese had developed their cosmology of yin and yang and begun to understand the world in terms of the dynamic interplay and mutual influence of these two universal elements.[1]

Disavowing the existence of divine power, Mingjia constituted the first group of thinkers to recognize the power of symbols in shaping perceptions of the world. Since the time of Deng Xi, therefore, ming was regarded as a linguistic and rational tool for understanding the universe and achieving political control. According to this view, to the extent that ming (names) reflected the reality of shi (the objective world), social order was assured. Consequently, it was believed that manipulating the relationship between ming and shi would directly affect the outcome of persuasion.

Chinese Mingjia were more interested in epistemological issues than in moral ones. In this context, Hui Shi's approach was more holistic than that of Gong-sun Long. In addition to being included in texts by Deng Xi, Hui Shi, and Gong-sun Long, such epistemological emphasis in relation to speech and argumentation was also found in the works of Xunzi, Mozi, and the Later Mohists. For example, according to Xunzi, bian entailed the use of one's reason. In fact, Xunzi was the first Confucian thinker to conceptualize ming bian in the direction of rational argument. Though Chinese logic in the ming bian system may not appear as systematic and clearly defined as Aristotelian logic, Chinese thinkers, especially the Mohists, were concerned with the logical aspects of persuasion. For example, Mozi and the Later Mohists formulated their own rational notions of *lei tui* (classification by kind) and *ming gu* (understanding cause and because), which share certain similarities with Greek deductive and inductive reasoning processes. The most valuable contribution made by Mozi and the Later Mohists was their treatment of bian as both an art and a science, a way of achieving social justice as well as a mode of inquiry for establishing truth and knowledge.

Dialectical Emphasis

The Chinese cosmology of yin and yang juxtaposes seemingly opposite elements in a system of dialectical interrelatedness. This dialectical cosmology as applied to ancient Chinese rhetoric is most evident in philosophical and political discourse, which challenges the audience to grasp the subtle interplay of things and, in the process, to awaken to more profound levels of truth. Oftentimes the challenges are expressed in the form of poetic and paradoxical language, as, for example, in the *Dao De Jing* and *Zhuangzi*.

Based on their mystical belief in the total interpenetration of things, Laozi and Zhuangzi proposed wu ming and viewed bian as a spontaneous activity capable of bridging opposites and achieving the dao. The activity of bian, accordingly, was not polarizing; nor did it consist of imposing one's view on others. Instead, bian was a process for connecting and transcending apparent differences and polarized positions. In this way, one was freed of all dogma, illusions, and attachment. In their quest for what was unsaid and unheard, Laozi and Zhuangzi looked beyond the world of being. For them, one acquired wisdom and rhetorical artistry through an acute perception of the situation.

Psychological Emphasis

As China entered the Warring States period, the ideal of a moral king and benevolent government became less important than acquiring land and political power through militaristic and utilitarian means. As a result, morally based persuasive strategies gave way to psychological appeals that had little or nothing to do with morality. Instead, these appeals catered to base human motivations—for example, fear of being shamed in public or losing face, and the desire for fame and fortune. A skillful you shui adapted his message to the audience's (the ruler's) likes and dislikes, offering advice as to the estimated gains and losses involved in taking certain actions. In fulfilling his responsibilities to the king, a you shui employed all the available means of persuasion. In addition to arguments made in reference to historical example through the use of chain reasoning and the identification of advantages and disadvantages, the predominant form of persuasion employed by Chinese you shui and bian shi was metaphorical and analogical reasoning. Though not unique to Chinese rhetorical practice and culture, the use of metaphor and analogy was prevalent and pervasive in the ancient Chinese texts. It was certainly the most common rhetorical practice and skillful technique employed by the ancient Chinese in their rhetorical activities. Moreover, Han Feizi, who challenged but also adopted the elements of all the schools of thought that preceded him, envisioned bian as a political force involving an acute understanding of the psychological mindset of the audience. In his view, shui and bian were tools of political expediency rather than moral and rational activities.

Generally speaking, in the ancient Chinese rhetorical tradition, forms of speech and persuasive discourse vary, as do formulations of ming bian. Furthermore, Chinese rhetorical perspectives, as expressed by various interdependent schools of thought, are rooted in Chinese philosophical, social, and cultural contexts. These perspectives have evolved and expanded over time, in large part as a result of their interactions with one another.[2]

Furthermore, they appear to have much in common with ancient Greek rhetorical views dating from the fifth to third century B.C.E. The following pages present a comparison of the rhetorical traditions of these two ancient cultures.

A Comparison of Chinese Ming Bian and Greek Rhetoric

No evidence has been found to suggest a connection between ancient Greece and ancient China.[3] However, the two cultures shared similar social and cultural values in addition to their rhetorical perspectives. For example, as discussed in chapter 2, poetry was a common form of rhetorical expression in Chinese cultural life even before Confucius's time. Likewise, Homeric poetry was a dominant form of communication in ancient Greece as early as the eighth century B.C.E. Ancient China of the fifth century B.C.E. was in a period of cultural transition and social upheaval. The highly elitist Zhou dynasty had collapsed. Consequently, the nobility had lost its power and the common people were taking control of their own lives. During this time China was divided into many vassal states, which were constantly at war with one another for power and autonomy. In the midst of such social chaos, the ancient Chinese valued communal life and routinely made sacrifices for the common good. On a spiritual level, they viewed the world as a synthetic unity of yin and yang.

During the same time period in ancient Greece, "the nobles were beginning to lose their political monopoly" (Andrews 1967, 56). The country was divided into many city-states. The Persians invaded in 480 B.C.E., and there was a war between the Athenians and the Spartans from 431 to 404 B.C.E. Despite all this, the ancient Greeks placed high value on community life and public service. Furthermore, they "looked at the world with a steady gaze that did not see any part of it as separate and cut off from the rest, but always as an element in a living whole" (Jaeger 1965, xx). These historical and cultural similarities gave rise to similar rhetorical sensibilities between the two ancient cultures.

Similarities between Greek Rhetoric and Chinese Ming Bian

Based on this survey of Chinese ming bian as well as studies of Greek rhetoric undertaken by Western historians, it appears that Greek rhetoric and Chinese ming bian share common ground in the following five categories: the art of persuasion, ethical emphasis, rational engagement, psychological activity, and evolutionary nature. It should be noted, however, that these rhetorical elements are relatively distinct and explicit in the Greek context, while in the Chinese context they appear to be more implicit and less clearly defined.

(1) The Art of Persuasion. Despite differences in rhetorical forms in the two cultures,[4] it is evident that both Chinese ming bian and Greek rhetoric involved the arts of persuasion. This point is best made in the Chinese context by an examination of the rhetorical styles of Mingjia, Xunzi, the Later Mohists, Han Feizi, and the Daoists. For example, Mingjia such as Deng Xi, Hui Shi, and Gong-sun Long were portrayed by other scholars as eloquent speakers and masters of persuasion. In their practice of bian, these men strove to persuade others through their eloquent and artistic use of language. This sense of bian was further developed by Xunzi and the Later Mohists, who expanded its scope into the realms of morality and logic. For Han Feizi, bian [shui] rose to the level of art to the extent that one managed to penetrate into the mind of the audience. Finally, for the Daoists, bian was accomplished by making artistic choices rather than by following rigid rules.

While for the Chinese Mingjia the art of bian was generally employed in making a legal argument or attempting to win over an audience, for the Greek sophists rhetorical artistry carried magical power, capable of exerting influence over people in any instance. At the same time, the concept of probability was at the core of Greek rhetorical theory, and this was true of Chinese Mingjia as well. While Mingjia were often called "glib tongued" by the Chinese philosophers, the sophists were described as "linguistic craftsmen." Similarly, Mingjia were known for arguing from "right to wrong and wrong to right," while the sophists were accused of making a "strong case appear weak" since they "pursue probability through thick and thin in every kind of speech . . ." (Plato *Phaedrus* 272e).

Even Confucius and Mencius, who were more concerned with the moral and social implications of ming bian, emphasized the appropriate use of language in elevating persuasion to an art. The same can be said for Plato, who condemned the sophistic use of rhetoric while, at the same time, using dialogical and poetic language to convey his philosophical ideas. Furthermore, Aristotle's synthesis and development of the rhetorical theories of the Greek sophists and Plato made rhetoric a discipline of both art and science. Likewise, Xunzi, in the formulation of his own rhetorical perspective, borrowed and developed the notion of ming bian from his predecessors. Both Aristotle and Xunzi considered the artistic use of language a highly important and effective means of persuasion.

(2) Ethical Emphasis. In both China and Greece of the fifth century B.C.E., philosophers moved away from cosmological speculation toward a

concern for moral and ethical issues, the primary issue being how to be a good person and live a good life.[5] The entire discussion of ming bian by Chinese thinkers centered around how to live as moral human beings and how to construct a moral society through the use of symbols.

Out of this overriding concern, ming bian was regarded as a moral, ethical, and social activity. For Confucius, the purpose of speech was to elevate oneself to the level of a junzi; for Mozi, the goal was to become a person capable of universal love; and for Daoists, it was to achieve transcendent knowledge of the dao. Similarly, Greek rhetoric emphasized molding human character in accordance with aretê. The purpose of rhetoric, for Plato, was to uplift one's soul through dialectical discourse. For Aristotle, Isocrates, and even the Roman rhetoricians Cicero and Quintilian, the perfect orator was first of all a moral person with a well-rounded and broad education. In this sense, both the ancient Chinese and the ancient Greeks perceived speech as a persuasive tool for altering individual behavior and transforming the social order. In both cultures sophistic forms of rhetoric were considered immoral and harmful by philosophers. For example, just as Confucius accused Mingjia of speaking superficially and hypocritically, Plato condemned Greek sophistic rhetoric as "knack" without moral substance. In Chinese philosophical texts ming bian and ethics are interrelated; a bian shi should at all times be a moral person. Likewise, in ancient Greek rhetorical texts, a strong connection is made between rhetoric and ethics, and wisdom and eloquence, especially in the works of Plato and Aristotle. Confucius's assertion that a good bian shi was a junzi who possessed the virtue of ren strikingly resembled Quintilian's definition of a rhetor as a good, well-spoken person. It also directly paralleled Plato's contention that a good orator "does well in all his actions" (*Gorgias* 507c) and Aristotle's claim that the term rhetorician may "describe either the speaker's knowledge of the art, or his moral purpose [choice]" (*Rhetoric* 1355b20). Both Confucius and Mencius believed that only a person with a good, knowledgeable, and righteous mind was deserving of the title bian shi and capable of effecting positive changes in society. In a like manner, Plato argued: "The good orator, being also a man of expert knowledge, will have these ends [morality] in view in any speech or action by which he seeks to influence the souls of men" (*Gorgias* 504d). Similarly, in the words of Aristotle, "Persuasion is achieved by the speaker's personal character when the speech is so spoken as to make us think him credible" (*Rhetoric* 1356a5), while for Isocrates, the power to speak well was an indication of a good and faithful soul (*Isocrates II* 253–56).

Both Chinese and Greek cultures perceived ming bian and rhetoric as means of maintaining social order. This understanding of rhetoric and ming bian can be identified in both Aristotle's and Confucius's work, with the primary difference being one of emphasis concerning the type of rhetoric and ming bian needed to achieve these shared goals. Aristotle emphasized deliberative rhetoric for its communal function and values. A good rhetor, in Aristotle's opinion, should not be concerned with individual benefits but devoted to the public good. Similarly, Confucius's rectification of names aimed at achieving social order and benefiting the public. When everyone speaks and acts according to his/her position or status in a society, order will be maintained. When society is peaceful, everyone benefits.

(3) Rational Activity. Both the ancient Chinese and their Greek counterparts shared the belief that human beings were rational animals and that rational argument was inherently persuasive. From the works of Gong-sun Long, Xunzi, Mozi, and the Later Mohists, clear evidence can be discerned equating ming bian with rational argument. For example, classification and categorization were primary concerns of these thinkers in their quest to gain knowledge, establish truth, and win arguments.

The search for rational procedures to construct arguments were also central concerns of Greek philosophers and rhetoricians. For example, Plato taught that when undertaking an argument, a speaker must first be able to define the subject or concept being discussed and divide it into specific categories backed up by relevant examples until he reaches the limit of divisibility. Likewise, Aristotle considered rhetoric a counterpart to dialectical discourse in that it dealt with deduction (the enthymeme) and induction (examples).[6]

The concepts of deductive and inductive reasoning are not the exclusive inventions of the ancient Greeks, however. Xunzi discussed a rational system similar to deductive and inductive reasoning processes and was interested in logical concepts such as discrimination, coherence, and proofs. Interest in rational engagement is even more evident in the works of Mozi and the Later Mohists. For example, the concept of gu requires that both major and minor reasons for a conclusion be given; the concept of lei assists in the making of rhetorical classifications and generalizations; and, finally, the word *tui* signifies the logical process by which inferences are made deductively and inductively.

(4) Psychological Activity. Rhetoric and ming bian, as formulated by both ancient Greek and Chinese thinkers, include not only aesthetic, moral, and rational components but also psychological elements. This is especially true in the context of understanding and adapting to an audience. The focus of the Greek philosophical strand of rhetoric, according to George

Kennedy (1980), lay in the consideration of and adaptation to one's audience. In ancient China, similarly, Confucius considered talking to the right audience the key to success, while for Laozi appropriateness and naturalness were essential skills for adapting to one's audience.

The idea of audience adaptation in terms of timing and appropriateness is more prevalent and explicit in Greek sophistic rhetoric. As Poulakos explains, "In conjunction with the notion of Kairos, the Sophists gave impetus to the related concept of prepon (the appropriate) apparently prescribing that what is said must conform to both audience and occasion" (1983, 41). Audience adaptation was also a concern for Plato. In his words, "The function of speech is to influence the soul. It follows that the would-be speaker must know how many types of souls there are" (*Phaedrus* 271d). For Plato, the art of speech involved adapting one's message to one's audience. For this reason, he considered interpersonal communication more conducive to moral improvement than public discourse.

Similarities can also be discerned between Han Feizi and Aristotle with regard to understanding persuasion as a psychological activity. In his essays on speaking and persuasion, Han Feizi identified different kinds of audiences, analyzing how a message might be interpreted differently by audiences with different motives and moods. Aristotle offered a similar analysis—namely that a person's judgment was affected by his or her differing moods. In his words, "when they feel friendly to the man who comes before them for judgement, they regard him as having done little wrong, if any; when they feel hostile, they take the opposite view" (*Rhetoric* 1378a1).

Likewise, Han Feizi advised his readers that the key element to understanding one's audience was to understand their feelings of love and hate. Although Han Feizi did not offer a detailed description of different types of emotions as Aristotle had done in book 2 of his *Rhetoric*, he did discuss the importance of appealing to different kinds of emotions in the interest of successful persuasion. Hence, both Aristotle and Han Feizi's strategies of persuasion can be regarded as psychological in nature.

(5) Evolutionary Nature. When viewed in their respective historical contexts, it can be seen that neither Greek rhetoric nor Chinese ming bian was rigid, static, or permanently defined. Rather, they were fluid, dynamic, and constantly in the process of being redefined. Edward Schiappa's (1990, 1992) exploration of the original Greek terms related to language and rhetoric, from the fifth to fourth century B.C.E., exposes the evolutionary nature of such terms. For example, according to his study, the term logos, used in the fifth century B.C.E., entailed a relatively holistic view of rhetoric, whereas

the term *rhêtorikê*, coined by Plato in the fourth century B.C.E., separated rhetoric from philosophy. Schiappa's investigation suggests that the formulation of a Greek system of rhetoric was built upon the technical and sophistic understandings of rhetoric that preceded Plato and Aristotle. The evolutionary nature of the term *rhetoric* is demonstrated by Greek philosophers' efforts to criticize, challenge, and construct a philosophical rhetoric.

This evolutionary process was similar to the development of Chinese ming bian. Prior to the emergence of the School of Mohism and the appearance of *Mo Bian*, the term *ming* was used by Deng Xi and Confucius to connote symbol usage and social control. Subsequently, however, it was used by Zhuangzi, Xunzi, Gong-sun Long, and the Later Mohists to mean language, rational thinking, and epistemology. Like Plato and Aristotle, they may have redefined and extended the meaning of *ming* in order to distance themselves from earlier thinkers—in this case, the early Mingjia and Confucianists. As a result, they were able to identify themselves with other philosophers whose views regarding ming were similar to their own. The sense of bian remained implicit until the Mohists attempted to use the word *bian* to formulate theories and principles of persuasion and argumentation. Over time the word *bian* grew from its original meaning of making distinctions and classifications to mean disputation and argumentation, in the works of Xunzi and the Later Mohists. What is more, in Han Feizi's writing, *bian* was consistently used in reference to speech, persuasion, and argumentation. The various schools of thought and individual thinkers influenced one another's views of ming bian through a process of mutual criticism and eventual synthesis. In general, all philosophical views and rhetorical perspectives were formulated in relation to Confucius, who was one of the earliest thinkers.

The Greek word *logos* may not have the same meanings as the Chinese word *ming*. Likewise, the Greek word *rhêtorikê* may not be identical to the Chinese word *bian*. Still, these terms are indicative of the similar evolutionary paths of Greek rhetoric and Chinese ming bian. If the naming of social realities can serve to re-create, develop, or change those realities, the new naming or redefining of a discipline can serve to keep that discipline vital and relevant.

Differences between Chinese Ming Bian and Greek Rhetoric

From the above comparisons, similarities between Chinese ming bian and Greek rhetoric are evident. This does not mean the two rhetorical systems are identical, however. Differences exist between the two cultures regarding social contexts and cultural values, as well as rhetorical perspectives.

Ancient Greece and China differed in their political structures, types of speech, and racial demographics. In terms of political structure, the ancient Greeks formed the *polis*, through which the elite citizens of Athens voiced their opinions on political, cultural, and judicial issues.[7] In ancient China no such equivalent emerged. Although each small state was relatively autonomous, political decisions were made by the kings and ministers rather than by citizens or through a democratic process.

Concerning speech patterns, while "the Greeks thought of the *polis* as an active, formative thing, training the minds and characters of the citizens" (Kitto 1961, 75) and involving deliberative, epideictic, and forensic types of public oration, the ancient Chinese engaged in shui, jian, and bian activities, taking the form of political consultations and philosophical debates conducted in private and public settings. While the ancient Greeks were involved with one another in courts considering issues related to their individual lives, in the Chinese context bian shi attempted to persuade the ruler to heed their advice on matters of governance and personal morality. In ancient Greece the problem of land redistribution was resolved primarily at the individual level, with the landowner making his case in a court of law; in ancient China the redistribution of land took place at the state level when one state conquered another and took possession of its land. Furthermore, before the advent of Buddhism and Indian cosmology, the Chinese culture was largely indigenous and racially homogeneous; in contrast, the Greek culture was part of a larger mixed cultural region that included Egypt and Mesopotamia (Bernal 1987).

These general differences between ancient Chinese and Greek cultures contributed to differences in philosophical and rhetorical views. For our purposes, we will examine the differences in the role of language, mode of inquiry, treatment of emotions, the domain of rationality, and rhetorical education.

(1) The Role of Language. The ancient Greeks and Chinese Daoists differed significantly in their senses of rhetoric and ming bian. In the Greek tradition, more attention was paid to the power and impact of verbal communication. However, in the Daoist tradition verbal symbols were treated with ambivalence and skepticism. In Zhuangzi's view, the function of language was limited. More specifically, language was only a means, not an end in itself. Therefore, according to Zhuangzi, one should not allow oneself to be enslaved by language. Persuasion was achieved not by the quantity of one's speech but by its quality, by how appropriately and spontaneously one used language in response to a particular situation. Furthermore, Daoist

ming bian placed much emphasis on nonspeech and nonverbal communication. It advocated a mystical way of life based on artistic sensibilities and an understanding of multiple interpretations of reality.

In at least one very important sense, Chinese ming bian cannot be identified with Greek rhetoric. That is, the purpose of ming bian was to embrace the whole by balancing and reconciling apparent opposites. In this sense, the Daoist perspective has the potential to serve as an antidote to the problem of many authorities. Given the Daoist principle of noncontention, Chinese ming bian seems to offer a spirit of cooperation and compromise, while Greek rhetoric appears relatively confrontational and antagonistic (as demonstrated in the dialogue between Socrates and the sophists in *Gorgias*). Another Daoist strength related to communication strategies is its careful consideration of the subtlety and intricacy of human interactions. This approach offers more depth and breadth of understanding than would a mechanical model of communication.

(2) Mode of Inquiry. Schiappa (1992, 1993) contends, in his revised account of the history of Greek rhetoric, that by the fourth century B.C.E. rhetoric and philosophy were split conceptually and morphologically. Plato was perhaps largely responsible for this split, given the fact that he placed philosophy above rhetoric, identifying it as a superior form of intellectual inquiry and means of seeking truth. Rhetoric was subsequently limited in scope to mere persuasive activity. Ironically, though Aristotle attempted to reconcile rhetoric with philosophy, his preoccupation with science further atomized rhetoric as a separate discipline. For the Greeks, rhetoric was practiced in such a way as to divide—for example, body from mind, right from wrong. This divisive aspect has affected the Western approach to the study of Greek rhetoric. For example, George Kennedy divides Greek rhetoric into three strands: technical, sophistic, and philosophical; while Ernesto Grassi divides it into "practical" and "theoretical" components; and Thomas Conley identifies four distinctive types of Greek rhetoric: "motivistic," "controversial," "dialectical," and "problematic."[8]

In contrast, the Chinese rhetorical tradition has never separated rhetoric and philosophy. Though certain Chinese thinkers have condemned speech lacking in moral and practical value, all Chinese thinkers considered the use of language an integral part of gaining truth and knowledge, as well as a powerful means of achieving social order and justice. In this sense, ancient Chinese rhetoric and philosophy are inseparable and of equal importance. As Charles Moore observes, the Chinese "look at life and philosophy in its totality, not in its parts" (1967, 3). "The oneness of substance and form, of reason and experience, and of knowledge and action are the foundation

CONCLUSIONS AND IMPLICATIONS 301

principles of the Chinese perspective" (Kincaid 1987, 332). This holistic outlook continues to pervade Chinese life to such an extent that, to this day, rhetoric is not identified as a separate discipline in China's institutions of higher learning. Moreover, unlike the Greek civilization, which borrowed heavily from other cultures and thus was able to develop vocabulary to describe types of speech, the Chinese culture was largely formed indigenously, which restricted the development of vocabulary for speech.

(3) Treatment of Emotions. Another significant difference between the Greeks and Chinese, in their respective approaches to rhetoric and ming bian, is in their treatment of emotions. Unlike the Greek rhetoricians, who treated pathos as a separate rhetorical means to an end, the Chinese, especially in the philosophical and rhetorical system of Mencius, included emotion in their moral and cognitive system. For the Chinese, the heart is considered the locus of true moral understanding and an integral part of the intellectual process of making judgments and decisions. Furthermore, the emotional appeals discussed by Han Feizi were concerned with establishing trust and building relationships. For Han Feizi, emotions, expressed in verbal and nonverbal forms, could be employed for both good and evil purposes. Skillful emotional appeals could inspire the listener to commit selfless acts of bravery or despicable acts of cowardice. In contrast, for Plato, emotions were an inferior and immoral form of communication, cut off from reason and harmful to the well-being of the soul.

With the exception of Mencius and Han Feizi, the Chinese did not consider emotions a primary concern with regard to ming bian. In contrast, Greek rhetoricians considered emotion, or pathos, one of the most important means of persuasion. For example, Gorgias is well known for casting a spell over his audience with his eloquence and emotions. Although Aristotle was aware that arousing passion in his audience could be dangerous, he nonetheless identified pathos as one of the three artistic proofs in rhetoric. In book 2 of his *Rhetoric* he discussed, at great length and in much detail, different types of emotion and the importance of knowing their functions.

(4) The Domain of Rationality. The survey of Chinese ming bian strongly suggests that the ancient Chinese engaged in logical thinking in a manner similar to the ancient Greek practice of deductive and inductive reasoning. However, the Chinese system of rationality differs from Greek logic in certain respects. While Greek logic prioritized essence and certainty in the deductive and inductive processes, the Chinese made allowances for flexibility and probability (as indicated by the notions of lei, gu, tui), arguing that one's conclusion does not necessarily derive from or depend upon one's premises and examples. While Greek logic may be more universally

applicable, by virtue of its formalized system, Chinese "logic" may serve a more practical function because of its recognition of contingencies and variables. Another important difference between Greek logic and the Chinese system of rationality is the former's use of abstract and scientific language, contrasted with the latter's use of a broad range of rhetorical means, particularly metaphor and analogy.

(5) Rhetorical Education. Differences between Greek rhetoric and Chinese ming bian are also reflected in the two cultures' approaches to rhetorical education. Rhetoric was originally taught as an art of persuasion by the Greek sophists. Subsequently, it was developed by Isocrates, who considered it the core of a liberal arts education. The technical rhetorical tradition initiated by Corax and Tisias in Sicily was expanded by the Romans. For example, Quintilian standardized rhetorical education by offering a more complete and well-rounded curriculum. The tradition was further codified with the introduction of textbooks such as *Rhetoric of Alexandrum* (allegedly written by Anaximenes), the anonymous *Rhetoric of Herennium*, and Hermagoras's *Stasis Theory*. The teaching of rhetoric, in both Greek and Roman traditions, involved a pedagogical approach designed to educate the "perfect orator" for public life.

In ancient China the teaching of ming bian was not the concern of the philosophers. Although bian and shui were common practices of argumentation and persuasion in the fifth to third century B.C.E., ming bian was neither treated as a separate discipline nor systematically taught. Although Confucius, Mencius, Xunzi, and Mozi were all well-known teachers, their explicit topics of study were ethics, history, literature, and philosophy. Theories of language and ming bian were embedded and implicit in their teachings but not explicitly addressed. Interestingly, the teaching styles of these men, documented in their written works, were often in the form of dialogues and discussions, questions and answers.

In summary, Chinese ming bian was not as well established and systemized as Greek rhetoric. This is because ming bian was treated as an integral aspect of ethics and politics rather than a separate discipline. In the surviving texts the standard approach to ming bian seems to be philosophical and practical rather than pedagogical. Furthermore, though the Mohists managed to formulate a more explicit theory of ming bian, they failed to exert their influence on subsequent dynasties. Consequently, their theory of ming bian did not prevail. And, while the understanding of ming bian has evolved over time, in the context of Chinese history, no attempts have been made at codification in order to make it more technically accessible.

Chinese ming bian and Greek rhetoric are revealed primarily through the philosophical and rhetorical works of philosophers and rhetoricians of ancient times. Within each culture there is a great deal of diversity regarding schools of thought and individual thinkers. The parallels between the two cultures in the practice and formulation of rhetoric and ming bian may have been caused by one or more of the following factors: similar or different social and cultural contexts; geography; economic and political structures; thought patterns affected by language, values, and experience. Future efforts to explore these factors may provide additional insights into the reasons for these similarities and differences.

However, the similarities and differences between Greek rhetoric and Chinese ming bian may not be entirely attributable to social, cultural, and linguistic factors. To some extent they may also have resulted from discussions about the role of persuasive discourse in ancient China and Greece, respectively. Accordingly, the meanings of ming bian and rhetoric should be viewed in the context of the evolution of these discussions. The "shared senses" of ming bian and rhetoric may point to the possibility of a universal sense of rhetoric which transcends culturally specific factors even while embracing them.[9] Different cultural understandings of rhetoric and ming bian may provide insights into the nature and function of rhetoric and ming bian that are lacking in each culture. The uniqueness of each rhetorical system could serve to broaden the vision of human rhetoric in the direction of multiculturalism. Since rhetoric and ming bian continue to affect us today, understanding points of similarity and difference is clearly of great significance.

Implications of Contemporary Chinese Communication

It is generally believed that the Chinese mind and culture were essentially shaped by classical texts and philosophical ideas formulated in the pre-Qin period, in particular by Confucianism, Daoism, and Legalism. The same can be said for Chinese communication and rhetorical practices. Although Confucianism, considered synonymous with traditional Chinese culture, has been severely criticized since the beginning of this century and is no longer recognized as a state ideology, its cultural influence, along with the influence of other schools of thought and individual thinkers, is still making its presence felt in Chinese thought and communication. In the words of Kam Louie, "each generation of any civilization maintains and continues its cultural traditions; otherwise, that civilization cease to exist" (1986, preface vii). In the following, I will examine two areas of contemporary Chinese communication which have been demonstrably influenced by the schools of thought and individual thinkers introduced in this book: political communication and interpersonal communication.

Political Communication

With the takeover of mainland China by the Communist Party in 1949, Marxism was adopted and enforced as the official ideology of the mainland Chinese government. Although Karl Marx had formulated his theory of social change and revolution in response to the economic and political situation in western Europe in the nineteenth century, Mao Zedong, the leader of the Communist Party, strongly believed that Marxist theory, which had been successfully applied in the Chinese overthrow of imperialism and feudalism, would also be well suited to the tasks of political control and ideological construction of the new China. In a series of ideological campaigns designed to eliminate traditional values, Mao's government appropriated the political philosophy and rhetorical perspectives of the ancient Chinese thinkers covered in this study.

To begin with, a moral/ethical emphasis has been characteristic of Chinese political communication throughout Chinese history. While Confucius and Mencius engaged moral persuasion in reference to the pronouncements and activities of sage kings, Mao's government-controlled media pursued their ideological conversion by referring to the moral words and deeds of Mao Zedong and his comrades. In addition, they also based their appeals on the moral examples of ordinary people. At the beginning of the so-called Cultural Revolution (1966–1976), Mao launched a national campaign that involved studying his "little red book" as a moral guidance for speech and action. Mao seemed to share Mencius's belief that human nature was inherently good and that, therefore, selfish motives and acts could be controlled and corrected; in other words, one's character could be dramatically improved with proper guidance, informed by Marxist and Maoist ideology and moral examples. Through an ambitions campaign of indoctrination under way since the 1950s, the Chinese people were asked to learn from the moral examples of those who selflessly sacrificed their personal interests and even their lives for the good of the country. Those singled out by Mao as moral examples, such as Lei Feng, would qualify as junzi by Confucius's criteria. The desire for material gain, considered by Confucius the domain of xiaoren, was described by Mao as a function of the bourgeoisie, the class enemy to be denounced and overthrown. This moral emphasis in the arena of public and political communication generated a strong sense of ethical idealism and hero worship among the Chinese, both of Confucius's and Mao's China.

Moreover, Mozi's proposition of shang tong prescribed a purpose and process of public communication very much like the practice of political communication in contemporary China. Today, whenever there is an important message from the top leader, it is first conveyed to high officials in oral or written form. These high officials then pass the word down to local party branches, who in turn communicate the message to the common people in the work unit. The only difference between Mozi's shang tong and contemporary China's political communication is that today when the top leader's message is passed on, it is not completely conveyed. Certain "important" messages are kept "secret" by the leaders at the different levels. The more secret and important messages one holds, the more power one has over others and the more likely that power will be abused by corruption and undemocratic government. This practice resembles in certain respects the practice of *shu* 術 (strategy, scheme, game plan), proposed by Han Feizi for the rulers.

Another feature of shang tong that can be identified in contemporary China's political communication is the absolute moral infallibility of the ruler. The leader is almost always right; his thinking cannot be challenged. One must identify with one's superiors, and the whole nation must be unified in thought and action. In this cultural climate, the ruler's moral character is all that stands between him and abuses of power. This was the case during Mao's rule and is still true today, in that the Communist Party formulates its own laws, which the party leader has the authority to revoke (not in theory but in practice). The belief in the absolute moral infallibility of the Chinese leader has been the fatal fallacy of Chinese political thought throughout Chinese history. Tragically, despite many painful lessons, this belief—the root of which can be traced to Mozi— remains prevalent in today's China.

Furthermore, China's authoritarian tendencies can be traced to Xunzi's doctrine of the rectification of names to create uniformity in thought and action. Through the government-controlled media and system of supervised social organizations, the Communist Party exerts its control of the people in every possible way. For example, the most repeated slogan throughout the 1980s was "Unification of thoughts, unification of policy, unification of planning, unification of commanding, and unification of action."

Though Confucianism has been the most popular philosophy in Chinese history, the undeniable fact is that Legalism was China's first state ideology. Furthermore, on a parallel course with Confucianism, Legalism has had a significant impact on Chinese political communication and statecraft from its inception to the present. In fact, the Chinese system of governance is an amalgam of the Confucian emphasis on virtuous rulership, in its promotion of economic prosperity, and Legalism, with its emphasis on strong political control through state-sanctioned ideology and social control. Legalistic practices resulted in the suppression of free public speech, while, at the same time, the government used all the rhetorical means at its disposal, including the government-controlled media, to indoctrinate the masses and promote unified thought and action. Ironically, political communication in China since the economic reforms of the early 1980s has also revealed traces of Daoist influence—to the extent that it has advocated the bridging of seeming opposites in its attempt to reconcile socialism with capitalism and a free market economy with tight political control.

Han Feizi's Legalistic notion that the ruler has the right to control and suppress subversive views is still prevalent among the Chinese ruling body with respect to dissidents. Legalism asserts that the ruler makes and enforces laws but is, himself, above the law. Furthermore, any speech or action taken against the ruler is, by definition, against the law. For this reason, when students openly challenged Premier Li Peng, demanding his resignation during the Tiananmen Square Democratic Movement of 1989, they were branded "counterrevolutionaries." Likewise, Deng Xiaoping 鄧小平 put Wei Jingsheng 魏京生 (a prominent political dissident) in prison for fifteen years for publicly denouncing Deng's dictatorship in 1972, and for another fourteen years for his efforts to "overthrow the government" by publicly calling for a democratic China. Unlike the Western legal system, which assumes a person's innocence until guilt has been established, a political prisoner in China is considered guilty until proved innocent. What is more, not until recent years has China begun to provide defendants with defense attorneys. However, in the case of serious political or antigovernment crimes, the impact of the defense attorney is minimal, with the Communist Party exercising primary influence over the verdict. Given this state of affairs, it is easy to understand why the Chinese government, in its practice of Legalism, has been perceived as ruthless.

Another feature of Han Feizi's political system was its condemnation of intellectuals and suppression of intellectual thought—hence the practice of "burning books and burying intellectuals." Unfortunately, history appears to have repeated itself in this regard. During the heyday of the Cultural Revolution between 1966 and 1976, Mao launched a ruthless attack on intellectuals, destroying artifacts that symbolized traditional Chinese cultural values in the name of establishing a new Chinese culture. Intellectual works promoting critical thinking were perceived as threats to the government and were banned.[10] Furthermore, intellectuals were required to be reeducated and reformed by workers, peasants, and soldiers.

Interpersonal Communication

The tradition of moral persuasion under the principle of *yi* 義 (morality, benevolence, righteousness, faithfulness), advocated by Confucius and Mencius, and the tradition of instrumental persuasion in the context of *li* 利 (benefit, profit), proposed by Mozi and Han Feizi, coexist to a large extent in the interpersonal communication patterns of contemporary China. Yi emphasizes the values of filial piety to one's parents, loyalty to superiors, faithfulness to friends, and selflessness for the sake of the collective good; while the principle of li recognizes the values of self-interests, activities for the sake of material gain, and individual expression.

Research on contemporary Chinese communication patterns indicates the presence of both collectivistic and individualistic orientations and employment of both moral and instrumental strategies of persuasion.[11] Concerning Chinese interpersonal communication, there are those who place the interests of family and state above their own, conducting themselves in a sincere and honest manner. Such communication is known in Confucian terms as *zheng ming* (the rectification of names), whereby individuals act according to prescribed roles, take responsibility for the well-being of family and clans, and conform to the dictates of a hierarchical social order and implicit cultural values. There are also those whose interpersonal communication is guided by utilitarian motives. Such communication is characterized by manipulation, deceit, and the never-ending exchange of favors. In general, the Chinese are both ideal and practical in their interpersonal communication styles. One can identify individuals possessing the characteristics of a junzi: such people are honest, candid, caring of others, frugal, and selfless. At the same time, one can also observe in them the qualities of a xiao ren: in other words, they are materialistic, callous, inscrutable, and dishonest when to be so is in their best interests. With the increasing orientation toward materialism in today's China, instrumental persuasion for the sake of utilitarian gain has become more prevalent and socially acceptable. In fact, interpersonal communication is predominantly characterized and regulated by *ren qing* 人情 (the exchange of favors) and *guan xi* 關系 (connections), with an emphasis on the acquisition of material goods and practical benefits.

Moreover, Han Feizi's notion of *shu* 術 (strategy, scheme, game plan) has been a technique employed in all facets of Chinese life: in political struggles between the ruler and the ministers, in the workplace between superiors and subordinates, and in trade and business transactions between sellers and clients. While to the Westerner's mind the practice of shu may seem deceptive and unethical, for the typical Chinese it is considered skillful, self-protective, and strategic, requiring much wisdom and insight into human psychology.[12]

Given the various philosophical traditions and their respective value systems, it is not surprising that the value orientations and communication patterns of the Chinese people are diverse and manyfold. Chinese culture has a history of accommodating different, even opposing, ideas. Accordingly, the cultural dynamics of mainland China are relatively subtle, complex, and sophisticated. In this context, individualism and collectivism, the principles of yi (morality, righteousness) and li (profit, benefit), and moral and instrumental styles of persuasion can coexist.

In some respects today's China resembles the Spring-Autumn and Warring States period of the ancient past. For example, China is currently in the midst of cultural transition and ideological transformation. Mao's orthodox is no longer idolized. Instead, economic freedom and foreign exchange with the West have stimulated diverse perspectives and promoted individualistic thinking. At the same time, traditional values and patterns of persuasive discourse have resurfaced. China's rich rhetorical tradition, an understanding of which helps explain current political and interpersonal realities, can offer the Chinese guidance in many facets of communication.

Implications of Multicultural Rhetoric

The challenge that rhetorical scholars will face in the twenty-first century is not simply to dismantle the notion that only Greek rhetoric legitimately belongs within the rhetorical canon, but, more importantly, to produce unpolarized, subtly nuanced, postethnocentric intellectual discourse and multicultural modes of rhetorical inquiry. As Arran Gare asserts, "What is needed is not merely the subversion of Eurocentric narratives, but construction of grand narratives elaborating ways of thinking that allow the achievement, and the failure of all people in the world to be properly appreciated" (1995, 325).

Multicultural rhetoric can be defined as rhetoric that is not based on any particular canonized system but rather recognizes and celebrates a diversity of rhetorical styles and persuasive discourse. It is a system capable of honoring both universal values and cultural insights in the practice and formulation of rhetorical perspectives. For example, metaphorical and analogical forms of persuasion, prevalent in the Chinese ming bian tradition, should be given equal status with the deductive and inductive styles of reasoning prevalent in Western rhetoric. The purpose of promoting multicultural rhetoric is not merely to be well informed with regard to the world's rhetorical traditions, but also to reduce stereotypical misunderstandings cross-culturally, to challenge outmoded assumptions and habits of mind, to increase one's empathic abilities vis-à-vis people from different cultures, to expand one's horizons, and to reach a more profound and comprehensive understanding of what it means to be human.

These ambitious goals can be accomplished by applying multicultural hermeneutics. Specifically, sincere attempts must be made to cross-cultural, linguistic, and philosophical boundaries in the quest for native meanings of rhetorical concepts, in examining original texts (especially those historically ignored and neglected), and in understanding the social and cultural contexts that give rise to rhetorical theories and practices. A comparison of different rhetorical traditions is always helpful in identifying both universal themes and unique cultural contributions, as well as in deepening one's understanding of various rhetorical traditions.

Multicultural rhetoric should emphasize shared experiences and perceptions concerning the use of symbols and symbolic interactions. By so doing, communication across cultures will be made more humane and effective despite differences of race, language, and culture. This comparison of classical Chinese ming bian and Greek rhetoric suggests the tentative conclusion that, at least during the period from the fifth to third century B.C.E., these two cultures held similar beliefs about speech, persuasion, and argumentation. This was true despite the fact that they spoke radically different languages and lived in very different cultures. It would appear that universal rhetorical elements exist and that these elements connect humans of different cultures, building a bridge across the communication gaps between them.

A multicultural rhetoric should consider cultural diversity in speech, persuasive styles, and argumentation as opportunities to enrich human experience through the use of symbols. The differences between and among rhetorical traditions should not be seen as conflicting or mutually unintelligible. Efforts should be made in crossing linguistic and cultural barriers and boundaries to reach and understand one another. In the words of Robert Allinson, "East and West require each other for their own existence, and future development depends not on one system of thought replacing the other, but on an integrated growth which maintains and expands both tendencies" (1989, 23).

It is my sincere hope that this effort provides useful information and insights for scholars interested in the study of Chinese ming bian, culture, and communication, and that it inspires future research toward building a multicultural rhetoric as well as enriching our understanding of how rhetoric operates in various cultures. Given the fact that multiculturalism is built and accomplished largely through a multicultural rhetoric and discourse, the importance of formulating such a rhetorical system cannot be overstated. The survival of humankind may well depend upon it.

Notes

Introduction

1. Cole argues that the fabric of rhetoric existed in the late fifth century and was embedded in Greek poetic, literary, ritualistic, and educational experiences, but that the conceptualization of rhetoric did not take place until the fourth century B.C.E. Schiappa critiques George Kennedy's model of three rhetorical strands in the Greek tradition, characterizing it as an "unhistorical," "tripartite schematization" "leading to distortion." Enos discusses the evolutionary nature of Greek rhetoric caused by increased literacy and political expediency before the time of Aristotle, concluding that Greek rhetoric must be understood in Greek contexts and that the history of rhetoric is shaped by multiple forces. In the article "Rhêtorikê: What's in a Name? Toward a Revised History of Early Greek Rhetorical Theory" (1992) Schiappa contends that Plato coined the word *rhêtorikê* and separated rhetoric from philosophy. See also de Romilly, 1992. In the book de Romilly informs the reader of the contribution made by Greek sophists in moralistic and political thinking, and discusses the sophists' philosophical views of relativism.

2. As the Chinese thinkers under consideration in this book are men, I will use "he," as opposed to "he and she."

3. The Chinese term *zi* here is not part of these thinkers' names, but rather a marker indicating established and prominent scholars in ancient times.

4. Chinese philosophical schools of thought were first classified in the chapter of *Yi Wen Zhi* (Records of Classics and Arts) of *Han Shu* (the Book of Han) authored by Ban Gu (32–92 A.C.). Chinese scholars and sinologists use the category "schools" to refer to the pre-Qin thinkers and their ideological affiliations. For convenience, I have titled each chapter according to the schools of thought, grouping individual thinkers under each school.

5. The word *zhe* 哲 first appeared in Shang Shu to mean wisdom and ability. In *Shuo Wen Jie Zi*, the first Chinese dictionary compiled by Xu Shen (58–147 A.C.), it is defined as "knowing and understanding." The Chinese term for *philosophy* is *zhe xue* 哲學, which is translated and introduced to China by a Japanese philosopher. For more information and additional reference on the adaptation and translation of the term *philosophy*, see Allinson, *Understanding the Chinese Mind*, 5.

6. To avoid overburdening the English reader with too many Chinese characters, I will only use Chinese characters for important names, book or chapter tiles, places, and concepts.

7. My own translations are verified by Professor Li-cheng Gu from the Department of Asian and African Languages, Northwestern University.

Chapter 1

1. Among them were Claudio Grimaldi (1638–1712), Matteo Ricci (1552–1510), Nicholas Longobardi (1565–1655), Antoine de Sainte-Marie (1602–1669), and Joachim Bouvet (1656–1730). For more information on Western missionary activities in China, see Ronan and Bonnie, *East Meets West.*

2. Matteo Ricci lived in China for twenty-eight years and spoke fluent Chinese. He studied Chinese language, philosophy, and culture; met the Chinese emperor; and made friends with Chinese intellectuals. He was well known and respected by the Chinese and was also the first person to bring Western science and religious ideas to China.

3. The book contains a collection of 116 popular American illustrations featuring images of Chinese in the nineteenth-century United States. The illustrations reveal stereotypical and racist American perceptions of Chinese people and culture of the time period.

4. Other Western scholars who shared this view on Chinese language and thought patterns include Whorf (*Language*), who claimed that only Western language is capable of producing science. Also see Nakamura, *Ways of Thinking,* 13.

5. Also see the letter on pages 24–27 from Lin Zexu 林則徐, a Chinese commissioner sent by the emperor to the city of Guangzhou to deal with the opium problem. The letter had an obvious tone of superiority and ethnocentrism.

6. Using biased language and incomplete information on American culture and people, the book sends a strong sentiment of nationalism and anti-Americanism.

7. Caws further explains in the rest of the quote that multicultural identity versus a pancultural one means nobody is at home everywhere.

8. See Kroll, "Disputation." In Kroll's description, "The China of the *Chan-Kuo/Han* [Zhan Guo/Han] period (400 B.C.E.–200 C.E.) seems to have abounded with *pien shih* [bian shi], the name applied to 'wandering persuaders'" (p. 126). The romanization by Kroll and Crump, and Dreher is the system of Wade-Giles. The bracket romanization represents the conversion of the Wade-Giles system into the pinyin system that I will use throughout this project.

9. For additional works on Chinese logic and reasoning and controversy by sinologists over whether ancient China has categorical syllogism, see Needham, Science and Civilization, vol. 2; Chung-ying Cheng, "Logic and Language in Chinese Thought"; and Chemielewski, "Concerning the Problem."

10. There are a number of versions of English translation of Shang Shu, such as James Legge's in his The Chinese Classics, vol. 3; and Clae Waltham's in Shu Ching: Book of History.

11. For a critique of the Corax and Tisias legend, see Schiappa, "The Beginnings."

12. Although the translation in *A New English-Chinese Dictionary* is 詭辯者 (deceptive speaker), it does not encompass the contextual meaning of sophist in the Greek rhetorical tradition. Bian zhe is an equivalent to bian shi here.

13. *Mingjia* has been translated into "School of Ming," "School of Naming," "School of Logicians," and "School of Dialecticians" in works on Chinese philosophy.

14. The first known attempt to explore foreign land was made by Zhang Qian 張騫 in 138 B.C.E. A few other attempts were made to contact what is today's Middle East or central Asia. In the early fifteenth century Zheng He 鄭和 went on six overseas explorations to western Asia, the Persian Gulf area, and some African countries. During the Tang dynasty (618–907 A.D.) China was subject to a lot of foreign influence, in particular, the influence of Buddhism from India.

15. The most well known scholar is Yan Fu, who translated into Chinese Thomas Huxley's *Evolution and Ethics*, Herbert Spencer's *Synthetic Philosophy*, Montesquieu's *L'Esprit des lois*, Adam Smith's *Wealth of Nations*, and William Jevons's *Elementary Lessons of Logic*. See Xiaosui Xiao, "China Encounters Darwinism: A Case of Intercultural Rhetoric," 83–99.

16. Chinese scholars and scholarship of this group include Fung, Yu-Lan, *History*; Wing-Tsit Chan, *Source Book*; Zhang Dainian, *Zhong-guo*; and Lao Siguang, *Xin-bian*.

17. Chinese scholars and scholarship of this group include Wu Feibai, *Zhong-guo*; Wen Gongyi, *Xian-qin*; Zhou Yunzhi and Liu Peiyu, *Xian-qin*; Yu Yu, *Zhong-guo*; and Wang Dianji, *Zhong-guo*.

18. Hou Wailu et al., *Zhong-guo*, 415–16. I did my own translation on secondary sources of Chinese language. I will use the pinyin system to spell out the names of Chinese scholars and retain whatever forms were used for the Chinese scholars in their English publications. I will spell the Chinese scholars' names (in pinyin) by the order of family name followed by first name, as practiced in Chinese culture. In the Spring-Autumn and Warring States period, many thinkers contended in response to the social, political, and philosophical questions proposed as the result of social change. *Han Shu* classified them into schools of thoughts as we know them today. Among those schools of thought, School of Ming, Confucianism, Daoism, Mohism, and Legalism seemed to be the most popular. For more information on other schools and disputation among them, see Fung, *A History*; Graham, *Disputers*.

19. Among the ancient texts to be examined in the later chapters, a few are particularly devoted to the discussion of language, speech, and rational thinking by the School of Ming. These works were compiled by Wu Feibai in 1949 and reprinted in 1981.

Chapter 2

1. For example, descriptions of the Xia dynasty could be found in *Mencius, Zhuangzi, Huai Nanzi, Shang Shu, Lu Shi Chun Qiu,* and *Zuo Zhuan*. The term *Xia* is still used as an equivalent for Chinese culture; the Chinese calendar was once called *xia li* 夏歷 (the Xia Calendar).

2. Some popular myths created at the time were: *pan-gu kai-tian* (creation story); *chang-e ben-yue* (a woman named Chang-e went to the moon). There are also myths of cultural heroes such as Fu Xi, who discovered nets for capturing birds, fetched fire from the god of thunder, and invented the Eight Diagrams for prediction and divination; Shen Nong, who invented means of agriculture and discovered all edible plants; and Huang Di, a wise tribal leader, and his wife, who invented the technique of silkworm breeding.

3. Myths and legends of *nu-wa bu-tian* (a woman named Nuwa patched the sky), *Hou-yi chu-hai* (a person named Hou-Yi shot down nine suns), and *Da-yu zhi-shui* (a person named Da-yu conquered flood) are examples of this nature.

4. The legend was mentioned in *Shi Jing, Mozi, Shi Ji, Mengzi, Guo Yu, Zuo Zhuan, Xunzi, Zhuangzi, Han Feizi,* and *Lu Shi Chun Qiu*.

5. For example, the myth of Huang Di, the high god of a local tribe, is regarded as the common ancestor of all Chinese. The myth has been used as a rhetorical appeal for the unity of all Chinese at home and overseas.

6. According to Enos, *Greek Rhetoric,* Homeric poets also performed ritualistic ceremonies that carry cultural significance.

7. R. A. D. Forrest cites Father Wieger's speculation that the art of writing can be known to the Chinese as early as the twenty-second century B.C.E. (*Chinese Language,* 35).

8. Western scholars of Chinese language have claimed that a great number of Chinese characters are phonetic and abstract in nature. See Karlgren, *Analytic Dictionary;* DeFrancis, *Chinese Language.*

9. See William Watson, *Early Civilization,* for a detailed description of the process.

10. This stylistic feature that facilitates chanting and memorization has been attributed to classical Chinese texts. See David Ze, "Ong's Paradigm," 523–40.

11. In *Zhan Guo Ce* numerous stories are told about persuasive interactions between kings, ministers, and counselors. For more information see Crump, *Intrigues.*

12. See Zhang Bingnan, *Jixia,* for a complete coverage of the Jixia scholars and their topics of debate.

13. All the texts except *Guo Yu* have complete or partial translations available. However, some translations are not adequate, in my judgment. I will do my own translation of the excerpts to be discussed.

Chapter 3

1. Examples of mistranslation Conley gives are *kyriotaten* and *pistin* as "the most potent of all the means of persuasion" and *diapseudontai* as "speakers are untrustworthy."

2. Diachronic explanation relates to the trajectory or the change in meaning of a term over time. For example, the word *rhetoric* changes its meaning from "cookery" and "a knack" in *Gorgias* to "a dialectical process of reasoning" in *Phaedrus* by Plato. Synchronic understanding explores the use and meaning of a term at a particular moment without reference to historical text. For example, in the fifth century B.C.E. the word *logos* meant "forms of argumentation, discussion, questions and answers, and speeches" (Schiappa, "Rhetorike," 8).

3. In the translation of *Shi Jing* by Bernhard Karlgren (1950), *yan* at times was translated as the first person pronoun. Hu Shi (1921) argued that there was not sufficient evidence to prove that *yan* served as a first person pronoun and proposed

three grammatical functions of *yan* in *Shi Jing*, namely as a conjunction, an adjective, and a demonstrative.

4. The same kind of example can be found in a number of places in *Zuo Zhuan* and *Guo Yu*.

5. The concept of *yan* was developed by Liu Xie (465–532 A.C.) in his well-known *Wen Xin Diao Long* 文心雕龍 (The Cultivating of the Mind and the Carving of the Dragon), a literary critique (eds. Fu and Wei, 1989). Liu proposed three types of philosophy of *yan*. The first is *jing yan* 精言 (fine language), referring to language of reason and language of philosophy. The second type is *kua shi* 誇飾 (exaggeration), a language used in literature that is filled with imaginations and emotions. The third type of *yan* is *zheng shi* 征實 (requiring truth), a language that states and explains facts (50–55). In Chinese classics, the uses of these three types of *yan* are not clearly marked, and they are often integrated. Therefore, it is difficult to decide whether works such as *Zuo Zhuan*, *Guo Yu*, and *Zhan Guo Ce* are historical or literary texts. See H. Zhao, "Rhetorical Invention," for more information on the language art of *Wen Xin Diao Long*.

6. The word *rhetoric* is translated as *xiu ci* in modern English-Chinese dictionaries compiled by Chinese scholars. As a result, the understanding of rhetoric as a field of study is limited to modification of terms or stylistic devices in written discourse for the contemporary Chinese.

7. *Ke qing* refers to those officials who come from other states and work as top advisers for the king. It was a common practice for top officials to travel to other states and change their citizenship either out of their disillusion with the former state or to better their financial circumstances.

8. In *Shang Shu*, although *jian* is not used, a few other words are used to refer to persuasion and advisory activities. For example, *shi* 誓 (oath) and *gao* 誥 (proclamation) are used to mean public speech; *xian* 咸 (p. 207) means giving advice; *song* 訟 refers to argument; and *yi* 逸 means to explain (p. 65). These terms were not used for the same meanings in the later texts, and new terms were used to replace them.

9. The characters *yue* 說 and *yue* 悅, as a result, are different in shape but have the same sound and same meaning in classical Chinese.

10. Another term that is related to *bian* is *lun* 論. The word is used infrequently in the pre-Qin texts to mean discuss, expound, and express opinions. It does not have the connotative meanings as *bian* in relation to persuasion and argumentation.

Chapter 4

1. Examples of these public speeches are *gan shi, tang shi, pan geng, mu shi, jiu gao*, and *da gao* in *Shang Shu*. For the sake of consistency in labeling the chapter titles, I will use the Chinese version of *Shang Shu* and do my own translation of the citations in this chapter. Some events recorded in the text are not attested by historians, although the Chinese in general regard them as historical facts.

2. Examples of such *jian* activity recorded in *Shang Shu* are *yao dian, xi bo kan li, zi cai*, and *wu yi*.

3. The chapter of *gao tao mo* typically exemplified this kind of group activity in *Shang Shu*.

4. The same line of argument is evident in two other speeches, namely *kang gao* and *jiu gao*.

5. According to Raphals, *Knowing Words*, "metic intelligence" is a universal mode of intelligence that emphasizes cunning strategies and practical knowledge rather than morality and rationality. The use and discussion of metic intelligence are evident in both ancient Chinese and Greek traditions.

6. The same claim of this book and a portion of the English translation of the book can be found in James I. Crump Jr.'s *Intrigues: Studies of the Chan-kuo Ts'e*, 1964. A more complete translation is done in Crump's *Chan-Kuo Ts'e*, 1970.

7. There are translations of *Sunzi Bing Fa* (The Art of War) in English, French, Russian, Japanese, and Italian. The English version is translated by T. Cleary, 1988.

8. *He-zong* advocates an alliance among the six states (the state of *Yan* in the North and the state of *Chu* in the South, joined by the states of *Qi*, *Wei*, *Zhao*, and *Han*). *Lian-heng* advocates that the three weak states form an alliance with the state of *Qi* in the East or with the state of Qin in the West. See Raphals, *Knowing Words*, for further explanation on this. Her translation of *he-zong* is "the Alliance," and the *lian-heng* is "the Syndicate."

Chapter 5

1. This notion of *ming* was developed by Legalists such as Shang Yang 商鞅, Han Feizi 韓非子, and Shen Bu-Hai 申不害 into *fa* 法 (law) and *shu* 術 (the rhetorical art of the government to assure the power of the king and effect of law). For more information on the School of Legalism, see Wang Zanyuan, *Zhong-guo*; and Young, *Philosophical Foundations*, 82–93. A more detailed discussion of Han Feizi and the Legalist School appears in chapter 9.

2. The same story was also told in *Liezi* 6.177–78.

3. The popular version of the persecution Protagoras received was that his books were burned and he was banished from Athens. Schiappa argues that such account is not reliable, claiming, "Perhaps the origin of the book-burning myth was Aristophanes' flaming conclusion to the sophistic 'thinkery' in the *Clouds*" ("Rhêtorikê," 145).

4. A. Forke has provided an English translation of the two chapters of *Deng Xizi* along with his article "The Chinese Sophists."

5. The Chinese practice of law at the time was different from today's Western notion and practice of law. There were no prosecution and defense lawyers or jury system. If two people or two groups got into a legal dispute, they all went to the "judge," a government official, and each presented his own case. The judge would cross-examine both sides at the same time. The decision as to who was guilty or innocent was based on the plausibility of the testimonies as well as on the judge's observation of the nonverbal behavior of the prosecutor and defen-

dant. Thus, the burden was placed on the prosecutor and defendant to make the best possible arguments and present them persuasively to the judge.

6. There are other interpretations of Hui Shi's ten propositions. Chang Pinglin, in Chan (*Source Book*), divides the ten paradoxes into three categories according to their implied meaning. For example, numbers 1, 2, 3, 6, 8, and 9 argue that all quantitative measurements and spatial distinctions are illusory and unreal. A different explanation is given by Hu Shih, who contends that the first nine paradoxes are intended to prove a monistic theory of the universe, which is concluded by the last paradox. In Hu's words, "The tenth paradox is, therefore, to be regarded as the 'moral' of the argument. All the nine paradoxes are intended to show that 'the universe is one' and that we should 'love things equally'" (*Development*, 113). Forke ("Chinese Sophists") simply concludes that Hui Shi's ten paradoxes deny the existence of worlds which resemble closely those of the Greek Eleatic philosophers Parmenides and especially Zeno.

7. In *Metaphysics* Aristotle said, "it is impossible to think of anything if we do not think of one thing [familiar]" (1006b9).

8. In Cicero's *De Oratore* and Quintilian's *Institutes of Oratory*, metaphor was treated as a linguistic device that connects two similar meanings to produce aesthetic and pleasing effect.

9. Contemporary Western scholars tend to treat metaphor as a universal concept in connection with thought. For example, I. A. Richards regards metaphor as fundamentally "a borrowing between and intercourse of thoughts, a transaction between context." Thought, as he argues, "is metaphoric, and proceeds by comparison, and the metaphors of language derive therefrom" ("Philosophy of Rhetoric," 51).

10. "Hard and white" and "white horse is not a horse" are arguments proposed by Gong-sun Long, the third Mingjia to be introduced in this chapter. In some pre-Qin writings, "hard and white" has become a metaphor for endless and useless argument, which is what Zhuangzi referred to here.

11. Segments of translations of *Gong-sun Longzi* can be found in Forke, "Chinese Sophists," 61–82; Fung, *History*, 205–6, 209–12; Graham, "Lung's Essay," 282–301; Chemielewski, "Notes," 7–22; Chan, *Source Book*, 237–38. There have been some conflicts in these translations and more controversies in the interpretations of the text. To avoid the problem of inconsistency and confusion in the use and translation of terms, I use my own translation of the text. For a more detailed discussion on Gong-sun's logical system, see Graham, *Disputers*, and Hansen, *Language and Logic*.

12. See Guthrie, *History of Greek Philosophy*, vol. 3, 176–219 for a discussion of views on language by Greek sophists.

13. Wittgenstein shared a similar view with Gong-sun on this point as he claimed, "In everyday language it very frequently happens that the same word has different modes of significance—and so belongs to different symbols" (*Tractatus*, 29). See Rieman, "Kung-Sun Lung," 305–19 for a comparison between Gong-sun Long and Wittgenstein on naming.

14. This is mostly with regard to the sophistic tradition. Although Plato con-

demned rhetoric for celebrating probable truth rather than absolute truth, Aristotle and Isocrates continued the sophistic tradition of rhetoric.

15. See Fang Ke, *Zhong-guo bian-zhengfa*; Wang Dianji, *Zhong-guo*; Zhou Yunzhi and Liu Peiyu, *Xian-qin*; Wen Gongyi, *Xian-qin*. The interpretations and criticism of Gong-sun in these works are very similar.

16. See Kennedy, *Classical Rhetoric*; de Romilly, *Great Sophists*; Barrett, *Sophists*; Kerferd, *Sophistic Movement*; and Poulakos, "Toward a Sophistic Definition," for the various definitions of sophists.

Chapter 6

1. The job of a *ru* (or *shi ru* 師儒) was to educate the children of noble families in the six arts known as *liu yi* 六藝—rituals, music, shooting, riding, writing, and arithmetic—for the elementary level and the six classics—*Shi Jing* (the Book of Odes), *Shang Shu* (the Book of History), *Yi Jing* 易經 (the Book of Change), *Yue Jing* 樂經 (the Book of Music), *Li Ji* 禮記 (Records of Rituals), and *Chun Qiu* 春秋 (Spring-Autumn Annuals)—for the advanced level.

2. See Louie, *Critiques*, for attacks on Confucianism in the modern Chinese history. For studies on the erosion of Confucianism in Chinese communication behaviors, see Xing Lu, "Theory of Persuasion," 108–22; Chang and Holt, "More than Relationship," 251–71; Chu and Ju, *Great Wall*; Garrott, "Chinese Cultural Values," 211–25; and Xing Lu, "Interface."

3. For example, when Duke Jing of Qi asked Confucius how Duke Mu of Qin had managed to become a ruler, Confucius replied that Duke Mu's ascendancy to the throne was an expression of the correct policy and humane government. He offered examples of Duke Mu's humanity. Duke Jing was pleased with Confucius's answers and continued consulting with him on state affairs (Si-Ma, "*kongzi shijia*," 202). Available translations of selected chapters of *Shi Ji* are by Burton Watson, *Records of the Historian*, 1969; and Yang Hsien-Yi and Gladys Yang, *Records of the Historian*, 1974.

4. There are a number of translations available of Confucius's *Analects*. I chose D. C. Lau's version, which I consider most faithful to the original. However, when at times I find the translation inadequate, I use my own translation and mark in text reference as *LY* standing for *Lun Yu*. Confucius's notion of morality excludes women. It is fair to say that Confucius is a sexist by modern terms. In Lau's translation of Confucius's *Lun Yu* (The Analects) and *Mengzi* (Mencius), the Chinese word *ren* 人 as person or people in the original text is translated into "man" as supposed to a gender-neutral term. Two reasons may contribute to such translation. First, though *ren* in a denotative sense may include women, the physical and political activities involved or referred to were most likely engaged in by men at the time. Thus, *ren* is translated as "man" according to the contextual and connotative meaning. Second, the translation of *Lun Yu* and *Mengzi* by Lau was done in the 1970s, when it was common to use the term *man* to refer to the concept of human.

5. The quote also indicates that Plato and Confucius both excluded women in their philosophical systems.

6. Here Confucius claimed that the rectification of names would be his number one priority if appointed to public office, and that the task would take three years.

7. Hall and Ames use the term "performance" in their *Thinking through Confucius* (273). Makeham refers to *ming* as a performative role which serves the nominal prescriptive function; the quote is from Makeham, *Names and Actuality*, 46.

8. See the meanings of *wen* in *Analects*, translated by D. C. Lau: book 1, chapter 6 (knowledge, learning); book 3, chapter 14, and book 9, chapter 5 (as culture); book 5, chapter 15 (fond of learning); book 6, chapter 18 (embellishment); book 7, chapter 25 (as classics); book 9, chapter 11 (knowledge); book 9, chapter 27 (knowledge of classics); book 12, chapters 8 and 24 (as embellishment, refinement); book 19, chapter 8 (as embellishment).

9. The discussion of the balance between *wen* and *zhi* can also be found in book 12, chapter 8, and book 6, chapter 18.

10. For example, *san si er xing* 三思而行 (think three times before taking action); *bu chi xia wen* 不恥下問 (never be ashamed of asking advice of those beneath you); *xue er bu yan* 學而不厭 (never tire of learning); and *ju yi fan san* 舉一反三 (generate three more examples by providing one example).

11. See *Analects* or *Lun Yu* book 4; chapters 11, 16, 24, book 6, chapter 13; book 7, chapter 37; book 12, chapter 16; book 13, chapters 23, 25, and 26; book 14, chapter 6; book 15, chapter 24; book 16, chapter 8 for comparison between *junzi* and *xiaoren*.

12. In order, the contrasts are made in *Lun Yu* or *Analects* book 12, chapters 8 and 14; book 4, chapter 16; book 2, chapter 15.

13. In these cases, the tenor (subject) follows the vehicle (means used to explain the subject).

14. In Lau's (1970) translation of *Mencius*, *yi* means "dutifulness" when it refers to relations between friends and superiors. At other times Lau translates the term as "rightness." *Li* can mean "rites" in its broader sense of rituals and "courtesy" in its narrower sense of politeness. Lau uses both translations at different times. To keep the meaning consistent, I translate *yi* as righteousness and *li* as rites when used by Mencius in an abstract sense related to values.

15. Among the available translations on Mencius, I find D. C. Lau's translation most faithful to the original text. However, I do my own translation when Lau's translation seems inadequate.

16. Bernal argues that the Greeks', including Platonic, philosophy was influenced by the Egyptian tradition of associating the heart with the intellect and of seeing the heart and the diaphragm as the seat of both the mind and feelings (*Black Athena*, vol. 1, 141–45). For a more recent account on Greek rhetoric before Aristotle and sophists' philosophy and rhetoric, see Enos, *Greek Rhetoric*, and de Romilly, *Great Sophists*.

17. There had been no evidence to indicate that any women participated in the advisory activities. Thus, presumably, all the advisers at the time were men.

18. These examples can be found in *Mengzi* or *Mencius* book 6, part A, chapter 2; book 6, part A, chapter 19; book 6, Part A, chapter 10; book 1, part A, chapter 6.

19. Knoblock's translation of *Xunzi* is the most recent and the most complete. It is also considered the most authoritative. However, I will use my own translation if at times I believe the translation is inadequate.

20. In this translation the original Chinese *ren dao* is literally translated as "the Way of Man." It means "moral standard and principles." As with the translation of *Analects* and *Mencius* by D. C. Lau, *ren* as person or people is translated as "man" in *Xunzi*.

21. *Li* here means "reason, criteria, and principles." It has the same sound with *Li* as "rites" but is a different character and has a different meaning.

22. Knoblock's translations for this crucial paragraph of *Xunzi* are not adequate. His translation of *xin* (heart) as "mind," and *bian* (distinction, argumentation) as "dialectics" does not fully capture the original meaning.

23. Knoblock translated *bian* as "discrimination." However, in classical Chinese, *bian* (argumentation) and *bian* (discrimination) are used interchangeably depending upon the context. In my opinion, in the paragraphs dealing with persuasion, speech, and counterargument concerning *jian yan*, Xunzi used *bian* primarily to mean argumentation that involves discrimination and classification in the process.

24. In this sense, Xunzi's vision of *bian* finds remarkable similarity with the four purposes of rhetoric proposed by Aristotle: (1) rhetoric is to find truth and to prevent injustice; (2) rhetoric is a means of instruction; (3) rhetoric is used to argue from both sides of the issue; (4) rhetoric is a means of self-defense. See Aristotle, *Rhetoric*, 1355a25.

25. The three types of argument by the three groups are described in more details in chapters 5, 6, and 22 of *Xunzi*.

Chapter 7

1. The first complete original of *Mozi* was compiled by Wang Zhong 汪中 in 1780 but lost. The first published work about Mozi was *Mozi Kan Wu* 墨子勘誤 by Su Shi-xue 蘇時學 in 1867. Fu Shan 付山 wrote *Mozi Da Qu Pian Shi* 墨子大取篇釋 in 1663, and it was published in 1854. The first work on the topic of Mohism was *Mo Xue Lun* 墨學論 by Yu Zheng-xie 俞正燮 in 1833. For a complete list of publications on the study of Mozi by Chinese scholars since the eighteenth century, see Yang Junguang, *Mozi Xin Lun*, 335–61.

2. Alfred Forke translated *The Works of Mozi with Commentaries*, written and edited by Sun Yi-rang 孫詒讓 (1894), into German in 1922. The first complete translation of *Mozi* from Chinese to English was done by Yi-Pao Mei 1929; A. C. Graham translated *Mo Bian* in his *Later Mohist Logic, Ethics, and Science*, 1978. For studies on Mohists texts, see Mei, *Motse*; Hu Shih, *Logical Method*; Needham, *Science and Civilization*; and Garrett, "'Mo-Tzu.'"

3. Yi-Pao Mei's English translation of *Mozi* is so far the most complete. However,

it does not include the section of *Mo Bian*. Though the style of the translation at times seems to be less smooth, the content is mostly adequate and faithful to the original version.

4. An equivalent of a sage.

5. The ancient manuscript *Shi Ji* (Records of the Historian), which contains biographical information on most of the well-known thinkers of the pre-Qin period, offers little information on Mozi.

6. Like those of Confucius, Mencius, and Xunzi, Mozi's moral and rhetorical system excludes women.

7. *Li* here means "profit, benefit, or utility." It shares the same sound with *li* as "rites" and *li* as "principles," but a different character with a different meaning.

8. The first four chapters of *Mo Bian: Jing Shang* 經上 (Canons, part 1), *Jing Shuo Shang* 經說上 (Expounding the Canons, part 1), *Jing Xia* 經下 (Canons, part 2), *Jing Shuo Xia* 經說下 (Expounding the Canons, part 2), were selected from *Mozi* by Lu Sheng in the third century A.D. Lu's introduction and interpretation of these four chapters is known as *Mo Bian Zhu* (the Explanation of Argumentation of Mo). Unfortunately, the book was lost. During the Qing dynasty Sun Yi-rang 孫詒讓 (1848–1908) took *Daqu* 大取 (Major Illustrations) and *Xiaoqu* 小取 (Minor Illustrations) from *Mozi*, grouped them with the other four chapters, and labeled them *Mo Bian*. *Jing Shang* and *Jing Xia* make statements or give definitions, while *Jing Shuo Shang* and *Jing Shuo Xia* offer explanations and elaboration of the statements and definitions introduced by the term *shuo zai* . . . 說在 (the explanation is . . .).

9. For a detailed description of this controversy, see Zhu Zhikai, *Mo Jing zhong*.

10. A. C. Graham offers a fine translation of *Mo Bian*, or *Mohist Canons*, in *Later Mohist Logic, Ethics, and Science*, though it is inadequate in certain places. For example, Graham's translations of *lu* 慮 into "thinking" and *zhi* 知 into "connecting" are not faithful to the original. *Thinking* is generally understood in the West as a mental activity of reasoning; *Lu*, on the other hand, means a psychological activity of worrying, and it is expounded in the text as a willingness of seeking. Therefore, I used my own translation from the original version in Chen Menglin (1983), "Canons, Expounding the Canons," 3–6, 137–38. Throughout the interpretation of *Mo Bian*, I will rely on the original version for the authentic meaning and use Graham's translation when, in my judgment and through the verification against the original, it adequately captures the original meaning.

11. Later Mohists' view of *ming* was influenced by the notion of relativism taught by their predecessors Hui Shi and Zhuangzi. In their perceptions of truth and knowledge, they also share similarities with Greek sophists such as Protagoras and Gorgias, as well as Aristotle.

12. *Fa* is also used as an equivalent to *li* 理 (reason), as basis, standard, or criteria for classifying sameness and difference.

13. In Chinese the four principles are worded as *yi ming ju shi, yi ci shu yi, yi shuo chu gu, yi lei qu,* and *yi lei yu* 以名舉實，以辭抒意，以說出故，以類取，以類予.

14. See Aristotle, *Prior Analytics,* 25a–26b, for an elaboration of the relationship.

Chapter 8

1. Lau used the Wade-Giles system, while I used the pinyin system for the title of the *Dao De Jing*. There are a number of translations of the *Dao De Jing*. In comparing the original version with several translations, I found Lau's translation the most adequate. The Chinese and English texts are placed side by side, which makes it easy to verify the meanings.

2. Despite the controversy over its authorship, the *Dao De Jing* has been identified by scholars as the work of Laozi.

3. Sources on Greek cosmology and philosophy are numerous. Some highly regarded ones are Burnet, *Early Greek Philosophy*; Guthrie, *History of Greek Philosophy*; Kirk and Raven, *Pre-Socratic Philosophers*. The five elements are discussed in *Shang Shu*, while the best book to illustrate the Chinese concept of yin and yang is *Yi Jing* (the Book of Change).

4. See the claims made in Allen, *Greek Philosophy*, 11; Cornford, *Plato and Parmenides*, 35; Guthrie, *History of Greek Philosophy*, vol. 2, 170; Kirk and Raven, *Pre-Socratic Philosophers*, 279; and Tarán, *Parmenides*, 59.

5. Buddhism was first introduced to China from India in the late Eastern Han dynasty (around 100 C.E.). The Chinese interpreted Buddhism through a Daoist lens, generating a secularized version of Buddhism characterized by its pragmatic approach to social and individual problems. Chinese thought and culture are in general characterized by the integration of Confucianism, Daoism, and Buddhism.

6. I chose to use Watson's translation of *Zhuangzi* in this section. The translation is ordered by chapters as well as the titles in the Chinese version. However, Watson used the Wade-Giles system for the romanization of 莊子, while I use the pinyin system. Graham (1981) also translated the first seven chapters of *Zhuangzi*. Other English translations of *Zhuangzi* are available; however, they are either too old (the earliest is 1889) or incomplete. Translating *Zhuangzi* poses great difficulty for the translator, as it was written in literary form. As Watson tells the reader, "my translation is as much an interpretation, and as tentative in many places, as any other" (Introduction, 20–21). However, I do think Watson has done a more adequate job than others in terms of both content and style.

7. In chapter 26 Zhuangzi's family is described as very poor. For example, according to legend, Zhuangzi once had to borrow some grains from the marquis of Chien-ho.

8. Controversies exist over the authorship of *Zhuangzi*. Most scholars agree that the inner chapters (the first seven) were written by Zhuangzi himself. The remaining chapters may have been written by Zhuangzi or his followers. At any rate, *Zhuangzi* represents both an individual and collective mind concerning Zhuangzi's philosophy and rhetorical styles. For convenience, I will treat Zhuangzi as the author of the whole text.

9. It is also possible that the author of *Zhuangzi* influenced the author of the *Dao De Jing*, as the date of the latter text is not confirmed and there has been speculation that Laozi may not in fact be the author of *Dao De Jing*.

10. See chapter 6, 90–91, for a conversation between Confucius and his student Yen Hui. Yen Hui tells his teacher that he has forgotten benevolence, righteousness, rites, music, and finally everything. Confucius praises him, calls him a worthy man, and proclaims him his teacher.

11. See chapter 2, "Discussion on Making all Things Equal," 37. In *Gorgias* Plato defined false rhetoric as knack and cookery. In *Phaedrus* Plato redefined true rhetoric as an art akin to dialectic in finding knowledge and truth.

12. Wittgenstein shares some similar views with Zhuangzi on the limitations of language, believing also that language does not represent the whole of reality.

13. According to *Zhuangzi*, imputed words make up nine-tenths of Zhuangzi's writing, and repeated words make up seven-tenths of Zhuangzi's persuasion. See *Zhuangzi* or *Chuang Tzu*, chapter 33, "The World."

14. See chapters 4, 6, 14, 21, and 22 for examples of such dialogues and the portrayal of "invented" Confucius.

15. In chapter 9 of *Zhuangzi* Zhuangzi used two other allegories to illustrate the value of *wu wei*, suggesting that primitive society was the ideal society, because there was no desire or greed, and people were equal and happy.

Chapter 9

1. So far, Liao's translation is the only complete translation of *Han Feizi*. At times the translation is not very smooth in terms of style, but it is adequate in capturing the original meaning. I will use the Chinese version of *Han Feizi* to interpret and verify the original meaning. Watson (1963) has translated some sections of *Han Feizi* along with those of *Mozi* and *Xunzi*.

2. Li Si 李斯 was instrumental in assisting the king of Qin to unify China after Han's death. For more information on Li Si and how he assisted Emperor Qin to unify China, see Bodde, *China's First Unifier*.

3. *Li* here means "principle and standard," the same sound with *li* as "rites" but different character and different meaning.

4. *Kunzi*, translated by Allyn Rickett, 1965, "*Fa fa*" (On Conforming to the Law), 90–106, Kuan-Tzu is spelled by the Wade-Gile's system while *Guanzi*, conforms to the pinyin system of Chinese Romanizations.

5. The English translation of *Shang Jun Shu* is done by Duyvendak, *The Book of Lord Shang*, 1963.

6. Shen Bu-hai helped Duke Zhao of Han reform and strengthen the state of Han. Shen studied under Daoist philosophers and was interested in *xing ming* 刑名 (penal laws and names).

7. Historians have not confirmed that Gui Guzi was a real historical figure. However, it is recorded in *Shi Ji* that Su Qin and Zhang Yi, well-known *you shui* of the Warring States period, studied under him. It is theorized that *Gui Guzi* was produced during the Warring States period, possibly by some hermit, and refined by Su Qin and Zhang Yi.

8. Machiavelli, *The Prince*, 1981. A brief comparison is made between legalism and Machiavellianism in Rubin, *Individual and State;* and Schwartz, *World of Thought*.

9. There are said to be five vermin in society. The other four are: *you shui*, wearers of private swords, courtiers, and tradesmen and craftsmen. See chapter 49 for a discussion of the five vermin.

10. This analogy of the patriarchal family in connection with the rulership of the state is still prevalent in contemporary China. The ruler of the state or country is regarded as a father figure who is "strict, but kind" exerting absolute authority to the ultimate benefit of his people. In fact, the Chinese term for country, *guo jia* 國家, is made up of two characters: state and family.

11. For example, chapters 7, 10, 44, and 49 of *Han Feizi* provided a number of historical examples for this purpose.

12. Chapters such as 13, 14, 20, and 21 of *Han Feizi* are filled with anecdotes for this rhetorical purpose.

Chapter 10

1. The concept of yin (negative, female) and yang (positive, male) first appeared in *Yi Jing* (the Book of Change), which was said to be written by Zhou Wen Wang or Duke Zhou in the Zhou dynasty and later edited by Confucius.

2. Debates at the intellectual, political, and public levels continued in the subsequent years in China. For example, there had been organized religious debates during the Tang dynasty (618–907), particularly the debating tactics of Han Yu 韓愈 and Liu Zongyuan 柳宗元 against Buddhism. Debates for and against Wang Anshi's 王安石 political reform were evident in the Song dynasty (960–1279). At the public level in Chinese modern history, there was passionate rhetoric against the Japanese during the Anti-Japanese War (1937–1945) and fervent debates and rhetoric during the Cultural Revolution (1966–1976).

3. According to Stuart Piggott, the Greeks began to hear about China and regarded the Chinese as mythical Hyperboreans in the eighth or seventh century B.C.E. Not until the sixth century had "the Greek colonies on the Black Sea . . . established sufficient contacts for Chinese silk to find its way into a barbarian Iron Age chieftain's grave in South Germany, and thereafter the two great worlds of antiquity were at least conscious of each other's existence" (William Watson, *Early Civilization in China*, general editor's preface).

4. For example, Chinese persuasion takes place mostly in private situations, while Greek rhetoric is practiced generally in public realms.

5. See Jaeger, *Paideia*, xxii. Therein Jaeger observes, "Man is the centre of their thought. . . . Their philosophy moved from the problem of the cosmos to the problem of man, in which it culminated with Socrates, Plato, and Aristotle." Also see Chan, *Source Book*, 3; and Creel, *Chinese Thought*, 31, for discussion on Chinese humanism.

6. See Plato, *Phaedrus*, 277; and Aristotle, *Rhetoric*, 1356a–57a. In this section

Aristotle also discussed the basis of enthymeme, which can generate "necessarily true" and "generally true" conclusions allowing room for probability.

7. Women and slaves were not considered citizens and thus were excluded from participation in politics.

8. See the elaboration of each type of rhetoric in Kennedy, *Classical Rhetoric;* Grassi, *Rhetoric as Philosophy;* and Conley, *Rhetoric.*

9. Postmodern scholarship would disagree with the discussion of anything "universal," as resemblance is believed to be a subjective judgment. However, while I acknowledge the human variety and differences caused by social conditions from an intellectual point of view, I do think that humans share common grounds that often transcend external conditions and, thus, cannot be reduced to culture. This is especially so from a mystical and spiritual point of view.

10. For a good analysis of Chinese intellectuals, historical and present, see Link, *Evening Chats.*

11. For example, Jensen ("Values and Practices") explored the moral emphasis of Chinese communication. For studies on Chinese instrumental communication, see Bond and Hwang, "Social Psychology"; Chang and Holt, "More than Relationship." For studies on transitions in cultural values from moral to instrumental emphasis, see Xing Lu, "Interface." For studies claiming that China is a collectivistic culture, see Gudykunst and Kim, *Communicating;* and Hui and Triandis, "Individualism-Collectivism." For studies claiming that China is switching to an individualistic orientation, see Chu and Ju, *Great Wall;* and Garrott, "Chinese Cultural Values."

12. For example, in *The Asian Mind Game,* authored by Chin-ning Chu, Chu discusses Chinese psychology and the art of *shu* as applied in business persuasion and transaction.

Bibliography

Chinese Texts

Primary Texts

Most of the primary texts I used were reprinted and published in the 1990s. Each text has the original version in the classical Chinese language along with explanations or translations in the modern Chinese language.

Chen, Menglin 陳孟麟. *Mo Bian luo-ji xue* 墨辯邏輯學 (The Logic of Argumentation of Mo). Shandong: Qi Lu Books, 1983.
Chun Qiu Zuo Zhuan Zhu 春秋左傳注 (Zuo Commentaries). Compiled by 左丘明. Edited by Yang, Bojun 楊伯峻. Beijing: China Books, 1990.
Confucius. *Lun Yu bai-hua jin yi* 論言白話今譯 (The Translation of Analects). Edited by Gou, Chengyi 勾承益 and Li, Yadong 李亞東. Beijing: China Books, 1992.
Deng, Xi 鄧析. "Deng Xizi" 鄧析子. In *Zhong-guo luo-ji shi zi-liao xuan* 中國邏輯史資料選 (Selected Essays on Chinese Logic). Edited by Chinese Logic Studies. Lanzhou: Gansu People's Press, 1985.
Gong-sun, Long 公孫龍. *Gong-Sun Long jin zhu jin yi* 公孫龍今注今譯. Edited by Chen, Guimiao 陳癸淼. Taipei: Shang Wu Printing House, 1986.
Guo Yu quan-yi 國語全譯 (Discourse of the States). Compiled by 左丘明. Edited by Huang, Yongtang 黃永堂. Guiyang: Guizhou People's Press, 1995.
Han, Feizi. *Han Feizi quan yi* 韓非子全譯 (The Explanation of Han Feizi). Edited by Zhang, Jue 張覺. Guiyang: Guizhou People's Press, 1992.
Laozi. *Dao De Jing* 道德經 (Canon of Way and Virtue). Edited by Liu, Yandeng 劉彥燈 and Fan, Youqi 範又琪. Wuhan: Central China University of Science and Technology Press, 1990.
Mencius. *Mengzi bai-hua jin yi* 孟子白話今譯 (The Translation of Mencius). Edited by Li, Shuang 李雙. Beijing: China Books, 1992.
Mozi. *Mozi bai-hua jin yi* 墨子白話今譯 (The Translation of Mozi). Edited by Wu, Longhui 吳龍輝等 et al. Beijing: China Books, 1992.
Shang Shu. In *Bai-hua Shang Shu* 白話尚書 (Book of Documents). Edited by Zhou, Bingjun 周秉鈞. Changsha: Yue Lu Books, 1990.
Shi Jing. In *Shi Jing jian-shang ci-dian* 詩經鑑賞詞典 (The Critique of Canon of Poems). Edited by Ren, Zibin 任自斌 and He, Jinjian 和近健. Beijing: Hehai University Press, 1989.
Xunzi. *Xunzi bai-hua jin yi* 荀子白話今譯 (The Translation of Xunzi). Edited by Wang, Sen 王森. Beijing: China Books, 1992.
Zhan Guo Ce quan yi 戰國策全譯 (The Explanation of Zhan Guo Ce). Edited by Wang, Shouqian 王守謙 et al. Guiyang: Guizhou People's Publishing House, 1992.

Zhuangzi. *Bai-hua Zhuangzi* 白話莊子 (The Explanation of Zhuangzi). Edited by Zhang, Yuliang 張玉良. Xi An: San Qin Publishers, 1990.

Secondary Works

This portion of bibliography includes both the classical and contemporary works by Chinese scholars. All the classical works were reprinted and published in recent years.

Ban, Gu 班固. *Han Shu xin-zhu* 漢書新注 (The Explanation of Han Books). Edited by Shi, Ding 施丁. Xian: San Qin Publishers, 1992.

Chen, Guying 陳鼓應 "Ni Cai zhe-xue he Zhuangzi zhe-xue de bi-jiao yan-jiu" 尼采哲學和莊子哲學的比較研究 (A Comparison between the Philosophy of Nietzsche and Zhuangzi). In *Lun Zhong-guo chuan-tong wen-hua* 論中國傳統文化 (Discussions on Chinese Traditional Culture). Beijing: Life, Reading, and New Knowledge Books, 1988.

Chen, Song 陳崧. "Ping 'wu-si' qian-hou dong-xi wen-hua wen-ti de lun-zhan" 評五四前後東西文化問題的論戰 (The Polemics on the Relationship between Eastern and Western Civilizations around the May 4th Movement). In *Zhong-guo wen-hua* 中國文化 (*Chinese Culture*), 72–98. Shanghai: Fudan University Press, 1985.

Fang, Ke 方克. *Zhong-guo bian-zheng fa si-xiang shi* 中國辯證法思想史 (*The History of Chinese Dialectical Thought*). Beijing: People's Press, 1985.

Fang, Lizhong 房立中. *Gui Guzi mou-lue* 鬼谷子謀略 (Strategies of Gui Guzi). Beijing: China Broadcasting and Television Press, 1992.

Feng, Youlan 馮友蘭. *Zhong-guo zhe-xue shi xin-bian* 中國哲學史新編 (New Compiled Version of Chinese History of Philosophy). Beijing: People's Publications, 1964.

Guo, Moruo 郭沫若. *Shi pi-pan shu* 十批判書. Beijing: Science Press, 1959.

He, Zhaowu 何兆武 and He, Gaoji 何高濟. "Du Li Ma Dou de zhong-guo ri-ji" 讀利瑪竇的中國日記 ("Reflection after Reading Matteo Ricci's *I Commentary della China*.") In *Zhong-guo wen-hua yan-jiu ji-kan* 中國文化研究集刊 (*The Collection of Chinese Cultural Studies*). Shanghai: Fudan University Press, 1985.

Hou, Jiaju 侯家駒. *Zhou Li yan-jiu* 周禮研究 (The Study of the Zhou Rites). Taiwan: Lian Jin Publishers, 1987.

Hou, Wailu 侯外廬 et al. *Zhong-guo si-xiang tong-shi* 中國思想通史 (*History of Chinese Thoughts Vol. I*). Beijing: People's Press, 1966.

Hu, Shi 胡適. "Shi san-bai pian yan zi jie" 詩三百篇言字解 (The Interpretation of Yan in Shi Jing). In *Hu Shi wencun* 胡適文存 (The Works of Hu Shi). Shanghai: Oriental Book Company, 1921.

Lao, Siguang 勞思光. *Xin-bian zhong-guo zhe-xue shi* 新編中國哲學史 (New Compiled Version of Chinese History of Philosophy). Taipei: San Min Books, 1984.

Li, Jianzhao 李建釗. "Lun Mengzi hao bian" 論孟子好辯 (Mencius's Fondness for Argument). In *Zhong-guo luo-ji si-xiang lun-wen xuan* 中國邏輯思想論文選 (Selected Papers on Chinese Logical Thinking), edited by Liu, Peiyu 劉培育 et al. 149–64 Beijing: Life Reading and Knowledge Publication, 1981.

Liezi 列子 (Liezi). Edited by Wang Qiangmo 王強模. Guiyang: Guizhou People's Press, 1993.

Liu, An 劉安. *Huai Nanzi yi-zhu* 淮南子譯注 (Explanations of Huai Nanzi). Edited by Chen, Guangzhong 陳廣忠. Jilin: Jilin Classics Press, 1990.

Liu, Xie 劉勰. *Wen-xin diao-long* 文心雕龍 (Cultivating the Mind and Carving the Dragon). Edited by Fu, Weixun 付偉勳 and Wei, Zhengtong 韋政通. Taipei: Dongda Library Inc., 1989.

Lu, Buwei 呂不韋. *Lu shi Chun Qiu* 呂氏春秋 (The Spring-Autumn of Mr. Lu). Beijing: China Books, 1992.

Peng, Lin 彭林. *Zhou Li zhu-ti si-xiang yu cheng-shu nian-dai yan-jiu* 周禮主體思想與成書年代研究 (*The Study of Central Ideas of Zhou Li and Its Completion*). Beijing: China Academy of Social Science Press, 1991.

Shen, Fuwei 潘福偉. *Zhong-xi wen-hua jiao-liu shi* 中西文化交流史 (*The History of Exchange Between Chinese and Western Cultures*). Shanghai: People's Press, 1985.

Shen, Xirong 潘錫榮. *Gu han-yu chang-yong ci-lei shi* 古漢語常用詞類釋 (Illustration of Commonly Used Terms in Classical Chinese). Shanghai: Xue Lin Publisher, 1992.

Shuo Yuan 說苑 (The Garden of Talks). Edited by Liu, Xiang 劉向. Guiyang: Guizhou People's Press, 1992.

Si-Ma, Qian 司馬遷. *Shi Ji* 史記 (Records of the Historian). Beijing: Beijing Broadcasting Institute Press, 1993.

Sun, Miao 孫淼. *Xia Shang shi gao* 夏商史稿 (History of the Xia and Shang Dynasties). Beijing: Classics Publishers, 1987.

Sunzi. *Sunzi jiao-shi* 孫子校釋 (The Explanation of Sunzi). Edited by Wu Jiulong 吳九龍. Beijing: Military Science Press, 1991.

Wang, Dianji 汪奠基. *Zhong-guo luo-ji si-xiang shi fen-xi* 中國邏輯思想史分析 (Analysis of the History of Chinese Logic). Beijing: China Books, 1961.

Wang, Li 王力. *Gu han-yu chang-yong ci-dian* 古漢語常用詞典 (Dictionary of Common Words of Chinese Classical Language). Hong Kong: Central Publications, 1976.

Wang, Zanyuan 王贊源. *Zhong-guo fa-jia zhe-xue* 中國法家哲學 (Chinese Philosophy of the Legalist School). Taipei: Tong Ta Books, 1989.

Wen, Gongyi 溫公頤. *Xian-qin luo-ji shi* 先秦邏輯史 (History of Logic in Pre-Qin). Shanghai: Shanghai People's Press, 1983.

Wu, Feibai 伍非白. *Zhong-guo gu Mingjia yan* 中國古名家言 (Speech of Chinese Ancient Mingjia). Beijing: China Academy of Science, 1981.

Wu, Yi 吳怡. *Zhong-guo zhe-xue fa-zhan shi* 中國哲學發展史 (Development of the History of Chinese Philosophy). Taipei: Sun Ming Stock Limited Company, 1984.

Xu, Shen 許慎. *Shuo Wen Jie Zi* 說文解字 (Explanations of Meanings of Words). Hefei: Yellow Mountain Books, 1993.

Yang, Junguang 楊俊光. *Mozi xin lun* 墨子新論 (New Discussion of Mozi). Nanjing: Jiangsu Educational Press, 1992.

Yi Jing 易經 (Canon of Change). Edited by Wang, Ji 王驥. Beijing: China Social Science Press, 1990.

Yu, Yu 虞愚. *Zhong-guo ming-xue* 中國名學 (Chinese Study of Ming). Taipei: Shang Wu Printing House, 1959.

Yu, Ziliu 余紫榴. *Zhong-guo shi-hua wu-qian nian: long de gen* 中國史話五千年龍的根 (Chinese History of Five Thousand Years: The Root of Dragon). Hong Kong: Shang Wu Printing House, 1985.

Zhang, Bingnan 張秉楠. *Jixia gou-chen* 稷下鉤沉 (The Study of Jixia). Shanghai: Shanghai Classics, 1991.
Zhang, Chuanxi 張傳璽. *Zhongguo gudai shi* 中國古代史 (The History of Ancient China). Beijing: Beijing University Press, 1991.
Zhang, Dainian 張岱年. *Zhong-guo zhe-xue da-gang* 中國哲學大綱 (Canons of Chinese Philosophy). Beijing: China Social Science Press, 1982.
Zhao, Guangxian 趙光賢. *Zhou-dai she-hui bian-xi* 周代社會辨析 (Distinction and Analysis of Zhou Society). Beijing: People's Press, 1980.
Zhao, Ming 趙明 et al. *Xian-qin da wen-xue shi* 先秦大文學史 (The History of Literature in the Pre-Qin Period). Changchun: Jilin University Press, 1993.
Zhong Yong 中庸 and *Da Xue* 大學. In *Si shu yi zhu* 四書譯注 (The Explanation of Four Classics), edited by Wu, Enpu 烏恩溥. Changchun: Jilin Classic Press, 1990.
Zhou Li 周禮 (The Rites of Zhou). Edited by Cheng, Yuanmin 程元敏. Taiwan: National Editing and Translation Office, 1987.
Zhou, Yunzhi 周雲之 and Liu, Peiyu 劉培育. *Xian-qin luo-ji shi* 先秦邏輯史 (History of Logic in the Pre-Qin Period). Beijing: China Academy of Science Press, 1984.
Zhu, Zhikai 朱志凱. *Mo Jing zhong de luo-ji xue-shuo* 墨經中的邏輯學說 (The Logic in Mohist Canon). Chengdu: Sichuang People's Press, 1988.

Translations of Chinese Texts

There are many other available versions of English translations of Chinese classical texts. I only offer information on the sources that I have used or consulted in this study.

Chen, Ku-Ying. *Lao Tzu Text, Notes, and Comments*. San Francisco: Chinese Materials Center, 1977.
Cleary, T. *The Art of War: Sun Tzu*. Boston: Shambhala, 1988.
Crump, J. I. Jr. *Chan-Kuo Ts'e*. Oxford: Clarendon Press, 1970.
Duyvendak, J. J. L. *The Book of Lord Shang: A Classical of the Chinese School of Law*. Chicago: University of Chicago Press, 1963.
Graham, A. C. *Chuang-tzu: The Seven Inner Chapters from the Book Chuang-tzu*. London: George Allen & Unwin, 1981.
———. *Mo Bian*. In *Later Mohist Logic, Ethics, and Science*. 239–494 Hong Kong: Chinese University Press, 1978.
Karlgren, Bernhard. *The Book of Odes*. Stockholm, Sweden: Museum of Far Eastern Antiquities, 1950.
Knoblock, John. *Xunzi: A Translation and Study of the Complete Works Vols. I–III*. Stanford, Calif.: Stanford University Press, 1988.
Lau, D. C. *Confucius the Analects*. New York: Penguin Books, 1979.
———. *Mencius*. New York: Penguin Books, 1970.
———. *Tao Te Ching*. Hong Kong: Chinese University Press, 1982.
Legge, James. *The Book of Poetry (Shi Jing): Chinese Text with English Translation*. New York: Paragon Book Reprint Corporation, 1967.
———. *Shang Shu*. In *The Chinese Classics*, vol. III. Hong Kong: Hong Kong University Press, 1960.

Liao, W. K. *The Complete Works of Han Fei Tzu Vol I*. London: Arthur Probsthan, 1939.
———. *The Complete Works of Han Fei Tzu Vol II*. London: Arthur Probsthan, 1959.
Mei, Yi-Pao. *The Ethical and Political Works of Motse*. London: Arthur Probsthan, 1929.
Rickett, Allyn. *Kuan-Tzu: A Repository of Early Chinese Thought, Vol. I*. Hong Kong: Hong Kong University Press, 1965.
Waltham, Clae. *Shu Ching: Book of History*. London: George Allen & Unwin, 1972.
Watson, Burton. *Basic Writings of Mo Tzu, Hsun Tzu, and Han Fei Tzu*. New York: Columbia University Press, 1963.
———. *The Complete Works of Chuang Tzu*. New York: Columbia University Press, 1968.
———. *Records of the Historian*. New York and London: Columbia University Press, 1969.
Yang, Hsien-Yi and Gladys Yang. *Records of the Historian*. Hong Kong: Commercial Press, 1974.

Scholarly Works in English

Abegg, Lily. *The Mind of East Asia*. London: Thames and Hudson, 1952.
Allen, E. Reginald. *Greek Philosophy: Thales to Aristotle*. 2nd ed. London: Collier Macmillan Publishers, 1985.
Allinson, Robert E. "An Overview of the Chinese Mind." In *Understanding the Chinese Mind: The Philosophical Roots*, edited by Robert E. Allinson, 1–25. Hong Kong: Oxford University Press, 1989.
Ames, Roger. *The Art of Rulership: A Study in Ancient Chinese Political Thought*. Honolulu: University of Hawaii Press, 1983.
Andrews, Antony. *The Greeks*. New York: Norton Library, 1967.
Aristotle. Categories, Metaphysics, Physics, Poetics, Posterior Analytics, Prior Analytics, Rhetoric, The Nicomachean Ethics, Topics. In *The Complete Works of Aristotle*, edited by Jonathan Barnes. Vols. I and II. Princeton, N.J.: Princeton University Press, 1984.
Barrett, Harold. *The Sophists*. Novato, Calif.: Chandler & Sharp Publishers, 1987.
Bassnett-McGuire, Susan. *Translation Studies*. New York: Methuen, 1980.
Becker, Carl. "Reasons for the Lack of Argumentation and Debate in the Far East." *International Journal of Intercultural Relations* 10 (1986): 75–92.
Benjamin, Walter. "The Task of the Translator." In *Illumination*, translated by Harry Zohn, 69–82. New York: Schocken, 1969.
Bernal, Martin. *Black Athena: The Afroasiatic Roots of Classical Civilization*. New Brunswick, N.J.: Rutgers University Press, 1987.
Bodde, Derk. *China's First Unifier: A Study of the Chin Dynasty as Seen in the Life of Li-SSu*. Leiden: E. J. Brill, 1938.
———. "Myths of Ancient China." In *Mythologies of the Ancient World*, edited by Samuel Noah Kramer, 367–408. Garden City, N.Y.: Anchor Books, 1961.
Bond, M. H., and K-k Hwang. "The Social Psychology of Chinese People." In *The Psychology of the Chinese People*, edited by M. H. Bond, 213–65. Hong Kong: Oxford University Press, 1986.

BIBLIOGRAPHY

Bruns, Gerald L. *Hermeneutics: Ancient and Modern.* New Haven and London: Yale University Press, 1992.
Buber, Martin. *I and Thou*, 2nd ed. New York: Scribner's, 1958.
Burnet, John. *Early Greek Philosophy,* 4th ed. London: A & C Black, 1963.
Cassirer, Ernst. *An Essay on Man: An Introduction to a Philosophy of Human Culture.* New Haven: Yale University Press, 1944.
Caws, Peter. "Identity: Cultural, Transcultural, and Multicultural." In *Multiculturalism: A Critical Reader,* edited by David Theo Goldberg, 371–87. Oxford, U.K. and Cambridge, Mass.: Blackwell, 1994.
Chan, Wing-tsit. "Chinese Theory and Practice, with Special Reference to Humanism." In *The Chinese Mind: Essentials of Chinese Philosophy and Culture,* edited by C. A. Moore, 11–30. Honolulu: East-West Center Press, 1967.
———. *A Source Book of Chinese Philosophy.* Princeton, N.J.: Princeton University Press, 1963.
———. "Syntheses in Chinese Metaphysics." In *The Chinese Mind: Essentials of Chinese Philosophy and Culture,* edited by Charles Moore, 132–48. Honolulu: East-West Center Press, 1967.
Chang, Chung-yuan. *Creativity and Taoism: A Study of Chinese Philosophy, Art, and Poetry.* New York: Harper Torchbooks, 1963.
Chang, Hui-Ching, and Richard G. Holt. "More Than Relationship: Chinese Interaction and the Principle of Kuan-Hsi." *Communication Quarterly* 39 (Summer 1991): 251–71.
Chang, Kwang-Chih. *Early Chinese Civilization: Anthropological Perspectives.* Cambridge, Mass.: Harvard University Press, 1976.
———. *Shang Civilization.* New Haven and London: Yale University Press, 1980.
Chemielewski, Janusz. "Concerning the Problem of Analogic Reasoning in Ancient China." *Rocznik Orientalistcyzny* 40, no. 2 (1979): 65–78.
———. "Notes on Early Chinese Logic." *Rocznik Orientalistcyzny* 26 (1963): 7–22.
Cheng, Chung-ying. "Chinese Philosophy and Contemporary Human Communication Theory." In *Communication Theory: Eastern and Western Perspectives,* edited by D. Lawrence Kincaid, 23–43. San Diego, Calif.: Academic Press, 1987.
———. "Dialectic of Confucian Morality and Metaphysics of Man." *Philosophy East and West* 21 (April 1971): 111–23.
———. "Logic and Language in Chinese Thought." In *Contemporary Philosophy: A Survey,* edited by Raymond Klibansky. Vol. III. Firenze, La Nuova Italia, Italy, 1969.
———. "Nature and Function of Skepticism in Chinese Philosophy." *Philosophy East and West* 27 (April 1977): 137–48.
Cheng, Chung-ying, and Richard H. Swain. "Logic and Ontology in the 'Chih Wu Lun' of Kung-Sun Lung-Tzu." *Philosophy East and West* 20 (April 1970): 137–54.
Choe, C. "Rhetoric: A Comparison of Its Evaluation in East and West." Paper presented at the annual convention of the International Communication Association, Honolulu, Hawaii, 1985.
Choy, Philip, P. L. Dong Choy, and M. K. Hom. *The Coming Man.* Hong Kong: Joint Publishing Co., 1994.
Chu, Chin-ning. *The Asian Mind Game.* New York: Rawson Associates, 1990.
Chu, Godwin C., and Yanan Ju. *The Great Wall in Ruins: Communication and Cultural Change in China.* New York: State University of New York Press, 1993.

Cicero. *De Oratore Book I.II.* Trans. E. W. Sutton. Cambridge, Mass.: Harvard University Press, 1976.
Cikoski, John. "On Standard of Analogic Reasoning in the Later Chou." *Journal of Chinese Philosophy* 2–3 (June 1975): 325–57.
Clifford, James. *The Predicament of Culture: Twentieth-Century Ethnography, Literature and Art.* Cambridge, Mass.: Harvard University Press, 1988.
Cole, Thomas. *The Origins of Rhetoric in Ancient Greece.* Baltimore and London: Johns Hopkins University Press, 1991.
Conley, Thomas M. "The Greekless Reader and Aristotle's Rhetoric." *Quarterly Journal of Speech* 65 (1979): 74–79.
———. *Rhetoric in the European Tradition.* New York and London: Longman, 1990.
Cornford, Francis M. *Plato and Parmenides.* New York: K. Paul, Trench, Trubner and Co., 1939.
Crawford, Robert. "The Social and Political Philosophy of the Shih-chi." *Journal of Asian Studies* 22 (1963): 401–16.
Creel, H. G. *Chinese Thought from Confucius to Mao Tse-Tung.* Chicago: University of Chicago Press, 1953.
Crump, James I. Jr. *Intrigues: Studies of Chan-kuo Ts'e.* Ann Arbor: University of Michigan Press, 1964.
Crump, James I. Jr., and John Dreher. "Peripatetic Rhetors of the Warring Kingdoms." *Central States Speech Journal* 2 (1951): 15–17.
Cua, Antonio S. *Ethical Argumentation: A Study in Hsun Tzu's Moral Epistemology.* Honolulu: University of Hawaii Press, 1985.
———. "Hsuntes' Theory of Argumentation: A Reconstruction." *Review of Metaphysics* 36 (1983): 867–94.
Cushman, Donald P., and D. Lawrence Kincaid. "Introduction and Initial Insights." In *Communication Theory: Eastern and Western Perspectives*, edited by D. L. Kincaid, 1–10. San Diego, Calif.: Academic Press, 1987.
DeFrancis, John. *The Chinese Language: Fact and Fantasy.* Honolulu: University of Hawaii Press, 1984.
De Groot, J. J. M. *The Religion of the Chinese.* New York: Macmillan, 1910.
De Romilly, Jacqueline. *The Great Sophists in Periclean Athens.* Trans. J. Lloyd. Princeton, N.J.: Princeton University Press, 1992.
Dobson, W. A. C. H. "Studies in the Grammar of Early Archaic Chinese." In *T'oung Pao.* Vol. LI, 295–321. 1964.
Dreher, John, and James Crump Jr. "Pre-Han Persuasion: The Legalist School." *Central States Speech Journal* 3 (March 1952): 10–14.
Dubs, H. Homer. "The Date of Shang Period." In *T'oung Pao.* Vol. XL. Livr. 4–5 322–35. 1951.
Egan, Ronald. "Narratives in Tso-chuan." *Harvard Journal of Asian Studies* 37 (1977): 323–52.
Enos, Richard L. *Greek Rhetoric Before Aristotle.* Prospect Heights, Ill.: Waveland Press, 1993.
Fairbank, John. *China Perceived: Images and Politics in Chinese-American Relations.* New York: Alfred A. Knopf, 1974.
Fingarette, Herbert. *Confucius: The Secular as Sacred.* New York: Harper and Row Publishers, 1972, 6–7.

Forke, Alfred. "The Chinese Sophists." *Journal of the North China Branch of the Royal Asiatic Society* 34 (1901–2): 1–100.
Forrest, R. A. D. *The Chinese Language.* London: Faber and Faber, 1948.
Foss, Sonja. *Rhetorical Criticism: Explorations and Practice.* Prospect Heights, Ill.: Waveland, 1989.
Foucault, Michel. *The Birth of the Clinic: An Archeology of Medical Perception.* Trans. A. M. Sheridan Smith. New York: Vintage, 1975.
Fox, Michael V. "Ancient Egyptian Rhetoric." *Rhetorica* 1 (1983): 9–22.
Fung, Yu-Lan. *A History of Chinese Philosophy.* Vol. 1. Trans. D. Bodde. Princeton, N.J.: Princeton University Press, 1952.
Gadamer, Hans-Georg. *Truth and Method.* 2nd ed. Trans. Joe Weinsheimer and Donald G. Marshall. London: Sheed and Ward, 1989.
Gare, Arran E. "Understanding Oriental Cultures." *Philosophy East and West* 45 (July 1995): 309–28.
Garrett, Mary. "Asian Challenge." In *Contemporary Perspectives on Rhetoric,* edited by Sonja Foss, Karen Foss, and Robert Trapp, 295–306. Prospect Heights, Ill., Waveland 1991.
———. "Classical Chinese Conceptions of Argumentation and Persuasion." *Argumentation and Advocacy* 29 (1993a): 105–15.
———. "The 'Mo-Tzu' and the 'Lu-Shih Ch'un-ch'iu': A Case Study of Classical Chinese Theory and Practice of Argument." Diss., University of California, Berkeley, 1983.
———. "Pathos Reconsidered from the Perspective of Classical Chinese Rhetorical Theories." *Quarterly Journal of Speech* 79 (1993b): 19–39.
Garrott, June R. "Chinese Cultural Values: New Angles, Added Insights." *International Journal of Intercultural Relations* 19 (1995): 211–25.
Geertz, Clifford. *The Interpretation of Cultures.* New York: Basic Books, 1973.
Gill, Ann. *Rhetoric and Human Understanding.* Prospect Heights, Ill.: Waveland Press, 1994.
Goldberg, David T. "Introduction: Multicultural Conditions." In *Multiculturalism: A Critical Reader,* edited by David Theo Goldberg, 1–41. Oxford, U.K. and Cambridge, Mass.: Blackwell, 1994.
Goodman, Russell B. "Skepticism and Realism in the Chuang Tzu." *Philosophy East and West* 35 (July 1985): 231–37.
Graham, Angus Charles. *Disputers of the Tao.* LaSalle, Ill.: Open Court Publishing Company, 1989.
———. "Kung-Sun Lung's Essay on Meanings and Things." *Journal of Oriental Studies* 2 (July 1955): 282–301.
———. "The Logic of the Mohist Hsiao-Chü." In *T'oung Pao.* Vol. LI. Livr. 1, 1–54. 1964.
Grassi, Ernesto. *Rhetoric as Philosophy: The Humanist Tradition.* University Park and London: Pennsylvania State University Press, 1980.
Gudykunst, William B., and Young Yun Kim. *Communicating with Strangers.* New York: McGraw-Hill, 1984.
Gulick, Sidney. *The East and The West: A Study of Their Psychic and Cultural Characteristics.* Rutland, Vt., and Tokyo: Charles E. Tuttle Company, 1963.
Guthrie, W. K. C. *A History of Greek Philosophy.* Vols. I–III. Cambridge, U.K: Cambridge University Press, 1962, 1965, 1969.

———. *The Sophists*. Cambridge, U.K: Cambridge University Press, 1971.
Hall, David L., and Roger T. Ames. *Thinking Through Confucius*. Albany: N.Y.: State University of New York Press, 1987.
Hall, Edward. *Beyond Culture*. New York: Doubleday, 1976.
Hansen, Chad. *A Daoist Theory of Chinese Thought*. New York: Oxford University Press, 1992.
———. *Language and Logic in Ancient China*. Ann Arbor: University of Michigan Press, 1983.
———. "A Tao of Tao in Chuang-tzu." In *Experimental Essays on Chuang-tzu*, edited by Victor H. Mair, 25–55. Honolulu: University of Hawaii Press, 1983.
Hart, James. "The Speech of Prince Chin: A Study of Early Chinese Cosmology." In *Explorations in Early Chinese Cosmology*, edited by Henry Rosemont, 35–65. Chico, Calif.: Scholars, 1984.
Havelock, Eric. *The Literate Revolution in Greece and Its Cultural Consequences*. Princeton, N.J.: Princeton University Press, 1982.
———. *Preface to Plato*. Cambridge, Mass.: Harvard University Press, 1963.
Heidegger, Martin. *Being and Time*. Trans. John Macquarrie and Edward Robinson. New York: Harper and Row, 1962.
Hofstede, Geert. *Culture's Consequences*. Beverly Hills, Calif.: Sage, 1980.
Homer. *The Iliad*. Trans. W. H. D. Rouse. New York: New American Library, 1938.
———. *The Odyssey*. Trans. W. H. Rouse. New York: New American Library, 1937.
Hsu, Cho-yun. *Ancient China in Transition*. Stanford, Calif.: Stanford University Press, 1965.
Hu Shih. *The Development of the Logical Method in Ancient China*. 2nd ed. New York: Paragon Book Reprint Corp., 1963.
Hughes, Ernest Richard "Epistemological Methods in Chinese Philosophy." In *The Chinese Mind: Essentials of Chinese Philosophy and Culture*, edited by C. A. Moore, 77–101. Honolulu: East-West Center Press, 1967.
Hui, C. H., and H. C. Triandis. "Individualism-Collectivism: A Study of Cross-Cultural Researchers." *Journal of Cross-Cultural Psychology* 17 (1986): 225–48.
Huxley, Thomas H. *Evolution and Ethics*. Trans. Yan Fu. Shanghai: Shang Wu Books, 1923.
Isocrates. "Antidosis." In *Isocrates II*. Trans. George Norlin. London: William Heinemann, 1928.
Jaeger, Werner. *Paideia: The Ideals of Greek Culture Vol. I*. New York: Oxford University Press, 1965.
Jensen, Vernon. "Rhetorical Emphasis of Taoism." *Rhetorica* 5 (1987): 219–32.
———. "Values and Practices in Asian Argumentation." *Argumentation and Advocacy* 28 (1992): 155–66.
Karlgren, Bernhard. *Analytic Dictionary of Chinese and Sino-Japanese*. Paris, 1923.
———. *The Chinese Language: An Essay on Its Nature and History*. New York: Ronald Press Company, 1949.
Keightley, David. "The Religious Commitment: Shang Theology and the Genesis of Chinese Political Culture." *History of Religions* 12 (1978): 211–25.
Kennedy, George. *The Art of Persuasion in Greece*. Princeton, N.J.: Princeton University Press, 1963.
———. *Classical Rhetoric and Its Christian and Secular Tradition from Ancient to Modern Times*. Chapel Hill: University of North Carolina Press, 1980.

Kerferd, G. B. *The Sophistic Movement*. Cambridge: Cambridge University Press, 1981.
Kincaid, L. D. "Communication East and West: Points of Departure." In *Communication Theory: Eastern and Western Perspectives*, edited by L. D. Kincaid, 331–40. San Diego, Calif.: Academic Press, 1987.
Kirk, Geoffery S., and John E. Raven. *The Pre-Socratic Philosophers: A Critical History with a Selection of Texts*. 2nd ed. Cambridge, U.K.: Cambridge University Press, 1983.
Kirkwood, William G. "Revealing the Mind of the Sage: The Narrative Rhetoric of the Chuang Tzu." *Rhetoric Society Quarterly* 22 (Summer 1992): 6–19.
Kitto, Humphrey D. F. *The Greeks*. Baltimore: Pelican Books, 1961.
Kroll, J. L. "Disputation in Ancient Chinese Culture." *Early China* 11–12 (1985–1987): 118–45.
Kwok, D. W. Y. *Scientism in Chinese Thought: 1900–1950*. New Haven and London: Yale University Press, 1965.
LaFargue, Michael. *Tao and Method: A Reasoned Approach to the Tao Te Ching*. Albany: NY: State University of New York Press, 1994.
Lee, Cyrus. "A Short History of State Higher Education in China." In *Chinese History Vol. I: General and Ancient History*, edited by Kuei-yung Chang 59–74. Taipei: China Academy, 1977.
Leibniz, Gottfried W. *Discourse on the Natural Theology of the Chinese*. Trans. Henry Rosemont Jr. and Daniel J. Cook. Honolulu: University Press of Hawaii, 1977.
Liang Chi-Chao. *History of Chinese Political Thought: During the Early Tsin Period*. New York: Harcourt, Brace & Company, 1930.
Lin Yu-tang. *The Wisdom of China and India*. New York: Random House, 1942.
———. *The Wisdom of Confucius*. New York: Modern Library, 1938.
Link, Perry. *Evening Chats in Beijing*. New York: W. W. Norton & Company, 1992.
Liu, Wu-Chi. *A Short History of Confucian Philosophy*. New York: Penguin Books, 1955.
Lloyd, Geoffrey Ernest Richard. *Polarity and Analogy*. Cambridge: University of Cambridge Press, 1966.
Louie, Kam. *Critiques of Confucius in Contemporary China*. New York: St. Martin's Press, 1980.
———. *Inheriting Tradition: Interpretations of the Classical Philosophers in Communist China, 1949–1966*. Hong Kong: Oxford University Press, 1986.
Lu, Sheldon Hsiao-peng. *From Historicity to Fictionality: The Chinese Poetics of Narrative*. Stanford, Calif.: Stanford University Press, 1994.
Lu, Xing. "An Interface between Individualism and Collectivism in Chinese Cultural Orientation and Social Relations." *Howard Journal of Communications*, forthcoming.
———. "Recovering the Past: Identification of Chinese Senses of Pien and a Comparison of Pien to Greek Senses of Rhetoric in the Fifth and Third Centuries B.C.E." Diss., University of Oregon, 1991.
———. "The Theory of Persuasion in Han Fei Tzu and Its Impact on Chinese Communication Behaviors." *Howard Journal of Communications* 5 (Fall 1993–Winter 1994): 108–22.
Lu, Xing, and David Frank. "On the Study of Ancient Chinese Rhetoric/Bian." *Western Journal of Communication* 57 (Fall 1993): 445–63.
Ma, Hing Keung. "The Chinese Taoistic Perspective on Human Development." *International Journal of Intercultural Relations* 14 (1990): 235–49.

Machiavelli, Noccolo. *The Prince*. Trans. George Bull. New York: Penguin, 1981.
Makeham, John. *Names and Actuality in Early Chinese Thought*. Albany: NY: State University of New York Press, 1994.
Mei, Yei-pao. *Motse, the Neglected Rival of Confucius*. London: Probatain, 1934.
Moore, Charles A. "Introduction: The Humanistic Chinese Mind." In *The Chinese Mind: Essentials of Chinese Philosophy and Culture*, edited by C. A. Moore, 2–10. Honolulu: East-West Center Press, 1967.
Morrison, Toni. "Unspeakable Things Unspoken: The Afro-American Presence in American Literature." *Michigan Quarterly Review* 28 (Winter 1989): 1–34.
Mote, Frederick. *Intellectual Foundation of China*. New York: Alfred A. Knopf, 1971.
Murphy, James. *A Synoptic History of Classical Rhetoric*. Davis, Calif.: Hermograras Press, 1983.
Nakamura, Hajime. *Ways of Thinking of Eastern Peoples: India, China, Tibet, Japan*. Honolulu: University of Hawaii Press, 1964.
Needham, Joseph. *Science and Civilization in China Vol. 2, History of Scientific Thought*. Cambridge: Cambridge University Press, 1956.
Northrop, Filmer S. C. "The Complementary Emphases of Eastern Intuitive and Western Scientific Philosophy." In *Philosophy: East and West*, edited by Charles A. Moore, 168–234. Princeton, N.J.: Princeton University Press, 1944.
———. *The Meeting of East and West*. New York: Macmillan Company, 1946.
Oliver, Robert. *Communication and Culture in Ancient India and China*. Syracuse, N.Y.: Syracuse University Press, 1971.
Ong, Walter. *Orality and Literacy: The Technologizing of the World*. New York: Methuen, 1982.
Organ, Troy W. *Western Approaches to Eastern Philosophy*. Athens: Ohio University Press, 1975.
Palmer, Richard E. *Hermeneutics: Interpretation Theory in Schleiermacher, Dilthey, Heidegger, and Gadamer*. Evanston, Ill.: Northwestern University Press, 1969.
Plato. *Cratylus*. Trans. Benjamin Jowett. In *The Collected Dialogues of Plato*, edited by Edith Hamilton and Huntington Cairns. New York: Bollingen Foundation, 1961.
———. *Gorgias*. Trans. Walter Hamilton. New York: Penguin Books, 1960.
———. *Phaedrus*. Trans. Walter Hamilton. New York: Penguin Books, 1973.
———. *The Republic of Plato*. Trans. Francis M. Cornford. London: Oxford University Press, 1941.
Poulakos, John. "Toward a Sophistic Definition of Rhetoric." *Philosophy and Rhetoric* 16 (1983): 35–48.
Quintilian, M. F. *On the Teaching of Speaking and Writing: Translations from Books One, Two, and Ten of the Institutes of Oratory*. Edited by James Murphy. Carbondale and Edwardsville: Southern Illinois University Press, 1987.
Raphals, Lisa. *Knowing Words: Wisdom and Cunning in the Classical Traditions of China and Greece*. Ithaca and London: Cornell University Press, 1992.
Reding, Jean-Paul. *Les fondements philosophiques de la rhétorique chez les sophistes grecs et chez les sophistes chinois*. New York: Peter Lang, 1985.
Resnik, Michael David. "Logic and Scientific Methodology in the Writing of Mencius." *International Philosophical Quarterly* 8 (1968): 212–30.
Richards, I. A. "Mencius Through the Looking-Glass." In *Richards on Rhetoric: I. A. Richards' Selected Essays 1929–1974*, edited by Ann Berthoff. New York: Oxford University Press, 1991.

———. "The Philosophy of Rhetoric." In *Philosophical Perspectives on Metaphor*, edited by M. Johnson, 48–62. Minneapolis: University of Minnesota Press, 1981.
Rieman, Fred. "Kung-Sun Lung, Designated Things and Logic." *Philosophy East and West* 30 (July 1980): 305–19.
Rodzinski, Witold. *A History of China*. Vol. 1. Oxford: Peramon Press, 1979.
Ronan, Charles E. S., and B. C. Bonnie. *East Meets West: The Jesuits in China, 1582–1773*. Chicago: Loyola University Press, 1988.
Ross, William D. *Plato's Theory of Ideas*. Oxford: Clarendon Press, 1951.
Rubin, Vitaly A. *Individual and State in Ancient China: Essays on Four Chinese Philosophers*. Trans. Steven I. Levine. New York: Columbia University Press, 1976.
Said, Edward. *Orientalism*. New York: Vintage Books, 1979.
Saussy, Haun. *The Problem of a Chinese Aesthetic*. Stanford, Calif.: Stanford University Press, 1993.
Schiappa, Edward. "The Beginnings of Greek Rhetorical Theory." In *Rhetorical Movement: Essays in Honor of Leland M. Griffin*, edited by David Zarefsky, 5–33. Evanston, Ill.: Northwestern University Press, 1993.
———. "Did Plato Coin *Rhetorike*?" *American Journal of Philology* 3 (1990): 457–70.
———. "Rhetorike: What's in a Name? Toward a Revised History of Early Greek Rhetorical Theory." *Quarterly Journal of Speech* 78 (1992): 1–15.
Schwartz, Benjamin. *In Search of Wealth and Power: Yen Fu and the West*. Cambridge, Mass.: Harvard University Press, 1964.
———. *Reflections on the May Fourth Movement*. Cambridge, Mass.: Harvard University Press, 1972.
———. *The World of Thought in Ancient China*. Cambridge, Mass.: Belknap Press of Harvard University Press, 1985.
Scollon, Ron, and Suzanne Wong Scollon. *Intercultural Communication: A Discourse Approach*. Oxford, U.K. and Cambridge, Mass.: Blackwell, 1995.
Scott, Robert L. "On Not Defining 'Rhetoric.'" *Philosophy and Rhetoric* 6 (1973): 81–98.
Smith, Richard J. *China's Cultural Heritage: The Ch'ing Dynasty 1644–1912*. Boulder, Colo.: Westview Press, 1983.
Steinkraus, Warren E. "Socrates, Confucius, and the Rectification of Names." *Philosophy East and West* (April 1980): vol. 30, 261–63.
Sullivan, Dale L. "Kairos and the Rhetoric of Belief." *Quarterly Journal of Speech* 78 (1992): 317–32.
Sun, Siao-fang Sun. "Chuang-tzu's Theory of Truth." *Philosophy East and East* 3 (July 1953): 137–46.
Takaki, Ronald. *Strangers From a Different Shore: A History of Asian Americans*. New York: Penguin Books, 1989.
Tarán, L. *Parmenides: A Text with Translation, Commentary, and Critical Essays*. Princeton, N.J.: Princeton University Press, 1965.
Taylor, Charles. *Philosophy and the Human Science*. Cambridge: Cambridge University Press, 1985.
Teng, Ssu-yu, and John K. Fairbank. *China's Response to the West: A Documentary Survey 1839–1923*. Cambridge, Mass.: Harvard University Press, 1954.
Thompson, Laurence G. *Chinese Religion*. 3rd ed. Belmont, Calif.: Wadsworth Publishing Company, 1979.
———. *The Chinese Way in Religion*. Belmont, Calif.: Wadsworth Publishing Company, 1973.

Timmerman, David. "Ancient Greek Origins of Argumentation Theory: Plato's Transformation of Dialegeshai to Dialectic." *Argumentation and Advocacy* 29 (Winter 1993): 116–23.
Ting-Toomey, Stella. "Intercultural Conflict Styles: A Face-Negotiation Theory." In *Theories in Intercultural Communication*, edited by Young Yun Kim and William B. Gudykunst. 213–35. Newbury Park: Sage, 1988.
Tseu, Augustinus A. *The Moral Philosophy of Mo-Tze*. Taiwan: China Printing, 1965.
Tung, Tso-pin. *An Interpretation of the Ancient Chinese Civilization*. Taipei: Chinese Association for the United Nations, 1952.
Verwighen, Albert F. *Mencius: The Man and His Ideas*. New York: St. John's University Press, 1967.
Vickers, Brian. *In Defence of Rhetoric*. Oxford: Clarendon Press, 1988.
Waley, Arthur. *Three Ways of Thought in Ancient China*. New York: Doubleday/Anchor Books, 1939.
Watson, Burton. *Early Chinese Literature*. New York: Columbia University Press, 1962.
Watson, William. *Early Civilization in China*. London: Thames and Hudson, 1966.
Weber, Max. *The Protestant Ethic and the Spirit of Capitalism*. Trans. Talcott Parsons. New York: Scribner's, 1976.
Welch, Kathleen E. *The Contemporary Reception of Classical Rhetoric: Appropriations of Ancient Discourse*. Hillsdale, N.J.: Lawrence Erlbaum Associates, 1990.
Whitson, Steve, and John Poulakos. "Nietzsche and the Aesthetics of Rhetoric." *Quarterly Journal of Speech* 79 (1993): 131–45.
Whorf, Benjamin L. *Language, Thought, and Reality*. Cambridge, Mass.: M.I.T. Press, 1956.
Winch, Peter. "Understanding a Primitive Society." *American Philosophical Quarterly* 1 (1964): 307–24.
Wittgenstein, Ludwig. *Tractatus Logico-Philosophicus*. Trans. D. F. Pears and B. F. McGuinness. London: Routledge and Kegan Paul, 1961.
Wu, Kuang-Ming. *Chuang Tzu: World Philosopher at Play*. New York: Crossroad Publishing Company, 1982.
Xiao, Xiaosui. "China Encounters Darwinism: A Case of Intercultural Rhetoric." *Quarterly Journal of Speech* 81 (1995): 83–99.
Young, S. "The Philosophical Foundations of Han Fei's Political Theory." *Philosophy East and West* 39 (1989): 82–93.
Ze, David. "Walter Ong's Paradigm and Chinese Literature." *Canadian Journal of Communication* 20 (1995): 523–40.
Zenji, Dogen. *Shobogenzo Vol II* (The Eye and Treasury of the True Law). Trans. Kosen Nishiyama and John Stevens. Sendai, Daihokkaikaku, Japan: Nakayama Shobo, 1977.
Zhao, H. "Rhetorical Invention in Wen Xin Diao Long." *Rhetoric Society Quarterly* 24 (Summer/Fall 1994): 1–15.
Zhong, Longxi. "The Tao and the Logos: Notes on Derrida's Critique of Logocentrism." *Critical Inquiry* 11 (March 1985): 385–98.

Index

Actor orientation, 22
Aesthetic rhapsodies, 27
Analects, 30, 31, 67, 75, 76, 154, 157, 158, 163, 166–68, 199, 228. *See also* Confucius
Analogic reasoning. *See* Reasoning
Analogy, 139
Anaximenes, 302
Ancestor worship, 45, 48–53, 55, 61, 99, 108, 159, 183, 197, 290
Animal sacrifice, 51, 61
Antiphon, 45
Arete, 91, 295
Argumentation, 139, 143, 194, 291. *See also* Bian
    and bian, 30, 88, 89, 93, 177, 191, 203, 214, 247, 289, 298
    and Mencius, 174, 177, 194
    and Mingjia, 40, 147, 152, 223
    and Mozi, 205, 208, 209
    and rhetoric, 27, 28, 33, 92, 258
    and School of Mohism, 32, 41, 196, 214–16, 221, 222, 224
    and Taoism, 39, 225, 233, 234
    and Xunzi, 155, 183, 191, 192, 194
    and Zhuangzi, 220, 243, 247
Aristotle, 32, 36, 37, 39, 44, 66, 69, 105, 137, 140, 147, 148, 150, 151, 155, 160, 165, 167, 168, 175, 177, 182, 183, 191, 193, 196, 209, 210, 212–14, 218, 220, 223, 224, 229, 231, 278, 285, 286, 291, 294, 295–98, 300, 301
Art of War, 117. See also *Sunzi Bing Fa*
Athens, 17, 152, 239, 299

Bai Jia Zheng Ming, 40, 66
Bi, 57, 97
Bian, 84–90, 132–36, 254. *See also* Argumentation; Bian shi; Ming bian
    and argumentation, 38, 71, 81, 174, 177
    and ci, 171, 181
    and Han Fezi, 280–83, 287
    and ming, 40, 71, 72, 92, 153, 155, 272
    and Later Mohists, 215, 220, 222
    and Mozi, 206–9, 214
    and rhetoric, 288–92, 294, 298, 299, 302
    and School of Mohism, 223
    and shui, 71, 139, 272
    and shuo, 81, 92
    and Xunzi, 183, 186, 191–94
    and yan, 155, 171, 181
    and Zhuangzi, 219, 226, 241, 247
Bian shi, 26, 27, 30, 40, 41, 64, 86, 87, 128, 254, 290, 299. *See also* Bian zhe; You shui
    and Confucius, 165, 169, 260, 295
    and Gong-Sun Long, 143
    and Han Fezi, 283
    and Later Mohists, 212, 220
    and Mencius, 177, 178, 181, 182, 295
    and Mozi, 197, 198, 203–5, 208
    and rhetoric, 127, 292
    and Xunzi, 186, 187, 190, 193, 194
    and Zhuangzi, 219, 239, 240, 247
Bian shuo, 81
Bian zhe, 41, 129, 131–33, 136, 137, 144. *See also* Bian shi
Biao (principle), 204
Bible, 19
Book of Changes. See *Yi Jing*
Book of Documents. See *Shang Shu*
Book of Han. See *Han Shu*
Book of Music. See *Yue Jing*
Book of Odes. See *Shi Jing*
Buber, Martin, 250

341

INDEX

Buddhism, 91, 154, 209, 228, 236, 242, 245, 299
Bu Guan, 51
Bu Zheng, 233

Canon building, 24, 43, 288
Canonical texts, 25, 154
Capitalism, 29, 306
Celestial Dynasty, 18
Chinese Response to the West, 18
Christianity, 18, 91, 196, 200
Chuang Tzu. *See* Zhuangzi
Chun Qiu Zhan Guo. *See* Spring and Autumn & Warring States Period
Ci (modes of speech), 51, 72, 73, 77, 78, 82, 88, 89, 93, 96, 97, 122, 171, 177, 181, 183, 192, 220
Cicero, 295
Classification. *See* Lei
Communication goals, 29
Communism, 29, 304–6
Confucianism, 15, 32, 59, 66, 105, 127, 128, 136, 154, 176, 182, 194–96, 198, 199, 201, 203, 204, 206, 232, 241, 259, 260–65, 273, 280, 287, 289, 291, 303, 305, 306.
 See also Confucius
Confucius, 17, 30–32, 74, 86, 107, 128, 137, 143, 148–50, 154, 155, 169, 170, 171, 173, 177, 178, 181–87, 191, 194, 196, 197, 201, 214, 224–26, 228, 230, 238–40, 243, 246, 248, 251, 253–55, 260, 261, 263, 282, 293–98, 302, 304, 305
 bian, 85, 219, 281
 Chinese society, 49, 54, 57, 62, 157, 198–200, 231
 editor, 95, 96, 101
 ming, 90, 129, 134, 175, 211
 rectification of names, 41, 82, 160, 161, 187–90, 234, 290, 307
 teacher, 63–5, 76, 156, 158, 159, 167, 227, 229, 262, 277
 use of language, 75, 162, 164, 166, 168, 174
 yan, 163, 165
Cosmology, 248

Cross-cultural, 22, 24, 28, 43, 91, 92, 309
Cultural Revolution, 154, 304, 306
Cultural stereotypes, 15, 16, 18, 22, 25, 28, 33

Dao (The Way), 137, 183, 185, 186, 192, 205, 206, 226, 228, 231–37, 241–55, 264, 265, 290, 292, 295, 299. *See also* Laozi
Dao De Jing, 38, 39, 67, 76, 82, 87, 225–30, 232–34, 238, 241, 252, 291. *See also* Laozi
Daoism, 32, 35, 38, 41, 66, 76, 127, 154, 170, 183, 185, 195, 199, 219, 220, 225, 226, 228, 231–33, 252, 257, 258, 261, 262, 264, 265, 270, 280, 289, 290, 294, 295, 299, 300, 303, 306. *See also* Laozi
Da Xue, 9, 157
De (Virtue), 55, 59, 91, 100, 206, 226, 229–31, 233, 234, 241–43, 244, 264, 290
Debate, 30, 41
Deduction. *See* Reasoning, deductive
Democracy, 29, 44
Deng Xi (founder of Mingjia), 83, 87, 128–38, 141, 143, 147, 150, 151, 161, 187, 222, 223, 272, 291, 294, 298
Deng Xiaoping, 306
Derrida, Jacques, 237
Descartes, Rene, 235
Dialectics, 20, 21, 28, 88, 129, 139, 214, 224, 225, 236–38, 289, 291, 295, 296
Dilthey, William, 19–21
Divination, 45, 51–53, 55, 61, 99, 108, 290
Doctrine of Mean, the. *See Zhong Yong*
Dogmatism, 14

Eight Uniformities, 60
Emperor Shun. *See* Shun, Emperor
Emperor Yao. *See* Yao, Emperor
Empire building, 24
Emptiness, 185
English language, 23
Enthymemic persuasion, 103
Epistemology, 30, 41, 65, 67, 84, 87, 88, 90, 129, 134, 142, 144, 146, 150–52,

171, 183, 196, 197, 199, 208–11, 222, 225, 228, 233, 234, 238, 240, 242, 248, 289–91, 298
Essentialism, 14
Ethical decision making, 32
Ethnocentrism, 15, 18, 24, 28, 33, 91
Ethos, 175, 193, 278
Eurocentrism, 17
Evil, 185, 202, 263, 264

Fa (Law), 185, 216–18, 259, 261–63, 265, 272
Fables, 252
Feelings (Qing), 112, 113, 141
Feudalism, 304
Five elements, 104, 228
Five kinds of happiness, 104
Foreign policy, 30
Four conducts, 60
Fu, 57, 97

Gadamer, Hans-Georg, 20, 21, 91
Garrett, 27, 28, 32, 71, 89, 124, 173, 219, 276,
Geertz, Clifford, 22
The Great Learning (*Da Xue*), 157
Greece, 45, 52, 56, 133, 142, 268, 294, 295, 299
Greek
    culture, 46, 167, 301
    logic, 32
    oratory, 29, 58
    philosophers, 145, 150
    texts, 168
    thought, 33, 94, 144, 166, 194, 209, 219, 229, 247, 291, 296
Greeks, 17, 92, 93, 95, 101, 168, 218, 220, 228, 290, 296, 300
God, 49, 50
The Golden Mean, 160
Gong-Sun Long, 83, 84, 87, 129, 132, 142–51, 189, 211–13, 222, 223, 239, 240, 272, 291, 294, 296, 298
Gong-Sun Longzi, 130, 143, 150
Gorgias, 118, 136, 142, 147, 151, 173, 219, 244, 300, 301
Grammar, Chinese, 73

Gu (Cause and because), 37, 180, 181, 207, 208, 215, 217–20, 222, 291, 296, 301
Gui Guzi, 270
Guofeng (National Wind), 96–98
Guo Yu (*Discourse of the State*), 67, 74, 75, 78, 94, 107, 108

Han Dynasty, 59, 129, 153, 195, 224
Han Feizi, 81, 86–88, 118, 182, 185, 228, 258–71, 273–87, 292, 294, 297, 298, 301, 305–7
Han Feizi, 67, 261, 265, 280, 283–85
Han Shu (*Book of Han*), 9, 76, 129, 132, 136, 140, 141
Harmony, 30, 38, 114, 159, 160, 167, 200, 231
Heaven, 50, 59, 61, 98–100, 102, 103, 106, 109, 110, 138, 159, 171, 172, 181, 201, 202, 228, 229, 241, 246, 274, 286
Heaven, Way of (Tian Dao). *See* Way of Heaven
Heaven's Will. *See* Will of Heaven
Heidegger, Martin, 20, 21
Heraclitus, 139
Hermeneutical circle, 19
Hermeneutics, 19–25, 93, 288, 309
    historical, 21
    methodology of, 25
    multicultural, 25, 28, 43
    scriptural, 21, 22
High context language, 16
Homer, 46, 52, 56, 57, 94, 96, 101, 293
Hsun Tzu. *See* Xunzi
Huai Nanzi, 9, 198
Hui Shi, 129, 135–40, 142, 143, 147, 149–51, 162, 187, 189, 196, 217, 222, 223, 226, 238–40, 253, 291, 294
Human nature, 180, 181, 183, 185
Hume, David, 235
Hu Shi, 39, 40, 87

I Ching. *See Yi Jing*
Ideographic characters, 16
Iliad, 96, 101
Imperialism, 304
Indian philosophers, 144, 299

Individuality, 30, 308
Inductive thought. *See* Reasoning
Inference. *See* Tui
Intercultural, 23, 34
Intuitive thought patterns, 16, 32, 236, 237
Isocrates, 295
Isolating language, 16

Jesuits, 18
Jian (Advising), 53, 72, 78–82, 89, 93, 299
Jian shi (Advisors), 79, 80, 84, 100, 102, 111, 112, 116, 118, 125
Jian shu (Letters of persuasion), 261
Jixia Academy, 65, 85, 128, 142, 151, 152, 170, 183, 186, 270
Jixia scholars, 65, 142, 143, 183
Junzi (Gentleman), 116, 165–67, 172–74, 185, 186, 190–93, 211, 243, 262, 290, 295, 304, 307

Kairos, 39, 132, 151, 219, 247, 297
Kant, Immanuel, 235
King George III, 18
King Wen of Zhou, 99, 102, 102, 106, 110–12
King Wu (or King of Wu), 99, 111, 112, 114, 125
Koan, 116
Koran (see Qur'an)

Language
    Chinese, 32, 34, 90, 222
    English, 23
    "language of ambiguous similarity," 92, 93
    low context, 17
    target, 23
Lao Tzu. *See* Laozi
Laozi, 30, 226–39
    and bian, 87, 206, 219, 291
    and Confucius, 253, 254
    and Gong-Sun Long, 143
    and Han Fezi, 264
    and ming, 82, 83, 211, 291
    and rhetoric, 35, 38, 39, 297
    and shi, 64
    and Xunzi, 185
    and yan, 27, 77, 251
    and yi, 137
    and Zhangzi, 241–43, 246, 248, 252, 255, 257, 292
Later Mohists, 32, 83, 84, 86, 143, 149, 152, 189, 196, 197, 199, 203, 208–22, 281, 289, 291, 294, 296, 298
Legalists, 59, 66, 127, 128, 131, 134, 136, 170, 182, 183, 195, 201, 228, 238, 258, 259, 261, 264, 266–70, 272, 284, 285, 287, 289, 303, 305, 306
Lei (Classification), 37, 144, 207, 211, 212, 219, 220, 222, 223, 230, 234, 291, 296, 301
    lei ming, 213, 215, 216, 218
    zhi lei, 207
Li (Benefits; profits), 201, 307
Li (Rites), 55, 57, 59, 62, 75, 100, 130, 155, 157–59, 162, 163, 166, 167, 170, 171, 172, 174, 183–85, 191, 193, 197, 214, 230, 238, 254, 261–63, 265, 266, 268, 289, 308
Liezi, 176
Li ji (*Records of Rituals*), 98, 157
Linguistics, 16, 82, 88
Lin Yutang, 38, 170, 226, 233
Li Si, 182, 261
Logic, 16, 31–33, 36, 37, 40–42, 84, 193, 196, 208, 222–24, 237, 283, 285, 287, 290, 291, 296, 301, 302
    Greek. *See* Greek, logic
Logicians, 40, 129, 150, 258
Logocentric, 237
Logos, 37, 68, 92, 145, 148, 193, 219, 235, 298
Lu, State of, 32, 75, 107, 197, 199
Luoji, 37, 42
Lu Shi Chun Qiu, 9, 131, 133, 136, 143

Machiavelli, 272
Mandate of Heaven (Tian Ming), 49, 50, 53–59, 100, 102–4, 108, 171, 200, 289
Mao Tse Tung. *See* Mao Zedong
Mao Zedong, 48, 154, 304–6, 308
Marx, Karl, 304

Marxism, 304
Meditation, 236
Mei (beautify; praise), 96, 122
Mencius, 169–75
   and bian, 87, 294, 295, 301, 302
   and ci, 77
   and Confucianism, 155, 186, 194, 196, 260, 261
   and Han Fezi, 263
   and human nature, 304
   and jian shi, 80
   and Jixia Academy, 65, 86
   and Mozi, 197, 204, 290
   and ren, 184, 186
   rhetorical style of, 178–82
   and Xunzi, 182, 183, 185, 187
   and yan, 37, 76
   and yi, 307
   and Zhuangzi, 226, 238
Mengzi, 67, 76, 154, 155, 171, 178, 180
Metaphor, 113, 121–23, 139, 140, 152, 168, 169, 178, 182, 215, 232, 236, 237, 289, 292
Metaphysics, 41, 152, 209, 225, 228–30
Methodological problems, 15, 21
Metis, 270
Middle Ages, Europe, 50, 287
Middle Kingdom, 18
Middle Way, 159
Military strategy, 30
Ming (Naming). *See also* Ming bian; Mingjia; Zheng ming
   and bian, 40, 71, 72, 84, 85, 88–90, 92, 153, 155, 194
   and Confucius, 128, 129, 161, 162
   and Deng Xi, 128, 134, 135, 161
   and Gong-Sun Long, 145–47
   and Laozi, 230, 234, 235
   and Later Mohists, 83, 197, 211, 212, 215, 220, 223
   and Mencius, 175
   and Mingjia, 42, 128, 161
   and Pre-Qin period, 129, 209
   and rhetoric, 272, 273, 287–89, 291, 298
   and shi, 134, 144–47, 161, 211, 212
   and Xunzi, 183, 186, 193
   and yan, 90, 155, 194
   and zheng ming, 41, 82, 161, 162, 211
   and Zhuangzi, 238
Ming bian, 40, 42, 85, 92, 93, 127, 130, 132, 134, 136, 137, 141, 142, 150, 151, 155, 194, 195, 220, 222–25, 257, 288, 289, 291–303, 309, 310
Mingjia (School of Ming), 32, 36, 40–42, 66, 83, 86, 87, 89, 90, 126–29, 132, 134, 142, 146, 150–52, 161, 183, 195, 196, 199, 208, 211, 222–25, 234, 238, 241, 246–48, 261, 280, 281, 289–91, 294, 295, 298
Ming shi, 132, 147, 238, 272
Mo Bian (Argumentation of Mo), 81, 83, 195–97, 199, 208, 209, 215, 219, 298
Mohism, School of, 32, 41, 66, 86, 87, 90, 127, 134, 136, 143, 170, 183, 195, 196, 201, 204, 213, 241, 248, 280, 281, 289, 291, 298, 302. *See also* Later Mohists
Monocultural, 24
Mozi (Motzu), 32, 41, 177, 197–208, 211, 213, 216, 217, 222, 226–29, 234, 249, 261, 263, 265, 266, 281, 291, 295, 296, 302, 305
Mozi, 67, 85, 196, 197, 203, 208
Multiculturism, 24, 25, 288, 303
Mythology, 45, 201

Naming. *See* Ming
Narratives, 27
Nature, oneness with, 28, 137
Neo-Mohists, 151
Nietzsche, Friedrich, 225, 250
Non-Western cultures, 15, 17, 24, 25, 28, 34, 42, 69
Nuo (Seven kinds of agreement), 221, 222

Occidentalism, 16, 17, 19, 35, 43
Odyssey, 96, 101
Old Testament, 49
"On the Propogation of Christianity Among the Chinese." *See* Ricci, Matteo

Ontology, 20, 84, 129, 142, 149–51, 159, 175, 219, 228–30, 248
Opium War, 15
Opposites, pair of, 33
Oracle bones, 229
Orientalism, 14–19, 25, 28, 33, 43
Oxymoron, 252
Pali Canon, 19

Parable, 178
Paradox, 28, 35, 226, 228, 230, 232, 236, 237, 240, 251, 252, 291
Parmenides, 229
Pathos, 301
People's Republic of China, 29
Persuasive strategies, 27, 32
Phaedrus, 244
Phenomenology, 20
Phronesis, 270
Pi, 140
Plato, 66, 68, 71, 145, 146, 150, 158, 165, 167–69, 172–74, 181, 191, 209, 228, 229, 231, 244, 246, 247, 254, 294–98, 300, 301
Poetics, 140. See also Aristotle
Poetry, 52, 56–58, 61, 73, 78, 97, 100, 102, 156, 237, 251, 289, 290, 293, 294
Polarities, 33
Pre-Platonic, 168
Pre-Qin Period, 42–45, 47, 58, 96, 107, 117, 125, 129, 155, 240, 258, 288, 289, 303
Prepon, 247, 297
Protagoras, 130–34, 147, 151, 173
Pythagorism, 219

Qi (Energy), 155, 174, 176, 177, 181, 290
Qi Gong, 228
Qian Long (Emperor), 18
Qin Dynasty, 44, 182, 224, 228
Qing. *See* Feelings
Qin Shi Huang, 268
Quintilian, 229, 302
Qu'ran, 19

Racism, 15
Reasoning, 32, 167, 180, 290
  analogic, 27, 32, 41, 178, 215, 289, 290, 292, 309

chain, 27
deductive, 32, 37, 104, 106, 118, 120, 152, 178, 179, 193, 208, 217, 218, 285, 291, 296, 301, 309
inductive, 32, 37, 103, 106, 118, 120, 152, 193, 208, 291, 296, 301, 309
Records of the Historian. See *Shi Ji*
Rectification of Names. *See* Zheng ming
Red Guards, 154
Relativism, 138, 139, 150, 151
Ren (Benevolence), 32, 75, 155, 157–59, 162, 163, 166, 167, 171–74, 177, 178, 180–82, 191, 193, 199, 200, 201, 203, 206, 211, 230, 231, 238, 254, 262, 266, 290
  xiao ren, 201, 304, 307
The Republic, 172. *See also* Plato
Rhetor, 26, 41, 64
Rhetoric, 39, 69, 70, 297, 301. *See also* Aristotle
Rhetoric, 93, 96, 122, 131, 134, 150, 152, 177, 183, 204, 220, 235–38, 244, 246, 295–97, 299–301, 303, 308, 310
  Chinese, 17, 21, 23, 25, 26, 28–30, 33–40, 42–44, 69, 71, 77, 89, 90, 92, 105, 116, 145, 152, 163, 203, 224, 288, 289, 291, 292. *See also* Ming bian
  Greek, 21, 24, 29, 30, 42, 44, 57, 63, 68, 69, 90, 92, 94, 131, 134, 145, 151, 152, 288, 289, 293–98, 300–303, 308, 309
  Indian, 29
  Mohist, 196
  Shi Jing, 100
Rhetorica, 17
Rhetorical
  activities, 65, 86, 101, 102, 108, 136, 152, 170, 176, 182
  appeal, 112, 229, 250
  characteristics, 102, 127
  concepts, 68, 71, 82, 309
  context, 234
  device, 99, 102, 133, 251, 283, 289
  doctrines, 199
  education, 299
  effect, 114

experience, 97, 293
  function, 237
  inquiries, 155
  means, 283, 289
  paradox, 165
  perspectives, 155, 157, 160, 168, 186, 194, 196, 243, 258, 304
  possibilities, 257
  practice of Mingja, 129, 288
  purposes, 200
  scholars, 308
  skill, 63, 64, 131, 260
  strategies, 108, 111, 116–18, 222, 233, 236, 247, 284
  style, 136, 178, 247, 283
  technique, 100, 105, 106, 113, 121, 152, 285
  texts, 95, 117, 270
  theories, 45, 67, 143, 258, 287
Rhetorical practices
  Asian, 32
  Chinese, 27, 72
  Daoist, 35, 38, 39, 225
  Multicultural, 25, 288, 308, 310
  Western, 31, 34, 36, 39, 42, 43, 113, 125, 225, 309
Rhetorical Studies, 24
Rhetoricians
  Chinese, 51, 54
  Roman, 295
Rhêtorikê, 68, 90, 92, 93
Ricci, Matteo, 15, 70, 195. *See also* "On the Propogation of Christianity Among the Chinese"
Rites. *See* Li
Ritual, 52, 57, 59, 61, 159, 289
Romans, 302

Saint Augustine, 235
Schleiermacher, Friedrich, 19, 21
Scholars, Western, 26, 28, 30, 31, 33, 34, 36, 37, 70, 152, 153, 229, 288, 289, 293
School of Ming. *See* Mingjia
School of Mohism. *See* Mohism
School of Names and Forms. *See* Mingjia
School of Vertical and Horizontal. *See* Zonghengjia

Scientific thought, Western, 16–18, 32, 196, 209, 224
Selflessness, 29
Self-realization, 154
Sextus Empiricus, 235
Shang Di (High God), 49, 50, 52, 55, 289
Shang Dynasty, 45–49, 51–55, 57, 66, 95, 102, 103, 179
Shang Shu (*Book of History*), 46, 50, 53, 56, 58, 59, 74, 75, 77, 79, 94–96, 101, 103, 104, 106, 108, 121, 122, 124, 125, 143, 157, 229, 289
Shang Song (Eulogies of Shang), 52
Shang Tong, 201–3, 261, 265, 266, 305
Shang Yang, 170, 260, 266, 267, 269
Shell Bone Script, 48, 51, 52, 72
Shi, 26, 27, 65, 80, 156, 195. *See also* Rhetor
Shi (Actuality; Objective world), 82, 128, 129, 134, 146, 147, 150, 161, 168, 211, 212, 291
Shi (Intellectual elite), 63, 64, 96
Shi (Position of power), 270–72
Shi Guan, 53
Shi Ji (*Records of the Historian*), 9, 65, 107, 117, 156, 157, 170, 183, 227, 239, 261, 266
Shi Jing (*Book of Odes*), 52, 56, 58, 72–75, 79, 80, 94–96, 99–101, 106, 110, 114, 115, 122, 125, 157, 166, 229, 289
Shu (Reciprocity), 166
Shu (Strategy), 268, 269–73, 276, 279, 305, 307, 308
Shui (Persuasion), 71, 72, 81, 82, 88, 89, 93, 139, 272, 274, 287, 288, 292, 299, 302
Shui nan (Difficulty of persuasion), 275
Shu Jing (*Book of Documents*)
Shun, Emperor, 46, 159
Shuo (Explanation), 71, 72, 80–82, 84, 88, 89, 92, 93, 183, 191, 192, 219, 220
Shuo shu, 97
Shuo Wen Jie Zi (*Oldest Chinese Dictionary*), 88
Shuo Yuan (*Garden of Talks*), 9, 136, 139
Sinocentrism, 17
Six kinds of misfortune, 65
Skepticism, 235, 243

INDEX

Socialism, 29, 306
Socrates, 31, 148, 158, 167, 169, 300
Socratic dialogue, 141
Song (Eulogies), 96, 97, 99
Son of Heaven, 18, 53, 55, 201, 202, 204
Sophistry, 41, 143
Sophists, 26, 36, 62, 92, 118, 127, 129, 131, 136, 144–46, 148, 151, 152, 162, 173, 174, 214, 224, 225, 246, 247, 286, 294, 295, 297, 300, 302
Speech. *See* Yan
Spring and Autumn Period, 29, 45, 61, 62, 66, 85, 87, 95, 106–8, 110, 114, 127, 130, 154, 156, 157, 166, 195, 197, 287, 308
Stereotypes. *See* Cultural stereotypes
Submission, to central authority, 29
Sunzi, 117, 270
Sunzi Bing Fa, 117, 270
Su Qin, 87, 117, 119, 123

Taiwan, 29
Tao. *See* Dao
Tao Te Ching. *See* Dao De Jing
Te (Virtue). *See* De
Texts
    Chinese, classical, 27, 37
    Daoist, 38
    Han, 46
    Pre-Qin, 45, 46, 59, 64, 67, 95, 100, 106, 209, 254, 255
Third World, 23
Three acts of speaking, 133
Three dynasties, 179
Three modes of speech, 251
Traveling persuaders. *See* You shui
Tui (Inference), 37, 180, 181, 190, 192, 208, 218–20, 285, 291, 296, 301

Universal change, 149
Universal law, 265
Universal love, 197, 199–201, 207, 229, 290, 295
Utilitarianism, 197

Vertical and Horizontal, School of. *See* Zonghengjia
Virtue. *See* De

Warring States period, 26, 29, 40, 45, 61, 62, 65, 66, 85, 87, 95, 106, 107, 117, 123, 127, 136, 142, 144, 154, 170, 182, 195, 197, 198, 209, 238, 359, 260, 266, 270, 287, 288, 292, 308
Way, The. *See* Dao
Way of Heaven, 141, 229
Wen, King of Zhou, 56–58
Wen (Language art), 163, 166–68, 210. *See also* Rhetoric
Wen bian (Inquiring into argumentation), 86
Western
    culture, 17
    languages, 16
Will of Heaven, 53, 55, 102, 103, 109, 172, 199, 229, 266
Wu, King of, 57, 58
Wu, State of, 109–13
Wu ming (Nameless), 234, 235, 291
Wu wei (Non-action), 35, 226, 227, 229–33, 242, 257, 261, 264, 269
Worldviews, 20
Wittgenstein, Ludwig, 245

Xia Dynasty, 44–48, 51, 52, 54, 57, 66, 95, 101, 106, 179, 289
Xiao (Filial piety), 166, 167
Xin (Heart), 112, 173
Xin (Trustworthiness), 75, 162, 166, 277
Xing (Form), 272, 273
Xing (Practice of morality), 57, 78, 97, 128, 166
Xunzi (Hsun Tzu), 67, 81, 84, 85, 130, 154, 182–194,
    argumentation (bian), 32, 88, 208, 291, 294
    bian shi, 87, 260
    Confucianism, 155, 168, 196, 262
    Han Fezi, 263, 264
    Hui Shi, 136
    Jixia Academy, 65, 86
    ming, 129, 296
    ming bian, 296, 298, 302
    rectification of names, 41, 305
    Xunzi, 67, 81, 85, 86, 136, 154, 155, 182, 183, 191, 193

INDEX

Xu Shen, 88

Ya (Elegance), 73, 96, 97, 99
    da ya (big elegance, 98
    xiao ya (small elegance), 98
Yan (Speech), 31, 72–78, 84, 86, 88–90, 92, 93, 96, 155, 160, 163, 164, 171, 181, 183, 194, 211, 241, 243, 246, 288, 289
    bang yan (condemning speech), 75
    cha yan (to verify), 279
    chan yan (slandering speech), 98, 203
    chang yan (beautiful speech), 31, 74
    cheng yan (sincere speech), 175, 176
    chong yan (repeated speech), 251–53
    da yan (great words), 244, 246, 247
    de yan (virtuous speech), 164,
    duo yan (too talkative), 234
    e yan (evil speech), 187
    fu yan (assertive speech), 74
    gui yan (noble speech), 77, 234
    hui yan (remorseful speech), 74
    ji yan (recording speeches), 53
    jian yan (treacherous speech), 187, 191
    jing yan (clever speech), 74
    liu yan (rumor), 187
    mei yan (beautiful speech), 77
    na yan (adopted for use), 104
    nan yan (difficulty of speaking), 275
    pian yan (deceitful speech), 74
    qiao yan (clever speech), 31, 98
    ren yan (benevolent speech), 34, 76, 164, 174, 175
    shan yan (good speech), 31, 76, 77, 174, 175, 204, 234
    shen yan (cautious speech), 164, 165
    shi yan (hypercritical speech), 31, 74, 75, 174, 175
    shi yan (wrong speech), 165
    ting yan (listen to), 279
    wei yan (upright speech), 164, 165
    wang yan (forget language), 245, 246
    wu yan (no language), 245, 246
    xi yan (talking less), 233, 234
    xiao yan (small speech), 244, 245
    xin yan (trustworthy speech), 31, 76, 77, 164, 204, 234
    ya yan (correct speech), 164, 165
    yi yan (easy speech), 234
    yu yan (imputed speech), 251, 252
    zen yan (accusing speech), 98
    zhen yan (king's speech), 74
    zhi yan (goblet speech), 251–53
    zhi yan (wise speech), 76, 176
    zhong yan (mass speech), 74
Yan Fu, 10
Yang, 228, 241, 291
Yao, Emperor, 46, 110, 111, 159, 185, 271
Yellow peril, 15. *See also* Cultural stereotypes
Yi (Difference), 216
Yi (Righteousness), 75, 137, 162, 168, 170–72, 174, 181, 201, 203, 206, 214, 307, 308
Yi Jing (*Book of Changes*), 52, 55, 56, 96, 157
Yin, 228, 241, 291
Yin Dynasty, 48
You shui (Traveling persuaders), 26, 64, 79–81, 117–21, 124, 125, 128, 132, 136, 137, 143, 147, 152, 156, 163, 169, 173, 175, 178, 186, 187, 198, 239, 260, 274, 283, 292. *See also* Bian shi
Yu. *See* yan
Yu, 45
Yuan (Adduction), 220
Yue (Music), 57
Yue Jing (*Book of Music*), 157

Zen, 116, 244, 245
Zhan Guo Ce (*Intrigues*), 67, 78–80, 83, 94, 116–18, 120–25, 128, 136, 140, 289
Zhang Yi, 87, 117, 119, 136, 140

INDEX

Zhengming (Rectification of names), 41, 82, 84, 155, 160, 161, 186–90, 211, 234, 272, 273, 296, 305, 307
Zhi (References), 150, 209, 210
Zhi (Wisdom), 170–72, 244
Zhi cheng (Ultimate state of sincerity), 175
Zhou Dynasty, 45, 47, 53–61, 63, 64, 66, 72–74, 95, 98, 99, 101, 102, 106, 116, 130
Zhou Li (Rites of Zhou), 56, 59–61, 156
Zhong (loyality), 162, 166
Zhong Yong (the Doctrine of Mean), 157, 175
Zhong Yong (The Middle Way), 159, 160, 162, 166
Zhuangzi (Chuang Tzu), 185, 238–57
  anecdotes, 284
  argumentation (bian), 86, 219, 291, 292
  Daoism, 35, 226, 233

Deng Xi, 138
eloquence, 87
function of language, 299
Gong-Sun Long, 142
Hui shi, 136–38, 141, 142
ming, 298
mingjia, 129
Mozi, 199
rhetoric, 35, 152
Xunzi, 185
yan, 77
Zhuangzi, 67, 85, 130, 136–38, 141, 142, 146, 225, 226, 239–43, 250, 252–55, 291
Zhu guan, 51
Zonghengjia (School of Vertical and Horizontal), 65, 117
Zuo Zhuan (Zuo Commentaries), 66, 74, 75, 78, 79, 94, 107–13, 115, 117, 118, 120, 122, 124, 125, 128, 166, 229, 266, 289